Higher Learning in America

1980–2000

EDITED BY ARTHUR LEVINE

THE JOHNS HOPKINS UNIVERSITY PRESS
BALTIMORE AND LONDON

©1993 The Johns Hopkins University Press
All rights reserved. Published 1993
Printed in the United States of America on acid-free paper

The Johns Hopkins University Press
2715 North Charles Street, Baltimore, Maryland 21218-4319
The Johns Hopkins Press Ltd., London

Johns Hopkins Paperbacks edition, 1994
05 04 03 02 01 00 99 98 97 96   6 5 4 3 2

Library of Congress Cataloging-in-Publication Data
Higher learning in America, 1980-2000 / edited by Arthur Levine.
    p.   cm.
  Includes bibliographical references and index.
  ISBN 0-8018-4457-6   ISBN 0-8018-4861-X (pbk.)
  1. Education, Higher—United States—History—20th century.
2. Universities and colleges—United States—History—20th century.
3. Kerr, Clark, 1911–   I. Levine, Arthur.
LA227.4.H55 1993
378′.7304—dc20   92-19746

A catalog record for this book is available from the British Library.

To Clark Kerr

Contents

Preface

ARTHUR LEVINE

This book is about the modern American system of higher education. It honors the person who was perhaps most instrumental in creating that system, Clark Kerr.

Since 1911, when Kerr was born, the United States has moved from a system of higher education open to a very small proportion of the population and largely peripheral to the economic activities of the country to a system of higher education offering access to all high school graduates and functioning at the center of the nation's economic, social, and political life.

At the beginning of the twentieth century, fewer than 5 percent of America's eighteen-year-olds attended college. There were just twenty-five thousand college faculty and staff and ninety-three hundred graduate students in the entire United States. There were fewer than a thousand colleges and universities; only thirty-eight institutions offered doctoral degrees; there was no such thing as a community college. The legendary college presidents, the university builders of the nineteenth century, remained national leaders: Eliot of Harvard, Jordan of Stanford, and White of Cornell.

Since that time the number of students attending college has grown more than fortyfold, and the proportion of eighteen-year-olds enrolled is up by a factor of ten. The faculty is thirty-five times as large, and the number of institutions has been multiplied by almost four. There are 160 times as many graduate students and 12 times as many doctoral-granting universities. And there are nearly thirteen hundred community colleges, enrolling over half of America's freshman students.

If one person can be called the architect of this change, it is Clark Kerr. He made four major contributions that define higher education today. First, as president of the University of California, he modernized and mass-produced the research university. With roots in the 1876 founding of Johns Hopkins, the American research university remained an impractical hot-house flower, particularly in the public sector, until World War II. Even as late as 1958, when Kerr came to the presidency, the number of top-ranked research universities could be counted on one's fingers and toes.

As the new president of the University of California, Kerr began the process of strengthening and enlarging each of six campuses—Berkeley, UCLA, an agricultural school, a teachers college, a liberal arts college, and a medical school and associated appendages—and then added three new campuses, at Irvine, San Diego, and Santa Cruz. In the process of building the modern University of California system, Kerr did for higher education what Henry Ford did for cars. He mass-produced low-cost, high-quality education and research potential for a nation that hungered deeply for both.

Second, Kerr developed a vocabulary and philosophy to define the modern university. He called it the "multiversity" in his 1963 volume *The Uses of the University*. It was

> an inconsistent institution . . . not one community, but several—the community of the undergraduate, the community of the graduate, the community of the humanist, the community of the social scientist, the community of the scientist, and the community of the professional schools; the community of nonacademic personnel; the community of administrators. Its edges are fuzzy—it reaches out to alumni, legislators, farmers, businessmen—who are all related to one or more of these external constituencies. . . . It is a community of varied, even conflicting interests. . . . Many parts can be added and subtracted with little effect on the whole, or even little notice taken or any blood spilled.

The "multiversity" was a controversial vision, troubling to many. It replaced outdated, though perhaps more appealing, classical visions of the pristine teaching college advocated by John Cardinal Newman and of the pure research university advanced by Abraham Flexner. The advantage of the multiversity was that it was an accurate portrait of the modern university. It described actual practice in the largest public higher education system in the country, California's. It provided a social and educational rationale the rest of the country would embrace.

Third, Kerr led in developing the modern higher education system, incorporating planned diversity of institutional types and universal access to colleges. When he entered the presidency, there were continuing collisions among the various public sectors of higher education in California (universities, four-year colleges, and two-year schools), characterized by burgeoning growth, conflicting roles, inconsistent missions, and unrestrained competition and intense jealousies between institutions. Kerr responded to the internecine warfare by bringing California's colleges and universities together. The result was a master plan specifying unique roles for each sector of higher education. The university was charged with doctoral education and research, enrolling the top eighth of California's high school graduates. The four-year state colleges would be teaching institutions focusing primarily on undergraduate education, career programs, and selected graduate courses below the doctorate. They would enroll the top third of high school students. Junior colleges would offer two-year transfers and vocational programs open to every California high school graduate.

The importance of the California Master Plan was that it stopped the stampede toward a single, homogeneous model of higher education. Excellence in many purposes was chosen over mediocrity in a single mission. Beyond this, the plan formalized California's transition from mass to universal access to college—every high school graduate was offered a college education. It also provided a mechanism for planning the future of higher education. In the years that followed, all of these elements—diversity, excellence, access, and planning—would become rallying cries for American higher education. And, by means of master plans or comparable measures, most states would create open-access, public higher education systems similar to California's.

Fourth, Kerr directed the largest scale assessment and reform effort in the history of American higher education. As chairman of the Carnegie Commission on Higher Education and the Carnegie Council on Policy Studies in Higher Education, he led the nation's leading thinkers and policy makers in documenting, debating, evaluating, and proposing improvements for the system of higher education he had been so instrumental in developing. Between 1967 and 1980, the Carnegie Commission and Council produced 175 volumes described by Waldheim Nielsen as the "most important body of descriptive and analytical literature about American higher education ever produced." It resulted in reform from the campus to the federal and state capitols, from the classroom to the courts. It was nothing less than a fundamental reassessment of a system of higher education which had matured in the years since World War II.

To write as large across the pages of higher education history as Clark Kerr has is a historical rarity. It requires an uncommon mix—the right person, the right place, and the right time. In 350 years of American higher education history, that combination has existed only twice—in the years after both the Civil War and World War II. During the first period, private higher education developed; during the second, public higher education came of age.

The final report of the Carnegie Council published in 1980 was titled *Three Thousand Futures*. It was a valediction to an era. It marked a conclusion to the post-World War II expansion and growth of higher education. The days of seemingly endless dreams and ever-increasing resources were over. They would be replaced by new realities, constraints, and limits. The future rested with each of three thousand colleges and universities. National leaders of historic proportion would give way to three thousand separate campus leaders. The era of creating a uniquely American twentieth-century university was completed; now its limits would be tested.

This is a book about that period of testing. It focuses retrospectively on continuity and change within higher education during the decade of the 1980s and looks prospectively at the trends, issues, and challenges of the 1990s. The book is divided into five parts. Part 1 focuses on the environment of higher education during a period of dramatic political, economic, and demographic change. A chapter by Patrick Callan examines the politics of higher education and the changing role of government with regard to the campus. Margaret Gordon looks at the economy—job markets, cost, student aid and enrollment patterns in colleges and universities. Demographics are discussed later in the book in a chapter on college students.

Part 2 is concerned with the different types of institutions that make up higher education. Martin Trow sets the stage with a chapter describing the historical development of the contemporary model of higher learning: how the United States came to create a decentralized and institutionally differentiated system of higher education. Against this backdrop, the fates of specific types of colleges and universities during the 1980s and 1990s are discussed. Roger Geiger describes the research university. David Breneman examines the liberal arts college. Leslie Koltai writes about community colleges. And Neil Smelser is concerned with large, multicampus public systems of higher education. The U.S. experience is placed in international perspective in chapters by Lyman Glenny, comparing the United States to Australia, and Ladislav Cerych, looking at renewal in central and eastern Europe today.

The third part of the book deals with the constituencies that compose the college and university community. There are chapters by Burton Clark on the faculty, Judith Block McLaughlin and David Riesman on the presidency, Philip Altbach on students, and Joseph Kauffman on trustees.

The curriculum and educational program are the subject of the fourth part of the volume. Virginia Smith discusses one of the most hotly debated aspects of collegiate education today—general education, the education that should be common to all people. The focus then shifts to the interior of the academy—specialization and the disciplines. Chapters by Alberta Arthurs and Marian Diamond examine what C. P. Snow called the two cultures, the most dramatically diverging fields within the university, the humanities and the sciences.

The fifth and final part of the book deals with the critical issues facing higher education today. K. Patricia Cross writes about the tension between teaching and research. Flora Mancuso Edwards is concerned with college access and retention of disadvantaged students. The campus climate, a subject of scourging front page headlines by the national press, is discussed by Ernest Boyer. Arthur Levine explores diversity on campus in a time when conflict over race, ethnicity, gender, and sexual preference is rife in colleges and universities. And Don Stewart looks at assessment in a period when the majority of states demand that institutions of higher education prove their achievements and demonstrate accountability.

The chapters follow a common design. With a few necessary exceptions, each is divided into two portions—one tracing the developments of the past decade and the other indicating likely trends for the 1990s and the strategies colleges and universities might consider for dealing with them.

This book takes its cue from Clark Kerr's classic work *The Uses of the University*. From the perspective of the 1990s, this volume looks at how and why the uses of the university have changed, are likely to change, and need to change in the years ahead.

This book is written with deep affection and admiration for Clark Kerr.

I thank William Bowen, Neil Rudenstine, and the Andrew W. Mellon Foundation for making it possible.

I am also exceptionally grateful to two people without whom there would be no book. JB Hefferlin, my close friend and teacher, edited each chapter with more caring and conviction than we had any right to expect or hope. Without exception the authors viewed it a privilege to work with him. The fruits of our labors are far better as a consequence of his work. Betty

Walker served as administrative coordinator and secretary for the project. With style and grace, she managed to juggle the efforts of twenty-five different offices and out of the chaos make a book appear. No mean task.

Finally, I thank Jacqueline Wehmueller of Johns Hopkins University Press for taking on this project and bringing it to a successful conclusion.

Introduction

ERIC ASHBY

Copies of this book will come to rest on the shelves of university libraries and in the hands of those who are interested in the development and politics of academe. Readers will be many, for the present state and the future of higher education in the United States are of consequence for the entire nation—indeed, for the entire world.

Clark Kerr's role in higher education has had international consequences. Because Kerr is an international figure, it is fitting that at least one contribution to this volume should come from abroad. Scores of Kerr's fellow Americans know him more intimately than I do, but I can testify to his reputation in lands across the Atlantic and Pacific oceans. In the British *Who's Who* he is described as "educator." His career has covered much more than education, but yes: if you include among his pupils not only students but trade-union leaders, captains of industry, and congressmen, then he deserves the title of educator *sans pareil*.

If your first introduction to Clark is by a handwritten note from him, you have a slight problem, for his handwriting runs in faint ripples, each word resembling a seismograph tracing when earth tremors are near to zero. When you have deciphered the note—it will rarely be more than two or three lines long—it will convey a warm invitation, or the dedication of an offprint, or a generous appreciation of something you have sent him. When you meet him, you find no faint ripple about the man himself. You have the impression of someone at ease but concentrating on whatever has to be talked about. In speech deliberate and quiet, weighing his words; a level tone of voice; his statements precise without being emphatic, assured without being assertive, salted with dry wit; his pattern of speaking neatly catalogued and presented with clarity.

Watch Clark Kerr at work and you can discern the sources of his style. It began way back in the Quaker tradition, where listening is part of the art of conversation and seeking consensus is more important than winning an argument. Then came years of practice as arbitrator and conciliator, where he acquired the skill of resolving disputes between management and the shop floor not by papering them over but by meticulous attention to detail. Long ago William Blake pronounced the formula for success in such negotiations: "He who would do good to another must do it in Minute Particulars."

Under Kerr's leadership, the Carnegie Commission on Higher Education and then the Carnegie Council on Policy Studies in Higher Education produced the most searching and comprehensive study of higher education issues ever made. "The Commission's task," Kerr has written, "was to examine the issues facing higher education in the United States as we approach the year 2000." There was a rather easy way to discharge the task. The commission and then the council could have settled for bland statements of principle, with impressionistic scenarios, something like the sketches an architect would make to attract a client. Not under Clark Kerr's leadership would such an approach suffice: as chairman he would settle for nothing less than a shelfload of detailed reports, something like an architect's full-scale drawings, down to details of plumbing and the layout of drains.

The commission's recommendations may be seen as a product of the scientist's tool of reductionism applied to higher education as though it were an organism. The commission began by dissecting the issues into manageable subissues, such as are discussed in the chapters of this book, followed by consultation with experts and the amassing of hard data. Then, on each subissue, the commission and council sought a consensus on conclusions and recommendations. Some of the issues were controversial; on a similar commission in Britain they would surely have led to minority reports, which are a well-known ploy among academics when they play politics. (You find yourself in a minority over some issue. During discussion you squeeze concessions out of the majority, who weaken the impact of their draft to get unanimity. Then at the last moment, when the majority have agreed on their draft, you persist after all in your minority reservation, which is likely to have more bite to it than the majority report because it has made no concessions to majority opinion. The redoubtable social reformer Beatrice Webb was a virtuoso in this technique.)

So far as I recollect, there is not in all the thirty-seven reports produced by the commission one minority report. That they are a triumph of consensus politics over conviction politics gives the recommendations a reassuring credibility. Of course, this also means that they are somewhat dull to read. They lack the pretentious glitter of some writing on higher learning in America (such as you find in R. M. Hutchins's books), and they do not have the strident emphasis of Thorstein Veblen's writing. Recommendations by consensus are less colorful. But they have a longer shelf life.

And what of the shelf life of the Carnegie commission's and council's reports? Some of their recommendations were so quietly adopted that they have become common practice and their origin forgotten. Others were not tried and found wanting but were found difficult and never tried, and several have trodden on the toes of self-interest and have been smothered by that dismissive formula dear to professors: "I am far from convinced" (which means "I am implacably opposed to this").

Indeed, at a time when society is in need of new kinds of initiative from universities, Clark Kerr notes "with sadness" a general reluctance among academics to entertain innovation. Universities, like the religious institutions from which they are descended, hold certain articles of faith which are nonnegotiable, for example, integrity in the pursuit and transmission of knowledge. It is fit and proper that any innovation which would contravene these articles of faith should be opposed. But universities also cherish certain traditions and privileges. Over the centuries, some of these have had to be renounced because they were out of tune with the values of contemporary society and were not essential in the academic ethic—for example, the ineligibility of women to take degrees in the universities of Oxford and Cambridge and the early American colleges. Efforts to distinguish what needs to be changed and what must never be allowed to change fill shelves of sophistry. The merit of the Carnegie commission and council reports is that they examined these questions with cool detachment and supported their conclusions with abundant evidence.

In Britain the prime problem facing universities is how to reconcile accountability to their paymasters (now effectively the government) with their tradition of autonomy conferred upon them by royal charters. This gave rise by 1990 to open hostility between the body appointed by the government to administer grants (the Universities Funding Council) and the body that speaks on behalf of universities (the Committee of Vice-Chancellors and Principals). There are faults on both sides: some peevish intransigence from the universities up against a crude attempt by government to impose the techniques and style of commercial competition upon institutions of learning. Does Clark Kerr's diagnosis of the failure of higher education in America to respond fully to its challenges have relevance, too, for the decay of confidence between universities and the state? I think it does. Let me illustrate this with one example.

In the second postscript to his book, *The Uses of the University,* Kerr singled out two defects in governance which have contributed to the inflexibility of academics faced with challenges to their profession. One is participatory democracy as he defines it, the kind that gives "each identifiable group not only a voice but a veto." The other defect is "weakened leadership." Until recently these have not been notable defects in university governance in Britain. They are now becoming handicaps.

The British brand of participatory democracy has hitherto worked fairly well. This pattern of governance promotes a collegiate spirit. Innovation often begins with informal talk at the laboratory bench or over coffee in the departmental seminar, among young scholars, to percolate upward through faculty boards, senates, and finance committees; some of it survives to become university policy. Of course, directives do come down from above in the customary way over nonacademic issues, especially financial. But by and large academic policy is not initiated at the top and certainly not by the administration.

This pattern of governance leaves little scope for aggressive or autocratic leadership over academic policy from the president. His very title in English universities—"vice-chancellor"—denotes the historical origin of his position: a member of the faculty appointed by his colleagues to discharge some of the chancellor's duties. (As recently as 1970 the vice-chancellor of Cambridge did not even have an office on the premises of the university and he had no university-paid secretary.) Of course, in modern British universities the vice-chancellor is the chief executive officer, but his powers are not commensurate with that title. He presides over his colleagues as *primus inter pares,* with no right to hire or fire faculty and no authority to spend as much of the university's funds as would buy a ballpoint pen. He is, to a small degree, still a victim of the historical origin of his office. He can persuade, urge, encourage, oppose, warn, deplore, but he cannot command. His colleagues would agree that leadership is a quality required of him, but it has to be subtle, oblique, and with their consent. As to initiative over academic affairs, let me quote from my own experiences as vice-chancellor of two universities.

> If a British university president has a bright idea . . . it would be the height of ineptitude to publish it to his faculty, and fatal to issue a directive about it. He must unobtrusively—if possible anonymously—feed it into the organization at a low level, informally over lunch, and watch it percolate slowly upwards. With luck it will come on his desk months later . . . and he must greet it with the surprise parents exhibit when their children show them what Santa Claus has brought them for Christmas.

This comfortable style of governance worked well when less of the financial cake came from government sources and when the slices were big enough for each department to get a reasonable share. In the 1980s chronic under-funding and inept intervention from doctrinaire politicians badly bruised the collegiate spirit and weakened the influence of vice-chancellors, at a time when their effects ought to have been just the opposite. Clark Kerr's diagnosis of the failures in good governance in American universities now applies in a different form and for a different reason to British universities.

Although vice-chancellors have had no power within universities, they have had an important collective influence through the Committee of Vice-Chancellors and Principals. This body has no official standing, but in the past it has commanded the respectful attention of governments and it has initiated many valuable reforms in the university system (e.g., a centralized admissions procedure in which all universities cooperate.) The committee had amicable relations with the University Grants Committee, the body appointed by government and entrusted with the distribution of a block grant of public money among universities. When the two bodies conferred they did not sit as adversaries but as collaborators to further the interests of universities.

That cozy consensus has vanished. The University Grants Committee, for generations a reliable barrier to protect universities from political pressures, has been dismantled and replaced by a Universities Funding Council, with authority to base its funding on contracts with universities to supply goods and services (the goods being graduates and the services research) as may be needed to fuel the enterprise economy. Consider the statement by the man who became the chief officer of the funding council.

> Ministers are no longer thinking in terms of grants [to universities] however calculated, but in terms of buying certain services from universities. The bulk of these services are research and teaching. The Government is here a single purchaser, faced with an array of competing suppliers. It will use the power which this situation gives it to press for higher quality and greater efficiency just as Marks and Spencer (for example) do in similar circumstances.

Competition among universities is undoubtedly healthy. But competition on what criterion? The funding council's answer is clear: it recently invited universities to submit bids for the cost of producing graduates in each discipline, with the intent to show preference to the lowest bidders. Scholarship was up for auction. The serious aspect of this intent is the assumption that the government "is a single purchaser." Since the Middle Ages universities have had a place in a market economy, but the customers were the students, not the bishop or prince. The students chose the disciplines they wanted to master and the teachers they wanted to hear. There was healthy competition based on the intellectual appeal of the professor, not on offers from him to teach at cut-rate fees. Student preferences now have to give way to the preferences of a megacustomer who will decide what graduates are needed to promote what the government considers to be its own economic and social policies.

Compliance with this doctrine is the price British universities are asked to pay for their dependence on public funds. Clark Kerr wrote that universities need leadership as never before and that the leaders need to have "nerves like sewer pipes." British universities have a similar need for leaders who will affirm what universities stand for and what privileges they must be permitted to have even though they are financed by the taxpayer. High among these privileges is noninterference from the paymaster in the way that academics use their time. In a brilliant essay, "The Academic Ethos," Walter Rüegg described the university as "an institution of disciplined leisure" (1986). University teachers, he wrote, "are practically unique in the amount of time at their disposal, free from specific prescriptions as to how they should use it." How can that be justified? Rüegg's thesis is that society needs an institution devoted to "diminish the uncertainty of the future by providing . . . rationally verifiable criticism, proof, renewal and expansion of knowledge. . . . Disciplined leisure is needed for this task, because it is no longer possible to depend on experience and tradition." And he concluded that leisure, as time that does not have to be accounted for, is an essential condition for the effectiveness of a university teacher. The end products of this leisure have included antibiotics, nuclear power, computers, and—certainly not least—that grounding in humanities which makes it possible to communicate with nations that speak other languages and hold other beliefs: the whole apparatus of diplomacy and trade.

The notion that people paid out of public funds should have time during "working hours" for which they do not have to account is repugnant to a society where success is measured in a productivity-per-dollar ratio. Some politicians seem to be assuming that the more accountable time is, the more cost-effective the pursuit of knowledge will be. This is a new heresy in academe. It will not be dispelled by indignant protest. University teachers do have a tacit, self-imposed code of discipline, analogous to the Hippocratic Oath. They need to publish and declare it. And universities need, these days, to have leaders such as Clark Kerr, who can persuade their paymasters that uncommitted time, in a market where competition is for ideas, not profits, leads to the ultimate enrichment of society in cash as well as culture.

Reference

Rüegg, Walter. 1986. "The Academic Ethos." *Minerva,* 24:393–412.

I A Dynamic Environment

1 Government and Higher Education

PATRICK M. CALLAN

In a recent essay in which he discussed American higher education during the nine previous decades of the twentieth century and anticipated the issues of the 1990s, Clark Kerr characterized the 1980s as a "status quo decade." Examining a number of quantitative indicators, including student, faculty, institutional, and financial characteristics, Kerr found the decade "nonhistorical in the sense that so little happened that made history . . . 1989 was mostly a replica of 1979." Like the decades of 1900–1910 and 1920–30, Kerr saw the eighties as a time of minor changes, which placed little burden on policy-making and decision-making entities (1990, 5–6).

Seeds of important changes may, however, be sown in periods of apparent "normalcy," even though their full effects are felt or measured in future decades. With respect to the relationship of American higher education to government, it is too soon to know which of the many seeds planted in the 1980s will take root or what kinds of fruit they will bear. Yet it is not too early to note that the decade of the 1980s was profoundly different from those that immediately preceded it and was one of significant change in the roles of federal and state governments and in the influences of both levels of government on colleges and universities. This chapter describes and identifies some of those changes and then closes with some speculations about the relation of government to higher education in the 1990s. One caveat at the beginning: the fifty American states are not monotypic. They vary

greatly in conditions, traditions, and policies. This chapter seeks to interpret broad national trends rather than to describe the unique circumstances
of particular states.

The Resurgence of the States

The most significant change during the 1980s in the relation of government to higher education was the resurgence of the states. The federal
government remains an important presence in higher education, primarily
in its support of need-based student financial aid and of university-based
research and development. However, as in most areas of domestic policy,
federal initiative and influence on higher education have declined. Federal
higher education programs failed to keep pace with inflation from the early
to late eighties, and the major federal initiatives were rhetorical—attacks by
Secretary of Education William Bennett on the shortcomings of curriculum, the greed of universities, and the extravagant lifestyles of students and
the proclamation of national education goals by President Bush.

Governors and legislators in the early and mid-1980s were confronted
with painful economic realities. It was left to them to formulate responses to
dislocations brought on by recession, federal reductions of aid to state and
local governments, international economic competition, demographic and
technological changes, double-digit unemployment rates, and revenue
shortfalls that brought many states to the brink of insolvency at a time of
peak demand for public services. As David Halberstam put it in a discussion
of the role of governors, "If their states lose factories, they are the ones faced
with declining tax bases and less money with which to prepare their citizens
for new kinds of work. . . . What are political abstractions on the floor of
the House or Senate are realities in state budgets. In the governors' world,
politics are closely tied to economics, which has become vastly more important in America in the past ten years" (Halberstam 1991, 13).

Whatever the intentions may have been, President Reagan's "New
Federalism" did not result in wholesale reduction or elimination of public
services at the state level. Indeed, diminished federal assistance reinvigo-
rated state leadership. The eighties were a decade of state-led initiatives and
innovations in domestic policy that have been compared to the Progressive
Era reforms of state and local government in the early years of the twentieth
century (Osborne 1988, 1–3, 330–332). Whatever one's philosophical view
of the appropriate roles of state and federal governments, there is little
doubt that such a shift did occur and that it enhanced the influence of
governors and state legislatures. As one democratic governor stated, "Basi-

cally since Mr. Reagan has been president whether the Democrats or even the Republicans agree with everything he's done, he's made [all governors] more powerful" (Neuharth 1988, 4).

Economic development was the focus of the new state policy leadership. Education reform became a centerpiece of most state policy agendas and the basic component of many state programs to develop a competitive work force, improve living standards and quality of life, and even reform public assistance programs. In August 1986, the governors of the fifty states adopted *Time for Results*—a set of recommendations for improvement of education at all levels. The impetus for this report was clearly stated by Lamar Alexander, Chairman of the National Governors' Association, in his summary of the document. "Well, what has gotten the Governors' attention? Jobs. More than anything else, it is the threat to the jobs of the people who elect us" (National Governors' Association 1986, 5). Three years later the first education summit in the nation's history brought all the governors together with the President of the United States, reflecting recognition of the degree to which educational policy leadership had passed to the states.

By the mid-1980s, a school reform movement had been launched in virtually every state—more often than not stimulated by an activist governor. The time was ripe for state political leaders to direct their attention to higher education. A series of national reports emanating from within the academy had questioned the effectiveness of undergraduate education. A task force of the Education Commission of the States (ECS) responded to state interest in the quality of teaching and learning at the undergraduate level. This Task Force on Effective State Action to Improve Colleges and Universities, led by Governor Thomas Kean of New Jersey, challenged states and colleges and universities to work to strengthen student preparation for college, improve the effectiveness of undergraduate education, assess its outcomes systematically, improve rates of completion, better serve diverse student needs, and sharpen definitions of institutional missions (Education Commission of the States 1986).

Similar concerns were raised in the 1986 National Governors' Association report, *Time for Results*. The association's Task Force on College Quality, chaired by Governor John Ashcroft of Missouri, called on states to define institutional missions clearly, emphasize the importance of undergraduate education, see that colleges and universities implemented systematic approaches to the assessment of student learning, provide incentives for the improvement of quality, and emphasize the importance of commitment to access (National Governors' Association 1986, 153–165).

By the middle of the decade, it was clear that the calls for refocusing federal higher education policy to stimulate "those transformations necessary to meet the emerging demands of American society" were falling on deaf ears in Washington (Newman 1985, xviii). But by this time national economic conditions, the resurgence of state government, gubernatorial leadership, the national reports, and the absence of federal initiative had combined to focus state attention on higher education and, in particular, on the states' role in quality, equity, and financing.

Quality

The traditional role of state government has been to provide institutions of higher education with the resources believed to be the necessary conditions for instructional quality. State support has included the construction and maintenance of facilities, including classrooms, laboratories, and libraries, and financial support sufficient to employ qualified faculty and staff. State officials and higher education leaders have seldom fully agreed on the level or adequacy of the support provided, but there is little disagreement about the responsibility of the state to make available the physical and human infrastructure within which public institutions strive for quality.

The traditional state perspective of instructional quality in higher education has been deferential. In the past, states were willing to rely heavily if not exclusively on institutional mechanisms—faculty governance, peer review, etc.—and on assurances of presidents and provosts that the system was functioning effectively. Both state and federal governments relied on accreditation to protect the public interest by assuring at least minimum standards of instructional quality.

In the 1980s states began to develop more explicit policies that addressed the quality of undergraduate education and institutional accountability for the effectiveness of instruction. No state sought to dictate higher education curricula or to do away with accrediting bodies. But responding to concerns that had spilled over from the elementary and secondary reform movement and from national reports on such problems as teacher education, the neglect of undergraduate teaching, and low community college transfer rates, as well as complaints from some employers about the competence of new employees, many state leaders began to raise questions about the educational outcomes of baccalaureate programs. What did graduates know? What did colleges and universities know about the effectiveness of student learning beyond the evaluations of student performance in individual courses? In the absence of such information, how could improvement strategies be designed and resources targeted for improvement?

The issue of educational quality gave rise to issues of accountability. In return for their financial support, states have always demanded accountability—but most accountability in higher education has been fiscal and procedural. That is, states have generally sought assurance that money was spent for the general or specific purpose for which it was appropriated, and they have demanded varying degrees of compliance with laws, regulations, and procedures governing the spending of public money. Some of the latter has been thought to be excessively bureaucratic, intrusive, and inefficient (Newman 1987, 23–38).

The shift of state interest to educational outcomes was unprecedented. The policy tool most frequently adopted to press state concerns about educational quality was student assessment.[1] In 1990, twenty-seven states responded affirmatively to an ECS survey that asked whether a state assessment initiative was in place as a result of legislative or board action. Another half-dozen states had taken steps to stimulate or encourage assessment initiatives. Only eight of the forty-eight responding states reported no assessment activities and no plans to undertake them.

Initial fears of many administrators and faculty that states would replicate the dismal experience of public school assessment by mandating statewide standardized tests were not realized. With few exceptions, institutions were given flexibility to develop their own approaches. Some state leaders who had argued for institutional discretion expressed concerns that colleges and universities, particularly those that had not been provided special funding for assessment, might take the calls for assessment of outcomes less than seriously, which might in turn lead to pressures for more heavy-handed state approaches. In the meantime, according to the American Council on Education, 70 percent of public colleges and universities reported that they were assessing outcomes of learning, and the overwhelming majority said they were doing so in response to a state requirement (Ewell, Finney, and Lenth 1991). Some leaders of higher education interpreted the state interest in learning outcomes and assessment as a new wrinkle in an old and cyclical tension over accountability. However, there were important differences from traditional accountability demands. Many of the governors who promoted the new state focus on educational outcomes were supporters of increased support of higher education, not proponents of cutbacks; most of the state respondents to the ECS survey reported that they had no interest in micromanaging or standardizing the process of assessment; and an overwhelming majority of the state respondents asserted that educational improvement was the primary purpose of assessment in their states (Ewell, Finney, and Lenth 1991, 2–3).

Proponents of state-stimulated outcome assessment believe that it is a plausible strategy for raising the importance of undergraduate education, stimulating curricular reform, strengthening quality control at the institutional level, and diagnosing student and programmatic weaknesses. Skeptics fear that it will fail to engage the faculties, who must ultimately be responsible for improvement, become a compliance function performed by administrators and institutional researchers, and lead ultimately to homogenization of instruments and curriculum and to standardized testing for minimum achievement standards. There are also fears that assessment may someday be tied to resource allocation in a punitive way. It is too early to know which set of hopes or fears is most likely to be realized.

What may be more important than the fate of assessment initiatives is the assertion by states of a public policy interest in the quality of higher education and their unwillingness to defer to the traditional mechanisms of quality assurance. This was a new phenomenon of the 1980s with significant but uncertain consequences for the future relationship of government and higher education.

Equity

Historically, government has been the force for greater inclusiveness in American higher education. The major initiatives for extending access to new populations have been federal and state policies that stimulated the development of land-grant universities during the nineteenth century, the expansion of state higher education systems, educational opportunities for veterans, the creation of community colleges, need-based student financial assistance, and prohibition of race and gender discrimination in the twentieth century. Colleges and universities have tended to reflect public and governmental commitments to access and quality. The periods of national progress in expanding and equalizing educational opportunity have always been times when access was high on the agenda of government. The periods of government withdrawal from or resistance to the expansion of access have been those of least progress.

Without state and national commitment, issues of access and equity seldom find their way into the highest priorities of colleges and universities. As Derek Bok has stated, "The fact remains that, left to their own devices, academic communities are no less prone than other professional organizations to slip unconsciously into complacent habits, inward-looking standards of quality, self-serving canons of behavior. To counter these tendencies, there will always be a need to engage the outside world in a lively, continuing debate over the university's social responsibilities" (1990, 111). The difficulties colleges and universities experience in establishing and sustaining commitment to the education of minorities were reflected in two surveys conducted in the late 1980s.[2] The American Council on Education reported that, according to its Campus Trends 1989 survey, "although most administrators perceive more commitment to minority participation now—as compared to ten years ago—only one-third rated the level of commitment as high" (Carter and Wilson 1989, 17). And in its 1989 survey of over five thousand faculty in American colleges and universities, the Carnegie Foundation for the Advancement of Teaching found that 49 percent of respondents agreed with the statement, "I am satisfied with the results of affirmative action at this institution" (1989, 105).

In no area of domestic policy was the lack of federal leadership more conspicuous in the 1980s than that of equal educational opportunity. Historically, every major attack on inequality of opportunity in American life since the Civil War had been stimulated by the federal government. This was particularly the case for higher education from the mid-1960s to the mid-1970s when federal civil rights enforcement, student financial assistance, and moral leadership stimulated unprecedented progress in the enrollment and graduation of underrepresented ethnic minority groups. In contrast, the 1980s were a lost decade for federal leadership and for institutional progress in equal educational opportunity at all levels of education.

To grasp fully the magnitude of the federal retreat from equality in the field of education and the long-term consequences for higher education, one must examine federal educational commitments at all levels. Since most federal education programs serve disadvantaged populations, reduction of federal education support takes its greatest toll on the groups least well served—the poor and historically disadvantaged ethnic minority groups. Between 1980 and 1988 federal assistance to elementary and secondary education, adjusted for inflation, was reduced by 12 percent. During the same period federal funding for higher education, which consists mainly of student financial assistance, netted an increase of 7.4 percent, which fell far short of keeping pace with rising college costs. Most of the largest cuts occurred in the programs targeting disadvantaged populations:

- Compensatory assistance for disadvantaged children, where participation declined by 9 percent while the number of children in poverty rose;
- Office of Civil Rights—a 42 percent reduction in real funding;
- Supplemental Opportunity Grants—the size and number of awards decreased; and
- Work-study programs in higher education, where participation declined by 10 percent

Although the number and size of Pell grants increased over this period, the most significant change in student financial assistance was the shift from need-based grants to loans as the predominant federal student financial aid program—a change highly unlikely to make higher education more inviting to the poorest and most underrepresented populations. The magnitude of this shift was reflected in a 96 percent increase in lending under the guaranteed student loan program between 1980 and 1988 (Verstegen 1990, 366–370).

For the states the equity agenda grew out of the economic agenda. State public policy initiatives early in the eighties were adopted to stimulate growth and job creation through economic innovation and education. As we have seen, concerns about the quality of the labor force provided the primary impetus to education reform. The first sets of reforms in most states did not focus on the educationally or economically disadvantaged. However, as the decade wore on, state strategies for economic renewal began to take into account the projections of slow work-force growth and the reality that, for many states, new entrants to the labor force would increasingly come from the ranks of minorities, immigrants, and women. The capacity of states to compete for high-wage industries and jobs would depend in no small part on the skill and competence of these emerging workers (Hudson Institute 1987, 75–103).

In the middle and late years of the decade it also became apparent to many state policy makers that few of the state initiatives affecting public schools or higher education were addressing the lack of success of education at all levels with black, Hispanic, and native Americans. These are the groups that make up an increasing proportion of young Americans and that by any measure—progression through levels of schooling, graduation rates, scores on standardized tests, college attendance rates, enrollment in graduate and professional schools, etc.—are the least well served by American education. The bottom line for states was that both economic and educational logic led to the same conclusion: without improvement in the education of minority groups, few states could hope to be successful.

In elementary and secondary education, states began aggressive attacks on the problems of urban education. New policies provided for parental choice of public schools for at-risk students (e.g., Minnesota), placing "academically bankrupt" school districts into receivership (e.g., New Jersey), and radical reorganization establishing parent and community control of schools and school site management (e.g., Illinois).[3] State higher education policy agendas also began to reflect greater emphasis on the participation and achievement of minorities. An array of policies and programs were advanced, adopted, refocused, or expanded to reduce barriers to minority student enrollment, assist students in adapting to college, and encourage institutions to improve learning. These included the explicit identification of increased minority enrollment and graduation rates as a state priority or goal (e.g., California); funding for new initiatives or expanded programs, such as state student financial assistance, outreach, transition, and mentoring programs (e.g., Pennsylvania, New Jersey); assessment of incoming students for diagnostic purposes (e.g., New Jersey); learning assistance programs to help students compensate for poor preparation (e.g., New York); collaboration with public schools to raise student aspirations and improve preparation for college (e.g., Michigan); holding colleges and universities accountable for improved access and achievement of underrepresented groups (e.g., New Mexico); and incentives for achieving these outcomes (e.g., Connecticut) (Pipho 1988a, 1988b; Firestone, Fuhrman, and Kirst 1989; Education Commission of the States 1990b; Richardson 1990).

Despite these initiatives and despite the successes of a small number of colleges and universities, national, state, and institutional progress on the higher education equity agenda in the 1980s was accurately summed up in a single word, "stalled" ("Stalled," 1990). The gap between minority and majority college participation and degree attainment was not narrowed. Most of the state initiatives came too late to make much difference in the eighties. However, even if the states continue to be proactive in this area, it seems unlikely that significant progress will be made until federal, state, and institutional efforts are aligned in addressing achievement and participation gaps related to income and ethnicity.

State Financing of Public Higher Education

Aid to public schools is the largest expenditure in most state budgets, but higher education receives the second largest share of most state budgets. State financial support for colleges and universities depends upon the condition of state treasuries and the competitive position of colleges and universities relative to other public services provided by the states. In the 1980s state support for higher education reflected the volatility of state finances. During the early years of the decade the fiscal condition of most state governments was seriously eroded by (1) the taxpayers' revolt that began in the late seventies and that terminated three decades of state and local government expansion and reduced revenues, (2) increased demands for public services due to the national recession, and (3) reductions of federal assistance to state and local government that created increased financial pressures. Public higher education found itself squeezed along with the states. Inflation-adjusted appropriations per student dropped for three consecutive years, from 1981 through 1983. Tuition in public colleges and universities jumped dramatically.[4]

The fiscal circumstances of state governments improved during the middle years of the decade because of a national economic recovery and tax increases adopted in 1982 and 1983. On the inflation-adjusted per student basis, higher education support increased sharply in 1984, 1985, and 1986 and leveled off in 1987. According to Steven D. Gold, Director of Fiscal Studies for the National Conference of State Legislatures, spending per student in 1982 dollars increased from $3,691 in 1980 to $4,002 in 1987. Of course, these figures conceal large annual fluctuations during this period.

Another useful measure of state financial support of higher education is state spending per hundred dollars of personal income. Overall, state revenue per hundred dollars of personal income increased from $7.41 in 1980 to $7.86 in 1987. By this measure state spending for higher education declined from $0.94 to $0.92 during the same period. This suggests some erosion in the competitiveness of higher education within state budgets. Two sectors of state services that significantly improved in state support by this measure during these years were Medicaid and corrections.

Greater reliance upon tuition was the other significant financial trend of the 1980s. The rate of increase in tuition at public colleges and universities outstripped increases in state appropriations by almost 30 percent from 1980 to 1987. The portion of current operating expense borne by tuition rose from 24.7 percent at the beginning of the decade to 29.2 percent in 1987.

Despite some loss of competitive position and some difficult years at the beginning and end, it is likely that public colleges and universities realized gains in state revenues during the decade of the 1980s. The outlook for the next decade seems considerably less positive. State finance appears to be entering another difficult period, according to some experts the most difficult since the Great Depression. Growing public concerns about the escalating costs of higher education to the public as well as to students and taxpayers have been articulated with increasing frequency and rising intensity. Some studies have shown that administrative costs have been the fastest-growing component of many institutional budgets ("The Lattice and the Ratchet," 1990). The federal government has shifted responsibilities for mandated services to states as part of its strategy for dealing with deficits. And a number of governors who sought major tax increases were "burned" in the 1990 elections. The prospects for public services that rely heavily on state financial support are poor. It is likely that the first recourse of public colleges and universities will be another round of steep tuition increases.

Public Policy and Independent Higher Education

The conditions of the 1980s presented special issues for government and the independent nonprofit sector of American higher education. Private nonprofit colleges and universities are located in forty-nine of the fifty states and account for 22 percent of all enrollments, 28 percent of bachelor's degrees, and 36 percent of all Ph.D.s. By educating students who, in the absence of this sector, would be enrolled at public expense at state-supported institutions, they save taxpayers more than $12 billion annually. They contribute considerably to the quality, diversity, and competition that have kept the United States preeminent in higher education (Education Commission of the States 1990c).

The rising costs of higher education threaten the affordability of many private colleges and universities. The gap between average tuitions of public and private institutions widened to $5,300 per year in current dollars between 1975–76 and 1987–88. Private institutions spend two billion dollars each year on need-based aid to narrow the affordability gap. The cost of this aid, in turn, has become one of the forces driving private tuitions upward. From 1980–81 to 1987–88, federal need-based aid to undergraduates at private colleges and universities dropped from $2.604 billion to $1.101 billion, and the average grant per recipient is estimated to have declined from $2,360 to $1,610. The states vary in their dependence upon private institutions, in the extent to which their constitutions permit financial support of independent institutions or students who attend them, and in their history and traditions of support. Among the states that provide support, the most common mode is student financial aid. A few states provide direct institutional support on the basis of enrollments or degrees granted (Education Commission of the States 1990c, 8–13, 70–95).

In 1990 a task force convened by the Education Commission of the States, chaired by Governor John Ashcroft of Missouri and Clark Kerr, issued its report, *The Preservation of Excellence in American Higher Education: The Essential Role of Private Colleges and Universities*. The task force found in the trends of recent years, "threats to the continuing fiscal health of the private sector" and concluded that "any weakening of the private sector . . . threatens to place the American system of higher education at risk." A number of the task force recommendations were addressed to federal and state governments and called for recognition of the role and importance of independent institutions, removal of financial impediments to access and choice "among a broad range of public and private institutions," and restoration of the growth of need-based financial aid (Education Commission of the States 1990c, 3, 38–41).

Governance

Most public policy domains discussed in this chapter, including access, accountability, and finance, are characterized by sharing of responsibility between state and federal governments. The final area of discussion—governance, and particularly governance of public higher education—is a responsibility and right exercised exclusively by the states. It is the states that establish the structures of governance and control for their institutions.

Structural changes did not loom as large on the state policy agenda of the 1980s as they had during the two preceding decades. The 1960s saw the creation of statewide coordinating boards and of new multicampus systems. The late sixties and the seventies witnessed the creation of consolidated statewide governance in five states, including two with major state universities, Wisconsin and North Carolina. There had been a number of predictions that the trend toward central multicampus statewide systems of governance would continue into the 1980s (Graham 1989).

The 1980s turned out to be a time of much ferment about the structures of public higher education in the states but very little change. The Education Commission of the States reported that, between 1985 and 1990 alone, twenty-seven states undertook major reviews and evaluations of their higher education systems and twenty-six states considered major or minor structural changes.

The major organizational changes of the decade were the establishment of statewide multicampus governing boards in two states, Massachusetts and Maryland. Statewide coordinating or planning boards were given increased responsibility and authority in eight states. Several states reorganized subsystems, such as community colleges or vocational-technical institutes (Education Commission of the States 1990d, 16–20).

If structural change was limited to a few states, the changes that did occur tended toward increased centralization at the state level, whether through consolidated governance or, more frequently, greater authority for statewide coordinating boards. Another noteworthy trend, sometimes subtle and sometimes overt, was the growing influence of governors. In 1985 Clark Kerr had noted the enlarged role of governors and caustically referred to state chief executives as the new "chief academic officers" of higher education (Kerr 1991, 267). A few states seemed to be moving in that direction. In Oregon, the coordinating board was abolished. Its functions and staff became part of the governor's office. In Maryland, the coordinating board was reorganized and strengthened and its executive officer became a member of the governor's cabinet, whose appointment was subject to gubernatorial approval. West Virginia created a cabinet position with responsibility for coordination of higher education. Some governors and their staffs actively sought to influence the selection and dismissal of executive officers of coordinating boards. These were isolated cases that were not without precedent and that do not constitute national trends. But they raise the possibility that the alternative to coordinating boards in some states may be gubernatorial coordination rather than, as the conventional wisdom would have it, consolidated governing boards.

The Legacies of a "Nonhistorical" Decade

Recent history has provided abundant evidence of the futility of making predictions about the forthcoming decade based upon our experience of the last one. What follows is not prediction. Instead, it is an impressionistic attempt to identify aspects of the legacy of the eighties which may influence the public policy environment for colleges and universities in the 1990s.

State Initiative

The public policy initiative will remain primarily at the state level. This has been the case through most of the history of higher education in the United States. As Clark Kerr pointed out, "The states, by and large, have taken good care of higher education; otherwise we would not have the best system of higher education in the world" (1991, 264). The deficit and financial constraints at the federal level are not likely to permit major federal initiatives, even if the political environment is more supportive than that of the 1980s. The national government had an unutilized opportunity to reassert its leadership role in traditional areas of federal policy, particularly in student financial assistance, through the reauthorization of the Higher Education Act in 1992.

Limited State Funds

The financial health of the state government is critical to higher education. It is clear from the experiences of the last twenty years that higher education funding tends to suffer disproportionately when state revenues are severely constrained. This occurs because demand for social programs, including entitlements, always escalates during hard economic times. And, unlike most public services, higher education can replace public dollars with tuition revenues. The fiscal problems most states are experiencing in 1990 and 1991 will not automatically end when the national recession runs out. Changes in state revenue policies in the 1980s left state tax systems less progressive (following the federal pattern) and less responsive to demographic fluctuations (increasing numbers of school-age children or of senior citizens) and to demands for education and human services. Without an overhaul of state tax policies, higher education could find itself squeezed very hard in state budgets. If projected enrollment declines occur in a number of states, the competitive position of colleges and universities within the state budgets could be further weakened.

Increased Skepticism about Undergraduate Teaching

The skepticism of governors and legislators about the importance and effectiveness of undergraduate education seemed to be growing at the beginning of the nineties. Some support for the validity of these concerns came from within the academy in the Carnegie Foundation's national surveys of faculty members (1989). In the 1990 report of the National Governor's Association on achieving national education goals, the association urged governors to adopt aggressive policies to stimulate and hold colleges and universities accountable for improvement of teaching and learning and for increasing enrollment and graduation rates of underrepresented minorities (National Governors' Association 1990). In the absence of confidence that institutions are addressing these issues, the credibility of higher education could be hurt, financial support could be affected, and the temptation to design regulatory devices to fill a perceived vacuum could become politically irresistible.

Increased Involvement of Higher Education in the Schools

An issue that is likely to rise on state agendas in the nineties is the responsibility of higher education to play a more significant role in the reform of public schools. The belief is widespread among state leaders that most colleges have stayed aloof from the school reform movement and been reluctant to make the changes necessary to support school reform. This was confirmed by the release in the fall of 1990 of John Goodlad's report on his national study of teacher education, which documented the low status and priority of teacher education at most of the universities studied and the neglect of these programs by university leaders (Goodlad 1990). The reform of public schools has been the single most significant policy issue in most states for a decade. Governors and legislators understand that higher education monopolizes many of the intellectual and educational resources needed to strengthen public school education. Their impatience is growing.

Reorganization

The interest of state leaders in governance does not usually emanate from the search for the perfect structure. Governance and structure tend to become issues when the confidence of the states in the quality or efficiency of public higher education is low. States that have embarked upon reorganization have often tended to look to governance changes for the solutions to problems that are educational or financial and to look to greater centralization as a way of assuring improvement and accountability. Tight state budgets, intensified competition for resources, and concern about higher education's responsiveness to societal needs—undergraduate education, teacher education, minority enrollment and achievement, etc.—could stimulate a new round of structural reorganizations.

The Level of Political Discourse

Finally, the most important element that will influence the character of the relationship between government and colleges and universities is the level and quality of the national political discourse. If the nation and the states focus on large public purposes—investing strategically in future productivity, achieving social justice, and strengthening democratic values and institutions—colleges and universities can be expected to respond constructively, as they have in the past. In such an environment, whatever specific public policies and appropriations are adopted, colleges and universities will be well treated by government because their contribution to the fulfillment of national aspirations is central. In the absence of high purpose and responsiveness, higher education is just another interest group jockeying for marginal advantage. The outcome could be another "nonhistorical" decade.

Notes

1. The information on state assessment policies draws upon the work of the Education Commission of the States under the direction of Joni E. Finney and particularly upon Paulson (1990); Ewell, Finney, and Lenth (1991); and Ewell (1990).

2. "Minority groups" and "minorities," as used in this chapter, refer to ethnic groups that have been historically underrepresented in American higher education. As the National Task Force on Minority Achievement in Higher Education noted, "The term is increasingly inaccurate. In several states African American, Hispanic, and/or Native American students are no longer the minority populations. However, they remain under-

represented in many aspects of American society, including higher education" (Education Commission of the States 1990a, 1).

3. Most state policy initiatives were not accompanied by increased financial commitments. Verstegen and McGuire estimated that, although state education assistance increased by 20 percent in real dollars between 1980 and 1988, less than 1 percent of the growth was allocated to disadvantaged populations (Verstegen 1990, 366).

4. The principal sources of data for this section are Gold (1989–90) and Wittstruck and Bragg (1988). The most reliable data on multiple dimensions of state support are available only through 1987.

References

Bok, Derek. 1990. *Universities and the Future of America.* Durham: Duke University Press.

Carnegie Foundation for the Advancement of Teaching. 1989. *The Condition of the Professoriate.* Princeton: Carnegie Foundation for the Advancement of Teaching.

Carter, Deborah J., and Reginald Wilson. 1989. *Eighth Annual Report: Minorities in Higher Education.* Washington, D.C.: American Council on Education.

Education Commission of the States. 1986. *Transforming the State Role in Undergraduate Education.* Denver: Education Commission of the States.

———. 1990a. *Achieving Campus Diversity.* Denver: Education Commission of the States.

———. 1990b. *Assessment and Accountability in Higher Education.* Denver: Education Commission of the States.

———. 1990c. *The Preservation of Excellence in American Higher Education: The Essential Role of Private Colleges and Universities.* Denver: Education Commission of the States.

———. 1990d. *State Postsecondary Structures Handbook.* Denver: Education Commission of the States.

Ewell, Peter T. 1990. *Assessment and the "New Accountability": A Challenge for Higher Education's Leadership.* Denver: Education Commission of the States.

Ewell, Peter T., Joni E. Finney, and Charles Lenth. 1991. "Filling in the Mosaic: The Emerging Pattern of State-based Assessment." *AAHE Bulletin,* 43(8):1–3.

Firestone, William A., Susan H. Fuhrman, and Michael W. Kirst. 1989. *The Progress of Reform: An Appraisal of State Education Initiatives.* New Brunswick, N.J.: Center for Policy Research in Higher Education.

Gold, Steven D. 1989–90. "State Support of Higher Education: A National Perspective." *Planning for Higher Education,* 18(3):21–33.

Goodlad, John. 1990. *Teachers for Our Nation's Schools.* San Francisco: Jossey-Bass.

Graham, Hugh D. 1989. "Structure and Governance in American Higher Education: Historical and Comparative Analysis in State Policy." *Journal of Policy History,* 1(1):80-107.

Halberstam, David. 1991. *The Next Century.* New York: William Morrow.

Hudson Institute, Inc. 1987. *Workforce 2000.* Indianapolis: Hudson Institute.

Kerr, Clark. 1990. "Higher Education Cannot Escape History: The 1990s." *New Directions for Higher Education,* 70(2):5-17.

———. 1991. *The Great Transformation in Higher Education, 1960–1980.* Albany: State University of New York Press.

"The Lattice and the Ratchet." 1990. *Policy Perspectives,* 2(4):1–8.

National Governors' Association. 1986. *Time for Results*. Washington, D.C.: National Governors' Association.

———. 1990. *Educating America: State Strategies for Achieving the National Education Goals*. Washington, D.C.: National Governors' Association.

Neuharth, Allen H. 1988. *Profiles of Power: How the Governors Run Our 50 States*. Washington, D.C.: Gannet.

Newman, Frank. 1985. *Higher Education and the American Resurgence*. Princeton: Carnegie Foundation for the Advancement of Teaching.

———. 1987. *Choosing Quality*. Denver: Education Commission of the States.

Osborne, David. 1988. *Laboratories of Democracy*. Boston: Harvard Business School Press.

Paulson, Christine P. 1990. *State Initiatives in Assessment and Outcomes Measurement: Tools for Teaching and Learning in the 1990s*. Denver: Education Commission of the States.

Pipho, Chris. 1988a. "Academic Bankruptcy—an Accountability Tool." *Education Week*, February.

———. 1988b. "Urban School Districts and State Politics." *Phi Delta Kappan*, 7(2):398–399.

Richardson, Richard C. 1990. *The State Role in Promoting Equity*. Denver: Education Commission of the States.

"Stalled." 1990. *Policy Perspectives*, 2(3):1–8.

Verstegen, Deborah. 1990. "Educational Fiscal Policy in the Reagan Administration." *Educational Evaluation and Policy Analysis*, 12:355–373.

Wittstruck, John R., and Stephen M. Bragg. 1988. *Focus on Price: Trends in Public Higher Education, Tuition, and State Support*. Denver: State Higher Education Executive Officers.

2   The Economy and Higher Education

MARGARET GORDON

During the course of the present century and especially since World War II, the enrollment of students in higher education and their choices of fields of study have become increasingly sensitive to the state of the economy and the job market for college graduates. Among the reasons for this development have been (1) the growth in demand for graduates with professional and managerial training; (2) the decline in the importance attached to a classical curriculum; and (3) beginning in the 1960s, the women's movement, with its emphasis on preparing women to enter professional and managerial occupations previously largely reserved for men.

As the Carnegie Commission pointed out (1973), however, preparation for the labor market is only one of the many functions of higher education. Any restriction of opportunities for enrollment in colleges and universities in response to what appear to be less favorable job prospects for graduates (as in the early 1970s) should be avoided. Or, as Keniston and Gerzon put it (1971, 40–41), "The *technical component* of education focuses primarily on preparing students to become economically productive citizens, while the *critical component* of education, in contrast, attempts to expose students to multiple and conflicting perspectives on themselves and their society."

The Job Market for Graduates

Toward the end of the 1970s, college and university administrators antic-ipated the need to adjust to a problem of declining enrollment associated with the anticipated decrease in the size of the college-age population stemming from the falling birth rates from the early 1960s on. As it turned out, enrollment in institutions of higher education was relatively stable during the 1980s; rising enrollment rates tended to offset the decline in the college-age population as students responded to a sharply rising demand for college graduates in a number of professional and managerial occupa-tions. A striking result of the favorable job market for graduates in those fields was a rise in the percentage by which the average income of college graduates exceeded that of high school graduates during the 1980s, whereas that percentage had declined slightly during the 1970s. For exam-ple, the average income of white male college graduates twenty-five to thirty-four years old rose during the late 1970s from 16 percent above the average income of high school graduates in the same age group to 30 percent above their average income by 1988. Similar changes occurred for white women, black men, and black women (Blackburn, Bloom, and Free-man 1990–91, 43; Carnegie Council 1980, 183).

The changing relationship of the average income of college graduates to that of high school graduates was attributable not only to a favorable market for college graduates in a number of professional and managerial occupa-tions but also to a deteriorating job market for high school graduates, especially in blue-collar employment.

The total number of bachelor's degrees conferred rose slightly in the 1970s and fell slightly in the 1980s, but there was a pronounced upward trend throughout this period in both the numbers and the percentages of degrees awarded in business and management, computer and information sciences, engineering, and health sciences (table 2.1). On the other hand, the decline in degrees awarded in education reflected in large part the declining demand for teachers in elementary and secondary education.

At the master's level, the most significant development was the pro-nounced rise in business and management degrees (M.B.A.s), while at the doctor's level there was relatively little change in either the total number of degrees awarded or their distribution among fields (tables 2.2 and 2.3). On the other hand, the number of first professional degrees in dentistry, medi-cine, and law conferred rose sharply, particularly in the 1970s, whereas in the 1980s the number of degrees declined slightly in dentistry and rose only slightly in medicine and law (table 2.4).

Table 2.1   Bachelor's Degrees Conferred by Institutions of Higher Education, by Field, 1970–71, 1979–80, and 1986–87

Type of Degree	1970–71		1979–80		1986–87	
	Number (× 10³)	% of Total	Number (× 10³)	% of Total	Number (× 10³)	% of Total
Total	839.7	100.0	929.4	100.0	901.3	100.0
Business	114.9	13.8	185.3	19.9	241.2	26.8
Computer sciences	2.4	0.3	11.2	1.2	39.7	4.4
Education	176.6	21.0	118.2	12.7	87.1	9.7
Engineering	44.9	5.3	58.4	6.3	73.8	8.2
Health sciences	25.2	3.0	63.6	6.8	63.2	7.0
Life and physical sciences and psychology	95.0	11.1	111.8	12.0	101.0	11.2
Social sciences	155.2	18.5	103.5	11.2	96.2	10.7
All other fields	226.7	27.0	277.9	29.9	198.3	22.0

Source: U.S. National Center for Education Statistics 1989.

Table 2.2   Master's Degrees Conferred by Institutions of Higher Education, by Field, 1970–71, 1979–80, and 1986–87

Type of Degree	1970–71		1979–80		1986–87	
	Number (× 10³)	% of Total	Number (× 10³)	% of Total	Number (× 10³)	% of Total
Total	230.5	100.0	298.1	100.0	289.6	100.0
Business	26.5	11.5	55.0	18.5	67.5	23.3
Education	89.0	38.6	104.0	34.9	75.5	26.1
Engineering	16.4	7.1	15.9	5.3	22.1	7.6
Life and physical sciences and psychology	12.1	5.3	11.7	3.9	10.7	3.7
Social sciences	16.5	7.2	12.1	4.1	10.4	3.6
All other fields	69.8	30.3	99.3	33.3	103.4	35.7

Source: U.S. National Center for Education Statistics 1989.

Table 2.3 Doctor's Degrees Conferred by Institutions of Higher Education, by Field, 1970–71, 1979–80, and 1986–87

	1970–71		1979–80		1986–87	
Type of Degree	Number (× 10³)	% of Total	Number (× 10³)	% of Total	Number (× 10³)	% of Total
Total	32.1	100.0	32.6	100.0	34.1	100.0
Business	0.8	2.5	0.8	2.4	1.1	3.2
Education	6.4	19.9	7.9	24.2	6.9	20.2
Engineering	3.6	11.2	2.5	7.7	3.8	11.1
Life and physical sciences and psychology	8.0	24.9	6.7	20.5	7.1	20.9
Social sciences	3.7	11.5	3.2	9.8	2.9	8.5
All other fields	10.4	32.3	12.3	37.6	13.3	39.0

Source: U.S. National Center for Education Statistics 1989.

It is readily apparent that the favorable job market for graduates in both the 1970s and the 1980s was in occupations in which the jobs were mostly outside educational institutions, and yet the sharply upward trend in compensation in many of these occupations had repercussions on faculty and administrative salaries, as we shall see.

One question that arises as we look at the data on degrees awarded concerns the absence of a significant increase in the number and percentage of doctor's degrees in business administration and engineering. There was ample evidence of the need for increasing faculty members in these fields, but, as the Carnegie Commission pointed out in 1973, the salary that a recipient of a bachelor's or master's degree in business administration or in engineering could obtain tended to exceed the salary that an assistant professor in these fields could expect after spending several years preparing for the doctorate. This has been true for blacks as well as whites and is at least partly responsible for the difficulty colleges and universities have in meeting affirmative action goals.

Starting salaries in 1980 in the various branches of engineering and in computer sciences were generally higher than in business fields, chemistry, and mathematics and were substantially higher than in the humanities and social sciences (table 2.5). However, during the 1980–85 period, which included the recovery from the severe recession of the early 1980s, the market for college graduates was generally favorable, with starting salaries

Table 2.4   First Professional Degrees Conferred by Institutions of Higher Education, by Field, Selected Years, 1959–60 to 1986–87

Year	Dentistry		Medicine		Law	
	Number (× 10³)	% of Total	Number (× 10³)	% of Total	Number (× 10³)	% of Total
1959–60	3.2		7.0		9.2	
1969–70	3.7	15.6	8.3	18.6	14.9	62.0
1979–80	5.3	43.2	14.9	79.5	35.6	138.9
1986–87	4.7	−11.3	15.6	4.7	36.2	2.0

Source: U.S. National Center for Education Statistics 1989.

Table 2.5   Average Monthly Salary Offers to Candidates for Bachelor's Degrees, by Field, 1980, 1985, and 1988

Field	1980	1985	Average Annual Increase 1980–85	1988	Average Annual Increase 1985–88
Accounting	$1,293	$1,697	5.6%	$2,010	5.8%
Business, general	1,218	1,636	6.1	1,772	2.7
Marketing	1,145	1,548	6.2	1,757	4.3
Engineering					
Civil	1,554	1,969	4.8	2,119	2.5
Chemical	1,801	2,369	5.6	2,584	3.0
Electrical	1,690	2,283	6.2	2,474	2.7
Mechanical	1,703	2,259	5.8	2,451	2.8
Nuclear	1,668	2,283	6.5	2,373	1.3
Petroleum	1,987	2,583	5.4	2,672	1.1
Engineering technology	1,585	2,137	6.2	2,290	2.3
Chemistry	1,459	1,897	5.4	2,192	5.0
Mathematics	1,475	2,047	6.8	2,237	3.0
Humanities	1,074	1,461	6.4	1,630	2.8
Social sciences	1,072	1,545	7.6	1,881	6.8
Computer science	1,558	2,082	6.0	2,276	3.0

Source: U.S. Bureau of the Census 1990b, 161.

rising at an annual average rate of about 6 percent (less, of course, in constant dollars). It must be kept in mind in interpreting these data that the fields were those in which the students were about to earn their degrees— not necessarily those in which they were hired.

Annual rates of increase were generally lower in 1985–88 than in 1980–85 and the spread was wider, with students graduating in engineering faring less well than those in such fields as accounting, marketing, chemistry, and the social sciences. Nevertheless, starting salaries in most branches of engineering continued to be relatively high.

In recession years such as 1981–82 and 1990–91, the job market was less favorable for graduates, but it is not clear that enrollment rates tended to fall during those years—instead the evidence is somewhat mixed. There was no sign of a decline of enrollment rates in the spring of 1991, and the Association of American Medical Colleges reported that applications for admission to medical schools rose sharply after having declined during the previous ten years. During the 1980s, the growing indications of a surplus of physicians had a discouraging effect on applications for entry into medical schools, which had risen sharply in the 1970s, partly as a result of increased federal aid to both medical schools and their students under the Health Manpower Act of 1971, which had been strongly influenced by the 1970 Carnegie Commission report on medical and dental education.

Among the applicants for admission to medical schools in the spring of 1991 were people who had been released from jobs in investment banking and business, into which students had flocked during the years of stock market price increases before the steep decline in the fall of 1987. Law had also been a popular field during most of the 1980s but looked less promising in a recession. Also playing an important role in the rise in applications to medical schools was a pronounced increase in the number of applicants of Asian ancestry, which had more than doubled since 1984. As is well known, moreover, students of Asian ancestry tend to have records of superior performance in the sciences.

Later, in the summer of 1991, it was reported that applications to graduate schools were at their highest level in years, as recent recipients of bachelor's degrees found a highly favorable job market. Moreover, the increase was in all fields, including the humanities.

The Rise in Higher Education Costs

As I have already suggested, the favorable job market for college graduates in such fields as business management and engineering had its repercussions on costs of instruction in colleges and universities, but a more general tendency for costs of instruction in higher education to rise more rapidly than the Consumer Price Index is well known and is associated with the failure of productivity to rise in education, as in a number of other service industries.

In most years, there has been a tendency for costs in higher education as measured by the Higher Education Price Index (HEPI) to rise more rapidly than the Consumer Price Index (CPI). This was not the case, however, in the 1970s, when the CPI rose sharply as a result of the repercussions of the oil crisis, but it was true in the 1980s and was at least to some degree associated with the increase in enrollments, especially, as we have noted, in certain fields.

From 1980 to 1985 the HEPI rose at an annual average rate of 7.8 percent, compared with 5.5 percent for the CPI. In the 1985–88 period, rates of increase for both the HEPI and the CPI were much lower—4.3 percent for the HEPI and 3.2 percent for the CPI—reflecting a number of influences which led to a decline in the rate of inflation.

Faculty Salaries

Faculty salaries in both public and private institutions rose more rapidly in the 1980s than they had in the 1970s and, on the whole, there was very little difference in the rates of increase in the various ranks (table 2.6). Interestingly, however, in the 1980–85 period, the rate of increase in private institutions exceeded that in public institutions and resulted in substantially higher salaries, especially at the full professor level, in private than in public institutions. In 1985, the average professor's salary in private institutions was $44,100 compared with $39,600 in public institutions; in 1989, the average in private institutions was $55,900 compared with $50,100 in public institutions.

How did this difference in the rate of increase come about, in a situation in which average salaries in private and public institutions had been almost equal? A probable explanation is that private institutions could respond more flexibly to a situation in which salary increases were needed to recruit faculty (or prevent a faculty member from accepting a job elsewhere). Public institutions operate with a framework of salary schedules, but private institutions can in some instances bargain without regard to a salary schedule. This does not mean that public institutions have no flexibility—they can bargain in terms of which step of a given rank will be offered. And there is little question that, by the end of the 1980s, as in former periods, prestigious faculty members could command salaries considerably above the average.

Table 2.6   Average Faculty Salaries in Public and Private Institutions of Higher
Education, Selected Years, 1970–89

Year	Professors	Associate Professors	Assistant Professors	Instructors
Public Institutions				
Average salary amount (× 10³)				
1970	$17.3	$13.2	$10.9	$9.1
1975	21.7	16.7	13.7	11.2
1980	28.8	21.9	18.0	14.8
1985	39.6	30.2	25.0	19.5
1989	50.1	37.9	31.7	23.9
Average annual percentage increase				
1970–75	4.6%	4.8%	4.7%	4.2%
1975–80	5.8	5.6	5.6	5.7
1980–85	6.6	6.6	6.5	5.7
1985–89	6.1	5.8	6.1	5.2
Private Institutions				
Average salary amount (× 10³)				
1970	$17.8	$12.6	$10.3	$8.6
1975	22.4	16.0	13.0	10.9
1980	30.1	21.0	17.0	13.3
1985	44.1	30.9	25.0	19.0
1989	55.9	38.8	31.9	24.1
Average annual percentage increase				
1970–75	4.7%	4.9%	4.8%	4.8%
1975–80	6.1	5.6	5.5	4.1
1980–85	7.9	8.0	8.0	7.4
1985–89	6.1	5.9	6.3	6.1

Source: U.S. Bureau of the Census 1990b (and prior years).

Salaries of faculty members were not the only element of cost that rose rapidly during the 1980s. Salaries of nonfaculty personnel also rose substantially, partly in response to a growing trend toward unionization of these employees. And there were increases in costs of maintenance, equipment, and construction. Moreover, there were periods during which state governments' support of public institutions of higher education was not adequate. In the spring of 1991, support of public institutions in California (and to some extent elsewhere) was cut sharply as the state faced a severe budget deficit.

Tuition and Fees

In view of the behavior of costs, it is not surprising that tuition and fees rose sharply throughout the 1980s (table 2.7). Nor is it surprising that the increases in dollar terms (though not always in percentage terms) gave rise to a growing gap in tuition and fees between public and private institutions. Thus, it is not surprising that the share of enrollment in private institutions fell somewhat during the 1980s—declining from 22.5 percent of all undergraduates in 1981 to 18.9 percent in 1988 and from 33.4 percent of graduate students in 1981 to 32.2 percent in 1988 (U.S. Bureau of the Census 1990a).

Table 2.7 Changes in Tuition and Required Fees in Public and Private Institutions of Higher Education, Selected Years, 1970–88

Year	All Institutions	Two-Year Colleges	Universities	Other Four-Year Institutions
		Public Institutions		
Average annual amount				
1970	$323	$178	$427	$306
1975	432	277	599	448
1980	583	355	840	662
1985	971	584	1,386	1,117
1988	1,160	690	1,750	1,320
Average annual percentage increase				
1970–75	6.0%	9.7%	7.0%	7.9%
1975–80	6.2	5.1	7.0	8.1
1980–85	10.7	10.5	10.5	11.0
1985–88	6.1	5.7	8.1	5.7
		Private Institutions		
Average annual amount				
1970	$1,533	$1,034	$1,809	$1,468
1975	2,117	1,367	2,614	1,954
1980	3,130	2,062	3,811	3,020
1985	5,314	3,485	6,843	5,135
1988	6,820	3,910	8,770	6,676
Average annual percentage increase				
1970–75	6.7%	5.7%	7.6%	5.9%
1975–80	8.2	8.6	7.8	9.1
1980–85	11.2	11.1	12.4	11.2
1985–88	8.7	3.9	8.6	9.2

Source: U.S. Bureau of the Census, *Statistical Abstract of the United States,* various issues.

Tuition and fees were not the only student charges that rose during the 1980s, but in general the costs of board and room rose in accordance with the CPI, whereas tuition and fees rose much more sharply than the CPI. For this reason, we shall pay particular attention to tuition and fees.

In public and private institutions alike, the percentage increase in tuition and fees was particularly high in the 1980–85 period. The gap between all private and all public institutions rose from $2,547 in 1980 to $4,342 in 1985, and the annual average percentage increase far exceeded that in the CPI. In universities, the dollar gap rose from $2,971 in 1980 to $5,457 in 1985, and by 1988 it had reached $7,020. Although complete data are not available for subsequent years, it is known that the trend toward rising tuition and fees continued. In the spring of 1991, Stanford University announced that tuition would rise from $14,280 to $15,102 in the fall and that the total cost of tuition, room, and board would be $21,262. Stanford officials, however, pointed out that the combined increase was the lowest (in percentage terms) since 1968–69 and commented that Stanford was continuing a recent trend among private universities to moderate tuition increases in view of protests on the part of students and families over tuition increases that had been far in excess of the nation's inflation rate (*San Francisco Chronicle* 1991). Meanwhile, the University of California increased its student fees by 40 percent in response to a sharp cut in state support as California's state government faced a severe deficit—a situation similar to one that the University of Michigan had faced in the early 1980s and that other state universities are likely to face in the near future.

Changes in Student Aid

Aid to students from low-income families became much more widely available when the federal government adopted a sizable program of student grants in 1972. This step had been strongly advocated by the Carnegie Commission (1968), and eventually the grants were known as the Pell grants in honor of Senator Claiborne Pell, chairman of the Senate Education Committee, who had played a major role in supporting the grants. During the 1980s expenditures under the program rose at an annual average rate of about 6 percent in current dollars (table 2.8) and rose modestly in constant 1989 dollars (College Board 1991, 4).

However, the most striking aspect of the data in table 2.8 is the rise in the cost of federal loan programs—the chief component of which is the guaranteed student loan (GSL) program. The loan program has, among other problems, experienced a high default rate, basically because the banks

Table 2.8 Expenditures on Student Financial Aid, 1980–81, 1985–86, and 1989–90 (in millions of current dollars)

				Average Annual Percentage Change	
Type of Aid	1980–81	1985–86	1989–90	1980–81 to 1985–86	1985–86 to 1989–90
Federal aid					
Pell grants	$2,387	$3,567	$4,476	6.2%	5.8%
Other grant programs	440	486	514	2.0	1.4
College work-study	660	656	780	0	4.4
Loan programs	6,897	9,542	13,144	6.7	8.3
Social Security	1,883	0	0	−100.0	0
Veterans	1,714	864	601	−13.0	−4.0
Other directed programs	384	782	828	15.3	1.4
State grant programs	801	1,311	1,785	10.4	8.0
Institutionally awarded aid	2,060	3,674	5,728	12.3	11.7

Source: College Board 1991.

involved in making loans have not had a strong incentive to police collection in a situation in which the federal government would "pick up the tab." There have also been problems associated with equal access of students from low-income and/or minority-group families. In a report issued in 1979, the Carnegie Council made a number of recommendations for improving student aid programs, including a proposal to convert the GSL program to a National Student Loan Bank, and the case for such a step remains strong despite some improvements in the GSL program over the years.

In its recent report on student aid, the College Board commented that "there is wide consensus in Washington that the aid system has come to rely too heavily on student debt, but no agreement on how to correct the imbalance" (1991, 14). The board also suggested that "many legislators of both parties believe too many of the working poor, lower middle-class and . . . needy middle-class students have been squeezed out of federal assistance" (p. 15). In this connection, it is interesting to note that President David Gardner of the University of California—faced with the increase in student fees previously mentioned—has advocated a program to provide financial aid to students from hard-pressed middle-class families (*San Francisco Examiner* 1991). It had recently been reported that the percentage of University of California students from families earning $30,000 to $45,000 had dropped nearly 14 percent during the 1980s, while overall enrollment rose 20 percent.

Enrollment Patterns

Clearly there is room for disagreement on a number of aspects of existing aid programs, but to understand the leading needs we should examine briefly the changes in enrollment patterns that occurred in the 1980s. (The following paragraphs draw most of their data from U.S. Bureau of Census [1990a, 1990b] and relate to eighteen- to twenty-four-year-olds except as otherwise noted.)

1. Trends in enrollment for men and women are presented in figures 2.1 and 2.2 The enrollment rate of men had dropped sharply toward the end of the Vietnam War but began to rise somewhat in the 1980s, whereas the enrollment rate of women had shown an upward trend throughout the period since the late 1960s but leveled off somewhat in the recession of 1981–82 and then resumed its rise—although it was still somewhat below the rate for men in 1988.

2. The percentage of black men enrolled continued to be considerably below that of white men and rose very little in the 1980s, reaching 18.0 percent in 1988.

3. The enrollment rate of black women exceeded that for black men and rose more steadily in the 1980s, reaching 23.8 percent in 1988. In this connection it is pertinent to note that the high school graduation rate of black women exceeded that of black men in 1988—77.9 percent for women compared to 71.9 percent for men.

4. Enrollment rates of Hispanics were considerably below those of blacks.

5. The percentage of undergraduates enrolled on a part-time basis increased slightly, but this was primarily attributable to an increase in part-time enrollment in two-year colleges. (This fact relates to the population fourteen to thirty-four years old but, of course, largely reflects college enrollment by eighteen to twenty-four-year-olds.)

6. The percentage of undergraduates enrolled in two-year colleges continued to climb modestly, reaching 34.8 percent in 1988.

7. And, as previously noted, private institutions experienced a modest loss in their share of enrollment, especially at the undergraduate level.

Figure 2.1 top, eighteen- to twenty-four-year-old men in the United States, 197–88; *middle,* percentage of eighteen- to twenty-four-year-old men in the United States enrolled in college, 1967–88; *bottom,* number of eighteen- to twenty-four-year-old men in the United States enrolled in college, 1967–88.

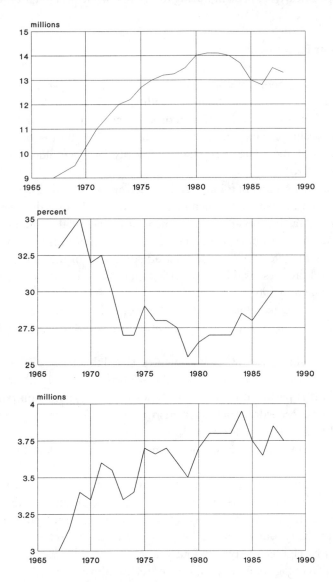

Source: U.S. Bureau of the Census, *Current Population Reports,* 1990, series P-20, no. 443.

Figure 2.2   *top,* eighteen-to twenty-four-year-old women in the United States, 1967–88; *middle,* percentage of eighteen- to twenty-four-year-old women in the United States enrolled in college, 1967–88; *bottom,* number of eighteen- to twenty-four-year-old women in the United States enrolled in college, 1967–88.

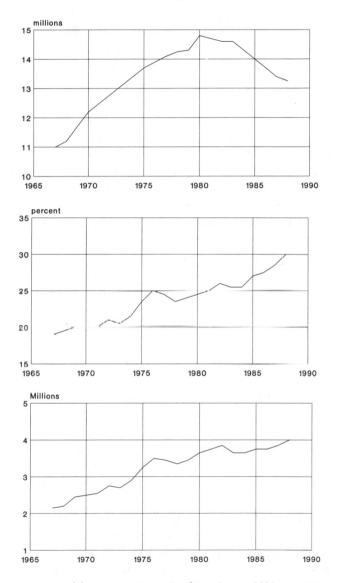

Source: U.S. Bureau of the Census, *Current Population Reports,* 1990, series P-20, no. 443.

Concluding Remarks

During the last few years, there have been a number of studies pointing to weaknesses in American education, especially at the secondary school level, but in some cases relating to higher education. Particularly distressing is the fact that the performance on standardized tests of American students nearing graduation from high school is substantially inferior to that in Japan and in a number of the countries of Western Europe. And yet, despite general recognition of the seriousness of the problem and the stance of President Bush that he wishes to be the "Education President," increases in expenditures in support of education have been very modest at the federal level in the face of the growing budget deficit, and cuts are being made in some of the states (with particular severity in California) as they face budget deficits.

At the heart of the problem is the reluctance of legislators to raise taxes since the enactment of California's proposition 13 in 1978 and the popularity of the stance against raising taxes on the part of Presidents Reagan and Bush, as well as the unpopularity of Walter Mondale's advocacy of raising taxes in the 1984 presidential campaign. And, when tax increases are proposed, they are likely to take the form of regressive taxes on consumption. In view of the serious need for financial support of education and other domestic programs, I believe that a modest increase in the progressivity of the income tax, together with a rise in the corporation tax and a more serious reduction in military expenditures than we have yet seen (despite the end of the Cold War), should be seriously considered. At the state level, there is a case for raising income taxes somewhat and for adopting an income tax in those states that lack one.

Failure to overcome the weaknesses of our education system, especially at the high school level but also in a number of fields at the college level, will seriously impair the capacity of American industry to compete with countries like Germany and Japan. There is growing recognition of the need for continuous training and retraining of employees—something that a number of large companies are emphasizing, in some cases through courses given by community colleges. Particularly important is the need to increase the high school graduation rate, which will increase the number of students prepared to enter college, and equally important is the quality of education at the secondary level. Recent studies have revealed superior performance of students graduating from Catholic high schools—something that departments and colleges of education should take into account as they prepare candidates to meet the demand for elementary and secondary teachers that is increasing as the children of the baby boomers reach school age, reversing the condition that prevailed from the 1970s into the 1980s.

Colleges and universities must prepare for the impending retirement of the many faculty members who were hired during the 1950s and 1960s. There will need to be replacements on a large scale, and there is little question that faculty salaries will continue to rise as colleges and universities compete with private industry, where, for example, salaries of chief executive officers have risen astronomically in recent years.

Finally, institutions of higher education will be faced with many changes during the next several decades, some of which may not be foreseeable today. Just as they have displayed flexibility in the recent past (Kerr 1991, ch. 10), it is to be hoped that they will display flexibility in the future, that they will survive the recent crisis in financing, and that they will adapt to changes in the labor market but at the same time adhere to the broader functions of higher education.

References

Blackburn, McKinley L., David E. Bloom, and Richard B. Freeman. 1990–91. "An Era of Falling Earnings and Rising Inequality?" *Brookings Review,* 9(1):38–43.

Carnegie Commission on Higher Education. 1968. *Quality and Equality: New Levels of Federal Responsibility for Higher Education.* New York: McGraw-Hill.

———. 1970. *Higher Education and the Nation's Health: Policies for Medical and Dental Education.* New York: McGraw-Hill.

———. 1973. *College Graduates and Jobs: Adjusting to a New Labor Market Situation.* New York: McGraw-Hill, 1973.

Carnegie Council on Policy Studies in Higher Education. 1979. *Next Steps for the 1980s in Student Financial Aid.* San Francisco: Jossey-Bass.

———. 1980. *Three Thousand Futures: The Next Twenty Years for Higher Education.* San Francisco: Jossey-Bass.

College Board. 1991. *Update from Washington.* Washington, D.C.: College Board, February.

Keniston, K., and M. Gerzon. 1971. "Human and Social Benefits." In *Universal Higher Education: Costs and Benefits,* pp. 40–41. Washington, D.C.: American Council on Education.

Kerr, Clark. 1991. *The Great Transformation in Higher Education, 1960–1980,* ch. 10. Albany: State University of New York Press.

San Francisco Chronicle. 12 February 1991.

San Francisco Examiner. 17 March 1991.

U.S. Bureau of the Census. 1990a. "School Enrollment: Social and Economic Characteristics of Students." *Current Population Reports,* series P-20, no. 443.

———. 1990b. *Statistical Abstract of the United States, 1990,* 110th ed. Washington, D.C.: U.S. Department of Commerce.

U.S. National Center for Education Statistics. 1990. *Digest of Education Statistics, 1989.* Washington, D.C.: U.S. Department of Education, Office of Educational Research and Improvement.

II Institutions in Transition

3 Federalism in American Higher Education

MARTIN TROW

Like Germany and Canada, but unlike most other countries in the world, the United States places the primary responsibility for education (including higher education) on the states rather than on the federal government. In the United States this mirrors the deep suspicion of central government reflected in the separation of powers in the Constitution. Moreover, the Tenth Amendment of the Bill of Rights states simply: "The powers not delegated to the United States by the Constitution, nor prohibited by it to the States, are reserved to the States respectively or to the people." Provision of education is one of these powers.

Federalism in the United States can be seen as the major determinant of the governance and finance of the nation's system of higher education. The concept of federalism focuses attention on the role of regional governments—in the case of American higher education, usually the states, although sometimes counties and cities are also relevant—and on their relation to the central authority of the national government. And federalism is also concerned with the role of private, nongovernmental sources of support, which are especially important for many of America's leading academic institutions, both "public" and "private." Thus, federalism in American higher education cannot be separated from the broader issue of how American higher education developed in the curious and unique ways that it has—so large, untidy, uncoordinated from the center, and without national (or even state) standards for the admission of students, the appointment of academic staff, or the awarding of degrees. For that reason, if no other, a discussion of the nature and emergence of American higher education must involve attention to the nature and emergence of federalism in American life.

Aspects of Federalism in Contemporary American Higher Education

The radical decentralization of control of American higher education (of which federalism is one aspect) is both required by and contributes to its size and diversity. Total college and university enrollments in 1990 were just short of fourteen million, in some thirty-five hundred institutions. Of these students, some 12.1 million were undergraduates and 1.9 million attended graduate or professional schools. Some 78 percent were enrolled in "public" institutions, though it is important to stress that many public institutions receive funds from private sources, and almost all "private" institutions are aided by public funds, through research support, student aid, or both.

Of the total enrollment of nearly 14 million, some 5.4 million, or over a third, were enrolled in two-year colleges, almost all of them public institutions. Over 7.9 million, or 56 percent, were classified as "full-time students" in that they met the requirements for full-time status as reported by the institutions, although many of these were also working part-time, while 6 million students were formally studying part-time (Evangelauf 1991). Indeed, the proportion of part-time students has been growing in recent years, as have the numbers and proportions of older students and students from historically underrepresented minorities, largely blacks and Hispanics. Students of nontraditional age—that is, twenty-five years and older—accounted for well over two-fifths of American college students, and racial and ethnic minorities made up nearly 20 percent. Women composed 54 percent of the total enrollment ("Almanac," 1988).

The size and diversity of the student body in American colleges and universities reflect the number and diversity of the institutions in which they are enrolled. No central law or authority governs or coordinates American higher education. The nearly two thousand private institutions are governed by lay boards that appoint their own members; the 1,560 public institutions (including nearly one thousand public community colleges) are "accountable" in varying degrees to state or local authorities but usually have a lay board of trustees as a buffer against direct state management, preserving a high if variable measure of institutional autonomy.

Differences in the forms of governance and finance among the public institutions are very large, both between and within states. For example, the universities of Michigan and California are able to call on state constitutional provisions protecting their autonomy against political intrusion; it is perhaps not coincidental that they are also the two most distinguished public universities in the country. Over the years both have used their freedom to diversify their sources of support; currently only 30 percent of the operating expenses of the University of California come from state government, and the proportion in the University of Michigan is even smaller—closer to 20 percent. (They are perhaps more accurately "state-aided" than "state" universities.) Other state institutions, by contrast, suffer constant state interference in their management and policies, interference facilitated by line-item budgeting, close state control over expenditures, and limited discretionary funds.

While an observer can see contrasting patterns in the legal and formal organizational arrangements from state to state, actual relationships between public institutions and state authorities vary also by historical tradition, the strength and character of institutional leaders, and the values and sentiments of governors and key legislators. Variations in the autonomy of public institutions can be seen not only between states, but also between sectors of higher education within states and even between institutions within the same state sector. Examples of the latter are the differences between the nine-campus University of California and the California State University system of twenty campuses, defined as primarily undergraduate institutions, also offering master's degrees, but without the power to award the doctoral degree (except in conjunction with a campus of the University of California or a private California university) and therefore doing little funded research. The California State University also does not have the University of California's constitutional protection and is funded on a line-item basis. Nevertheless, at least one of its campuses—California State University, San Diego—has encouraged its faculty to do research and to write proposals for outside funding; in these respects and in its success in gaining such support, it resembles a campus of the University of California rather than most other campuses in its own sector.

Diverse Sources of Funding

The diversity of funding is at the heart of the diversity of character and function of American higher education. American colleges and universities get support not only from national, state, and local governments, but also from many private sources such as churches, business firms, foundations, alumni, and other individuals; from students in the form of tuition and fees for room, board, and health services; and from many other clients of their services, for example, their hospitals' patients. In 1988–89 expenditures of all kinds on American colleges and universities were estimated to be over $131 billion—an increase over 1981–82 of 70 percent in current dollars and of 31 percent in constant dollars, representing roughly 2.7 percent of the Gross National Product (National Center for Education Statistics 1989, tables 126 and 133, pp. 30 and 36). Government at all levels together provides less than half of all current revenues for American higher education, currently about 42 percent. The federal government itself supplies only about 13 percent of the support for higher education, chiefly in the form of grants and contracts for research and development in the universities. That figure includes grants to students but excludes the federal government's loans and loan subsidies. (If it included those, the federal contribution would be closer to 20 percent and the students' contribution would be reduced by the same amount.) State and local governments (mostly state) provide a third of all support for higher education.

Students themselves (and their families) furnish about a quarter of the funds for higher education, and the institutions contribute about 27 percent from their own endowments and from other enterprises they operate and services they provide, such as hospitals. Another 6 percent is funded by gifts, grants, and contracts from private individuals, foundations, and business firms. In brief, students provide about a quarter of the revenues for higher education (perhaps half of which comes from student aid from various sources); the institutions provide about a third from their own endowments, gifts, and enterprises, and the rest comes from "government"— that is, cities and counties, the fifty state governments, and the many federal sources and agencies whose expenditures are not coordinated by any policy or office (National Center for Education Statistics 1989, table 269, p. 292; "Almanac," 1990).

These proportions differ, of course, between American "public" and "private" colleges and universities, though it must be stressed that all American colleges and universities are supported by a mixture of public and private funds. For example, while public colleges and universities currently get about half of their operating budgets from their state governments, private institutions get less than 2 percent from state sources. But the private colleges get a slightly larger proportion of their support funds from the federal government than do public institutions—17 percent as compared with 11 percent. The other big difference lies in the importance of student tuition payments that go directly to the institution; these account for less than 15 percent of the revenues of public institutions but nearly 40 percent of the support for private institutions (National Center for Education Statistics 1989, tables 270 and 271, pp. 193–294). And those proportions differ sharply among subcategories of colleges and universities (e.g., between research universities and four-year colleges in both public and private categories). The University of California last year got roughly $1 billion in research grants and contracts from agencies of the federal government, most of it directly to individual researchers and faculty members on its nine campuses, out of a total budget of $6 billion. (About a third of the $1 billion, incidentally, took the form of "overhead," which is split half and half between the state government, where it goes into the General Fund, and the university, for whom it is a discretionary fund.)

Diverse Sources of Student Aid

In 1989–90, total student aid from all sources was running at over $27 billion a year, 62 percent higher in current dollars and 10 percent higher in real terms than in 1980–81. Of this sum, nearly $2 billion came from state grant programs, and about $6 billion came from the resources of the institutions themselves, such as gifts and endowment funds. The remainder, over $20 billion, came from federal sources in a complex combination of student grants, loans, and subsidized work-study programs. Of that large sum nearly two-thirds, or $12.6 billion, was distributed through various loan programs (which are not included in the estimates of federal support cited above). As the total amount of federal aid has grown, the proportion taking the form of loans has grown; in 1975–76, three-quarters of federal student aid was awarded in the form of grants (Lewis 1989), but by 1989–90 the share of federal student aid in the form of grants had fallen to about a third (*Chronicle of Higher Education* 1989, A-31; "Almanac," 1990, 13).

In 1986–87 nearly half (46 percent) of all undergraduates received some form of financial aid; over a third (35 percent) were receiving federal aid ("Almanac," 1990, 13, 20). In real terms, student support from all sources increased by about 10 percent over 1980–81, a little less than the increase in total enrollments (up about 12 percent over that period) but probably close to the increase in "full-time equivalent" enrollments. Aid from federally supported programs decreased by about 3 percent from 1980–81 when adjusted for inflation. But large increases in student aid at the state and institutional levels (which now compose over a quarter of the total student aid from all sources) have more than offset the drop in federal funds for student aid. State student grant programs grew by 52 percent, and aid awarded directly by the institutions grew by 90 percent, both in real terms, during the decade of the eighties (*Chronicle of Higher Education* 1989,

A-31). In this area, as in others, the states, the institutions, and their constituencies are providing more of the support for higher education, although the shift is slow and is not reflected in absolute declines in the federal commitment.[1]

Differences in State Coordination and Support

The states differ markedly among themselves in the way they organize, govern, or "coordinate" their systems of higher education. In some states, such as Utah, coordinating councils are very powerful, serving as consolidated boards that govern the whole of the public sector of postsecondary education in the state. In contrast, California's Postsecondary Education Commission has relatively little formal power, serving chiefly as a fact-gathering advisory body to state government, and is itself largely governed by representatives of the institutions that it coordinates. In still other states, like Vermont and Delaware, there are no statutory coordinating bodies at all (Kerr and Gade 1989).

Similarly, how the states support higher education varies enormously from one region of the country to another, compared with regional differences in European countries. For example, in the New England and North Central states, private colleges and universities developed early and have tended to resist the competition of big publicly supported institutions. Public institutions have grown there as elsewhere in recent decades, but the effects of that heritage can still be seen, for example, in Massachusetts and New York, where great universities like Harvard, M.I.T., Columbia, and Cornell and a host of other vigorous private institutions overshadow and overpower the public colleges and universities. By contrast, in some western states there is little private higher education at all; public institutions, such as land-grant universities and public community colleges, have a virtual monopoly on the provision of degree-credit education within their borders. These differences are clearly evident in terms of per capita state support. For example, in 1990, per capita appropriations by the fifty states for higher education within their borders averaged $159 but ranged from $312 in Alaska to $67 in New Hampshire—a difference of nearly 5:1. If those two extreme states are set aside, a comparison of the second with the forty-ninth—Hawaii and Vermont—gives a ratio of 2.5:1. A slightly different index—state appropriations per $1,000 of state income (which attempts to control for state wealth, thus giving a measure of "effort")—shows similar results; again a ratio of 5:1, although the extreme states on this measure are Wyoming ($18 per $1,000) and New Hampshire ($3.50 per $1,000) (Layzell and Lyddon 1990, table 2, pp. 23–24).

As a consequence of its system of educational federalism, the United States is evidently prepared to sustain differences (or inequities) in support for higher education among the several states of this order of magnitude. This is perhaps one of the most significant and least remarked differences between the American and European systems. Any effort to achieve or approximate equality in America's provision of public services between and among states or regions would require considerable direct intervention by the central government. The federal government has been prepared to intervene strongly in education to defend the civil rights of students and faculty, most notably in connection with the potential for discrimination on the basis of race or gender, and it can also modestly reduce inequalities among states by providing federal funds directly to students and to researchers. With a few exceptions, however, the federal government does not try to stimulate state spending on higher education to compensate for differences in state wealth or effort or give the states unrestricted funds for support of higher education.

The most important historical exceptions to this policy were the contribution of the federal government to the states through the first Morrill Act, which clearly aimed to stimulate state spending for agricultural and technical education, and the introduction of the principle of requiring the states to provide "matching dollars" (to some ratio) for specific purposes, most notably in the second Morrill Act (Brubacher and Rudy 1958, 227). After World War II, President Truman's Commission on Higher Education recommended that the federal government undertake a massive program of "general support of institutions of higher education" precisely by channeling federal funds to the states "on an equalization basis" and limiting the recipients to public colleges and universities (Finn 1978, 122). The defeat of this effort to equalize higher education across the states and the further defeat in the Education Amendments of 1972 of efforts to channel federal funding directly to the institutions through unrestricted grants have established federal policy for the present and foreseeable future. The current reluctance (or constitutional inability) of the federal government to intervene directly to affect state policy toward higher education outside the realm of the protection of civil rights and liberties underlies the considerable power of the states to organize and fund their systems of higher education relatively free of the leveling hand of the federal government. The rather stronger egalitarian instincts of Europeans and Canadians lead them to view that "freedom" with some skepticism and on the whole critically.

This brief overview of the diversity of funding, student aid, and state support has sought to put into perspective the federal role in American higher education—one that is substantial in overall size but much smaller in its direct influence or power over the system than is the role of the several states. Since its founding, the federal government has come to play a role, and often a dominant role, in many areas of social and economic life in ways its founders never anticipated. Nevertheless, its role in American higher education is limited primarily to its support for research and student aid.

In the following pages, I explore the roots of this unique character of American higher education in the colonial experience, then explain the influence of the American Revolution on the attitudes and arrangements for higher education that came out of the colonial period, and finally trace the emergence after the Revolution of a national "policy" toward higher education—a policy nowhere articulated as such but defined by a series of events over a century and a half that have shaped today's federal relations with institutions of higher education.

The Roots of American Federalism in the Colonial Experience

Despite all the changes and transformations of state, society, and economy in modern times, the American system of higher education has its roots in the colonial period, when it developed characteristics distinguishable from all other systems of higher education in the world, notably in its governance patterns, marked by a strong president and lay governing board; its extraordinary diversity of forms and functions; and its marked responsiveness to forces in society as well as in state and church.[2] In one other respect the colonial colleges are familiar to us, and that is in the importance attached to them by the societies and governments of the colonies. At a time when most European universities were not really central to the vitality of their societies and were more or less preoccupied with the preparation of theologians and divines serving an established church or with defining the virtues and polishing the accomplishments of a ruling elite, seventeenth and eighteenth century colonial colleges in America were regarded by their founders and supporters as forces for survival in a hostile environment. They were seen as crucial, indeed indispensable instruments for staving off the threat of reversion to barbarism, the threatened decline into the savagery of the surrounding forest and its Indian inhabitants. They also played a familiar role for these early Calvinists in maintaining a learned ministry and a literate laity. Moreover, in the young colonies as on the later frontier, civilization and its institutions could never be assumed to be inherited. It had always to be created and recreated; for this purpose, learning and learned persons and the institutions that engendered them were needed. As

Henry May has noted, "From the very beginnings, the expressed purpose of colonial education had been to preserve society against barbarism, and, so far as possible, against sin" (1976, 32–33).

The colonial colleges were founded as public bodies. They were established and then chartered by a public authority and were supported in part by public funds, in part by private gifts and endowments, in part by student fees. The mixing of public and private support, functions, and authority has persisted as a central characteristic of American higher education to this day, blurring the distinction between public and private colleges and universities. Americans have tended to regard all of their higher education institutions as having a public dimension, and they also allowed for a private dimension in their public institutions. As Jurgen Herbst argued (1982), one cannot see the colonial colleges as either "public" or "private" institutions, but as "provincial," stressing their function of service to their sponsoring and chartering colony, rather than to their source of support or authority. Although the distinction between "public" and "private" emerged with a certain clarity during the nineteenth century and especially after the Civil War, it is still more appropriate to see the broad spectrum of American colleges and universities as lying along a continuum from fully public to nearly purely private (Kerr 1991).

Both the geography of the Eastern Seaboard and the accidents of settlement created a series of distinct and largely self-governing colonies, each tied to metropolitan London through a charter and governor, yet separate from one another in character, social structure, and form of governance. That, in turn, meant that when colonial colleges were established they differed from one another in their origins, links to colonial government, and denominational ties (Trow 1979). As a result, the eight colonial colleges— the nurseries of so many of the Revolutionary leaders—legitimated diversity. But similarities also existed among them. They had to be created in the absence of a body of learned men. In the new world no guild of scholars, no body of learned men existed to take the governance of a college into its own hands. The very survival of the new institutions in the absence of buildings, an assured income, or a guild of scholars required a higher and more continuous level of governmental interest and involvement in institutions that had become much too important for the colonies to allow them to wither or die. Moreover, a concern for doctrinal orthodoxy, especially during the seventeenth century, provided further grounds for public authorities to create governance machinery in which its own representatives were visible or held a final veto and continuing "visitorial" and supervisory powers. The medieval idea of a university as an autonomous corporation comprising masters and scholars was certainly present in the minds of the founders of colonial colleges, but the actual circumstances of colonial life forced a drastic modification in the application of this inheritance.[3]

College charters expressly reserved for colonial governments a continuing role in the governance of colleges, placing colonial officers directly on boards of trustees or assigning to the courts and legislatures the power of review. For example, in the 1748 charter for the College of New Jersey (later to become Princeton), the province placed its governor on the board as its presiding officer, and the 1766 charter of Queen's College (later Rutgers) included among its lay trustees the governor, council president, chief justice, and attorney general of the province (Herbst 1982, 86–87, 111). And in the turbulent sectarian climate of eighteenth century America, all of the colonies carefully circumscribed the powers of the corporate universities, each making sure that the colonial governors and legislatures retained ultimate powers as "visitor." Even in Connecticut, where Yale's trustees were all Congregational ministers, the charter that incorporated the trustees as the President and Fellows of Yale College preserved to the colonial court the right "'as often as required' to inspect the college's laws, rules, and ordinances, and to repeal or disallow them 'when they shall think proper'" (Herbst 1982, 47). The charter, Herbst noted, "guaranteed the school's autonomy within specific limits" but "thus upheld the ultimate authority of the Court over the college." And in colonial America, these reserve powers were in fact used from time to time.

Both Harvard College and William and Mary College—America's only two seventeenth century foundations—were established with a two-board government, one representing the institution or corporation, the other the external trustees. In both colleges, however, "the governmental practice . . . soon lost its distinctiveness and came to resemble that of the one-board colleges. American colleges were to be ruled by powerful and respected citizens, who would govern them for their own and their children's benefit" (Herbst 1982, 61). Ironically, the nearest American colleges and universities ever came to recreating the first, or corporate, board was when they finally were able to gather together a guild of learned men who could command respect and gain a measure of professional authority. It was not until after the turn of the twentieth century that academic senates became significant parts of the governance machinery of American colleges and universities, and then this occurred only in the most prestigious institutions employing scholars who were able to use the academic marketplace to compel respect and attention from presidents and boards concerned with the status and distinction of their institutions. The relative weakness of the academic profession in the United States, as compared with its strength in the United Kingdom, especially at Oxford and Cambridge, has had large consequences for the diverging development of the two systems (Trow 1985).

With the exception of New Jersey which, because of religious diversity occurring at the end of the colonial period, chartered two colleges (now Princeton and Rutgers), each colony granted a monopoly position to its college. In this respect, each colony behaved toward its college as England behaved toward Oxford and Cambridge and as Scotland behaved toward its universities, granting them the power to award degrees within their respective "provinces." American colonial governments attempted to prevent or inhibit the appearance of rival and competitive institutions in much the same way that the government in England had prevented the dissenting academies from widening the educational market during the eighteenth century. Consequently (and other factors were doubtless involved), in England the dissenting academies never emerged as serious competitive degree-granting institutions and were destined to failure and, with one or two exceptions, to eventual extinction (Armytage 1955, 128–140, 153–156; Parker 1914, 124–136). But their existence—and relevance—was noted in the colonies, where reference was made to them, during a dispute over sectarian issues at Yale in the 1750s, as better models than the ancient universities (Herbst 1982, 77). As Beverly McAnear observed, "The founders [of the mid–eighteenth century colonial colleges] . . . transplanted the essentials of the educational system of the English dissenting academies and saw the system take root" (1955, 44). The dissenting academies were even more relevant to the proliferation of American colleges on the frontier between the Revolution and the Civil War, with the significant difference that the American colleges were encouraged and sometimes even modestly supported by public authorities.

All of the colonial colleges were provided with public funds of various kinds, though in varying amounts and degrees of consistency. Some received a flat sum or subsidy to make up an annual shortfall in operating expenses or salaries; others received assistance in the construction and maintenance of buildings. The Assembly of Virginia provided the College of William and Mary with a percentage of the duties collected on furs, skins, and imported liquor (Robson 1985, 19). These subventions reflected an organic connection between the colony and "its" college, and the colonies were not reluctant to use the power of the purse as a constraint on colleges when they were alleged to have carried their autonomy too far. The Connecticut legislature in 1755 refused its annual grant of £100 to Yale because of a sectarian dispute with the college's president (Herbst 1982, 76). As Bernard Bailyn stated the situation throughout the colonies, "The autonomy that comes from an independent, reliable, self-perpetuating income was everywhere lacking. The economic basis of self-direction in education failed to develop" (1960, 44).

In sum, the power of colonial governments over their colleges derived from three fundamental sources: the power to give or withhold a charter, the continuing powers reserved for government within the charter, and the power of the public purse. Within those constraints the colonies had the experience before the Revolution of having created a group of colleges or "university colleges" similar in certain respects but differing in others— and having created these institutions at the initiative or with the encouragement of public authorities and powerful private constituencies. Such support stands in marked contrast to the conspicuous lack of such encouragement and, indeed, the stubborn resistance of or deeply divided responses by political and ecclesiastical authorities in England to the creation of new institutions of higher education, especially and particularly those originating outside the Establishment, during the decades before 1830. As noted above, the many dissenting academies created in England during the second half of the eighteenth century never had the encouragement of central or local government, and their failure to be fully acknowledged or to gain a charter and the right to grant degrees was among the factors leading them to short lives and a dead end, of no real use or inspiration to those who created the new English colleges and universities during the next century. By contrast, America's colonial experience provided a training in the arts of establishing institutions of higher education. And the skills and attitudes necessary for the creation of new colleges that were gained during the colonial period, along with the models of governance afforded by the colonial institutions, led (in a more favorable environment than England provided) directly to the proliferation of colleges and universities after the Revolution: sixteen more between 1776 and 1800 that have survived to the present and literally hundreds over the next half century, many of which did not (Robson 1983).

The Effects of the American Revolution

Before 1776, the colonies displayed a stronger or at least as strong a connection between state and college as was apparent in the mother country, but the relationship changed drastically after the Declaration of Independence. In a formal sense, the Revolution transformed colonial governments into state governments and superimposed a national confederacy and then a federal government on top of them. However, at the same time the Revolution weakened all agencies of government by stressing the roots of the new nation in popular sovereignty, the subordination of the government to "the people," and the primacy of individual and group freedom and initiative. "The individual replaced the state as the unit of politics," wrote Robert H. Wiebe, "and the Constitution and Bill of Rights confirmed this Copernican revolution in authority. . . . Unlike the eighteenth-century venture in building a society from the top down [American society after the Revolution] originated in a multitude of everyday needs that responded to the long lines of settlement and enterprise, not the imperatives of union" (1984, 353).

At least as important as this new conception of the relation of the citizen to the state that emerged from independence was the opening of the frontier beyond the Alleghenies, which gave many Americans a chance to walk away from the settled and "European" states that succeeded the old colonies, requiring them to create, indeed invent, new forms of self-government on the frontier (Elkins and McKitrick 1968). Among the institutions of the frontier were new colleges, resembling the colonial colleges in some ways but differing in others and linking the recently opened territories to the original culture of the Atlantic. In the twenty-five years after the Declaration of Independence, of the sixteen colleges that were established (and have survived), no fewer than fourteen were created on the frontier (Robson 1983, 323). After 1800, the floodgates of education opened, and hundreds of institutions were established in both old states and new territories. Most of them were small and malnourished, and many collapsed within a few years of their founding. The reason for this explosion of educational activity was a change in the three conditions that had hitherto characterized government-college relations during the colonial period: restrictive chartering, direct interest by government in the administration of colleges, and public support of higher education.

The new states, both those that succeeded the old colonies and those carved out of the new lands in the West, did not give a monopoly to any single state college or university, reflecting the quite different relationship between state and societal institutions that emerged from the Revolution. The states granted charters much more readily than had colonies before the Revolution and on decidedly different terms. Herbst told of efforts in 1762 by Congregationalists dissatisfied with the liberal Unitarian tendencies of Harvard to create a Queen's College in western Massachusetts. The nation's oldest college and its overseers opposed the proposal and prevailed, using the argument that Harvard "was a provincial monopoly, funded and supported by the General Court for reasons of state" and "properly the College of the Government" (Herbst 1982, 136). The principle that reserved a monopoly to the "College of the Government," with its attendant rights and privileges, had to be overthrown for American higher education to break out of the restrictive chartering of higher education that had been historical practice. What is astonishing is not that it was subsequently overthrown, but that it was done with such ease as scarcely to occasion comment.

The ease with which new colleges were granted charters after the Revolution and especially after the turn of the century was both symbol and instrument of the triumph of society over the state that the Revolution had achieved. Charters were distributed rather promiscuously to any group that seemed prepared to accept responsibility for raising funds for a building and hiring a president.[4] Despite the efforts of the Federalists, central government itself over time came to be not a dominant institution (alongside the churches) but merely one player in social life, and not a very important one at that. By the fifth decade of the nineteenth century, the national government was scarcely visible in American life: no national bank, no military worth mentioning, no taxes that a growing majority of citizens could remember paying its officials (Wiebe 1984, 353). And even state governments, closer to the people and with constitutional responsibility for education, confined their role to serving as the instruments of groups and interests of the society at large, including groups that wanted to create colleges for a whole variety of motives—cultural, religious, and mercenary, in all weights and combinations.

Long-term Federal Policy toward Higher Education since the Revolution

The colonial period taught Americans how to create colleges and gave us diversity among them. The Revolution gave us freedom from central state power and especially from the power of government, both federal and state, to prevent the creation of independent colleges and universities. But these new freedoms were reinforced and given substance through a further set of decisions that together have defined federal policy toward higher education from the founding of the Republic to the present. This policy, never articulated but defined by those decisions, has been to encourage the provision of higher education, broaden access to college and university to ever wider sectors of the population, apply the contribution of higher education to the practical work of society as well as to learning and scholarship—and to do all this without directly impinging on the autonomy of the institutions or on the constitutional responsibility for higher education reposing in the states. This policy paradoxically encouraged an active federal presence in higher education, yet had the effect of driving power in higher education progressively further away from Washington, D.C., down toward the individual states, the institutions, and their individual members, students, and faculty. It became a kind of continuing self-denying ordinance by which the federal government has acted to facilitate decisions made by others, rather than forcing its own decisions on the states, institutions, or members.

Five of these decisions since the Revolution were so significant as to warrant separate discussion:

1. the failure of George Washington and his immediate presidential successors to establish a national university in the District of Columbia;
2. the Supreme Court's decision of 1819 in the Dartmouth College case;
3. the Morrill, or Land Grant, Acts of 1862 and 1890 and the Hatch Act of 1887;
4. the Servicemen's Readjustment Act of 1944, better known as the G.I. Bill; and
5. the Education Amendments of 1972, which created the broad spectrum of federal programs of student aid that we have inherited, much expanded and amended

The Failure to Establish the University of the United States

Consider first the failure to establish a national university. The defeat of a proposal is a policy decision, and in the case of the failure of the proposed University of the United States, it is perhaps the most momentous in the history of American higher education.

A multiplicity of forces and motives lay behind the establishment of colleges and universities throughout our nation's history. Among these, as noted above, were a variety of religious motives, a fear of relapse into barbarism at the frontier, and the need for various kinds of professionals, as well as state pride and local boosterism, philanthropy, idealism, educational reform, and even speculation in land, in all combinations. But the resulting number and diversity of institutions, competing with one another for students, resources, and teachers, bringing market considerations and market mechanisms right into the heart of an ancient cultural foundation—all of this also required the absence of any central force of authority that could restrain it, that could limit or control the proliferation of institutions of higher education. The states could not be that restraining force; under the pressures of competition and emulation, they have tended throughout our history to create institutions and programs in the numbers and to the standards of their neighbors. Crucially important has been the absence of a federal ministry of education with the power to charter (or to refuse to charter) new institutions and of a single preeminent university that could influence institutions in other ways.

The closest we came as a nation to establishing such a central force was the attempt first by George Washington and then, though with less enthusiasm, by the next five presidents to found a University of the United States at the seat of government in the District of Columbia (Trow 1979). Washington, in fact, made provision for such a university in his will and pleaded strongly for it in his last message to Congress, where he argued that it would promote national unity—a matter of deep concern at a time when the primary loyalties of many Americans were to their sovereign states rather than to the infant nation. In addition, he saw the possibility of creating one really first-class university by concentrating money and other resources in it: "Our Country, much to its honor, contains many Seminaries of learning highly respectable and useful; but the funds upon which they rest are too narrow to command the ablest Professors, in the different departments of liberal knowledge, for the Institution contemplated, though they would be excellent auxiliaries" (Hofstadter and Smith 1961, 1:158).

Here, indeed, Washington was right in his diagnosis. The many institutions that sprang up between the Revolution and the Civil War all competed for very scarce resources and all suffered to some degree from malnutrition. Malnutrition at the margin is still a characteristic of a system of institutions influenced so heavily by market forces. Defeat of the national university meant that American higher education would develop, to this day, without a single capstone institution. Had we instead concentrated resources in one university of high standard early in our national life, it might have been the equal of the great and ancient universities of Europe or of the distinguished new universities then being established in Germany and elsewhere. As it was, whatever the United States called its institutions of higher learning, the nation simply did not have a single genuine university—no institution of really first-class standing that could bring its students as far or as deep into the various branches of learning as could the institutions of the Old World—until after the Civil War.

A national university would have profoundly affected American higher education. As the preeminent university, it would have had an enormous influence, direct and indirect, on every other college in the country and, through them, on the secondary schools as well. Its standards of entry, its curricula, its educational philosophies, even its forms of instruction, would have been models for every institution that hoped to send some of its graduates to the University in Washington. A federal system of high standard would surely have inhibited the emergence of the hundreds of small, half-starved state and denominational colleges that sprang up over the next century. They simply could not have offered work to the standard that the University of the United States would have set for the baccalaureate degree and demanded of applicants to its own postgraduate studies. In the United States, after the defeat of the University of the United States, no one has challenged the principle of high academic standards across the whole system because no one has proposed it: there have been no common standards, high or otherwise. In that spirit, we have created a multitude of institutions of every sort, offering academic work of every description and at every level of seriousness and standard.

The Dartmouth College Case

Another major event in the early history of the Republic had powerful effects on the shape and character of American higher education as we know it today: the 1819 decision of the Supreme Court in the Dartmouth College case (Whitehead and Herbst 1986). This was a landmark decision in that it affirmed the principle of the sanctity of contracts between governments and private institutions. In so doing, it gave expression to the Federalist belief that the government should not interfere with private property even for the purpose of benefiting the public welfare. John Marshall, then Chief Justice of the Supreme Court, had written earlier: "I consider the interference of the legislature in the management of our private affairs, whether those affairs are committed to a company or remain under individual direction, as equally dangerous and unwise." That antistatist position today sounds deeply conservative, but from another perspective it is radically libertarian and had broad and liberalizing effects on higher education. Marshall and his colleagues on the Court decided in the Dartmouth College case that a charter of a private college or university was a contract that a state could not retroactively abridge. And that had important repercussions both for the growth of capitalist enterprises and for the future development of higher education in the United States.

The rationale for the proposed changes in Dartmouth's charter was the plausible argument that, as the college had been established (though as a private corporation) to benefit the people of New Hampshire, this could best be accomplished by giving the public, through the state legislature, a voice in the operation of the institution. The state wanted to improve the college as a place of learning by modernizing its administration, creating the framework for a university, and encouraging a freer, nonsectarian atmosphere conducive to republicanism.

These goals were very much in the Jeffersonian tradition that encouraged the creation of "republican" institutions—by the states—to meet the needs of a new nation. In this spirit, in 1816 the New Hampshire legislature had passed a bill giving the state government broad powers to "reform" Dartmouth. Chief Justice Marshall, ruling in favor of the college trustees, declared that state legislatures were forbidden by the Constitution to pass any law "impairing the obligation of contracts" and that the charter originally granted the college was a contract (Hofstadter and Smith 1961, 1:218). In many ways Marshall's opinion followed the traditional view of the role of educational institutions in English society.

The Dartmouth College decision, preventing the state of New Hampshire from taking over the college, sustained the older, more modest role of the state in educational affairs against those who looked to the government to take a greater role in the working of society and its institutions. Marshall's decision had the practical effect of safeguarding the founding and proliferation of privately controlled colleges, even poor ones. Thereafter, promoters of private colleges knew that once they had obtained a state charter they were secure in the future control of the institution. After this decision, state control over the whole of higher education, including the private sector, was no longer possible.

The failure of the University of the United States and the success of Dartmouth College in its appeal to the Supreme Court were both victories for local initiative and for private entrepreneurship. The first of these set limits on the role of the federal government in shaping the character of the whole of American higher education; the second set even sharper limits on the power of the state over private colleges. Together, these two events constituted a kind of charter for unrestrained individual and group initiative in the creation of colleges of all sizes, shapes, and creeds. Almost any motive or combination of motives and interests could bring a college into being between the Revolution and the Civil War, and thereafter its survival depended largely on its being able to secure support from a church, from wealthy benefactors, from student fees, and even perhaps from the state. The colleges thus created were established relatively easily but without guarantees of survival. As a result, there arose a situation resembling the behavior of living organisms in an ecological system—competitive for resources, highly sensitive to the demands of the environment, and inclined, over time, through the ruthless process of natural selection, to be adaptive to those aspects of their environment that permitted their survival. Their environment also has included other colleges and, later, universities. So we see in this frog pond a set of mechanisms that we usually associate with the behavior of small entrepreneurs in a market: the anxious concern for what the market wants, the readiness to adapt to its apparent preferences, the effort to find a special place in that market through the marginal differentiation of the product, and a readiness to enter into symbiotic or parasitic relationships with other producers for a portion of that market. That is, to this day, the world of American higher education.

The 1862 Morrill Act

The Morrill Act, which created the land-grant colleges and universities, is indeed a landmark in American higher education. It was very far from being the first provision of support for higher education by central government through grants of government-owned land; indeed, under the Articles of Confederation the Northwest Ordinance provided for tracts of land to be set aside for the support of institutions of higher education in the Western Reserve. Ohio University, among others, was a beneficiary of such an early grant. But the Morrill Act provided support on an altogether different scale; in 1862 the federal government gave land to the states for the support of colleges and universities of an area equal to the whole of Switzerland or the Netherlands, about eleven thousand square miles. And it did this in the most extraordinarily permissive way. The act made no fixed requirements as to type of institution or, beyond broad designations of fields of study, as to content of instruction. The only positive obligations were to dispose of the land or scrip in a manner or on terms left to state discretion; maintain the fund as a perpetual endowment invested at 5 percent; devote the income to one or more institutions which, while including the traditional college subjects, must provide instruction in agriculture, mechanic arts, and military tactics; and make an annual report on the results (Ross 1942, 68).

The beneficiaries of the act were whoever the states decided they should be—among them Cornell in New York, M.I.T. in Massachusetts, and Yale's Sheffield Scientific School in Connecticut. In some states the money went to an existing state-supported institution; in California, the university was created through a merger of an existing private liberal arts college with the land-grant endowment. In both Oregon and Kentucky the money went to denominational colleges that remained under church control (Ross 1942, 75). In many other states, especially in the South and West, a new "A&M" college was created to be the beneficiary of the land-grant fund.

Basically, the federal government put the money—or at least the scrip—

on the stump and walked away, partly because there was no federal educational bureaucracy to provide for federal direction and control of state policy and partly because there was no consensus about what these institutions should look like or should be doing. Indeed, very sharp differences developed in Congress and outside it about the relative emphasis to be placed in these new institutions on pure or applied science, on practical experience and manual work, or on the old classical curriculum. The federal government's solution was to allow these contending forces to fight it out in each state. The result, needless to say, was various and messy, marked by ineptitude and corruption in places, confusion almost everywhere, but also by great imagination, creativity, and even genius—as illustrated by the vision of Ezra Cornell and Andrew Dixon White in New York. Some states got fifty cents an acre for their land, others ten times that much, and the variation in educational practice and academic standard was of the same order of magnitude, adding to the already high level of diversity in American higher education.

One may ask what the results might have been of trying to create a tidier system, one more rationally coordinated and marked by a clearer common sense of academic direction, higher academic standards, more highly qualified and better paid staff, better prepared students, and more adequate initial funding for buildings and equipment. We are, of course, describing the creation of the modern European university systems—and they have been trying to break out of the straitjacket of those constricting commitments and structures since the end of World War II, with great difficulties and only partial success.

The G.I. Bill of 1944

We now rightly think of the Servicemen's Readjustment Act of 1944—the original G.I. Bill—as one of the best things that ever happened to American higher education. It enormously broadened the idea of college going, it moved the enrollment rate from 15 percent of the age grade in 1939 toward 50 percent or more currently, and it brought seriousness and maturity to undergraduate classrooms that were not accustomed to them and that have never quite lost them.

But no one at the time it was debated expected it to be quite as successful as it was. Most estimates during the debates were that perhaps 800,000 veterans would take advantage of the program. By 1956, when the last veteran had received the last check, 2.25 million veterans had attended college under its auspices (Olson 1974, 43). In contrast, the United Kingdom had a comparable program, the "Further Education and Training

Scheme," which raised university enrollments from about 50,000 before World War II to 80,000 shortly after the war, causing great concern in the Ministry of Education regarding a possible decline in standards (Preston and Preston 1974). In the United Kingdom, that problem was met by steadily raising standards for entry to the universities after the war. As a result, the proportion enrolled in British higher education in 1987 (14 percent of the age grade) was roughly the same as the proportion enrolled in American colleges and universities fifty years earlier.

Two features of the G.I. Bill deserve particular emphasis. First, veterans could take their tuition payments and stipends anywhere they wished, certainly to any accredited college or university that would accept them and to many other nonaccredited postsecondary educational institutions, too. Again, there were irregularities at the edges: some corruption, some institutions that took tuition money without doing much teaching, whose students enrolled for the modest stipends provided. But again, we must consider the costs of closing those loopholes; the proliferation of forms and surveillance, the steady pressure to rationalize and standardize to make assessment, management, and credentialing easier. The federal government accepted the probability of abuse of the legislation, perhaps recognizing that rationalization in higher education, as elsewhere, is the enemy of diversity. And, as we have seen, federal policies on the whole have consistently favored diversity.

Second, one crucial provision of the G.I. Bill stipulated that "no department, agency, or officer of the United States, in carrying out the provisions [of this Act] shall exercise any supervision or control, whatsoever, over any State, educational agency . . . or any educational or training institution" (Olson 1974, 17–18). Of course, that is in the tradition of our constitutional reservation of responsibility for education to the states. But beyond that, we see here the same self-denying ordinance—the sharp separation of financial support from academic influence—that marked earlier federal policy and that became the model and precedent for the Education Amendments of 1972 and thereafter, which provide substantial noncategorical need-based federal aid to students by way of grants and loans.

The Education Amendments of 1972

The federal legislation on education passed in 1972 established higher education as a national priority in its own right. Various agencies of the federal government were already providing support for targeted issues, such as science laboratories and libraries, and for targeted groups of students, as through fellowships for graduate students in certain areas deemed vital to the national security or economic welfare. But during the late sixties and early seventies, broad support developed for greatly expanded federal aid for higher education, both to aid institutions undergoing rapid growth and to encourage further expansion of access, especially by groups historically underrepresented in higher education.

Most of the major organizations in higher education came out strongly in favor of direct, unrestricted aid to the colleges and universities themselves. But key members of Congress and the influential Carnegie Commission on Higher Education led by Clark Kerr argued strongly for federal support in the form of need-based aid to students rather than block grants directly to the institutions that would be linked to enrollments.[5] The tradition of the G.I. Bill was surely an element in the debate, but the driving motivation of those in favor of federal support in the form of student aid was the wish to increase the power of the students in the market and thus encourage the responsiveness of the institutions to changing patterns of student demand. The amendments as enacted in fact centered on student aid; while continuing certain earmarked provisions for the institutions (such as support for college libraries and for the construction of certain academic facilities), the largest part of the new programs took the form of federal grants and guaranteed loans to students, with special attention to needy or disadvantaged students. But this was now broad-spectrum student aid, not limited to particular fields of study or professions.

That the legislation took the form it did almost certainly enabled it to survive periodic budget cuts and changes of political mood in Washington by creating a large, stable voting constituency of greater weight to politicians than the leadership of the higher education world itself. But closer to the motivations of those who wrote the legislation is the fact that federal support in the form of student aid is the surest way of defending the autonomy of institutions of higher education against the leverage that block grants would have given to the federal government when, in time, it surely would have wanted to exert its influence over those institutions.

Over time further legislation has extended federal student aid to broader segments of the society and substituted loans for grants for most of the students aided. Although many of the provisions for institutional aid have been phased out over the last two decades, student aid remains the largest element of the federal role in higher education, alongside the equally crucial support provided by federal agencies to university-based research.

How did these five decisions, taken together, constitute a policy, and why, in retrospect, might one think of them as "successful"? I suggest that in each case the decision contributed to the diversity of American higher education—a diversity of type, of educational character and mission, of academic standard, and of access. In each case, public policy tended to strengthen the competitive market in higher education by weakening any central authority that could substitute regulations and standards for competition. It accomplished this by driving decisions downward and outward, by giving more resources and discretion to the consumers of education and the institutions most responsive to them. Public policy decisions strengthened the states in relation to the federal government, as in the defeat of the University of the United States and the passage of the Morrill Acts; strengthened the institutions in relation to state governments, as in the Dartmouth College case and the Hatch Act; and strengthened students in relation to their institutions, as in the G.I. Bill and the Education Amendments of 1972.

The Current Expansion of Federal Interventions

From the early land grants to speculators encouraging settlement in the Northwest Territories to the latest Pell grants to needy students, the federal government's central policy has been to expand and extend access to higher education more and more widely throughout the society. And since World War II, the federal government, with an expressed interest in the economic and military strength of the nation, has been the major source of support of both basic and applied research in the universities. These commitments of funds, directly to researchers and students, are still the largest and most visible forms of federal involvement in American higher education, the extent of which is sketched above. There is also the substantial but largely hidden subsidy provided by the federal government (and most state governments as well) through provision in the tax code for full deduction for income tax purposes of contributions to institutions of higher education (along with most other kinds of nonprofit "charitable" institutions). A further subsidy in the tax code gives parents a dependent's exemption for children who are full-time college or university students for whom they provide more than half the support.

During the past three decades the federal government has extended its interest in higher education in ways that reflect the central role that this institution now plays in American society and the economy. Some of these further interventions reflect the hugely increased size of the federal role in support for research since the end of World War II. The federal government's decisions about how to allocate its research support funds now affect the whole shape and direction of American science.

One set of issues centers around the competitive claims of "big science"—such enormous and expensive enterprises as the superconductor-supercollider, the plan to map the human genome, the launching of the Hubble telescope, and the exploration of space—and the ordinary claims of university-based researchers doing studies on their own initiative individually or in small teams. Big science is necessarily competitive with small science for funds, but its decisions are each so expensive and consequential that they inevitably bring political considerations (and pressures) into the heart of the scientific decision-making process. Efforts continue to be made to insulate these decisions from the most crass political forces and to make them "on their merits," but these mechanisms are strained by the traditions of state competition for federal funds in the Congress and the White House, the traditions of political deals and pork-barrel legislation in a populist society.

Until recently, the nature and administration of research overhead funds, paid by the federal government as part of their grants and contracts with university researchers, would have nicely illustrated my theme of the federal government's self-denying principle with respect to American higher education. These overheads, intended to reimburse the universities for the costs of maintaining the research facilities in which the federally funded scientific work was done, were negotiated with the individual universities, public and private, and then very loosely monitored, in ways that suggested that government funders of research were primarily interested in supporting the infrastructures of research without trying to manage them. The recent embarrassing revelations of inappropriate and (in part) illegal charges for overhead costs at Stanford threaten to change this older, looser relationship between the universities and their federal funding agencies, not just for Stanford but for the whole universe of research and universities (Hamilton 1991, 1430). The case has also brought committees of Congress (and their staff members) directly into the overhead picture. To a considerable degree, the freedom of American colleges and universities from the kind of close governmental oversight familiar in other societies has been based on a relatively high degree of trust on the part of American society (and its governmental institutions) in higher education. If that trust is eroded through such scandals as at Stanford, the autonomy of universities may be similarly eroded. It is too early to tell the effects of this event on the larger question of the relations of higher education with agencies of the federal government.

Some observers of federally funded research believe that we may already have reached the point of no return. In an editorial in *Science,* Philip Abelson observed that

> a particularly dismaying feature of the government-university interface is that relationships continue on a long-term course of evolving deterioration. In the early days after World War II, there was a high degree of mutual trust and an absence of bureaucratic requirement. Scientists had freedom to formulate and conduct their programs of research. Later the bureaucrats took over and placed emphasis on project research with highly detailed budgets and detailed research proposals. That, of course, is the road to pedestrian research (1991, 605).

And he cited the proliferation of administrative requirements and regulations as a serious drag on the freedom and quality of scientific work in the universities.

In recent decades the federal government—through all three of its branches—has become increasingly active in connection with its interest in the protection of the civil rights of citizens, most notably in relation to possible forms of discrimination against racial and ethnic minorities, women, and other vulnerable groups in American colleges and universities. These activities, affecting such issues as the confidentiality of academic personnel files, the monitoring of student admissions and faculty appointment and promotion practices, the protection of human subjects in scientific research, and many rules and regulations governing federally funded research, have bypassed state agencies and brought the federal government directly into the daily life of the colleges and universities.

These developments are at odds with the pattern of federal support without the exercise of substantial directive power that I have suggested has been the historical relation of the federal government to American higher education. One can see these developments as dramatic but limited changes in policy, leaving issues of the basic character and mission of American colleges and universities to their own governing boards and state authorities. Others may see these developments and tendencies as marking a sharp change in the character and direction of federal policy in the realm of higher education, associated with the federal government's increased role as protector of civil rights (whose definition has been broadened by federal courts in recent decades) and also with the sheer growth in the size, cost, and national importance of the education, training, and research done in American universities and colleges. It remains to be seen whether a decline in public trust in the institutions of higher education or the federal government's legitimate interest in the defense of equal rights for all citizens will lead to fundamental changes in what has been a unique and fruitful three-cornered relationship among American colleges and universities and their state and federal governments.

Notes

1. Looking at trends in state support over the past decade, it is clear that many states cut their support for public colleges and universities during the severe recession of 1980–82 but that thereafter the levels of state support tended to rise about as fast as the economic recovery and rising revenues permitted. State tax funds for the operation of higher education (this does not include capital costs) were nearly $31 billion for 1984–85, up 19 percent over 1983–84 (Evangelauf 1985). By 1990 the states were spending nearly $41 billion on operating expenses for higher education, up 23 percent (adjusted for inflation) over 1980–81. The current recession is causing a decline, not in state spending in higher education but in the rate of growth of state spending. Spending on higher education by the states in 1990–91 was 11.6 percent higher than two years earlier, but this was the lowest rate of increase in state support for higher education in thirty years (Jaschik 1990, 1).

2. This section draws on my paper (with Sheldon Rothblatt), "Government Policies and Higher Education: A Comparison of Britain and the United States, 1630–1860" (Rothblatt and Trow 1992).

3. At Harvard, for example, the charter of 1650 "exemplified a carefully wrought compromise between a medieval tradition of corporate autonomy and a modern concern for territorial authorities over all matters of state and religion. The former was preserved, even though weakly, in the Corporation; the latter was institutionalized in the Board of Overseers" (Herbst 1982, 16).

4. On the founding of Allegheny College in western Pennsylvania in 1815, see Rothblatt and Trow (1992), pp. 14–17.

5. For a discussion of the debate in Congress and elsewhere leading up to the passage of this law, see Finn 1978, especially pp. 121–128.

References

Abelson, Philip. 1991. "Editorial: Federal Impediments to Scientific Research." *Science,* 251:605.

"Almanac." 1988. *Chronicle of Higher Education,* 35(1):3.

"Almanac." 1990. *Chronicle of Higher Education,* 37(1):3.

Armytage, W.H.G. 1955. *Civic Universities: Aspects of a British Tradition,* pp. 128–140, 153–156. London: Ernest Benn Ltd.

Bailyn, Bernard. 1960. *Education in the Forming of American Society.* Chapel Hill: University of North Carolina Press for the Institute of Early American History and Culture at Williamsburg, Va.

Brubacher, John S., and Willis Rudy. 1958. *Higher Education in Transition,* p. 227. New York: Harper.

Chronicle of Higher Education. 1989. (6 September).

Elkins, Stanley, and Eric McKitrick. 1968. "A Meaning for Turner's Frontier: Democracy in the Old Northwest." In Richard Hofstadter and Seymour Martin Lipset, eds., *Turner and the Sociology of the Frontier,* pp. 120–151. New York: Basic Books.

Evangelauf, J. 1985. "States' Spending on Colleges Rises 19 Pct. in 2 Years, Nears $31-Billion for '85–86." *Chronicle of Higher Education,* 30 October, p. 1.

———. 1991. "A Record 13,951,000 Students Enrolled in College Last Fall, Education Department Survey Shows." *Chronicle of Higher Education,* 37(24):1.

Finn, Chester E., Jr. 1978. *Scholars, Dollars, and Bureaucrats.* Washington, D.C.: Brookings.

Hamilton, David. 1991. "Stanford in the Hot Seat." *Science,* 251:1420.

Herbst, Jurgen. 1982. *From Crisis to Crisis: American College Government, 1636–1819.* Cambridge: Harvard University Press.

Hofstadter, Richard, and Wilson Smith, eds. 1961. *American Higher Education: A Documentary History.* 2 vols. Chicago: University of Chicago Press.

Jaschik, Scott. 1990. "States Spending $40.8-Billion on Colleges This Year; Growth Rate at 30-Year Low." *Chronicle of Higher Education,* 37(8):1.

Kerr, Clark. 1991. "The American Mixture of Higher Education in Perspective: Four Dimensions." In *The Great Transformation in Higher Education, 1960–1980,* ch. 3, pp. 27–45. Albany: State University of New York Press.

Kerr, Clark, and Marian L. Gade. 1989. *The Guardians: Boards of Trustees of American Colleges and Universities.* Washington, D.C.: Association of Governing Boards of Universities and Colleges.

Layzell, Daniel T., and Jan W. Lyddon. 1990. *Budgeting for Higher Education at the State Level. Enigma, Paradox, and Ritual,* table 2, pp. 23–24. Washington, D.C.: George Washington University.

Lewis, Gwendolyn L. 1989. "Trends in Student Aid: 1963–64 to 1988–89." *Research in Higher Education,* 30:547–561.

May, Henry. 1976. *The Enlightenment in America.* New York: Oxford University Press.

McAnear, Beverly. 1955. "College Founding in the American Colonies, 1745–75." *Mississippi Valley Historical Review,* 42(1): 24–44.

National Center for Education Statistics. 1989. *Digest of Education Statistics, 1989.* Washington, D.C.: U.S. Department of Education, Office of Educational Research and Improvement.

Olson, Keith W. 1974. *The G.I. Bill, the Veterans, and the Colleges.* Lexington: University Press of Kentucky.

Parker, Irene. 1914. *Dissenting Academies in England,* pp. 124–136. Cambridge: Cambridge University Press.

Preston, H., and H. M. Preston. 1974. "The Further Education and Training Scheme." In Selma J. Mushken, ed., *Recurrent Education.* Washington, D.C.: National Institute of Education, U.S. Department of Education.

Robson, David W. 1983. "College Founding in the New Republic, 1776–1800." *History of Education Quarterly,* 23(3):323–341.

———. 1985. *Educating Republicans: The College in the Era of the American Revolution, 1750–1800.* Westport, Conn.: Greenwood Press.

Ross, Earle D. 1942. *Democracy's College: The Land-Grant Movement in the Formative Stage.* Ames: Iowa State College Press.

Rothblatt, Sheldon, and Martin Trow. 1992. "Government Policies and Higher Education: A Comparison of Britain and the United States, 1630–1860." In Colin Crouch and Anthony Heath, eds., *The Sociology of Social Reform.* Oxford: Oxford University Press.

Trow, Martin. 1979. "Aspects of Diversity in American Higher Education." In Herbert Gans, Nathan Glazer, Joseph R. Gusfield, and Christopher Jencks, eds., *On the Making of Americans,* pp. 271–290. Philadelphia: University of Pennsylvania Press.

————. 1985. "Comparative Reflections on Leadership in Higher Education." *European Journal of Education,* 20(2–3):143–159.

Whitehead, John S., and Jurgen Herbst. 1986. "How to Think about the Dartmouth College Case." *History of Education Quarterly,* 26:333–349.

Wiebe, Robert H. 1984. *The Opening of American Society.* New York: Vintage Books.

4 Research Universities in a New Era: From the 1980s to the 1990s

ROGER L. GEIGER

The 1980s were in many ways a tranquil interlude for higher education. Enrollments were largely static, few noteworthy programs were introduced, and government policies were perhaps more sclerotic there than elsewhere. But beneath the surface there was movement. The 1980s were above all an evolutionary decade, and for no segment of American higher education was this evolution more consequential than for research universities, largely because of changes affecting academic research itself. For this reason, the 1980s marked the beginning of a new era for the university research system, the fourth distinctive stage since the end of World War II—following the postwar era of 1945–57, the Sputnik era of 1958–68, and a period of stagnation from 1969 to 1979 (Geiger 1990; Kerr 1990). At the beginning of the 1990s, the distinctive characteristics of this era appear intact, even though the environment for higher education continues to evolve. Accordingly, in this chapter four basic trends of the new era are first described and then several of the conditions affecting the lives of universities at the beginning of the 1990s are discussed.

The Trends of the 1980s

Despite initial trepidations, the 1980s turned out to be a time for research universities to exploit their inherent strengths and to bolster their resources.[1] Two perceptible changes in public attitudes toward higher education set the stage for this scenario. The first was a greater appreciation of—and greater rewards to—academic quality. The clearest evidence of this was the strong demand for places at selective colleges and universities throughout the 1980s. Another sign was the enthusiasm manifested by alumni and donors toward such institutions.

The second change was more specific in timing and message. It stemmed from the conjuncture of growing concern about the international competitiveness of American industry and the explosive development of biotechnology. The latter served, as the atomic bomb had for a previous generation, to show that the purest academic research could have a profound practical effect. This was a message that research universities yearned to hear: a quarter century after Sputnik, they once more discovered a compelling rationale for their distinctive mission.

Privatization

Privatization—the general term indicating a growing reliance on private sources of income—has been a relatively recent development in higher education. For thirty years after World War II, government investments in higher education increased far faster than private inputs. This trend was definitely reversed during the 1980s (Geiger 1988). In just the first half of the decade, funds from private sources grew from 83 to 86 percent of basic educational expenditures at private institutions and from 24 to 28 percent at public institutions. These changes represented an additional $2.3 billion of annual support for higher education provided through private means.

Increases in student tuition brought the greatest additions to revenues in the 1980s. Large annual percentage hikes were originally provoked by double-digit inflation at the end of the 1970s, but such increases then persisted even after inflation subsided. Universities readily justified these actions by their need to catch up with inflated price levels. When no significant backlash materialized, they continued to raise tuition to help meet their accumulated backlog of needs. For the decade, average university tuition rose more rapidly in the private sector than in the public, and it rose most rapidly at private universities. Their cost of attendance rose nearly 60 percent in real terms.

In a longer perspective, the resort to higher tuition was a continuation— indeed, an intensification—of tendencies that had been present since the early 1970s. Strong demand for quality undergraduate programs in the 1980s, however, took precedence over earlier fears that high tuition would reduce access. The relative decline of government support for higher education has nevertheless driven much of the tuition rise. Tuition was substituted for insufficient state appropriations at public universities, largely to maintain accustomed academic standards. At private institutions, a portion of the tuition rise was devoted to providing substantial amounts of student financial aid, thus compensating in part for shrinking federal programs.

Universities also turned to voluntary support with great effectiveness in the 1980s. Overall giving to higher education had declined in real terms from the late 1960s through the midseventies. A modest recovery then only regained the lost ground. The 1980s, however, emerged as the most propitious era for fund raising since the late 1950s. This new bounty chiefly enlarged existing patterns of giving, which benefited research universities, but a few new developments were evident. Among recipients, many public institutions that had lacked highly organized development efforts became aggressive fund raisers during the decade. Among donors, corporate giving significantly expanded to equal more than a fifth of all voluntary support—a development that also favored research universities, especially public ones. Overall, few institutions failed to take advantage of the propitious conditions for fund raising. In 1990, thirty-eight of the fifty-six universities that belonged to the Association of American Universities were either conducting or planning formal campaigns—and at least six of these had billion-dollar targets.

Donated funds have been directed unequally to university departments and thus have influenced the uneven expansion of university activities. Schools of business have been especially well treated, and corporations have been solicitous toward engineering and applied sciences. Voluntary support has thus invigorated those professional schools and departments that have greatest contact with the corporate world. This development was one component in the general turning outward of universities in the 1980s.

An additional and more subtle dimension of privatization has been the greater relative strengthening of private institutions. The roots of this trend go back a quarter century to the era when just the reverse was true. By the late 1960s, most private research universities had reached a point at which their aspirations had outrun their resources. Their first reaction was to scale back expansion plans and to seek additional revenues, often through more aggressive management of endowment funds. A second, more severe round of fiscal distress followed early in the 1970s, due to shrinkage of voluntary support, inflation, a weak economy, and the bursting of the bubble in research and graduate education. These universities then endured a more painful episode of actual retrenchment accompanied by a rationalization of operations. Private universities emerged by the late 1970s as leaner, more efficient organizations that were reluctant to make new commitments unless adequate financing was assured. The financial pressures caused by inflation and recession reinforced these lessons. On the whole, private universities expanded commitments with circumspection during the prosperous years that followed.

Public universities learned these lessons later and less thoroughly. Their funding held up well during the 1960s, and the shortfalls of the early 1970s seemed to be aberrations. Their dependence on state appropriations gave them less control over their finances, which translated into less incentive to streamline operations. Indeed, bad funding years struck suddenly but were usually followed, sooner or later, by some measure of restitution. Although the public research universities have expanded their private revenues considerably, these funds have tended to compensate for continued weak funding from the states. At no major state research university have state appropriations kept pace with the rise in tuition income.

Differences of this kind have a cumulative effect. During the generation of massive government investment in higher education between 1945 and 1975, state universities tended to outdistance private ones academically. Since then, however, movement seems to have been in the other direction. When the standings of leading universities in *An Assessment of Research-Doctorate Programs in the United States* by Jones, Lindzey, and Coggeshall (1982) are compared to those in the Roose-Andersen ratings (1970), private institutions show an overall gain in rank (Webster 1983).

Programmatic Support of Research

Universities in the 1980s performed more programmatic research (i.e., research intended to be useful to outside sponsors). This is not necessarily applied or "practical" research—the ratio of applied to basic research actually declined slightly during the decade. Despite longstanding public pressure to get more payoff from university research, it was not until the 1980s that conditions changed sufficiently to make this feasible. Not only was more funding available for programmatic research, but universities showed a new receptivity toward such work.

Among patrons, three developments highlight the drift toward programmatic research.

1. At the beginning of the decade, the vast expansion of military research and development begun during the Carter administration and greatly accelerated during the first Reagan administration affected universities. Only a small portion of these funds trickled down to support academic research, but that trickle was sufficient to make the Department of Defense the fastest-growing federal source of support for university research. Its outlays

doubled from 1978 to 1983, and it surpassed the National Science Foundation as the second largest patron of research. This particular development has run its course, but that has not affected the overall trend.

2. The National Science Foundation (NSF) currently aspires to become the fastest-growing federal patron, but ironically it has forwarded that claim on the basis of furthering programmatic ends. Under the stewardship of Erich Bloch, the NSF accorded engineering an equal status with science in foundation nomenclature and embraced economic competitiveness as a mission. Through the NSF Engineering Research Centers, it has actively nurtured university-industry cooperation.

3. This last area has provided the third major component of programmatic drift. Industry-sponsored research is programmatic by nature, and it has easily been the most rapidly growing component of academic research in the 1980s. Currently, industry supports 6.6 percent of university research directly, and perhaps half as much again from other sources is intended for this end. Industry thus accounts for approximately one-tenth of university research—double what it did fifteen years ago.

The drift toward programmatic research has on balance been a boon to research universities. It has made the 1980s a decade of significant progress in research rather than a repeat of the dismal seventies. It has helped to make the university research system more pluralistic, with four of every nine new dollars in the eighties coming from nonfederal sources. But this new emphasis in research has carried through to other facets of university behavior. Most disturbing to most observers has been the endeavor to commercialize university research.

Universities generally adopted new standards of entrepreneurial behavior in the 1980s. The justification was to further the transfer of technology—the linkage between university research and contributions to the productive economy. The means for this were, principally, patenting aggressively, cultivating "propinquity effects" in research parks or business incubators, and promoting the formation of new firms with venture capital and equity stakes (Geiger 1992a; Matkin 1990).

The criticisms of university involvement with industry have chiefly focused on such commercialization of research by institutions or individual faculty members. Fears include the loss of faculty loyalties and efforts, the conflict of interest between the free dissemination of knowledge and knowledge-linked investments, the misuse of graduate students on commercial ventures, and the withholding of knowledge because of possible commercial value. The basic problem is that these are matters toward which universities must maintain vigilant and responsible policies; however, as universities themselves increase their commercial activities, the apparent conflict grows between their academic responsibilities and their vested financial interests (Fairweather 1988; Kenney 1986).

To dwell on such negatives nevertheless obscures two important points. First, the fears of critics ring rather hollow when applied to institutions where these practices have long been conducted responsibly and well. Second, even in the case of institutions just initiating such practices, the arguments have had no influence whatsoever on university behavior. The inducements to engage in entrepreneurial behavior, in other words, have far outweighed the caveats.

There are in fact two large ambiguities at the center of the commercial relations of universities. No one doubts that Stanford can do these things effectively, but how many other universities can emulate Stanford? Successful commercial relations depend upon the "economics of opportunism," but potentially lucrative opportunities are simply not abundant at most institutions. The notorious successes of some universities in commercial activities such as patents and research parks have come from capitalizing on extraordinary opportunities, but attempts to stimulate such activities systematically make universities more like other market participants, thus lessening their unique advantage (Geiger 1992a).

The second ambiguity has to do with the rationale for engaging in commercial relationships: Are they an extension of the service role of universities, or do they represent an opportunity to make money? Universities would undoubtedly like to have it both ways, but, aside from the experienced players, most cannot. Very few universities would seem to be currently turning a profit from commercial relationships. This situation is not yet really alarming, since these are often long-term investments—and they can be justified in any case as part of the service mission. But for a university truly to embrace technology transfer as part of its institutional mission requires decisive actions to assure that discoveries are disclosed, that patents are marketed, that commercial possibilities are capitalized, and that propinquity effects are realized (Geiger 1991; Smith and Karlesky 1977–78). To do these things well demands the establishment of separate and costly organizational structures, staffed by nonacademic professionals and well removed from the academic core of the university.

In sum, entrepreneurship, technology transfer, contributions to the economy—all have coalesced into a service mission that is largely autonomous from the academic goals of universities. Private institutions like M.I.T. and Stanford have pioneered this role, but it has recently had its greatest appeal to public research universities. They often include large engineering or agricultural colleges to which much of this activity is linked. In this respect, the entire programmatic drift in research support has been more congenial to the strengths of state universities, which find themselves under greater pressure to provide services believed to have economic value. Private research universities, on the other hand, have tended to be hungry for additional sources of revenue and hence aggressive in seeking links with industry. Much increased activity in the private sector came from universities that had virtually no relationship with industry before 1980, such as Columbia, Duke, Northwestern, and Yale.

The Dispersion of University Research

It seems to be well fixed in the public mind that university research is dominated by a handful of large, wealthy, prestigious institutions. Insofar as this is the case, it has been becoming less so over time. Shortly after the war, the ten largest performers of research accounted for 44 percent of all academic research. Recently, the share of the ten largest has shrunk to less than half of that. This development had not been anticipated. It had been predicted, in fact, that heightened competition for research funding would favor the "haves" rather than the "have-nots." Instead, other factors seem to have predominated.

The stagnant seventies produced an oversupply of well-trained scientists. Finding competent researchers was no longer the constraint that it had been since World War II. In addition, the growing programmatic emphasis of the research economy provided opportunities for those departments or institutions that were accustomed to pursuing applications-oriented lines of research. Conspicuous on the list of universities that have significantly increased their shares of research are land-grant universities and institutes of technology. But conspicuous among the decliners are the largest performers of research.

An appreciable part of that decline occurred during the 1980s. The proportion of university research expenditures concentrated in the ten largest performers declined from 20.3 percent in 1979 to 17.9 percent in 1989. In 1979, four universities each performed better than 2 percent of academic research; by 1989, for the first time none did.

Greater participation in academic research by a wider group of institutions has, implicitly or explicitly, long been a national goal. The disquieting aspect of this trend, however, is the disjunction between quality and quantity. The institutions that are most recognized for academic quality have generally seen their share of the research economy diminish. Specifically, of those twenty-five universities with the most distinguished departments as rated by the 1982 *Assessment of Research-Doctorate Programs in the United States,* only four expanded their share of research while two marginally increased theirs, eight marginally decreased theirs, and eleven significantly decreased theirs (data from Korhn, in progress). Does this mean that scientific quality is becoming less important in the distribution of research funds? Or does it mean that the university research system is changing in ways that are too complicated for this simple dichotomy to capture?

Arguing for the first alternative would be the whole drift toward programmatic funding of research, as well as the growing propensity to award research-related funds through "pork-barrel" appropriations. Most likely, the portion of research funds awarded through peer review or meritocratic competition has been shrinking. Still, changes in the nature of the research system could be the more important development. Subdisciplinary and interdisciplinary specialties are becoming increasingly important for the conduct of research and the locus of expertise. These specialized areas of excellence, moreover, are scattered more widely than ever before. It is not yet apparent to what extent quantity and quality of research are related in the new research environment. It could well be that the traditional leaders have used the prosperity of the 1980s to invest in quality in areas that have little effect on research expenditures. Or the emphasis on programmatic research may have promoted the vigor and the salience of the different specialties of more applications-oriented institutions.

Centrifugal Forces

The fourth trend of the 1980s consists of a shift in the balance of activities in universities away from the center and toward the periphery. This is a subtle trend—and one that begs definition. Certainly, a generation ago most people would have agreed that the most central or integral function of the university was the pursuit of knowledge for its own sake in the basic arts and sciences. One classic analysis interpreted this function as exemplifying cognitive rationality, the core value of universities (Parsons and Platt 1973). According to this view, the graduate school of arts and sciences is at the center, and the professional schools, while still integral parts of the university, combine cognitive rationality with different degrees of orientation toward external constituencies and praxis. Undergraduate education combines variable degrees of cognitive rationality with general education and socialization. University units thus encompass different combinations of values and constituencies. Given such a picture, what evidence is there for the contention about movement from the center to the periphery?

First, if one looks at changes in instructional activity, as reflected in degrees, a very stark trend is evident. The number of bachelor's degrees awarded in arts and sciences has declined significantly since the early 1970s, particularly in the humanities and social sciences. If education is included, those degrees composed two-thirds of the total in 1973 but just over one-third fifteen years later. The number of bachelor's degrees in business meanwhile doubled to reach one-quarter of all undergraduate majors. A similar pattern occurred for doctoral degrees. Those in letters declined by one-half; those in social sciences declined by one-third. Fields registering major gains tend to be scattered throughout the smaller technical and professional areas. In the arts and social sciences, then, there are now simply fewer students to teach on both the undergraduate and graduate levels.

A second piece of evidence might be inferred from the recent proliferation of separately organized research units. A recent study found their numbers increasing by 42 percent during the first half of the eighties (Friedman and Friedman 1986). Such units are established for a variety of tasks that cannot be accommodated in academic departments. Many of those founded a couple of decades ago were meant to achieve greater integration between the basic disciplines and professional departments. In keeping with the movement toward programmatic funding of research, however, the organized research units of the 1980s seem to have been predominantly intended to serve outsiders, particularly industry. Such special centers, although they seem to be quite effective for their intended purpose, are usually peripheral in location, personnel, and mission. Their proliferation has occurred largely outside the normal ties between research and graduate education.

Finally, the elaboration of special units associated with technology transfer constitutes an organizational superstructure well removed from the university core. Most remote, perhaps, are the special corporations established to develop real estate, hold patents, own equity in start-up firms, or act as conduits to for-profit, venture-capital corporations.

A case can be made, then, that a kind of centrifugal process has been at work within universities, largely connected with the other trends of the 1980s. One result may be the increased separation of graduate and undergraduate education, a development that may well bear on the perceived crisis in undergraduate education (see below). Another result has been the fragmentation—further fragmentation, to be exact—of the university as an organization, to the extent that the very notion of a core might be called into question.

The Challenges of the 1990s

An Uncertain Financial Environment

The recession of 1990–91 in all likelihood marked a definitive break with the financial conditions of the 1980s. The basic forces underlying the trend toward privatization seem to remain intact, but they will now operate in a different economic context. The consequences of this change are likely to vary for public and private universities.

Student tuition supplied the stoutest pillar of privatization during the 1980s, but it seems unlikely that additional weight can be shifted here, at least by private universities. The 60 percent rate of real increase in the 1980s was inherently unsustainable. The sticker price for a bachelor's degree in residence at a leading private university has reached a daunting $100,000 for the class of '95. The willingness and/or capacity of parents to pay or students to borrow may well have been reached. Similar arguments were made throughout the 1980s, and earlier too. The difference in the 1990s is that private universities themselves seem to believe that a danger point has been reached, and they have acted accordingly.

A consistent pattern has emerged. Many private universities have stated their intention to hold tuition increases at or near the rate of inflation (Evangelauf 1991). Such a limit will require that expenditure growth be rigorously controlled, and accordingly programs of systematic cost containment have been announced. At the same time, private universities have continued aggressive fund-raising efforts, in effect making future qualitative improvements dependent upon gifts. Private universities are thus still looking to private sources to meet their future financial needs, while at the same time adopting a proactive stance toward controlling the activities that generate those needs.

Public research universities, which are more numerous than private universities and account for about two-thirds of academic research, face more parlous conditions. The declining health of state budgets became increasingly evident during the last years of the 1980s. With the onset of the 1990 recession, these conditions became virtually universal and were reflected in declining state appropriations to universities. Throughout 1990, state universities were struck with shortfalls, freezes, budget reductions, or givebacks. The next year, 1991, brought worse news. The University of California, hitherto the most generously funded of public research universities, had to absorb a massive reduction of its budget; seven months into the fiscal year the state-assisted universities of Pennsylvania had to return previously appropriated funds to the state treasury; and in Oregon a voter-approved initiative slashed state spending, including university appropriations. Almost every state can offer similar tales.

The pattern of response to these events by state universities has been consistent, too. For additional revenues they have resorted, above all, to tuition increases. The University of California, with relatively low tuition, has announced a 40 percent hike, from about $1,650 to $2,300 for in-state students. In Pennsylvania, where in-state tuition is $4,000 and students already contribute more toward their education than the state does, a more modest percentage jump would still equal a substantial additional charge. Universities like California's clearly have the flexibility to extend tuition considerably without significantly restricting access or overburdening students with debt, but high-priced state systems face pricing considerations that are beginning to resemble those of private universities.

The relative advantage of private over public research universities thus seems likely to persist in a recessionary environment, although the financial outlook is bleaker for less wealthy private universities facing possible enrollment declines. Private universities have, on the whole, reacted cautiously to the relative prosperity of the 1980s. They enter the 1990s strengthened financially and with their expenditures under control. Although they will be constrained in their activities, this plight may nevertheless be more manageable than that of their public counterparts. These latter face a double disadvantage: the imperative of cost containment has been thrust upon them abruptly, forcing hasty cuts, and the subsequent savings are not captured by the institutions but revert to the state as budget reductions.

The Research Economy

The level of resources made available for academic research affects both public and private universities. This research economy, in contrast with the national economy, entered the 1990s in fairly robust condition. University research expenditures for fiscal year 1989, for example, proved to be substantially larger than earlier extrapolations: $15 billion, compared with previous estimates of $13.9 billion (National Science Foundation 1989, 1990). The federal component of these expenditures declined precipitously during the latter 1980s, falling below 60 percent, or less than it was in 1960. The federal budget deficit is nevertheless the darkest cloud overhanging the research economy. The magnitude of the problem simply dwarfs the sums involved. All federal expenditures for academic research (some $9 billion in 1989) represent only a tiny fraction of the official deficit projections. Perhaps for that reason, federal appropriations for academic science have held up remarkably well. Behind the aggregate figures, however, a conflict has brewed about how best to sustain the academic research enterprise.

The initial problem would seem to be a coercive demand for research funds, or "proposal pressure" in the parlance of the agencies that fund research. In reaction, the agencies have tended to spread their funds more thinly by granting less than the requested amounts (Teich et al. 1990, 11–12). At least some of these shortfalls have to be met by universities as support for graduate students or institutional matching funds. As this trend accelerates, institutions will become even more reliant on their own resources to encourage research. During the 1980s, institutional funds were, after industry, the second fastest-growing source of university research expenditures. There is an important difference between public and private universities in this respect. In 1982, such funds accounted for 8 percent at private institutions and 19 percent at public ones. At the end of the decade, institutional funding of research at public universities had increased by 4 percentage points versus only ½ point more for private ones. The pressures on federal agencies will likely produce a further squeeze on institutional resources. At the same time, universities may receive less compensation for their research efforts.

Stanford has in many ways been the exemplary university of this era for internal management of research (see Matkin 1990, 118–132, on patent management and Gardner et al. 1990 on cost containment), but the revelations that it had been gouging the government on indirect costs and the subsequent pillorying of the university before congressional committees altered another factor in the cost equations of academic research (Hamilton 1991). Reimbursements for indirect costs inexorably came under pressure. Auditors became emboldened, institutions timorous in their claims. Longer term, this situation portends a lower level of reimbursement for the rising costs of sustaining institutional capacities for research.

Both these trends—greater direct institutional contributions and less indirect cost recovery—promise to add to the financial constraints facing universities in the 1990s. The relative costs of research may well be on the rise for universities at the same time that some voices are alleging that too great an emphasis has already been placed on research.

Research Universities and Their External Critics

The communities on whom universities ultimately depend have little direct contact with what universities actually do, particularly in research. Attitudes tend to be shaped by isolated and symbolic events or by rather vague associations. The favorable climate of the 1980s was conditioned by broadly positive attitudes toward quality in undergraduate education and toward the relevance of academic research for the economic weal. The recent criticisms of higher education, and particularly of research universities, are ominous chiefly because they threaten this favorable climate.

The last few years have brought a succession of attacks on universities from outsiders and academics; the titles well indicate their tenor and slant: *Killing the Spirit: Higher Education in America* (Smith 1990); *Stillborn Education: A Critique of the American Research University* (Von Blum 1986); *The Moral Collapse of the University* (Wilshire 1990); and *Profscam: Professors and the Demise of Higher Education* (Sykes 1988). What they all have in common is liberal amounts of "research bashing," generally in the form of allegations that teaching is being neglected by professors fixated on research and that academic research is of little value in any case. There are enough grains of truth in some of these charges to make universities and their leaders uncomfortable. But it is a contrived and highly misleading viewpoint.

Universities are, first of all, multipurpose institutions in which different roles jostle and conflict with each other to varying extents, but in the main coexist. Setting teaching as the single measure of worth is sophomoric— and plays well at that level. The critics ignore the 90 percent of institutions that teach but do no research. They also ignore graduate and professional education, which approximates half of the enrollment of most private research universities and up to a third at some publics. One could go on, but there is little point; the arguments against research are largely rhetorical and journalistic. What is most disturbing is that these critics largely have the stage to themselves. The research universities seem reluctant to speak out on their own behalf.

Other criticisms have emanated from government. Despite the generally positive view of higher education held by the public, both federal and state governments prefer to believe that much is wrong. This hostility has taken several unconnected forms. Many conservatives believe that higher education has become a bastion of the Left and wish to challenge that dominance. They have turned their heaviest fire toward the battle over the curriculum, seeking to preserve some semblance of the Western cultural heritage against the claims of "diversity," as politically interpreted. The attack on Western culture has been waged most conspicuously in research universities, which has not endeared these institutions to the traditionalists. Apparently this accounts for their quixotic propensity to attack research as well. Lynne Cheney's volley in *Tyrannical Machines* (1990), for example, includes the usual strictures against research. Conservatives might better see the integrity of the scientific process as a counterweight to the program of the cultural Left, in which the supposed social implications of the curriculum are accorded greatest importance. Instead, many would prefer to cast doubt on the very integrity of science.

Fraud in science is a real problem but not one of the magnitude that several congressmen would make of it. Its cause is fairly evident—the excessive bureaucratization of biomedical research, principally at the National Institutes of Health, which results in an emphasis on the process of science (number of publications, etc.) rather than its substance. For science and for universities, it is more of a public relations problem: congressional hearings aimed at grabbing headlines and the sheer duration of several prominent cases convey the erroneous image that science is rotten at the core.

Congressional disrespect for institutions of higher education has been manifest most recently in the legislation that requires full reporting of crime rates around universities as well as the graduation rates of athletes. Both tasks raise problems of definition as well as enumeration. Congress apparently believes that it is protecting consumers (students) against exploitation by self-serving institutions. In truth, because many students take more than five years to graduate and universities have no knowledge of students who transfer to other institutions, noncompletion rates are a fiction. Such exercises delude the government and the press with meaningless numbers while imposing yet another burdensome record-keeping chore on higher education (Lederman 1991).

The executive branch of the federal government has harbored an unfathomable desire to investigate the most selective private colleges and universities for supposed antitrust violations. The activity in question—regularizing financial aid packages across institutions—is a form of charity that scarcely seems to be covered under the concept of antitrust. More importantly, it is an entirely laudable endeavor to prevent "bidding" for students. Its purpose is to extend limited aid resources and encourage student choice based on other than financial criteria.

At the state level, negative attitudes toward higher education have been manifest in the movement toward assessment. The underlying notion is that institutions are not educating students sufficiently on their own and, thus, must be held accountable through some form of assessment procedure. In just five years, three-quarters of the states had either implemented or planned an assessment effort (Hutchings and Marchese 1990).

Research Universities and Their Internal Critics

The cultural Left shares with its conservative antagonists a disdain for research universities. Its proponents tend to exist in and depend on these institutions, while also engaging enthusiastically in the academic rites of publishing and conference going. But they essentially reject the most basic tenets of the scientific ethos. (For the four sets of institutional imperatives that make up the ethos of modern science—universalism, communism, disinterestedness, and organized skepticism, see Merton 1973.) Instead of the universality of science, race and gender are forwarded as categories of analysis; instead of objectivity, reality is posited to be comprehended subjectively through the mind of the investigator; instead of the free sharing of scientific knowledge, scientific meetings that excluded men have been organized; and instead of being systematically critical toward their subjects, the prevailing spirit is closer to *pas d'ennemis a gauche*—literally, "no enemies on the left." Faculty holding these views have made significant inroads upon the curriculum. They also tend to seek out individuals of like views in new appointments. There thus resides an entrenched constituency within research universities who are hostile to the premises on which those institutions are based. (For a critique of these tendencies, see Searle 1990.)

Another but well-meaning line of criticism emanates from those who lead and love these institutions. Their feelings are so strong that, under the general rubric of "social responsibility," they advocate a larger role in society for research universities. Donna Shalala, Chancellor of the University of Wisconsin at Madison, wishes "to enlist the university as a primary tool for changing the culture at large": it should "function as a moral force beyond the pragmatic," exhibit "a new dedication to public service as a cornerstone of higher education," and discover and apply social science to remedy social ills (1989, 15–16). Harvard's former president, Derek Bok, urged a similar point as criticism: "Both in teaching and research," he wrote, "universities are responsive, but what they respond to is what the society chooses to pay for, not what it most needs" (1990, 44). What is wrong with these noble sentiments? The negative connotation they carry is disturbing: that universities are not currently providing sufficient public service. More serious is the fact that both statements seem to promise more than universities can possibly deliver in determining "what society needs"— certainly a matter for the political process—or causing social change— surely the responsibility of government.

On the other hand, the issue of social responsibility is not one that universities, public or private, can ignore. Universities are consequential institutions in contemporary society. They have an obligation not only to conduct themselves responsibly but also to feel and convey a genuine concern over the social implications of their manifold activities. Such a stance is made more difficult by the inherent nature of research universities. Their commitment to excellence in student and faculty achievements connects them predominantly with the privileged strata of American society. Real concern for the underprivileged is thus an appropriate counterweight; however, social responsibility is poor ground for universities to stake their public worth. On the contrary, they seem for the most part to be discharging admirably those tasks for which they are best suited.

Ensuring the Strength of Research Universities

When measured against the actual conduct of research universities, the complaints of the critics appear rather pallid. Do they neglect teaching? Not if the preferences of students are any indication. Student demand has been extraordinarily strong at the research universities during the past decade. This demand has been the underpinning of their relative prosperity (and their annual tuition hikes). Graduate education offered in American research universities is the envy of the world. Its comparative strength, as detailed in studies by Burton Clark (1991 and forthcoming), lies precisely in its structured teaching, as well as with its integration with powerful traditions of research. Here the preferences of foreign students for study in this country are cogent testimony to the strength of our institutions.

Should our universities be distrusted, as so many in government seem to think? Individuals and corporations in the private sector have thought otherwise and have backed such belief in a most convincing manner—with outright monetary gifts. Donor behavior in the 1980s (as contrasted with the late 1960s, for example) gave evidence of great confidence in universities, both public and private, and in the importance of their missions.

Are the basic paradigms of the scientific method in need of reformulation? While an internecine struggle convulses areas of the humanities and social sciences, the techniques of academic science are being used more widely and effectively than ever in other departments of universities. Specifically, cognitive rationality, in the form of academic research, has been incorporated more rigorously in the diverse professional schools. The 1990 Nobel Prize in economics, for example, was awarded to Harry Markowitz, William Sharpe, and Merton Miller for advances in the field of finance that are now basic to business education.

This last point could be made even more strongly. The great success of research universities in the 1980s has partly been due to the fact that they harbor and cultivate expertise grounded in science across many subjects. The turning outward of the research universities has made that expertise more available to consumers of research, who have eagerly taken advantage of this opportunity. One measure of this trend is provided by industrial spending for research outside of industry (in nonprofit organizations or universities); in 1970, universities received only 42 percent of these expenditures, but in 1989 their share was 67 percent (Geiger 1992a). This burgeoning demand for university expertise bears on the final criticism.

From an economist's point of view, what society pays for is what it needs, or at least what it wants. In this respect, universities have emphatically demonstrated their usefulness in the 1980s with such breakthroughs as new superconducting materials, genetically engineered substances, and a host of other discoveries. These activities should be interpreted as the best fulfillment of their social responsibility.

The great strengths possessed by contemporary research universities should not be cause for gloating or complacency. Their essential mission of advancing knowledge and providing excellence in education is immensely challenging. The problems facing them are real and daunting, all the more so because the 1980s were a comparatively easy decade and the 1990s promise to be far more difficult (Kerr 1990). All of the resourcefulness that they can command will be required to sustain their complicated and costly enterprise. But critics who have argued that the research universities are somehow on the wrong track are simply missing the larger picture. The first responsibility of research universities ought to be to continue doing what they have done so well—cultivating challenging education for highly talented undergraduates, providing the strongest graduate training in the world, performing research at the frontiers of knowledge, and sustaining a reservoir of expertise that can be called upon by American society. The leaders of American research universities bear a heavy responsibility not just in facilitating the attainment of these objectives at their respective institutions, but also in helping to articulate the importance of these functions to the rest of American society.

Note

1. These trends are treated more thoroughly in the author's volume, *Research and Relevant Knowledge: American Research Universities since World War II* (1992). Data presented here are drawn from the National Center for Education Statistics' *Digest of Education Statistics, 1988,* the National Science Foundation's series on "Academic Science/Engineering R&D Expenditures," and the Council for Financial Aid to Education's *Voluntary Support of Education.*

References

Bok, Derek. 1990. *Universities and the Future of America*. Durham: Duke University Press.

Cheney, Lynne V. 1990. *Tyrannical Machines: A Report on Educational Practices Gone Wrong and Our Best Hopes for Setting Them Right*. Washington, D.C.: National Endowment for the Humanities.

Clark, Burton R. 1991. "Graduate Education and Research Training in Higher Education: The UK and the USA." In Thomas Whiston and Roger L. Geiger, eds., *Research in Higher Education: The UK and the USA*. Oxford: Open University Press.

————. ed. n.d. "The Research Foundations of Graduate Education." Berkeley and Los Angeles: University of California Press. Forthcoming.

Council for Financial Aid to Education. "Annual Report." In *Voluntary Support of Education*. New York: Council for Financial Aid to Education.

Evangelauf, Jean. 1991. "1991 Tuition Increases Expected to Outpace Inflation, but Some Private Colleges Will Slow the Upward Trend." *Chronicle of Higher Education*, 37 (6 March): A1, A27–28.

Fairweather, James S. 1988. *ASHE/ERIC Higher Education Reports*. Vol. 6: *Entrepreneurship and Higher Education: Lessons for Colleges, Universities, and Industry*.

Friedman, Robert S., and Renee C. Friedman. 1986. "Sponsorship, Organization, and Program Change at 100 Universities." University Park: Institute for Policy Research and Evaluation, Pennsylvania State University.

Gardner, Catherine, Timothy R. Warner, and Rick Biedenweg. 1990. "Stanford and the Railroad: Case Studies of Cost Cutting." *Change*, 22(6):23–27.

Geiger, Roger L. 1988. *Privatization in Higher Education: International Trends and Issues*. Princeton: International Council for Educational Development.

————. 1990. "The American University and Research." In *The Academic Research Enterprise within Industrialized Nations: Comparative Perspectives, Government-University-Industry Research Roundtable*, pp. 15–34. Washington, D.C.: National Academy Press.

————. 1991. "Universities and Research in the United States since 1945." In Thomas Whiston and Roger L. Geiger, eds., *Research in Higher Education: The UK and the USA*. Oxford: Open University Press.

————. 1992a. "The Ambiguous Link: Private Industry and University Research." In William E. Becker and Darrell Lewis, eds., *Higher Education and the Development of the U.S. Economy*, pp. 265–297. Boston: Kluwer.

————. 1992b. *Research and Relevant Knowledge: American Research Universities since World War II*. New York: Oxford University Press.

Hamilton, David P. 1991. "Stanford in the Hot Seat." *Science*, 251:1420.

Hutchings, Pat, and Ted Marchese. 1990. "Watching Assessment––Questions, Stories, Prospects." *Change*, September/October, 12–38.

Jones, Lyle V., Gardner Lindzey, and Porter E. Coggeshall, eds. 1982. *An Assessment of Research-Doctorate Programs in the United States*. 5 vols. Washington, D.C.: National Academy Press.

Kenney, Martin. 1986. *Biotechnology: The University-Industrial Complex*. New Haven: Yale University Press.

Kerr, Clark. 1990. "Higher Education Cannot Escape History: The 1990s." In *New Directions for Higher Education*, 70 (Summer): 5–17.

Korhn, Jennifer. n.d. "Advancing Universities of the 1970s and 1980s." Ph.D. diss., Pennsylvania State University Higher Education Program. Forthcoming.

Lederman, Douglas. 1991. "College Officials Worry That Graduation-Rate Data May Be Misread and Misused." *Chronicle of Higher Education,* 37 (27 March): A38.

Matkin, Gary W. 1990. *Technology Transfer and the University.* New York: Macmillan.

Merton, Robert K. 1973. "The Normative Structure of Science." In Norman W. Storer, ed., *The Sociology of Science,* pp. 267–278. Chicago: University of Chicago Press.

National Center for Education Statistics. 1989. *Digest of Education Statistics, 1988.* Washington, D.C.: U.S. Department of Education, Office of Educational Research and Improvement.

National Science Foundation. 1989. "Patterns of R&D Resources, 1989." Washington, D.C.: National Science Foundation.

———. 1990. "Selected Data on Academic Science/Engineering R&D Expenditures: FY1989." Washington, D.C.: National Science Foundation, October.

Parsons, Talcott, and Gerald M. Platt. 1973. *The American University.* Cambridge: Harvard University Press.

Roose, K. D., and C. J. Andersen. 1970. *A Rating of Graduate Programs.* Washington, D.C.: American Council on Education.

Searle, John. 1990. "The Storm over the University." *New York Review of Books,* 37 (6 December): 34–42.

Shalala, Donna E. 1989. *Mandate for a New Century: Reshaping the Research University's Role in Social Policy.* Urbana-Champaign: University of Illinois.

Smith, Bruce L., and Joseph Karlesky. 1977–78. *The State of Academic Science.* 2 vols. New York: Change Magazine Press.

Smith, Page. 1990. *Killing the Spirit: Higher Education in America.* New York: Viking.

Sykes, Charles J. 1988. *Profscam: Professors and the Demise of Higher Education.* New York: Regnery Gateway.

Teich, Albert H., Stephen D. Nelson, Susan I. Sauer, and Kathleen M. Gramp. 1990. "Congressional Action on Research and Development in the FY1991 Budget." Washington, D.C.: American Association for the Advancement of Science.

Von Blum, Paul. 1986. *Stillborn Education: A Critique of the American Research University.* Lanham, Md.: University Press of America.

Webster, David S. 1983. "America's Highest Ranked Graduate Schools." *Change,* May/June, 14–24.

Wilshire, Bruce. 1990. *The Moral Collapse of the University.* Albany: State University of New York Press.

5

Liberal Arts Colleges:
What Price Survival?

DAVID W. BRENEMAN

When one considers the various institutions of American society, the private liberal arts college stands out as one of its great success stories. Many independent colleges that thrive today can trace their origins back to the seventeenth and eighteenth centuries. Harvard College (now University) heads the list, dating to 1636, but other colonial colleges included William and Mary, 1693; Yale, 1701; Pennsylvania, 1740; Princeton, 1746; Columbia, 1754; Brown, 1765; Rutgers, 1766; Dartmouth, 1769; Salem, 1772; Dickinson, 1773; and Hampden-Sydney, 1776. Few business firms can point to such histories, and indeed only a handful of churches and newspapers seem to be contenders for equivalent lengths of service. It is ironic, then, that when one reads the literature on private colleges one discovers a nearly unbroken history of concern for their survival. Are we looking at one of the hardiest of institutions, or one of the most fragile? Or, in some sense, are both attributes present? And what of their future?

This chapter pursues these questions, with particular reference to the last thirty years. We will see that concern about the future of private colleges was present even during the expansive years of the late 1950s and 1960s, while the 1970s saw a veritable flurry of reports bemoaning their financial plight and possible demise.

The 1980s dawned with predictions that as many as two hundred of these small colleges would not survive until the mid-1990s. And yet, surprisingly, the 1980s seem to have been good years for these colleges, for reasons we are only now beginning to understand. Some observers believe that the financial threats that were avoided in the 1980s will fall upon the colleges in the 1990s, but such concern may be misplaced. The track record of forecasts regarding the future of these colleges is poor, and the course of wisdom might simply be to cease speculation; nonetheless, this essay closes with a look at what the future may hold for this valued sector of American higher education.

Early Trends

One of the reasons for the litany of concern about the survival of these colleges is grounded in the reality of past failures. Pfnister noted that, by 1860, as many as seven hundred colleges had been created and had gone out of existence (1985, 35). In the American "system" of higher education, small independent colleges are the most vulnerable institutions; often lacking sizable endowments, heavily dependent on tuition, and without direct support from government, these colleges can fail if times are hard enough.

Furthermore, their role has been steadily reduced over time, as other institutions have emerged as dominant forces in higher education. Starting from an initial position of unchallenged leadership, undergraduate liberal arts colleges still enrolled two-thirds of all students in higher education at the turn of this century (Pfnister 1985, 33). By that time, however, private colleges were facing a severe educational challenge from the newly developing universities that stressed research and the creation of new knowledge— a story told magnificently by Veysey (1965). Seen from the heights of this powerful new institution, the liberal arts college appeared both irrelevant and insignificant, not destined to last. According to historian Frederick Rudolph,

> President Harper of Chicago, at the turn of the century, expected three out of four existing colleges to be reduced to the status of academies or modified into junior colleges. President Butler of Columbia was convinced that, if the American college was to be saved, it would have to reduce its course of study to two or three years. David Starr Jordan of Stanford looked into his crystal ball in 1903 and decided that "as time goes on the college will disappear, in fact, if not in name. The best will become universities, the others will return to their places as academies" (cited in Curtis 1988, 5).

It was in the face of such real or perceived threats that 150 college presidents convened in Chicago in 1915 to found the Association of American Colleges, for the "promotion of higher education in all its forms, in the independent and denominational colleges in the United States" (Curtis 1988, 8).

Subsequent events proved the Harper-Butler-Jordan forecasts of demise to be extreme, but private colleges have been rendered increasingly marginal during this century as public universities and community colleges have grown dramatically in both size and number. In 1955, liberal arts colleges still accounted for nearly 40 percent of all institutions (732 of 1,854), and they enrolled 26 percent of all students in that year (Pfnister 1985, 33). By 1970, 689 private colleges (24 percent of the nation's 2,837 institutions) enrolled only 7.6 percent of all students. By 1987, the number of private colleges was down to 540 of 3,389 (16 percent), while enrollments had shrunk to 4.4 percent of the total (Carnegie Foundation for the Advancement of Teaching 1987, 3, 5). This drop in the number of private colleges resulted less from their failure than from the expansion of many of them into more comprehensive institutions, including universities. Nonetheless, while the apocalyptic vision of the early university presidents did not come to pass, it is hard to argue with the judgment that, by 1990, the small private college had become a much diminished part of America's educational landscape.

Developments, 1960–1980

What do we know about the recent path of development of these colleges? What were the issues that they faced, and how did they deal with them?

During the 1960s, financial worries took center stage, pushing aside even curricular debates. The early and mid-1960s, years of exceptional growth in higher education, were also marked by a strong, noninflationary economy, capable of yielding annual productivity increases of 2 to 3 percent. Many students of higher education have referred to this time as the "golden years," including Hans H. Jenny and G. Richard Wynn, who, in a series of three publications (1970, 1972; Wynn 1974), traced the financial condition of forty-eight liberal arts colleges from 1960 to 1973. These three publications were the first in a seemingly unending series of reports in the 1970s commenting upon the financial plight of private education in general and of the liberal arts college in particular.

In the third report, *At the Crossroads,* Wynn summarized the findings of the first two reports as follows (1974, 2–3):

> When Hans Jenny and I titled our first study of these 48 colleges *The Golden Years,* we were referring to the generally prosperous early and mid-1960s. Enroll-

ments grew slowly but steadily, a building boom was peaking, faculty and staff salaries were approaching desired levels, and peaceful campuses were the rule. The 48 colleges collectively finished each year with an operating surplus. But during the last several years of our study, ending in 1968, clear-cut signs of financial distress became apparent, even for this sample of fairly well-to-do colleges.

Our update to 1970 was *The Turning Point,* dramatizing how the addition of only two fiscal years brought an end to the golden years in a splash of red ink. Income was unable to keep pace with accelerating expenditure growth, particularly student aid. Enrollment dropped drastically in several institutions, benefactors proved fickle, and increasing price competition from public systems took its toll.

In response to the budget deficits of the early 1970s, Wynn reported that by 1974 the colleges had been able to reestablish balanced budgets, not by increasing revenues but by cutting expenditure growth. Rather than rejoice at this elimination of deficits, Wynn raised the specter of a new era in which "quality distress" would replace "financial distress" as the central problem. Under this vision, colleges would survive, but survival would become the dominant concern, with innovation and quality enhancements sacrificed to the necessity of restraining expenditure growth.

While Jenny and Wynn were charting the changing fortunes of 48 private colleges, the financial plight of all American higher education was being depicted by Earl F. Cheit in *The New Depression in Higher Education* (1971), written for the Carnegie Commission on Higher Education. The fundamental problem that Cheit documented was a tendency for costs to rise faster than income, producing a cost-income squeeze. He and his colleagues studied a representative sample of 41 colleges and universities, including 14 private liberal arts colleges. Based on that sample, Clark Kerr in the foreword to Cheit's book projected that 28 percent of the nation's 730 liberal arts colleges were in financial difficulty, 43 percent were headed for trouble, and only 29 percent were not in financial straits (p. x).

Interviews with presidents of the fourteen private colleges produced the following composite picture (p. 123): "The financing of private education is in a crisis because of rising costs, fears that tuition has reached a 'saturation point,' desire to extend access to those who cannot afford it, decline in growth in the income which made up subsidies, and, finally, increased competition from state institutions." Cheit concluded that,

> in brief, administrators of the liberal arts colleges are struggling with the cost-income squeeze in a context that raises a larger issue. Their institutions offer an educational program that was once unique. Today, however, state institutions

offer much the same program, often just as good qualitatively, and at much lower cost to the student. Not only does this pose a problem of financial competition, but it also raises the larger question of the role of the liberal arts college. Administrators of these institutions argue persuasively the case for diversity, for pluralism, and see the solution to their problem in gaining access to more federal and state funding while retaining their independence. They believe this should be done and can be done. For them the issue is when. The current financial squeeze adds urgency to this longer-range problem, for many of these institutions are getting into financial difficulty (pp. 128–129).

Enactment of the Education Amendments of 1972—one of the most far-reaching pieces of federal higher education legislation ever written—provided an important part of the response to these presidents' needs. This legislation established the basic pattern of federal student aid that remains to this day. Among other provisions, it established basic educational opportunity grants (now Pell grants) and state student incentive grants; reauthorized (with amendments) the college work-study program, guaranteed student loans, and national direct student loans; converted educational opportunity grants into supplemental educational opportunity grants; created the Student Loan Marketing Association (a government-sponsored private corporation, financed by private capital, to provide liquidity and facilitate transactions involving insured student loans); and established the National Institute of Education, the Fund for the Improvement of Postsecondary Education, and the National Commission on the Financing of Postsecondary Education (Breneman and Finn 1978, 453–454). There is no doubt that these student aid programs of grants, loans, and work-study have played (and continue to play) a vital role in enhancing student access to higher education, as well as choice among institutions. As a consequence, they contribute importantly to the survival of private colleges.

The remaining task in meeting the financial needs of these colleges was to focus attention on state policy and in particular to encourage states to introduce or expand tuition offset grants. Although such grants can take many forms, perhaps the most common is that of need-based grants, provided from state funds, which undergraduates can use to cover some or all of tuition costs at private colleges, usually within the state. In 1974, the Association of American Colleges strongly recommended the adoption or expansion of state student aid programs and helped to popularize the concept of tuition offset grants. According to its report, *A National Policy for Private Higher Education,* their purpose was to reduce or stabilize the public-private tuition gap, thought to be the central economic problem of many private colleges (National Council of Independent Colleges and Universities 1974). The states responded to these arguments with varying degrees of generosity, and by 1976 thirty-nine of the fifty had one or more such programs, including, in nearly every instance, a need-based grant scheme (Breneman and Finn 1978, 47). By providing a federal matching component, the newly enacted State Student Incentive Grant (SSIG) program provided a financial incentive for such state grants.

By the mid-1970s, the basic financial structure that operates to this day was in place. Although the federal student aid programs are reauthorized and modified every few years, changes still function within the framework established by the Education Amendments of 1972.

The 1980s—a Decade of Surprises

What most viewers thought the 1980s would be like can be read directly from the titles of books and monographs published in the late 1970s and early 1980s: *Surviving the Eighties; The Enrollment Crisis: Factors, Actors, and Impacts; Challenges of Retrenchment; The Three "Rs" of the Eighties: Reduction, Reallocation, and Retrenchment;* and *The Coming Enrollment Crisis: What Every Trustee Must Know.* Most of these publications were based on extrapolations of demographic facts and economic trends. It was widely assumed that a 25 percent drop in the number of eighteen-year-olds, beginning in 1979 and lasting into the mid-1990s, would produce a decline in undergraduate enrollments of between 5 and 15 percent (although there were extreme projections on both up and down sides). The poor performance of the U.S. economy in the 1970s had produced by 1980 a situation of double-digit inflation and high unemployment known as "stagflation," rapidly rising energy costs, a standstill in productivity growth, and declining real incomes. (For an excellent discussion of these trends, see Levy 1988.) Furthermore, the mainline economics profession had few clear remedies to propose, since the economic situation defied the logic of the Keynesian system that had guided policy during the post-World War II years. A further concern unique to higher education was the decline in the economic rate of return to higher education, publicized by Richard B. Freeman in a widely read 1976 volume, *The Over-educated American.* In short, it was understandable why most observers expected the 1980s to be a time of decline for much of higher education, with a clear focus on retrenchment and survival. With regard to liberal arts colleges, more than one analyst shared the view of Robert Behn, expressed in congressional testimony (1979), that as many as two hundred small, tuition-dependent institutions would fail during the 1980s.

The fact that the reality turned out to be so different from the projections must be attributed primarily to the upsurge in the economy and secondarily to responses and adaptations of colleges and universities. History's final judgment on the wisdom of Reagan's economic policies is not yet in, but a sharp recession triggered by tight monetary policy in the early 1980s broke the back of inflation, and expansionary fiscal policies and supply-side incentives helped to produce one of the longest periods of economic expansion in modern times. Although the federal budget slid into steadily deeper deficits, most state governments experienced sharp revenue growth—a positive factor for higher education. A redistribution of income toward the wealthy enhanced the fund-raising potential of both private and public colleges and universities (Phillips 1990). In the final analysis, the well-being of higher education is so closely tied to the well-being of the economy that planners can virtually ignore other factors; the only problem is that no one can accurately forecast the course of the economy.

There were other surprises in the 1980s that affected higher education. Largely because the bottom fell out of the job market for high school graduates, the economic return to a college education reversed itself, with the wage premium for college graduates increasing between 1979 and 1986 to levels larger than those during any earlier period (Murphy and Welch 1989). As a result, the college-going rate of eighteen- to twenty-four-year-old high school graduates reversed its decline of the 1970s (when it hit a low of 29.7 percent) and reached 34.0 percent by 1986 (National Center for Education Statistics 1989, 199). A combination of higher college-going rates and continued growth in the enrollment of older and part-time students kept total enrollments rising, from 12.1 million to 12.7 million between 1980 and 1987 (National Center for Education Statistics 1989, 167), rather than declining.

The revenues of most colleges also took an unanticipated jump during the 1980s. Between 1981 and 1989, tuition in private institutions increased by an unprecedented 106 percent, far outstripping the growth in personal income or cost of living (College Board 1989, 11). Coming after a decade or more of research that stressed the critical need to reduce, or at least stabilize, the tuition gap between public and private institutions and keeping tuition increases in private colleges to a minimum, the actual experience was a stunning reversal. Contrary to what might have been expected, students were not driven away by these rapidly rising prices, and at many institutions—particularly the more selective ones—applications actually went up. Some observers speculated that parents and students were seeking quality more fervently than in previous years and were, to some extent, judging quality by price. Indeed, this author, who was serving as the president of a private college during those years, observed during his conversations with other college presidents that some seemed to have little incentive to keep prices down, particularly if doing so had the effect of lowering their institutions' actual or perceived quality.

This change in pricing behavior was reflective of another striking change in the 1980s: the growing tendency on the part of administrators to think about higher education in terms of marketing and strategic planning—a trend given a strong push by George Keller's widely read book, *Academic Strategy* (1983). Presidents, admissions officers, business officers, and development staff focused intensely on their institution's niche in the market for higher education services and how it was positioned relative to competitors. Admissions officials conducted survey research on student applicants, including not only those who were admitted and did not enroll but also those who did not complete the formal application process. Business officers followed tuition levels closely to ensure that their college's price accurately reflected its place in the academic pecking order and to avoid the sin of underpricing it relative to colleges deemed weaker. Development staff spent untold hours on public relations activities, striving to bring the college's name forward in those communities where both students and dollars were sought. Although much maligned by presidents, the annual reports on "America's Best Colleges" published by *U.S. News & World Report* popularized the pecking order and gave it third party validity in the public mind.

The net effect of these changes was to instill in college leaders a marketing mentality much more pronounced than had existed before. Ideas about pricing behavior were taken from the private sector of the economy. It was observed, for example, that, in the retailing business, department stores were moving toward one of two poles—those that stressed low price through heavy discounting but with limited service and those that stressed quality and service but played down price. Stores caught in the middle by not clearly serving one market or the other were the ones most often hurt. The lesson for most private colleges was not to get caught in the middle trying to keep prices down, but rather to emphasize quality and service in the belief that there was a strong demand for such services. Whether this approach was a sound long-range strategy for many private colleges is debatable, but it was thinking in this vein that contributed to the willingness to raise tuition by double-digit percentages year after year in the 1980s.

Another surprise was the explosive growth of the stock market throughout much of the decade, achieving an unprecedented annual rate of gain of 17.4 percent in Standard & Poor's five hundred–stock index (*Wall Street*

Journal 1989, C1). Most colleges follow the "total return" method of spending, generally based on a fixed percentage of a multiyear moving average of the value of their endowment, and the result of the soaring stock market for them was a sharp increase in the market value of endowments, which translated into increased revenue for operating budget. The booming stock market also helped fund-raising activities, both annual giving and capital campaigns. Many small colleges did not have a history of sophisticated fund-raising activities before the 1980s, but most advanced far along the learning curve during that decade, launching campaigns and developing the necessary volunteer support organizations required for success. These efforts produced yet another increased flow of revenues for most colleges.

It is more difficult to generalize about trends in federal and state support for students attending private colleges, although a good summary appears in the College Board's *Trends in Student Aid: 1980 to 1989*. Federal grant programs did not increase as rapidly as college costs, thus falling in real terms. Loan volume grew sharply, however, providing students with access to capital at subsidized rates. State student aid programs also grew in most states, although often starting from low levels. Relative to expectations, state and federal programs were disappointing to many college leaders; nonetheless, they often provided the margin of difference that allowed a student to attend a private college.

In short, the major revenue sources of most private colleges—tuition (determined by price and enrollment), endowment earnings, annual giving, and major fund drives—moved in the same direction during the 1980s: up. If one thinks of these revenues as a portfolio, a more normal pattern over a decade might be gains in some areas and losses in others. What is interesting about the 1980s, particularly in light of the earlier forecasts, is the fact that revenues all went in a positive direction. It seems unlikely that the 1990s will see a continuation of that trend. (Detailed data on each of the revenue trends may be found in my forthcoming volume on the future of private liberal arts colleges, to be published by the Brookings Institution.)

But Are They Still Liberal Arts Colleges?

It is time to consider an issue first raised by Earl J. McGrath and Charles H. Russell in their 1958 essay, *Are Liberal Arts Colleges Becoming Professional Schools?* While studying the liberal arts component in undergraduate professional schools, they became interested in the extent to which professional programs had entered the curricula of liberal arts colleges. McGrath and his colleagues at the Institute of Higher Education at Teachers College

Figure 5.1   Professional degrees awarded, 1972 and 1988.

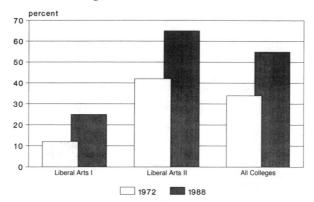

had found that, in a sample of twenty-five liberal arts colleges, 13 percent of all courses offered in the early 1960s were professional in nature—primarily education and business administration (Hungate, Meeth, and O'Connell 1964). That percentage probably increased considerably over the next quarter century—particularly in the most hard-up colleges—if the percentage of professional degrees they granted was any indication. Figure 5.1 shows the average percentage of professional bachelor's degrees awarded in 1972 and 1988 by all 540 private colleges classified in 1987 by the Carnegie Foundation as either Liberal Arts I (most selective) or Liberal Arts II (less selective). Professional degrees include such fields as business, education, nursing, engineering, computer science, agriculture, and health sciences. For all colleges, professional degrees awarded rose from 33 percent in 1972 to 54 percent in 1988; for Liberal Arts I colleges, the figures are 11 and 24 percent, respectively; and for Liberal Arts II colleges, 41 and 64 percent. By 1988, the answer to McGrath's question would appear to be a resounding "yes" for a majority of colleges.

This trend toward professional degrees is found throughout higher education during this time. Between 1968 and 1986, the percentage of bachelor's degrees awarded to students who concentrated in one of the fields within the arts and sciences (humanities, social sciences, mathematics, physical sciences, biological sciences, and psychology) plummeted from 47 percent to about 26 percent (Turner and Bowen 1990, 517). Among the factors explaining this dramatic shift are the changing labor market demands for increased technical training, the overcrowded labor market for new entrants (the baby boom effect), the new professional opportunities open to women, and the expansion of public higher education, with its

Figure 5.2   Freshman life goals, 1968–90.

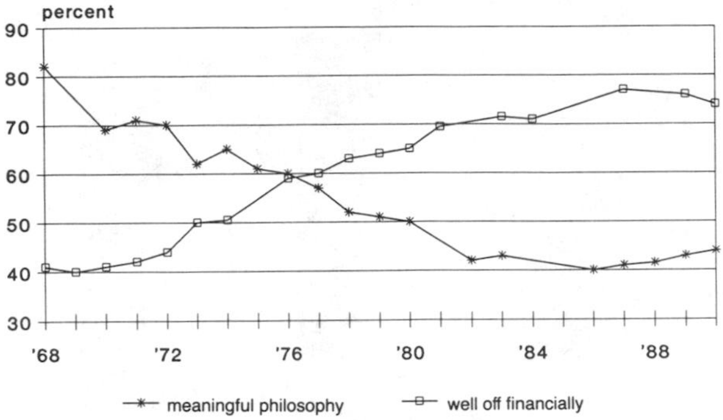

Source: The American Freshman: National Norms for Fall 1990 (Los Angeles, Calif.: Cooperative Institutional Research Program), p. 5.

emphasis on professional education. Changing student attitudes toward higher education and its role in meeting life goals mirror this shift as well. Between the late 1960s and the mid-1980s, a precipitous decline occurred in the percentage of freshmen who reported that developing "a meaningful philosophy of life" was an important reason for their attending college, while the percentage concerned with being "well off financially" increased dramatically (fig. 5.2).

In returning to the issue with which this essay began—the survival of the small private college—it seems that this striking shift from liberal arts to professional education was a central strategy followed by hundreds of colleges in the Liberal Arts II category. The shift has been so pronounced that it seems mistaken to call such schools "liberal arts colleges" any longer. Indeed, in a recent article, I argued that, by a liberal definition that includes any college awarding 60 percent or fewer of its degrees in professional fields, there are only about two hundred liberal arts colleges left in this country (Breneman 1990, 17). Were a more rigorous definition applied, such as one including only those colleges that awarded 25 percent or fewer of their degrees in professional fields, the number would be less than ninety. The several hundred small professional colleges excluded by these definitions would qualify for inclusion in the Carnegie category of "comprehensive institutions" if they were larger; given their small size, however, that label would be misleading, and a new category is needed. Although many of these colleges were able to survive by redefining their missions and changing their educational programs, it is nonetheless accurate to say that the country has lost hundreds of liberal arts colleges in recent decades.

A Look Ahead

As we have seen in this brief look at the history of liberal arts colleges and prior forecasts about them, the track record of prophesy in this arena is less than spectacular. As a result, caution and humility would seem to be necessary accompaniments to any effort to project their fate during this decade and beyond. A useful approach may be to identify the central concerns of thoughtful college presidents and others close to the institutions as the 1990s began.

First, a continuing decline in the number of high school graduates until mid-decade is a central concern; between 1989 and 1994 their numbers are projected to drop by nearly 11 percent (Western Interstate Commission for Higher Education 1988, 9). Although many small colleges enroll older students, this sector remains heavily dependent on enrolling full-time residential students of traditional college age.

The ability (and willingness) of students to pay the steeply higher tuition prices is a second, but related, concern. With tuition, room, and board charges totaling over $20,000 per year in many colleges, the age-old fear of pricing one's college out of the market has arisen again. Coupled to this is worry over the sharply rising amounts of college-funded scholarships (tuition discounts) required to help students meet their costs. In some colleges, such aid exceeds 20 percent of the total educational budget.

The ability to compete for new faculty (and retain current professors) is a third issue that keeps some presidents awake at night. If the shortfall of new faculty relative to demand materializes as projected by Bowen and Sosa (1989), small colleges may be particularly hard pressed to compete effectively for their share of talent. New doctorates with choices among academic jobs may steer away from colleges that have relatively low salaries and high teaching loads. The weakest colleges may simply not be able to compete for Ph.D.s, settling instead for master's degree holders or those with A.B.D.s (all but dissertation).

Growing competition with public universities for both students and donor support is a fourth concern and the final one noted here. Although not new, such competition may take on a sharper edge in the 1990s as the scramble for students continues and as state universities expand their efforts at private fund raising. It is too early to know whether the surprising trends of the 1980s will work to the benefit or detriment of private colleges in the 1990s, but increased competition for donor support is easily predictable, given the strapped circumstances of federal and state government budgets. With regard to student competition, in addition to issues of pricing and financing, the central concern is whether the trend away from arts and sciences will continue or reverse itself.

Grappling with these challenges will surely keep presidents, trustees, alumni, and other supporters of the private liberal arts college busy during the foreseeable future. Although it is easy to spin out grim scenarios for these small, tuition-dependent institutions with little organizational slack, the simple fact is that they have constantly confounded analysts and their forecasts of demise. Perhaps the flaw has been an excessive attention paid to tangible, as opposed to intangible, assets. When pressed, these colleges are often able to draw on resources hitherto untapped in the form of community support or financial sacrifices from faculty and staff. Their ability to adapt to changing educational interests of students is also evident. The course of wisdom is not to count them out.

Acknowledgment

Research for this chapter was supported by a grant from the Andrew W. Mellon Foundation.

References

"America's Best Colleges: An Exclusive Survey by the Editors of *U.S. News & World Report*." 1990. *U.S. News & World Report*.

Behn, R. D. 1979. "The End of the Growth Era in Higher Education." Statement presented to the Committee on Labor and Human Resources, United States Senate. Durham: Center for Educational Policy, Duke University.

Bowen, Howard R., and W. John Minter. 1975. *Private Higher Education*. Washington, D.C.: Association of American Colleges.

Bowen, William G., and J. A. Sosa. 1989. *Prospects for Faculty in the Arts and Sciences*. Princeton: Princeton University Press.

Breneman, David W. 1990. "Are We Losing Our Liberal Arts Colleges?" *College Board Review*, 156 (Summer): 16–29.

Breneman, David W., and Chester E. Finn, Jr., eds. 1978. *Public Policy and Private Higher Education*. Washington, D.C.: Brookings.

Carnegie Foundation for the Advancement of Teaching. 1987. *Carnegie Foundation Technical Report: A Classification of Institutions of Higher Education*. Princeton: Carnegie Foundation for the Advancement of Teaching.

Cheit, Earl F. 1971. *The New Depression in Higher Education*. New York: McGraw-Hill.

College Board. 1989. *Trends in Student Aid: 1980 to 1989*. New York: College Board, August.

Curtis, Mark H. 1988. "Crisis and Opportunity: The Founding of AAC." In *Enhancing, Promoting, Extending Liberal Education: AAC at Seventy-Five*, pp. 3–17. Washington, D.C.: Association of American Colleges.

Freeman, Richard B. 1976. *The Over-educated American*. New York: Academic Press.

Hungate, Thad, L. Richard Meeth, and William O'Connell, Jr. 1964. "The Quality and Cost of Liberal Arts College Programs: A Study of Twenty-Five Colleges." In Earl J. McGrath, ed., *Cooperative Long-Range Planning in Liberal Arts Colleges,* pp. 8–36. New York: Institute of Higher Education, Teachers College, Columbia University.

Jenny, Hans H., and G. Richard Wynn. 1970. *The Golden Years.* Wooster, Ohio: Ford Foundation and College of Wooster.

————. 1972. *The Turning Point.* Wooster, Ohio: College of Wooster.

Keller, George. 1983. *Academic Strategy.* Baltimore: Johns Hopkins University Press.

Levy, Frank. 1988. *Collars and Dreams.* New York: Norton.

McGrath, Earl J., and Charles H. Russell. 1958. *Are Liberal Arts Colleges Becoming Professional Schools?* New York: Institute of Higher Education, Teachers College, Columbia University.

Murphy, Kevin, and Finis Welch. 1989. "Wage Premiums for College Graduates: Recent Growth and Possible Explanations." *Educational Researcher,* 18(4):17–26.

National Center for Education Statistics. 1989. *Digest of Education Statistics 1989.* Washington, D.C.: U.S. Government Printing Office.

National Council of Independent Colleges and Universities. 1974. *National Policy for Private Higher Education: A Report of a Task Force of the National Council of Independent Colleges and Universities.* Washington, D.C.: Association of American Colleges.

Pfnister, Allan O. 1985. "The American Liberal Arts College in the Eighties: Dinosaur or Phoenix?" In *Contexts for Learning: The Major Sectors of American Higher Education by the National Institute of Education in Cooperation with the American Association of Higher Education,* pp. 33–48. Washington, D.C.: U.S. Government Printing Office.

Phillips, Kevin. 1990. *The Politics of Rich and Poor.* New York: Random House.

Turner, Sarah E., and William G. Bowen. 1990. "The Flight from the Arts and Sciences: Trends in Degrees Conferred." *Science,* 250(4980):517–522.

Veysey, Laurence R. 1965. *The Emergence of the American University.* Chicago: University of Chicago Press.

Wall Street Journal. 15 December 1989.

Western Interstate Commission for Higher Education. 1988. *High School Graduates: Projections by State, 1986 to 2004.* Boulder, Colo.: Western Interstate Commission for Higher Education.

Wynn, G. Richard. 1974. *At the Crossroads.* Ann Arbor: Center for the Study of Higher Education, University of Michigan.

6 Community Colleges: Making Winners out of Ordinary People

LESLIE KOLTAI

The modern community college movement in the United States is now entering its sixth decade. The forty-five years since World War II have witnessed its coming of age, and recent decades have seen community colleges take their place alongside four-year colleges and universities as clearly recognized institutions of postsecondary education. Since the 1947 publication of *Higher Education for Democracy*—the highly influential six-volume report of the President's Commission on Higher Education appointed by President Truman—public community colleges have grown faster than any other sector of higher education. Their numbers have more than doubled, and their enrollment has increased by a factor of twenty. Today, they serve fully one-third of the students in American higher education and employ over a third of American college and university faculty.

Community colleges have experienced significant success as well as growth over the past four and one-half decades. They provide low-cost but high-quality postsecondary opportunities for a broad array of clients, from first-generation college students to working adults and senior citizens. They are the major point of entry into higher education for America's low-income youth, underrepresented ethnic minorities, and new immigrants. They serve students of all ages who want to earn academic degrees, as well as nontraditional students seeking specific skills in nondegree programs. And, more than any other postsecondary sector, they have strong links to their communities, responding to local needs and interests in a manner and to an extent not seen in local public or private four-year colleges, proprietary schools, or research universities.

Changes in the 1980s

Despite the dynamism of the public community college movement, the early 1980s saw the end of its era of ready money, rapid expansion, and visionary dreams and the beginning of a period of financial retrenchment, fear of declining enrollments, and skepticism about the future. During the decade, demographic changes—including a radical shift in student profiles and an influx of underprepared students—forced community colleges to improve their planning, give greater clarity to their expectations, rethink their bifurcated mission of transfer education and career development, and try new approaches to remediation, occupational preparation, and accountability. Their growth rate fell dramatically. Their enrollment had increased by almost 200 percent in the decade from 1966 through 1976 (from 1.317 million to 3.939 million), but it grew by only 19 percent (to 4.703 million) during the next decade. Similarly, although the number of colleges grew by 82 percent or 465 new institutions between 1966 and 1976 (from 565 to 1,030), it grew by only 4 percent or 38 colleges between 1976 and 1986, to a total of 1,068 (El-Khawas, Carter, and Ottinger 1988, 7–8). Perhaps most significantly, the number of associate degrees that community colleges awarded actually decreased by 9 percent from 1983 through 1987—after having increased by 81 percent between 1971 and 1983.

The major reason for these changes was the large decline during the 1980s in the number of traditional college-age youth and a corresponding drop in the number of high school graduates. America's number of eighteen-year-olds peaked in 1979 at 4.3 million and since then has plummeted by one-fourth to 3.2 million today. Some observers predicted that, because of this drop, community college enrollments would decline during the past decade, but several factors accounted for their increased enrollments. Among them, the number of high school graduates going straight to college rose during the decade—from 50.9 percent in 1980 to 56.5 percent by 1987. In particular, the proportion of women high school graduates attending community college climbed steadily—increasing from 17.0 percent in 1977 to 19.8 percent in 1987 (Alsalam 1990, 16). But the major factor was increased enrollment in career and continuing education of adults beyond traditional college age.

Upgrading the Employed and Retraining the Unemployed

Community colleges turned to the already-employed as a source of students who could benefit from their varied menu of vocational and academic courses to prepare for either changes in existing jobs or moves to new ones. They attracted many adults who wanted to increase their skills to keep up with changes in their fields or advance their careers, as well as other workers who saw their jobs—or, in extreme cases, their entire occupations or companies—disappearing as a result of recession, changing technology, or the loss of the nation's manufacturing base. Many colleges signed cooperative agreements with local employers to upgrade their workers—often at the worksite rather than on campus. Many participated in government-sponsored projects to train the unemployed. And representatives of some colleges in the "rustbelt" eastern states joined envoy teams of municipal economic developers that traveled south and west to visit prospective firms, promising low-cost specialized training of new or existing workers to sweeten the deal of relocating in their region.

Besides the obvious interest of community colleges in occupational education at the two-year level, they had two advantages that other academic institutions lacked in attracting adult students: their accessibility in terms of location and their convenience in terms of extended classroom hours. With campuses nearby, adults could easily commute to class—and with evening offerings, they could schedule their coursework around their employment schedules. As Arthur Levine noted, community colleges that took into account the need for their students to work full time were often the "only choice" for working adults (1990, 28). Moreover, the willingness of community colleges to provide day care for children of students permitted many single mothers to enroll during daytime hours. By 1985, two of every three adults who met the federal definition of poverty were women, and more than half of America's impoverished families were headed by single mothers (Parnell 1985, 31). Helping such women move from welfare to work became a particular responsibility of two-year colleges.

As a result of these changes in clientele, the average age of community college students rose—from twenty-seven years in 1980 to twenty-nine in 1986. And as age increased, so did the number of part-time students (Cohen and Brawer 1989, 32–33). By 1988, 37 percent of all community college students were enrolled part-time. According to the *Community College Fact Book,* between 1976 and 1986 the part-time enrollment of women in two-year colleges increased 50 percent, while that of men grew by only 11 percent; thus, by 1988, 65 percent of all community college students were women (El-Khawas, Carter, and Ottinger 1988, 16).

As community colleges sought to prepare their students for as-yet-undefined jobs in an uncertain and shifting workplace, they rethought their career programs, making them more responsive to employment trends, employer needs, and student skills. Statistics have indicated that the greatest growth in the nation's job market into the twenty-first century will not be in occupations requiring a bachelor's degree but in those requiring some education beyond high school—the special province of the community college. As an illustration, *VocEd* magazine noted that, at the Kennedy Space Center, "85 percent of the technical positions require a community college-level education, and only 15 percent require a four-year or higher postsecondary level education" (Long 1985, 48). Among examples of innovative career programs whose graduates have no difficulty finding jobs, the industrial model building program of Northeast Wisconsin Technical College in Green Bay prepares students for positions making architectural models, prototypes for the automotive and toy industry, engineering and legal models, and even special effects for the movie industry ("NWTC's Industrial Model Program," 1991, 6). And North Carolina's fifty-eight-campus community college system has been called a possible model for "putting America back to work" because of its role in changing the state's economic basis from agriculture to high-technology manufacturing ("Jobs: Putting America Back to Work," 1982, 78–84).

While expanding their career programs, community colleges have sought to assure "career laddering" through articulating their programs with those of four-year colleges and universities—and even with high schools. The decade of the 1980s saw an increase in the number of community college students who transferred from career programs to universities despite an overall decrease in community college transfers generally. To encourage transfers by reducing the likelihood of students losing credit and wasting time because of moving from one institution to another, most two-year colleges have instituted transfer alliance programs with four-year institutions—as Alexander Astin recommended during the early part of the decade (1982, 192) and as Arthur Levine endorsed at the decade's close (1990, 176). Recently, community colleges have also reemphasized ways of helping students achieve an associate degree if not the baccalaureate, and businesses have been adding the degree to their preferred job qualifications (Cohen and Brawer 1989, 58, 215).

Partnerships between two-year colleges and high schools, as at LaGuardia Community College in New York, have attracted increasing attention and have been established in a number of states to facilitate students' introduction to postsecondary study. Some programs are occupationally oriented, such as courses of "techprep" study that begin in the junior year of high school and run through the two years of community college or "two-plus-two-plus-two" programs that extend from high school through community college to the baccalaureate. Others are learning-skill oriented, as is one at East Los Angeles College that involves 750 students from two local high schools, two junior high schools, and an elementary school who come to the college on Saturdays during the school year. This program initially concentrated on mathematics and science but now includes English, reading, and writing enrichment. Many of its former students have become teachers, and some have work in mathematics- and science-based professions ("East L.A. College," 1991, 20).

Community college enrollments have recently been affected by another factor: the largest wave of immigration in the nation's history, which began in the mid-1970s and has involved more than 11.5 million newcomers, more than 95 percent of whom are from Latin and Asian countries. When the United States pulled out of Vietnam, a stream of immigration from Southeast Asia began and has not yet stopped. And from the Latin countries came "freedom flotillas" from Cuba and Haiti and refugees from wars in Nicaragua and El Salvador, joining thousands who each year successfully cross the border from Mexico in search of a better life. This influx of new residents, most of whom are in need of English language instruction and many of whom are unable to read or write in their native languages, has strained the ability of community support systems, including colleges, to absorb them ("National English Literacy Demonstration Program," 1990, 1).

The 1986 federal Immigration Reform and Control Act allowed the addition of up to 2.5 million permanent residents to the American population, and it allocated funds to help affected states meet their basic health, education, and citizen needs. Community colleges across the nation expanded their English as a Second Language (ESL) and basic skills programs by means of these federal funds, but the expansion was greatest in the South and Southwest, where the weather and job markets attracted Asian immigrants, many of whom relocated there after initially settling in other parts of the country, and where the Spanish influence and language helped Hispanics find ready acceptance. Glendale College in California has offered a model program for these new citizens, providing a ladder of courses beginning with basic English for speakers of other languages and progressing through entry-level college instruction into transfer and vocational programs. In some states, however, colleges were reimbursed for these basic noncredit courses at only half the rate for credit courses, and in others federal funds have run out, leaving local communities to pick up the tab for much-needed services.

Because of all of the changes described thus far, 24 percent of all two-year college enrollments nationwide are now ethnic minority students. Community colleges enroll the highest proportion of underrepresented ethnic minorities of any postsecondary sector because of their low cost, their accessibility to commuters, and their open admissions orientation. Levine noted that all races, including whites, are likely to begin their college careers in public two-year colleges rather than in other institutions, but he reported that this is particularly true of Hispanics, and he observed that the proportion of black students enrolling in community colleges has been growing. "In 1980, 40 percent of black undergraduates were in two-year colleges; by 1988, this figure had grown slightly to 43 percent" (1990, 77).

In an effort to meet the needs of entering students for training in basic skills, two-year colleges have experimented with a variety of instructional innovations, from mastery learning through electronic technologies. For financial reasons, however, many have had to decrease their number of advanced courses or "second-level studies" for the sophomore year in favor of remedial and introductory first-year offerings. Some critics have claimed that community colleges have neglected their responsibilities for transfer, using as evidence the decline in the number of transfers during the 1980s (California Postsecondary Education Commission 1990). But some of this decline has stemmed from changes in the clientele of community colleges and from student interest during the 1980s in gaining job skills for immediate employment. It can be argued that community colleges have suffered unjustifiably by being inappropriately compared with four-year institutions in terms of their student persistence to the baccalaureate degree. For example, in analyzing the "High School and Beyond" study for the federal government, El-Khawas and associates found that far more high school graduates who aspire to a baccalaureate degree enroll in four-year institutions (59 percent) than in community colleges (16 percent) (1988, xvi). And Alexander Astin, in studying ethnic minority student persistence to the baccalaureate, attributed part of the low bachelor's degree completion rate for Hispanics and native American Indians, which is about half that of white students, "to the high concentration of both Hispanics and American Indians in community colleges" (1982, 40). Yet, for better or worse, community colleges play a larger role than most postsecondary institutions in what Burton Clark called the "cooling out" function of college, whereby students discover disparities between their hope for advanced degrees and their abilities to pursue these degrees—and as a result lower their educational ambitions (1960). Research studies that blame low community college transfer rates on the colleges themselves tend to suffer from not adequately considering this "cooling out" function of the two-year institutions. By including within a potential transfer pool of students large numbers of those at community colleges who hope to earn a baccalaureate but neither pursue the necessary courses of study nor achieve the required level of skill, such studies skew the results unfairly against two-year institutions. For example, Alexander McCormick found from a sample of 2,894 of the 12,000 participants in the "High School and Beyond" study that "the cooling out" not only persists but "appears strongest for those with the highest expectations regardless of ability" (1990, 14). He argued that studies of student persistence, both within an institution and in transfers between institutions, should take into account not only student expectations but student skills. Otherwise, he concluded, persistence studies are not informative in terms of understanding "students' negotiation of the higher education system," especially with respect to students' lowering of expectations for the bachelor's or a higher degree (1990, 1–2). For such reasons, some researchers have begun to call for a clearer definition of such terms as *transfer student* and *transfer rate* and for common data elements to facilitate analysis of transfer.

Changes in Faculty Characteristics

An encouraging change during the 1980s among community college faculty has been a decline in the proportion who have looked on two-year college teaching as a job of last resort because of a lack of faculty vacancies in four-year colleges and universities. Increasingly, community college faculty members have prepared for this work as a career goal rather than as a steppingstone to a university professorship. According to Arthur Cohen and Florence Brawer, "As a group, faculty members no longer look to the universities for their ideas on curriculum and instruction, nor do they see community colleges only as stations on their way to university careers. Community college instruction has become a career in its own right. Its flowering but awaits a more fully developed professional consciousness on the part of its practitioners" (1989, 90).

With this change has come increased interest among new faculty members in student assessment and placement and in the measurement of student outcomes, since these faculty have a clear commitment to meet the needs of community college students and are better trained for that pursuit. At the same time, "increasing numbers of instructors are obtaining doctoral degrees prior to employment or soon thereafter. . . . While 16 percent of the humanities instructors had doctorates in 1975, the percentage had increased to 23 by 1983. Among all liberal arts instructors, the percentage had increased to 27" (Cohen and Brawer 1987, 68).

Countering this trend toward a more committed faculty is the continued use of large numbers of part-time instructors. "Between 1976 and 1986 the number of part-time faculty increased by 47 percent, compared to a 26 percent increase in the number of full-timers and a 36 percent increase in the size of the administrative and professional staff. The use of part-time faculty is a firmly established and growing practice at community, junior, and technical colleges" (El-Khawas, Carter, and Ottinger 1988, xviii). Indeed, until community colleges are better funded, they will continue to employ disproportionate numbers of part-time faculty as a means to balancing their budgets while providing the small classes and individualized instruction required by their student population.

Another change evident during the 1980s was further diversification of two-year college faculty and staff. Increased numbers of women and ethnic minorities as faculty members and administrators of two-year colleges offer much-needed role models to many women and ethnic minority students on campus. Among efforts to this end, the League for Innovation in the Community College began its nationwide "Leaders for the 80s" project in 1980 with a focus on developing more women community college administrators; since then, offshoots of the national project have been organized in California, New Jersey, New York, North Carolina, Washington, and Wisconsin (Goodwin 1988, 10).

Changes in the Fiscal Environment

The passage of proposition 13 in California in 1978 signaled the beginning of a tax revolt that sent shock waves throughout the nation, since California—considered a bellwether state—seemed to face a multitude of tough decisions between imposing user fees or cutting back on such services as noncredit community education and classes for senior citizens and the disabled. By the early 1980s, community colleges in other states had cut back on classes, services, and faculty development in response to lack of funding. "With the advent of the 1980s," wrote Richard L. Alfred, director of the Community College Program at the University of Michigan in Ann

Arbor, "community colleges have felt the pressures of changing state and federal requirements guiding the allocation of resources, and the era of laissez-faire leadership has ceased" (1984, 8).

At the start of the decade, economists David Breneman and Susan Nelson argued that the most serious obstacle to a resolution of the tension between the expansive mission of community colleges and their shrinking financial base involved "the mission, not the finance of community college activities." With a mission that attempted to be "all things to all people," community colleges, according to Breneman and Nelson, had failed to justify the costs they deemed necessary for their operations (1981, 54).

By 1986, a community college vice-president commented:

> The most hallowed tradition of the community or junior college, the "open door," is under attack. Along with scores of other criticisms of education, a persistent questioning of the venerable open-door tradition has been evident and growing in the 1980s. And why not? Questions about the open door bring into focus two very popular concerns: standards of excellence and fiscal responsibility. As financial resources shrink, can the community college continue to justify excessive expenditures on high-risk students? As the taxpayer grows more dissatisfied with the quality of public education, can the community college continue to hope that educational exposure on a broad scale will produce enough success to justify continuation, or must it now ensure the quality of its service and the quality of its product? (Nigliazzo 1986, 33)

Community colleges have responded in a variety of ways to ensure quality. Their policy makers have focused more clearly on their institutions' missions of vocational and transfer education to answer legislators' and others' concerns about how well the colleges are fulfilling those missions. Some colleges have sponsored public opinion surveys to assess community attitudes—among them, the five two-year colleges in western North Carolina that used a comprehensive survey to determine public perceptions of their programs, services, and effectiveness in meeting community needs, as well as the value of education and training ("Telephone Survey," 1990). And most colleges have begun to locate potential sources of money other than government funds. As late as 1988, private gifts and endowments accounted for only 1 percent of the total revenues of the average college (El-Khawas, Carter, and Ottinger 1988, xvii), but since then community colleges have increased their links to the business community through contract education and sought contributions from corporations, foundations, and local philanthropists. In Mississippi, Meridian Community College has created a nationally recognized model technology transfer program in partnership with a local electronics company, with funds supplemented by the Job Training Partnership Act as well as $75,000 in company contributions for employee training ("Mississippi College," 1990, 7). In California, the Economic Development Network of the California Community Colleges has used $6.31 million to leverage $11.05 million in contributions from private sector partners, local and other state agencies, and other special projects (Board of Governors 1991).

Another means to improve the funding for two-year institutions has come through the presentation to funding agencies of hard data demonstrating student outcomes and successes. Offices of institutional research have become increasingly common on community college campuses as administrators have sought to demonstrate successful practices. Miami-Dade Community College in Florida has been especially well known for its integration of institutional research into institutional decision making. In California, Santa Barbara City College and Rancho Santiago College have outstanding research staffs who collect and analyze data on students to document program success. California's legislature has mandated that community colleges upgrade and expand their student assessment efforts as part of a "matriculation" program that also involves student counseling and follow-up to improve student achievement. That program is an example of concern both for student welfare and for the investment that the state's taxpayers are asked to make in higher education. Rather than imposing restrictive admission requirements, California's community colleges are adhering to their longstanding open-door policy of admitting at-risk students, including high school dropouts, and giving them the opportunity to demonstrate their abilities by "challenging" course prerequisites. At the same time, they recognize the need for better guidance as students select their courses, and the matriculation program was a natural response to this need. It not only allows for better advisement of students as they make their course selections, but also provides policy makers with a wealth of data concerning the results of student assessment, placement, and instruction procedures. In short, the demand of funding agencies for evidence of results is leading to the development of programs that are clearly related to students' educational needs.

Challenges for the Future

Changes buffeting community colleges during the past decade were summarized by Robert H. McCabe, president of Miami-Dade.

The accelerated evolution in our society over the past three decades parallels the most significant era of growth and development for the American community college. During the brief history of the community college movement, public attitudes toward social programs have seen some dramatic shifts. Today, the feeling that social programs have not worked, that there is too much government regulation, and that people should do more for themselves is strong. Yet, the problems of urban areas and minority populations have not lessened. Rather, the changing requirements for literacy in an information age and the stress of the substantial transitions that society is undergoing have caused already severe problems to deepen. Any public institution, especially one as closely tied to the needs of society as the community college, will also find itself deeply immersed in transition (1984, 44).

Community colleges will continue to face the problems of recent years into the coming century. A look at the enrollments of America's elementary and secondary schools gives a glimpse of tomorrow's students, who are very much like today's students, only more so. Minority enrollments will continue to increase. Underpreparedness in the basic skills will not abate. Elementary and secondary schools will face the same budget cutbacks, overcrowding, and increasingly outmoded equipment and buildings as postsecondary institutions, and, while many students in the schools grapple with learning English skills, they will continue to fall behind in other subjects, such as mathematics, science, and literature.

When considering student enrollments, there is a need to focus on serious students in the areas of both transfer education and career education. It is hoped that clarification of the dual mission of community colleges for occupational preparation and transfer education will help to address serious vocational students as well as their transfer-bound colleagues. Community college leaders must recognize and resolve the challenge presented by the need for additional remedial and basic skills courses, especially when increases in this part of the curriculum come at the expense of more advanced sophomore-level courses. Otherwise, fewer well-prepared, first-time college students fresh out of high school will choose to attend two-year colleges than they did a decade ago, if they have other options open to them.

The American community colleges have become increasingly diverse in terms of ethnic representation, and there is no reason to expect this pattern to change in the coming years. College leaders, therefore, must consider the potential changes needed on campus to meet the needs of an ever-changing student body. The curriculum, for example, has been a focal point over the past several years, with community college faculty members among the leaders nationwide calling for a multicultural curriculum. Among the leaders in this movement, San Juan College in New Mexico "has developed programs that serve the needs of its minority students that are not necessarily tailored to the needs of a specific minority group" (Henderson 1989).

At the same time, ethnic minority representation among the faculty and staff has only slowly increased, and many observers have pointed to the need for greater efforts to feed the pipeline from undergraduate to baccalaureate to graduate study so that community colleges can begin to hire more ethnic minority administrators and faculty members. Both of these issues, however, carry the potential for controversy on campus. Community college leaders need to be prepared to respond. They must take the lead in ensuring that both the curriculum and the college staff reflect the contributions of traditionally underrepresented groups, foster a campus community that tolerates and respects diversity, and facilitate the delivery of both vocational and transfer education in an intellectually lively environment.

While the community colleges serve as the educational entry point to postsecondary education for millions of low-income students and immigrants, they have not yet received from state or federal funding sources the funds they need. El-Khawas, Carter, and Ottinger noted that, "in spite of the historically unparalleled growth in both number of institutions and students enrolled, many educational and governmental leaders continue to overlook the critical importance and scale of this sector" (1988, xv). Leaders within the four-year higher education circle have been slow to recognize the service community colleges have provided for them. In taking responsibility for remedial education, for basic skills training, and for specialized learning skills acquisition, the community colleges have provided precollegiate education for hundreds of thousands of students who would otherwise seek a place in baccalaureate institutions ill-equipped to meet their needs. By providing vocational and career education, as well as transfer education, the community colleges prepare these students for job opportunities or transfer. Indeed, the institutions have moved well beyond the secondary status they held during the early part of this century and are ready to receive the position of financial security they need in order to continue to play that vital role.

The *Community College Fact Book* stated that "community colleges represent a financially efficient segment of higher education, educating 43 percent of the nation's undergraduates for a disproportionately small share of state and federal higher education monies" (El-Khawas, Carter, and Ottinger 1988, xviii). Although a majority of all entering freshmen begin their collegiate studies at community colleges and state funds account for 50 percent of community college revenues, two-year colleges receive only

19 percent of state funds for higher education and less than 10 percent of federal higher education funds. Community college spokesmen must begin to make a more persuasive case for more adequate funding.

In this regard, K. Patricia Cross stated that "the tough problem is not in identifying winners; it is in making winners out of ordinary people. That, after all, is the overwhelming purpose of education. Yet, historically, in most of the periods emphasizing excellence, education has reverted to selecting winners rather than creating them" (1984). More than any other segment of higher education, community colleges, with their open-admissions policies and their programs of remediation and English as a second language, have confronted this responsibility of creating winners rather than merely selecting them. By meeting their current challenges of responding to shifting student enrollment patterns, expanding the diversity of their faculty and staff, and finding additional funding sources, two-year institutions will increasingly serve as exciting teaching and learning centers that achieve the overarching purpose of education: "making winners out of ordinary people."

Acknowledgments

The author thanks research associates Karen S. Grosz, Marcia Murota, and Tracy O'Connell for their contributions to the development of this chapter.

References

Alfred, Richard L. 1984. "Maximizing Institutional Responsiveness to Changing Environmental Conditions." In Richard L. Alfred et al., eds., *Emerging Roles for Community College Leaders: New Directions for Community Colleges 46*. San Francisco: Jossey-Bass.

Alsalam, Nabeel, ed. 1990. *The Condition of Education 1990*. Vol. 2: *Postsecondary Education*. Washington, D.C.: U.S. Department of Education.

Astin, Alexander W. 1982. *Minorities in American Higher Education: Recent Trends, Current Prospects, and Recommendations*. San Francisco: Jossey-Bass.

Board of Governors, California Community Colleges. 1991. "Economic Development." 14–15 March 1991 Meeting Agenda. Sacramento: Board of Governors, California Community Colleges.

Breneman, David W., and Susan C. Nelson. 1981. *Financing Community Colleges: An Economic Perspective*. Washington, D.C.: Brookings.

California Postsecondary Education Commission. 1990. *Transfer and Articulation in the 1990s: California in the Larger Picture*. Report 90-30. Sacramento: California Postsecondary Education Commission, December.

Clark, Burton R. 1960. "The 'Cooling Out' Function in Higher Education." *American Journal of Sociology,* 65:569–576.

Cohen, Arthur M., and Florence B. Brawer. 1987. *The Collegiate Function of Community Colleges: Fostering Higher Learning through Curriculum and Student Transfer.* San Francisco: Jossey-Bass.

———. 1989. *The American Community College,* 2d ed. San Francisco: Jossey-Bass.

Cross, K. Patricia. 1984."Societal Imperatives: Need for an Educated Democracy." Paper presented at the National Conference on Teaching and Excellence, Austin, Texas, May.

"East L.A. College Partners Math Program Hopes to Found Institute." 1991. *Community College Week,* 1 April, p. 1.

El-Khawas, Elaine, Deborah J. Carter, and Cecilia A. Ottinger, compilers. 1988. *Community College Fact Book.* New York: Macmillan.

Goodwin, Gregory, ed. 1988. *Celebrating Two Decades of Innovation.* Laguna Hills, Calif.: League for Innovation in the Community College.

Henderson, James C. 1989. "Accommodating the Diversity Represented by Minority Students." In *Leadership Abstracts.* Laguna Hills, Calif.: League for Innovation in the Community College, April.

"Jobs: Putting America Back to Work." 1982. *Newsweek,* 18 October, pp. 78–84.

Levine, Arthur, et al. 1990. *Shaping Higher Education's Future: Demographic Realities and Opportunities, 1990–2000.* San Francisco: Jossey-Bass.

Long, James P. 1985. "Vocational Education in the Community Colleges." *VocEd,* 60(2):47–50.

McCabe, Robert H. 1984. "Dimensions of Change Confronting Institutional Leaders." In Richard L. Alfred et al., eds., *Emerging Roles for Community College Leaders: New Directions for Community Colleges 46.* San Francisco: Jossey-Bass.

McCormick, Alexander C. 1990. "Mobility of Educational Expectations: The Effect of Community Colleges." Paper presented at the Annual Meeting of the Association for the Study of Higher Education, Portland, Oregon, November.

"Mississippi College Is National Model for Community Partnership in Technology-based Training." 1990. *Community College Week,* 2 April, p. 7.

"National English Literacy Demonstration Program for Adults of Limited English Proficiency: A Research Study." 1990. *Amnesty Education Newsletter,* July.

Nigliazzo, Marc A. 1986. "The Fading Vision of the Open Door." In Billie Wright Dziech, ed., *Controversies and Decision Making in Difficult Economic Times: New Directions for Community Colleges 53.* San Francisco: Jossey-Bass.

"NWTC's Industrial Model Program Helps Firms Sell Ideas through Models." 1991. *Community College Week,* 16 April, p. 6.

Parnell, Dale. 1985. *The Neglected Majority.* Washington, D.C.: Community College Press.

President's Commission on Higher Education. 1947. *Higher Education for Democracy: A Report of the President's Commission on Higher Education.* Vol. 1: *Establishing the Goals.* New York: Harper.

"Telephone Survey Affirms NC Colleges' Effectiveness, Residents' Awareness." 1990. *Community College Week,* 24 December, p. 9.

7 California: A Multisegment System

NEIL J. SMELSER

In introducing its 1989 report on California's system of higher education, a team from the Organization for Economic Cooperation and Development (OECD) described that system as "self-consciously in the vanguard of educational development" (Education Committee 1989, 31). The description brings to mind three features: a degree of self-awareness, pride in leadership, and likely emulation by those not in the vanguard. The history of the system provides ample evidence to substantiate all three connotations.

Self-Awareness

First, California's political and educational leaders have studied its higher education system repeatedly and self-consciously. Major studies prior to the 1960 Master Plan for Higher Education appeared in 1934, 1947, 1955, and 1957. Most of these were somewhat defensive in character, seeking ways to stem the competition for status and higher degree-granting authority among California's colleges and to contain the costs associated with that competition (California State Council on Educational Planning and Coordination 1934; Strayer, Deutsch, and Douglass 1948; McConnell, Holy, and Semans 1955; Semans and Holy 1957). The Master Plan Survey Team also conducted a survey before submitting its recommendations for that plan, adopted in 1960. The Master Plan itself built in the requirement for its review by the legislature every decade. A joint legislative committee reviewed the Master Plan in 1971–73 (Joint Committee 1973), and both a lay commission and a joint legislative committee studied and reported on it in 1985–88 (Commission for the Review of the Master Plan 1987; Joint Committee 1989). The OECD selected California as a kind of non-European model for study in 1988–89 and, in connection with that investigation, the California Postsecondary Education Commission asked Clive Condren of the University of California to undertake a major study of the California system (1988).

Pride in Leadership

Second, "self-conscious" has often implied a degree of self-satisfaction. While most of the reviews up to 1960 were conducted in an atmosphere of apprehension of higher education's unmanageability, the review studies since have endorsed if not celebrated the system. Although both legislative reviews identified problem areas and ways to improve the Master Plan, neither called for any structural modifications. In 1987 the review commission described California's establishment as a whole as "an extraordinary education system" and the Master Plan itself as a "unique and timeless foundation" for higher education (Commission for the Review of the Master Plan 1987, 1, i). Two years later the joint legislative committee called the system as a whole "one of the most astonishing educational systems on earth" and spoke of a "postsecondary system of opportunity, quality, and diversity" (Joint Committee 1989, 1).

Likely Emulation

Third, California's system of higher education has been the object of much study and potential emulation from outside. The OECD examiners explained that one of the objectives of their survey of California's system of higher education was "to draw lessons as far as possible for . . . Member countries" (Education Committee 1989, 6). As citizen and scholar of California's system, I have spoken with dozens of individual visitors and scholars and with numerous delegations interested in that system; these visitors came from many other countries (among them Great Britain, Japan, Norway, Indonesia, and the Ivory Coast, as well as the OECD team) and from other American states. Californians tend not to reciprocate by studying other systems, a fact that constitutes some further evidence of their general self-confidence.

My objective in this chapter is to examine this evidently remarkable system from the standpoint of its history, its current structure, and its probable future preoccupations. I will organize my remarks along three lines: the system's ingenuity as a social invention, its distinctive vulnerabilities, and some future trends and problems derived from both our knowledge of the system and our sense of future social change in California.

The Structural Wizardry of the Master Plan

A Balance between Structural Rigidity and Structural Flexibility

The term *Master Plan* connotes comprehensiveness of scope and rationality of conception. Although history ultimately may judge it as such, it was certainly not bred in those conditions. The planners of the late 1950s, as well as the legislature who commissioned them, were faced with a history of restiveness and ungovernability of California's system—ambitions to transform junior colleges into four-year institutions, ambitions to transform four-year colleges into advanced degree-granting institutions, and ambitions to stem this tide on the part of the University of California (Coons 1968, 21–22). It was a situation—to paraphrase Gilbert and Sullivan's dreaded egalitarian utopia in *The Gondoliers*–of "everybody" trying to become (or remain) "somebody." In this context, the imposition of the Master Plan was an ad hoc act of lid clamping on this kind of instability. It achieved this in two ways. First, it formalized the principle of differentiation of function, which froze the several categories of institutions of higher education (the University, the state colleges, and the community colleges) into specialized educational missions from which they could not depart or—in the case of the community colleges and state colleges—climb.[1] Second, it built in a principle of differential elitism with respect to admissions, giving the University the top one-eighth of qualified high school graduates, the state colleges the top one-third, and the community colleges open admission to all students eighteen years or older, whether or not they were high school graduates, as long as they could benefit from instruction. The Master Plan was also a kind of ad hoc political compromise in that it gave—as critics complained—"something for everybody": a monopoly for the University, solid postbaccalaureate status for the state college system, and inclusion in the higher education system for the community colleges (Condren 1988, 30).

Subsequently, however, this situational compromise came to constitute an ingenious combination of structural rigidity on the one hand and capacity for growth and adaptation on the other. By virtue of the strictures imposed, ambitions to grow "upward" through change of educational mission were effectively thwarted. At the same time, the system built in the capacity to increase the size of individual colleges and universities and increase the numbers of institutions within each segment. The examiners from the OECD judged that the Master Plan "seemed to represent the most advanced effort through state action to organize mass education for a tripling enrollment [between 1960 and 1975]" (Education Committee 1989, 25). In practice, the expansion was mainly "mass" in character (i.e., in the second and especially the third segments). Between 1960 and 1970 the University expanded its student enrollments by approximately 57,000, the state college system by nearly 130,000, and the community college system by nearly 380,000 (Smelser 1973b, 49). It is extraordinary that a system with such a frozen structure can continue to accommodate as rapid and continuous a demographic growth as California's.[2]

A Balance between Excellence and Egalitarianism

It can be argued plausibly that no advanced or aspiring society in the world escapes the dilemma of how to maximize two educational purposes at once: the achievement of the highest quality and the most refined intellectual and cultural expression in its educational system on the one hand and the provision of a conduit for social mobility, credentialism, and societal participation on the part of the mass of its citizenry on the other. A variety of resolutions of the dilemma are observable in the panoply of the world's educational systems—for example, more or less ignoring mass participation, as in the case of Europe's past elitist arrangements; maximizing participation in the context of low quality, as in some phases of Philippine history; or attempting to stress both quality and participation in a single system, as was done by the City University of New York's experiment in open admissions.

California's Master Plan marked another distinctive attempt to come to terms with that dilemma involved in stressing both excellence and egalitarianism. Its solution rests on three foundations. The first, already mentioned, is differentiation of function. The campuses of the University of California maintain a virtual monopoly on one aspect of "quality": research and the doctorate. The second, also mentioned, is differential admission, which both "tracks" students into segments on the basis of demonstrated ability and performance (a stress on excellence) and opens the system to all who have reached age eighteen and can benefit from instruction (a stress on egalitarianism). The third foundation, which bridges the differentiated aspects (by function and by admission), is the transfer function, which permits those who enter community colleges to move subsequently to the other two segments and those who enter the community colleges and state universities to transfer to the University—if, in both cases, their collegiate academic performance gains them admission. (In practice there are flows in the reverse direction as well, but these are not as critical as the "upward" flows with respect to the fostering of egalitarianism.)

The OECD examiners found the combined effects of these three principles to be striking. Not only is the system able to expand on a mass basis, but it "[maintains] a quality of research and education at the top which [is] unsurpassed anywhere among the OECD countries and probably in the world" (Education Committee 1989, 25). Later we will discover a vulnerability contained in this compromise, but for the moment we underscore its ingenuity as a solution to the excellence-egalitarian dilemma. Summing up, the OECD examiners concluded that the Master Plan represents "a continuing compromise which is probably more effective than those found in Europe in the search for an optimum combination of equality and excellence" (Education Committee 1989, 29).

The Structuring of Individual and Institutional Mobility

The balances just noted can also be described in terms of their implications for individual social mobility (i.e., the movement of persons or, more precisely, students) on the one hand and institutional social mobility (i.e., the movement of university and college campuses) on the other. With respect to individual mobility, a certain sifting-and-blocking process takes place at the termination of secondary education: some students choose not to enter the system of higher education, all can enter the community colleges, one-third (judged by high school performance and test results) can enter the State University, and one-eighth (judged by the same criteria) can enter the University of California.[3] By virtue of the transfer function, however, the prospects for upward mobility remain open during the college career—that is to say, students can, if their performance merits it, move "upward" through the system.[4]

With respect to institutional mobility, the principle of the differentiation of function makes it impossible for college and university campuses to move upward or downward across the three levels: a situation of completely blocked mobility. This contrasts with the situation for individuals, who can move among the segments under some circumstances. However, institutions may compete and move within the segments. It is possible, for example, for a University or State University campus to improve both its status and its command of resources. The history of the San Diego campus of the University of California since its development in the early 1960s is a striking example. Moreover, an entire segment can compete with the others and thereby improve its relative position. The State University system has a long history of attempting to achieve parity with the University of California in appellation, salaries, libraries, sabbatical arrangements, and research support.

Described as such, the Master Plan achieved an ingenious splitting and structuring of opportunities for individual and institutional striving and, in doing that, evolved an unconsciously designed device for segregating and thus diffusing several potential kinds of individual and social conflict.

Governance

To continue the theme of conflict management: one positive aspect of the governance of the system of higher education has to do with the separation of governance by segment. Historically, the governing bodies of the three segments have evolved independently from one another. The Board of Regents of the University of California is a constitutionally established governing body dating from the beginning. The state university gained its own Board of Trustees when the Master Plan was enacted in 1960, but the board was granted only statutory, not constitutional status. The community colleges were governed under the State Board of Education until 1967, when the legislature and governor created a board of governors. In this process of independent evolution, each board has developed a sense of guardianship over its own institutions and a corresponding distaste for either weakening its powers through decentralization or surrendering its powers to a higher governing authority.

The wisdom of this independent evolution, unplanned and discoverable only by hindsight, is that it has avoided the inclusion of too many contending constituencies under the umbrella of one governance structure. The importance of this principle is underscored by noticing the brief and unhappy history (1960–74) of the Coordinating Council for Higher Education. This body was created by the Master Plan to superimpose a kind of voluntary coordination on the higher education system (the Coordinating Council included the private sector as well). The members of the council were mainly representatives of the segments—in particular, their chief executives—and they behaved as representatives to a large degree. Much of the history of the council was one of block voting and vetoing by the segments, which resulted in its ineffectiveness as a coordinating body. At the time of the 1971–73 review of the Master Plan, the legislature concluded that the coordinating efforts of the council had been inadequate (Joint Committee 1973, 22). In its place the legislature substituted another coordinating agency, the California Postsecondary Education Commission, which did not incorporate the principle of representation of the segments by staff but rather by members of their governing boards and which had a majority of public representatives rather than segmental representatives. At the same time, the legislature rejected the idea of a super board for all of higher education, largely on grounds that it would bureaucratize the system unduly. It should be noted, however, that a super board would probably have been plagued by segmental parochialism and jealousies.

The Structural Vulnerabilities of the Master Plan

Governance

While benefiting from the diffusion of conflict management, much of the governing structure of the system of higher education has labored under a number of ambiguities. The Board of Regents, most privileged by independent status, has proved the least problematical and has been subjected to the fewest calls for change. The Board of Trustees of the State University has rankled under the fact that its status is statutory. This not only symbolizes its lack of parity with the University, but it also places the state university system at a disadvantage with respect to budgetary intervention and control by the state. The Board of Governors of the community college system, superimposed on a large and dispersed body of campuses accustomed to local support and control, proved to be a chronically weak system, and the topic of community college governance occupied most of the attention of the Commission for the Review of the Master Plan in the first phase of its study (Commission for the Review of the Master Plan 1986).

Cost

Because the relative costs of (and returns to) different kinds of education defy accurate measurement and calculation, it is difficult to arrive at absolute judgments about the efficiency of different arrangements. In principle, however, it is possible to find several sources of duplication and possible waste in California's higher education system, which greater specialization might reduce.

The first source is that lower-division education is sustained in all segments. It is assumed (but not really proved) that lower-division education is least expensive at the community college level; considerations of efficiency might lead to the conclusion that these first two years might be removed from the programs of university and state university campuses. Yet scattered efforts to effect this further differentiation of function have engendered strong resistance.

The second source of inefficiency lies in competition within the segments. In the University of California system, for example, the large, general campuses of Berkeley and UCLA are often seen by the newer, smaller campuses as models to be emulated. This drive toward general campus status throughout the system generates pressure to develop very high-cost graduate programs and research facilities. Yet the internal status striving remains both endemic and strong, and the means to curb this impulse are not readily available.

Residual Ambiguities of Mission

The mission of each segment can be stated simply, but each retains a certain uncertainty and resultant uneasiness. The community colleges are restricted to two years of instruction leading to an associate degree and are expected to offer courses in three areas—vocational, transfer (liberal arts), and general instruction. Yet the proper weighing for each of the three is unclear and varies over time. In the interests of institutional survival, community colleges are often driven in the direction of expanding their "marketable" vocational programs—marketable, that is, both to students and in the economy.

The State University offers the baccalaureate and selected master's programs and is charged to carry out research related to teaching. Yet that system has proven to be the most restless segment, resembling the middle sibling that it is; it is chronically dissatisfied with the more privileged status of the University of California and strives continuously for parity on one front or another.

The University of California's mission includes those of the other segments plus doctoral training, research, and exclusive jurisdiction over certain kinds of professional training. By virtue of that scope, however, the university campus might be described as laboring under a certain kind of "functional overloading" of commitments to research, graduate training, professional training, undergraduate education, professional service, and public service (Smelser 1973a; Parsons 1973). Furthermore, given the reward structure of the national and international academic communities, University of California faculty tend to drift toward stressing the spheres of research, publication, and graduate training and national and international participation. In the eyes of critics, this means that they neglect other spheres, especially undergraduate teaching. These ambiguities of mission for each of the segments seem chronic and not easily alterable.

Short-changing Egalitarianism

The Californian compromise between excellence and equality was characterized above as a notable sociological invention. The possibility of transfer among segments, embodying an educational version of social mobility, is an essential ingredient in this compromise. In practice, however, the transfer function has proved problematic. During the first quarter century of the Master Plan, the number of community college transfers to the University of California system reached an annual high of just over eight thousand in 1973, a minuscule figure considering the more than one million students enrolled in community colleges. Furthermore, the transfer function has a tendency to atrophy. In the decade after that high point, transfers from community colleges to the University declined steadily to under five thousand in 1985 (Task Force on Lower Division Education 1986, 24).

This apparent "failure" on the egalitarian front generated an extensive debate on the Master Plan in the late 1980s. The debate was given greater heat by its racial/ethnic overtones. The vast majority of Hispanics and black minority students are in the community college system, and an atrophy of the transfer function implies a sluggishness in the efforts to advance these minority groups. These problems of admission and transfer were at the top of the agenda of both Master Plan review bodies in 1987–89 (Commission for the Review of the Master Plan 1987, 22–28; Joint Committee 1989, 17–42), and individual University campuses came under pressure to ease the transfer process, increase the numbers of transfer students, and increase the ratio between upper-division and lower-division students.

The forces determining the educational fate of disadvantaged minority and class groups are complex and multiple. They include the forces of culture, family, poverty, and discrimination, to say nothing of educational discouragement. It seems unrealistic and perhaps unfair to single out the system of higher education as accountable for failures in egalitarianism. Nevertheless, since the Master Plan was built on the premise that it would be a helpful institution in this regard, it stands to reason that it would also come to attention when blame is being assigned for those failures.

Managing Collective Conflict

Colleges and universities are institutionalized in large part in the name of values of individual achievement and are best equipped to deal with individuals. They admit individuals, give instruction to and grade individuals, discipline individuals, graduate individuals, and place individuals in occupational positions. We noted above that one of the effects of the Master Plan is to structure the mobility of individuals. We also noted that several features of that plan are geared to the containment of the competitive strivings of its colleges and universities.

There is, however, a third kind of conflict—group conflict—for which colleges and universities have few institutionalized mechanisms. This deficit of machinery geared to group conflict became evident during the turbulence experienced in higher education in the 1960s. Colleges and universities, reasonably able to handle traditional individual academic problems and individual disciplinary offenses, found themselves ill-equipped to deal with group phenomena such as mass demonstrations, protest, and violations of rules. They also discovered that they lacked—and had to invent—machinery to negotiate with groups as such. Even with several decades of experience with group conflict, colleges and universities are still more comfortable in dealing with individuals than with groups. This lack promises to become a more serious problem in the future, more-over, since a greater campus diversity promises to yield a situation in which groups define themselves in primordial ways—along gender, racial, ethnic, cultural, lifestyle, and environmentalist lines—and present themselves po-litically as groups, not individuals.

Some Glimpses into the Future

From these reflections we may generate some general predictions about the patterns of challenge, preoccupation, conflict, and accommodation that may be expected in California's higher education system.

The QUEEF Complex: Maximizing Everything

When the Commission for the Review of the Master Plan submitted its final report in 1987, it organized the contents around certain objectives that should guide the missions and policies of the higher education system. These objectives were summarized, in the Commission's words, as follows:

> Unity, to assure that all elements of the system work together in pursuit of common goals;
> Equity, to assure that all Californians have unrestricted opportunity to fulfill their educational potential and aspirations;
> Quality, to assure that excellence characterizes every aspect of the system; and
> Efficiency, to assure the most productive use of finite financial and human re-sources (1987, 3–4).

(We may alter the order and produce the acronym QUEE–Quality, Unity, Equity, and Efficiency.) Immediately after specifying these four objectives, the commission added a fifth, that those aims must be realized through voluntary coordination by the segments, not superimposed by the legislature or governor. This might be termed Freedom, which yields QUEEF as a guiding principle.

Several observations about the list of objectives come to mind. First, the language used to describe them was strong and absolute, containing words like *common, all, unrestricted, every aspect,* and *most productive,* all of which connote the logic of maximizing. Second, each ingredient was presented by the commission as independent, as though it existed in isolation from the others. Third, the rhetoric and affective tone of the presentation was such that, if asked, almost anyone is put in the position of having to assent to the positive value of each objective. Who can object to quality, unity, equity, efficiency, or freedom?

To represent QUEEF in this way, however, tends to obscure many of the realities of institutional life in higher education. In the first place, it is evident that many of the objectives stand in tension if not contradiction with one another—and thus cannot be simultaneously maximized. It is difficult to conceive, for example, how the values of unity and freedom can be simultaneously maximized. The goals of quality (excellence) and efficiency (cost control) also tug in different directions under some circumstances. And we noted above that the relations between excellence (quality) and equity pose some kind of dilemma. In the second place, if the state demands and the educational establishment agrees to maximize on all these fronts—which the commission's report asks that they do—this sets up the probability that cycles of overdemand and overpromise, failure to deliver, disappointment, and recrimination will be continuously generated.

QUEEF-like discourse appears frequently in the political and ideological rhetoric about higher education; it is part of the ambivalent give-and-take of public support of education and education's plea for that support. (More generally, it is probably part and parcel of the rhetoric that develops when multiple values are embedded in a single institutional complex.) It should be acknowledged, however, that the values of QUEEF constitute a utopian myth about its system of higher education. Such a myth probably gives comfort to many and may be necessary to drive people to higher goals, but at the same time it builds a note of unrealism into the institutional life of higher education and tends to generate episodes of exaggerated feelings of promise, hope, despair, and scapegoating. Since the QUEEF complex is rooted deeply in the cultural values of California (and America in general), I am certain that we will continue to live with that complex and its consequences for decades to come.

Asymmetries in the QUEEF Complex

As indicated, appeals of the QUEEF variety tend to generate agreement in principle with the general values invoked. In practice, however, the different objectives in the QUEEF complex are tilted to some degree in the direction of either the state or the educational establishment. Academics and educators tend to like quality and freedom most; representatives of the state tend to like unity and equity most. When academics (at least those in the University) speak of quality, they tend to have in mind quality of research, quality of graduate training, and quality of people in their institutions; when representatives of the state speak of quality, they tend to refer to the quality of undergraduate education.[5] When academics speak of efficiency, they look more to the resources necessary for high-quality output; when representatives of the state speak of efficiency, they usually mean cost containment.

Furthermore, values contained in the QUEEF complex are often arrayed against one another in debate. When representatives of the state invoke arguments based on equity, academics counterinvoke arguments based on quality. When representatives of the state invoke arguments based on unity (e.g., standardization), academics counterinvoke arguments based on freedom. Furthermore, these various values are most often invoked rhetorically as general principles and are often accompanied by unverified and possibly unverifiable assertions (e.g., research erodes good teaching; research fosters good teaching). For these reasons, debates within the QUEEF complex tend to be dialogues of the deaf, with both sides remaining unshaken in their commitments and beliefs. Such unprofitable conversations will also no doubt continue as long as the QUEEF complex persists.

Structural Continuity, Expansion, and Difficult Economic Times

It is reasonable to predict that the main structural contours of the Master Plan—including the principle of differentiation of function, differential admissions, transfer, and separate governance structures—will persist into the next several decades. The reasons for this prediction are, first, that these contours have persisted with notable continuity for three decades and, second, that they still constitute that nice compromise along the dimensions of change/stability and egalitarianism/excellence.

The structure will persist, however, in the context of two ongoing changes. First, the population of California will continue to expand. The state's population grew by almost six million in the 1980s, constituting an increase of about 25 percent in the nation's largest state. Although this astonishing rate may ease in the next two decades, the absolute numbers will continue to increase. This will sustain the pressure on higher education to continue its expansion of enrollments and, through them, the size and number of its campuses.

At the same time, it appears that higher education's share of the state economic pie will decrease further during the next decade or two. At present, the university and state university systems command about 10 percent of the state's revenue dollars. This percentage is expected to decrease to about 8 in a decade or so. The basic reason for this decline is competition arising from other state commitments, such as health care and social service. In particular, the schedule of payoff for existing bonds will increase significantly, and expenditures on new prisons and welfare will also rise. These burdens, combined with the continued demand for the expansion and renewal of the infrastructure of state and municipal facilities, will squeeze higher education, and it is not clear that sufficient offsetting resources will be found in federal revenues or private largesse.

In one respect this demographic/economic squeeze will encourage continuity in the structure in the Master Plan. In particular, it will reduce the probability that the State University will gain significantly in its efforts to secure the doctorate and to build more research into its mission. Both of these are high-cost items, and political leaders will be more reluctant than ever to admit such changes of mission. In another respect, however, the squeeze will push toward a change of mission for the University of California. Under pressure both to expand and to economize, the state may opt to grow in what it sees as the least expensive areas (i.e., in the lower tiers) and to hold back on the building of new campuses for the University. What may have to "give" under these circumstances is the University's commitment to admit the top one-eighth of the high school graduates of California. The past decade has witnessed some pressure on this component of the University's mission, and this will become more severe during the next two decades.

Contending with the Political and Social Effects of Diversity

No assessment of the future of California and its system of higher education begins without reciting the fact that by the year 2000 or so a majority of the state's population will be minority, with Hispanics, Asians, and blacks constituting main minority groups. Already the community colleges are heavily populated with minority students, as are the State Universities (but less so), and within the University of California both Berkeley and UCLA have passed the "majority of minorities" threshold with respect to student population. The future direction is clear, moreover, for all levels: greater racial, ethnic, and cultural diversity of student population.

The most immediate political effect of student diversification is to increase the pressure to diversify the administrative staff, graduate students, and faculty. (There is continued pressure to diversify with respect to gender as well.) The difficulties in responding to this pressure increase in the order mentioned, in large part because the "Ph.D. pipeline" of blacks and Hispanics has tended to diminish in the recent past. The fact that expansion of these minorities in graduate student and faculty ranks is difficult in the short run does not have much effect on those pressing to diversify, and the air is filled with a certain amount of ill will and charges of "elitism," "white male supremacy," "declining quality," and other rhetorical assertions. There is no reason to believe that this contradictory situation will not constitute one of the most severe political problems for California's system of higher education in the decades to come.

The other great dimension of diversity is social in character. Institutions of higher education—along with other institutions—have played an important historical role in socialization and in inculcating the values of citizenship, participation, tolerance, and professional commitment and have thus contributed in some degree to the integration of the larger society. That role will continue, and the examining committee of the OECD went so far as to predict that "the burden of incorporation into a pluralistic society has to rest centrally on the integrative capacity of the educational system" (Education Committee 1989, 6).

Yet the vision of "incorporation" is only one possible scenario, given the magnitude of the diversity and the depth of racial, ethnic, and cultural politics. I mention three scenarios, evidence for each of which might be cited.

- The program of assimilation of racially, ethnically, and culturally diverse groups to the existing values and roles of higher education. This is the "liberal" view, closest to that voiced by the OECD committee, and envisions continuing traditional patterns of liberal education and occupational and professional training, with students being socialized in these patterns, accommodating to them, and preparing themselves for participation in the institutions of the larger society.
- The program of altering the traditional missions of higher liberal education—which, it is argued, are biased along racial/ethnic, class, and gender lines in any event—to some mission that gives greater recognition to "nonmainstream" groups. The recent episodes of pressure for

curricular change are signs of this tendency, as are the recent debates about "political correctness" on campus and its possible threat to principles of academic freedom.

• The program of converting campuses into a microcosm of the pluralistic polity, with racial, ethnic, cultural, gender, and other groups competing for the resources as well as the symbolic and real control of the institutional life of colleges and universities. This scenario, too, although not novel in the history of education, would mark a further change in the traditional liberal mission of educational institutions. And, given the frail capacities of colleges and universities to manage group conflict (discussed above) such a "political pluralism" model would prove difficult to stabilize.

Like the future of any complex social institution that is based on multiple values and principles, the future of higher education with respect to diversity will not reveal a clear victory for any of these scenarios. Some aspects of all will continue to be visible. Each one will persist, and each one will have its vicissitudes. With respect to the issue of diversity, then, the future will bring "process" rather than "product" as an outcome, with all involved parties struggling for but never finally gaining advantages, new definitions of the situation, and satisfactory accommodations.

Notes

1. In this chapter I attempt to refer to institutions according to the name they are given at the time of the reference. The University of California has been called by that name since its inception. The second tier was known originally as *normal schools,* then *teacher's colleges.* When the Master Plan was put in place in 1960, this tier was called the California State College System; subsequently (1972), it became known as the California State University and College System; and in 1981 it took on the name of the California State University. In the beginning, two-year institutions were known as *junior colleges;* subsequently they were referred to as either *junior colleges* or *community colleges;* now they go almost exclusively by the name of *community colleges.* These name changes reflect the status striving of the second and third segments over the years, while the uneasy resistance on the University of California's part to the application of the name *university* to the second tier reflects the same preoccupation with prestige and status.

2. For a theoretical statement of the structural alternatives to change in the growth process, see Smelser (1973b, 36–38).

3. There are some minor exceptions to these rules (e.g., the "special admissions" procedures in the University of California, by which 6 percent of the entering class can be drawn from the population that does not fall in the top one-eighth as measured at high school graduation. Originally this category was designed to facilitate the admission of athletes, but more recently it has become a means to increase the representation of disadvantaged minorities.

4. There are some strictures on this process as well. For example, it is impossible for students to transfer during their first year at a given college, and universities and colleges require some minimum of residence (e.g., one year) to make a student eligible for graduation from that institution.

5. For example, in the report of the Joint Committee for Review of the Master Plan, fourteen pages were dedicated to "Undergraduate Education" in the section entitled "Educational Quality." In the same section four pages were dedicated to "Graduate and Professional Education," which was slightly more than the space allocated to "Vocational Education" and slightly less than that allocated to "Adult and Non-Credit Education" (Joint Committee 1989, 96–123). This kind of allocation of words is surely at variance with the priorities of many academics.

References

California State Council on Educational Planning and Coordination. 1934. *Statement of Basic Principles of the Respective Functions and Programs of the Junior College, the Teachers College, and the University.* Sacramento: California State Council on Educational Planning and Coordination.

Commission for the Review of the Master Plan for Higher Education. 1986. *The Challenge of Change: A Reassessment of the California Community Colleges.* Sacramento: Commission for the Review of the Master Plan for Higher Education.

————. 1987. *The Master Plan Renewed: Unity, Equity, Quality, and Efficiency in California Postsecondary Education.* Sacramento: Commission for the Review of the Master Plan for Higher Education.

Condren, Clive. 1988. *Preparing for the Twenty-First Century: A Report on Higher Education in California.* California Postsecondary Education Commission Report 88-1. Sacramento: California Postsecondary Education Commission.

Coons, Arthur G. 1968. *Crises in California Higher Education.* Los Angeles: Ward Ritchie Press.

Education Committee, Organization for Economic Cooperation and Development. 1989. *Review of Higher Education Policy in California.* Paris: Organization for Economic Cooperation and Development.

Joint Committee on the Master Plan for Higher Education. 1973. *Report of the Joint Committee on the Master Plan for Higher Education.* Sacramento: California Legislature.

Joint Committee for Review of the Master Plan for Higher Education. 1989. *California Faces . . . California's Future: Education for Citizenship in a Multicultural Democracy.* Sacramento: California Legislature.

McConnell, T. R., T. C. Holy, and H. H. Semans. 1955. *A Restudy of the Needs of California in Higher Education.* Sacramento: California State Department of Education.

Master Plan Survey Team. 1960. *Master Plan for Higher Education in California, 1960 to 1975.* Sacramento: California State Department of Education.

Parsons, Talcott. 1973. "Epilogue: The University 'Bundle': A Study of the Balance between Differentiation and Integration." In Neil J. Smelser and Gabriel Almond, eds., *Public Higher Education in California,* pp. 275–299. Berkeley: University of California Press.

Semans, H. H., and T. C. Holy. 1957. *A Study of the Needs for Additional Centers of Public Higher Education in California.* Sacramento: California Department of Education.

Smelser, Neil J. 1973a. "Epilogue: Social-Structural Dimensions of Higher Education." In Talcott Parsons and Gerald M. Platt, eds., *The American University,* pp. 389–422. Cambridge: Harvard University Press.

———. 1973b. "Growth, Structural Change, and Conflict in California Higher Education, 1950–1970." In Neil J. Smelser and Gabriel Almond, eds., *Public Higher Education in California,* pp. 9–143. Berkeley: University of California Press.

Strayer, George D., Monroe E. Deutsch, and Aubrey A. Douglass. 1948. *A Report on a Survey of the Needs of California in Higher Education.* Sacramento: State of California.

Task Force on Lower Division Education. 1986. *Lower Division Education in the University of California.* Berkeley: University of California.

8

Higher Education Coordination: Australia and the United States

LYMAN A. GLENNY

Since 1950, almost every industrialized nation in the world has attempted major reform of its higher educational system. The popular press plays up these reforms as revolutionary in character. Scholars know that such revisions come about more slowly and have many precursors, but their views rarely counter the popular version. Nonetheless, fundamental changes in systems of higher education have many preceding portents, as the history of state-level coordination in Australia and the United States illustrates. Both nations have similar cultural antecedents, and the character of their reforms regarding the broad goals of higher education has been similar, but the coordinating structures and procedures that they have developed for achieving these goals show quite different patterns.

Statewide coordination of higher education in the United States has often been controversial but now is generally accepted as a necessary bureaucratic form of governmental regulation. In contrast, state coordinating bodies have been tried but not accepted by all five of Australia's states—a condition that has led to the recent development of national, centralized coordination for Australian tertiary education. This chapter posits that this difference arose because of the failure of the Australian states and their tertiary education sectors to respond to the needs of complex educational systems, a diverse population, and an economy confronted by world competition.

The Government's Need for Coordination

Coordination of any social activity becomes imperative when decision makers are frustrated by the conflicting and competing claims of interest groups seeking additional funds, new functions, or more activities. Coordination can be defined as "involving regulating and combining so as to give harmonious results" (Glenny 1959) and "to achieve greater overall efficiency and to avoid unnecessary overlap of functions and wasteful use of scarce resources" (Gallagher 1982).

Coordination of higher education did not arise in the United States or Australia because of power-hungry bureaucrats or politicians, but because objectives thought to be in the public interest were not being met by colleges and universities acting in their traditional independent interests. Institutional desires for status, prestige, and large size create potential for much overlap in function and role as well as continuing controversy among institutions over the allocation of scarce resources. The resulting rampant competition for funds, programs, and buildings by universities and colleges in state legislative halls compels the establishment of stronger means for achieving desired ends. Some government body must make hard decisions on apportionment among institutions and give priority to state and national interests by limiting funding for particular programs of study and research to particular institutions. These governmental interests encompass a wide range of topics—from assuring equity in university admissions for different ethnic groups to preventing overlap or duplication of expensive programs and setting priorities on building construction among campuses. The growth of international competition and sophisticated technologies require that democratic societies, no less than authoritarian ones, set national priorities and goals and then use academic institutions as well as other organizations to achieve them. As a result, tensions have increased greatly between institutions of higher education, with their traditions of academic independence and internal control, and government agencies that try to achieve specific social goals requiring the close cooperation of colleges and universities.

In the United States, the lessening of conflict has occurred in large part through regulatory coordination in each state. Many imperfections in regulatory relationships exist, yet today a better understanding prevails between state officials and leaders of higher education than has at any time in the past thirty years. In most states, this understanding has stemmed from their creation of effective coordinating structures and procedures. The federal role vis-à-vis colleges and universities has been much more incremental, less intrusive, and as a result less volatile than that of the states—consisting as it does of federal financial aid for needy students to help assure their free choice of institutions and special-purpose federal grants and contracts that focus on national goals and that are open for bid by institutions but are not imposed on them. The situation is different in Australia. Tension between its institutions and government is at an historical high. Australia is on the road to a unified national system of universities and colleges that remain constitutional creatures of the states. In the process, Australia's colleges and universities are likely to forfeit to the care and protection of the Commonwealth much of the autonomy they have until now maintained.

The Commonalities and Contrasts between Higher Education in Australia and the United States

The higher educational systems of Australia and the United States are alike in many respects. Both nations established universities on the British/Scottish model and later modified them to include fundamental research as practiced in the German universities. In both countries, the vast majority of public institutions were created by state governments rather than the federal government. Both countries categorize their colleges and universities in a tiered system: universities that offer the doctorate and professional degrees and that conduct fundamental research and two-year institutions that offer diplomas, certificates, and at times associate degrees; in the United States a middle segment of former normal schools and teachers colleges has blossomed into comprehensive institutions that offer bachelor's and master's degrees and a sprinkling of doctorates. In both countries, lower-tier institutions want to offer doctoral degrees, conduct government-funded research, and be funded at the level of traditional universities. In both of them, coordination of higher education is legally a function of state governments. And, in both, similar complaints are heard: politicians often express concern that the older, traditional universities change too slowly, lack innovation, fail to teach effectively, give preference to research, and are more concerned with internal matters than with broad and vexing problems of concern to the larger society, whereas other institutions are more flexible, innovative, student oriented, and socially responsive.

Despite these important common characteristics, fundamental differences also exist that have import for the way that postsecondary education is perceived by the public and politicians as well as the way that coordination occurs in the two countries. Among the major differences are the eleven discussed below.

1. In Australia, the private higher education sector is in its infancy. A few very small religion-oriented colleges exist, but no private university was in operation until Bond University on the Gold Coast in Queensland initiated classes in 1988. Leaders of government, business, and industry support the idea of a private university sector, but most academics at public institutions look upon it with suspicion as likely to break their unions' longstanding policies on salaries, perquisites, and working conditions, and many vice-chancellors think that it will fail for lack of students willing to pay its necessarily high tuition.

In the United States a great many private colleges came into being before the first public institutions, and today at least half or more of the nation's top dozen universities are private.

2. Aside from early normal and technical/vocational schools, the Australian public has historically not supported postsecondary education—especially the major universities in the state capitals, which have been perceived as elitist, small, and remote from the everyday life of the communities in which they are located. Public indifference to higher education has waned slowly as the need for education has become better recognized. Even in 1987, however, when the disconcerting and often vitriolic criticisms of universities by a commonwealth minister caused a welter of newspaper articles and letters to the editor, they were written not by laypersons but instead by academics or reporters. The public maintained its indifference.

In the United States, the public maintains a proprietary interest in what it considers to be "its" institutions, as illustrated by its enthusiasm for local intercollegiate athletic events and its concern with student behavior and welfare.

3. Australians are much less mobile than U.S. citizens and maintain stronger emotional ties to their home states. Students seem less venturesome in seeking education in another state or even in another city, making it difficult to set up a "national system" in which institutions may become distinctive centers of teaching and research in different disciplines and professions. Until the mid-1980s, each state university maintained nearly the same array of degree and professional programs as all the rest—although some exceptions did exist.

In the United States, the states also vie to offer the full spectrum of professional and academic programs in their institutions, but many students attend college out of state, and a number of states have established interstate compacts to save resources and avoid duplication of high-cost specialized programs through agreements that permit their residents to enroll in those out-of-state programs and yet pay only in-state fees rather than nonresident tuition.

4. Australia's sector of two-year institutions, consisting of "technical and further education institutions"—is considered part of "tertiary" or postsecondary education but not "higher" education. In the United States, however, two-year community colleges—initially called *junior colleges*—became recognized as part of higher education by the late 1960s or early 1970s. Moreover, Australia's technical and further education institutions most frequently began with a strictly vocational curriculum, while U.S. community colleges first offered liberal arts and science courses and only later became predominantly vocationally oriented. Finally, although Australia's technical and further education institutions offer degrees as well as many diploma courses, student transfer from them to Australia's universities and colleges of advanced education is virtually nonexistent, whereas in the United States there is deliberate encouragement of transfer from community colleges to four-year institutions.

5. Student transfer among all of Australia's sectors is rare because all students must try by themselves to get their desired institution to accept their previously completed work, and they receive little encouragement to make the attempt. State policy to promote mobility is slow in developing. As technical and further education institutions have become more popular, the problem of transferring their credits to institutions of "higher education" has become a recognized issue but not yet a critical systemic problem. On the other hand, in America most states have deliberately facilitated student transfer through encouraging and, in some cases, mandating interinstitutional agreements to accept transfer credits. As a result the United States is sometimes derisively noted for the freedom with which students can transfer from one sector to another—up, down, and across—without great penalty.

6. The academic personnel of Australia's universities and colleges are unionized, with about 70 percent of the academic staff belonging to either of the two major national unions. These unions are a powerful force in higher education matters, being represented on the governing councils of the institutions, engaging in negotiations of working conditions, and dealing with policy issues with both the federal and state governments. In the United States, academic unionization is still rare at the state level and nonexistent at the national level. Although a fair sampling of community college faculty are unionized, the faculty in only a handful of large public

research universities have voted for collective bargaining. As a result, academic unions in the United States have little influence on state or national policy.

7. At the behest of Australia's academic unions and vice-chancellors, the Commonwealth has established a national salary scheme for academics that results in uniform salaries across all institutions of the same type. Thus, the highest-ranking professors at the University of Sydney make the same salary as those at the Universities of Adelaide or Melbourne. Critics of this egalitarian system conclude that no Australian university can become really world class under this policy. In contrast, the United States has over three thousand institutions and almost as many salary scales, and competition through differential salaries and perquisites for the "best" professors and researchers is intense among its leading institutions and those that hope to become world class.

8. The egalitarianism reflected in Australia's single-salary structure for higher education is a deep and long-held tradition and is mirrored in a dedication to equalizing treatment which makes for uniformity and homogenization in commonwealth policy. This contrasts markedly to the U.S. individualistic, competitive style that tends to diversity.

9. Since 1974, Australia's institutions have not charged tuition to native students, although in 1986 they began to collect an "administrative fee" of $250 that is tied to the cost of living and as a result increases each year. The loss of tuition income since 1974 has been offset by federal government funding and the administrative fee, but the ability of institutions to undertake any new endeavors without government financial support has been impaired. Institutions have also become more dependent on fluctuations of the economy and of governmental income. In contrast, virtually all U.S. colleges and universities charge tuition, although the amount varies greatly among public institutions and from state to state. In some states, institutions may use tuition income for their own priorities, but in others tuition income is simply an offset against government operating funds. On average, tuition in the United States produces about 15 to 20 percent of the cost of instruction—about the same proportion as Australian tuition before its abolition in 1974.

10. Australia's population is as urbanized as that of the United States, and until the 1980s all of Australia's large universities were located in the capital cities of its states. In contrast, some of the major U.S. public universities, such as those of Illinois and Michigan, were deliberately located in small towns well away from large metropolitan centers.

11. The most significant factors that distinguish Australian higher edu-

cation from that in the United States are differences in the two countries' governmental structure and their governmental practices for adopting and implementing policy. These differences make radical change in education more likely in Australia than in the United States. In both countries, individual states pattern their governmental structures and practices on those of the national government—in Australia a parliamentary form of government; in the United States a separation-of-powers doctrine that places legislative, executive, and judicial functions in separate but interdependent branches of government.

Under Australia's parliamentary system, the political party that controls the parliament also appoints the prime minister, and that person is not only leader of the party and leader of parliament but also the chief executive of the nation, appointing all cabinet ministers and heads of major executive agencies. The majority political party—the government—is held responsible for legislating its party platform and for implementing it, all through one person, the prime minister.

For Australian higher education, as a result, public policy first arises out of the underlying beliefs and philosophy of the political parties and only secondly out of current public issues. Political logrolling and negotiating takes place in party caucus, and once a commitment is made the party frames it for legislative action that may be heavily debated but rarely is in danger of not being passed into law. Party discipline comes first, and individual beliefs give way to the rule of the party caucus and an expected vote for the proposed policy in parliament.

Occasionally the party in power or a departmental minister may propose a policy so important or controversial that the party hesitates to make it law without first issuing a discussion document—a "Green Paper"—to get public reaction. Citizen and interest-group views are obtained through written critiques, conferences, public hearings, and the media. After these reactions, the party issues a "White Paper" that specifies the policies for parliamentary debate and adoption.

In the United States, the separation-of-powers principle invites a much more problematical series of steps before a proposed policy becomes law. The two political parties are not nearly as committed to a set of underlying social theories as are the Australian parties. Their "platforms" are likely to reflect current issues and the popular or expedient side of these issues rather than longstanding social priorities. Party loyalty is usually so weak that some majority party members will vote with the minority against proposed legislation on grounds that their local constituents oppose it. Under these conditions, proposed legislation—no matter who introduces it—is never certain of passage. Many legislative bills fail for this reason, while those that pass normally collect a great many amendments, sometimes modifying substantially the basic intent of the original proposal. To complicate matters, it is not uncommon for one party to control one house of the legislature and the opposing party the other or for the independently elected governor and legislature to represent different parties, both with their own set of priorities. If a bill passes both houses of the legislature, the governor may veto it or, in some states, line-item out important funding provisions. Finally, the executive branch must implement bills signed into law by the governor, and the governor's commitment to these statutes can determine the speed and enthusiasm with which this executive process takes place.

State Coordination in the United States

In both countries, agencies have been established by the states for the coordination of higher education. In the United States, the initial thrust toward statewide coordination came at the beginning of this century in Iowa, Florida, Oregon, and a few other states, where legislatures and governors placed all public institutions (normal schools, state colleges, and universities) under a single state governing board. In other states, as normal schools became teachers colleges during the 1920s, the states generally created a single board to govern them, even though they allowed the state university (or, where there were two, each university) to continue to be governed by its own board. But consolidation of these governing boards gained momentum during the Great Depression. State policy makers, motivated by a need for economy and efficiency, used strong legal language to empower the new boards, as in Georgia, to "consolidate, suspend, and/or discontinue institutions, merge departments, inaugurate or discontinue courses, and abolish or add degrees" (Georgia Code 1931). By the late 1930s, thirteen states each had a single governing board for all of its higher education.

After World War II, a newer type of coordination (initiated in the state of Oklahoma in 1941) gained popularity in states without consolidated governing boards as they confronted institutional requests for almost unlimited expansions of programs, faculties, and facilities stemming first from the enrollment of veterans under the G.I. Bill and then from the postwar "baby boom." This coordinating agency stands between the government and the separate governing boards of the institutions or segments, acting both as an adviser to the government on budgets, planning, new programs, and public policy and as a buffer between government and the institutions. During the 1950s and 1960s, when many new statewide governing boards were added and the majority of coordinating boards were first authorized, a good deal of skepticism prevailed about their usefulness. After much frustration, however, lawmakers concluded that such agencies could help protect state interests and gain greater rationality and efficiency in the entire enterprise while preserving the independence of higher education from partisan political attack. As a result, during the past dozen years, coordination as a concept has been thoroughly institutionalized in the states. The question is no longer whether or not coordination should occur, but what form of organization and which set of powers will best ensure it. Coordinating agencies or statewide governing boards now exist in all but two states, and their powers tend to increase over time as new problems arise and new demands are made on state resources.

State Coordination in Australia

In Australia, the milieu for the three tiers of postsecondary education did not change dramatically until after World War II. There was pronounced university expansion from 1957 to 1965, followed by even greater development of "colleges of advanced education" from 1965 to 1975, and then a vast expansion of "technical and further education" from 1975 to the present.

The First Tier: The Universities

By 1911, each state had created a university in its capital city, beginning with Sydney in 1850 and ending with Perth in 1911. Not until after the Second World War did the states create more. Then, from 1948 to 1977 they founded another thirteen. By 1987, there were twenty-three in the Commonwealth.

The states fully funded the universities until after World War II, when the commonwealth government began to offer direct institutional aid. By 1957, federal funds constituted about a quarter of recurrent funding. During the entire postwar period, despite increased interest and funding by the Commonwealth, the state governments continued to think of the universities as belonging first and foremost to them for meeting their education and research objectives. Simultaneously, the universities—each autonomous under its founding statute but concerned lest the state begin to encroach upon its autonomy—urged greater and greater funding from the Commonwealth through the Australian Universities Commission, an independent agency established in 1957 to recommend the level of funding by the central government. In 1974, with the abolition of student tuition, the Commonwealth took over full funding of the universities. The universities and faculties had finally achieved their goal of freedom from state control, and they continued to look upon the Universities Commission as their protector and supporter.

The Second Tier: Colleges of Advanced Education

Over the past century, a variety of agricultural schools, normal schools, teachers colleges, technical institutes, and specialized colleges for music, medicine, and pharmacy arose in Australia—some as large and almost as distinguished as the universities. Into the 1960s, the vast majority were "governed" by state bureaucracies of regular ministerial departments, such as education, agriculture, or health. In 1964, the Commonwealth's Martin Committee called for an expansion of postsecondary education different from the universities to provide greater diversity of programs and to meet the needs of a changing population and economy. Its report recommended that the states identify the most advanced of the melange of existing institutions as "colleges of advanced education" that would offer three- and four-year diploma and certificate work and be geared to providing occupational training of direct use to the community. It further recommended that the Commonwealth create a commission for these colleges similar in duties to the Australian Universities Commission and that the states fund these new colleges of advanced education on the same formula as the universities.

The Commonwealth accepted most of the Martin Committee's recommendations and thus began a vast expansion of the colleges—from twenty-six state institutions that were recognized in 1965 to be recipients of the commonwealth/state formula to eighty-three by the mid-1970s that were almost as different from each other as they had been before federal support. During this time, enrollments in the colleges increased very rapidly—from 44,850 in 1968 to approximately 140,000 ten years later (Williams 1982).

As could be expected, each college of advanced education sought more federal funds in competition with other colleges and the universities. Just as in the United States, this competition led to the creation of state coordinating agencies for the colleges—the first, Western Australia's Tertiary Education Commission, in 1970, followed after 1972 by the other states—but the state's problems of coordination were heightened as a result of commonwealth funding (Harman 1976). The Commonwealth's commission for the colleges relied heavily on the new state coordinating agencies, but by 1982 Don Anderson wrote that "the state coordinating bodies have tended to act, not so much as regulating and planning agencies, but as advocates for their systems, presenting the best possible case for resources to the federal commissions" (p. 79).

The Third Tier: Technical and Further Education Institutions

The vocational schools that have become "technical and further education institutions" functioned originally both at the high school and postsecondary levels and offered a wide range of trade, technical, and avocational courses. They were truly local institutions responding to community needs, although almost all of them lacked courses in the liberal arts. By 1975, when the Commonwealth created a new commission for them and they began their recent period of growth, there were 180 of these schools, with 300 separate metropolitan centers and 679 affiliated branches in 500 different locations outside the capital cities (Williams 1982). They are far and away the most accessible of all forms of postsecondary education in Australia, just as community colleges are in the United States, and their numbers and enrollments far exceed those of the other segments combined. Their funding and control has shifted less drastically away from state government to the Commonwealth than has funding for the colleges of advanced education and the universities, but as early as 1975 the Commonwealth was providing about a third of their support (Williams 1982). Their leaders have sought to obtain transfer privileges for their students into the universities and the colleges of advanced education, and they have tried to curb the tendency of colleges of advanced education to create programs duplicating theirs and then extend the number of classes so as to offer an advanced diploma or degree for them. However, no machinery at either the state or federal level has facilitated cooperation among the three sectors for student transfer or curricular coordination.

From the time of their origin, the technical and further education institutions were developed and controlled through state ministerial departments. The numbers of schools, branches, and centers increasingly required a larger central bureaucracy—but it did not coordinate them with the colleges of advanced education or the universities. In 1970, Peter Karmel, reporting on South Australian postsecondary education, commented that "the notions that tertiary institutions form part of a system of education and that there should be some coordination to ensure balanced development and a rational allocation of resources devoted to tertiary education have developed only slowly during the past decade" (quoted by Harman 1976). And Professor Harman added that "special coordinating machinery in fact was not developed as quickly as we might have expected, particularly at State level. Perhaps the main reason for this was simply a slowness to appreciate the need for coordination" (1976).

The 1964 Martin Report had encouraged cooperative relationships among institutions within and across sectors, but states were slow in following this advice. Although each state adopted some form of coordinating agency during the early 1970s and amended or radically altered original statutes in later years (with the most powerful agencies being in New South Wales, Victoria, and Western Australia, as noted above), these coordinating agencies focused on the colleges of advanced education. If universities were mentioned in the acts establishing the agencies, they were not included in the same control language as the colleges. Indeed, even the fairly strong coordinating language of the Victoria statute of 1978, which ostensibly included both higher education sectors, in practice left the universities with their autonomy virtually untouched. Also exempt from the new coordinating agencies were the technical and further education institutions, which continued to be governed by state ministerial departments. From 1965 to 1975—the first ten years of the colleges of advanced education—their coordinating agencies varied widely from one state to another, but eventually these agencies had much the same authority, which left little autonomy to the individual colleges, as can be seen from the following list of their functions compiled by Professor Harman in 1976.

- Foster the development of advanced education and achieve a "balanced system";
- Review and accredit all new or substantially revised courses and programs;
- Review and set priorities on state and federal funding;
- Allocate funds among the colleges in a reasonable way;
- Control new administrative and academic posts in the colleges;
- Plan for new colleges and promote rationalization among them;
- Supervise capital work projects, especially for new colleges;
- Collect and disseminate official statistics in advanced education;
- Set conditions of employment for all staff and salary classifications for non-academic staff; and
- Consult with other state agencies and provide advice to the ministers in relation to advanced education.

Academics in the colleges, especially in the mature multipurpose institutions, were not happy with these intrusive responsibilities of the coordinating agencies. Some principals and vice-chancellors complained bitterly that the agencies were too bureaucratic, employed inexperienced and poorly trained staff, and "governed everything we did." During 1986 and 1987, all states conducted inquiries into the usefulness of these agencies. Even before this, the commonwealth government saw the need for nationalization of various aspects of postsecondary education. As early as 1977 the Commonwealth had taken action to coordinate the sectors. That year it placed all three of the sector commissions under a new board—the Tertiary Education Commission. However, the law creating the commission failed to lessen the powers of the three sector commissions until two years later, when another law made them strictly advisory to the renamed Commonwealth Tertiary Education Commission. Thereafter, that commission paid much less attention to the sector commissions and to the state institutions in recommending policy. Academics began to accept the idea that the commonwealth commission was an arm of the government with little concern for buffering or presenting the needs of the institutions. Economic and social imperatives, not sufficiently foreseen or acted upon at the state level, resulted in the December 1987 publication of a commonwealth Green Paper, *Higher Education: A Policy Discussion Paper,* by J. S. Dawkins, Australia's Minister for Employment, Education, and Training under the Labor Party. In the Green Paper, Dawkins made no specific provision for state coordinating agencies; instead, he proposed to create a "unified national system" of tertiary education by making such changes as these:

- The Commonwealth would deal directly with individual institutions, not through the states or their agencies;
- Each institution was to produce an academic profile of itself to be used to determine the amounts of funding the Commonwealth would furnish for its operating and capital budget;
- Universities and colleges of advanced education would be consolidated to form large-sized universities that would improve diversity of course offerings and achieve economies of scale;
- The Commonwealth would create up to twenty-three more special research centers in universities and colleges of advanced education, based on the quality of their programs;
- Sources of income other than commonwealth funds would be encouraged from industry, contracts, grants, and the reimposition of student tuition, and the costs of expanding enrollments would be increasingly shared by the states;
- The salaries of academic staff and administrators would be adjusted by each institution to reward exceptional talent and according to the need for faculty in fields where they are scarce;
- A portion of the funds included in university faculty salaries for research would be withdrawn and assigned to research projects of high national

priority, with faculty of the colleges of advanced education to compete for these funds on equal terms with the universities;
- Transfer of credit from one institution to another would be encouraged; and
- A comprehensive and usable data base would be created.

The Green Paper was followed by extensive discussion between representatives of higher education and the commonwealth government, but the Commonwealth began effecting its recommendations even prior to July 1988, when Dawkins issued the party's White Paper, *Higher Education: A Policy Statement,* for parliamentary debate and approval. The new document was somewhat different than the Green Paper in its methods for implementing these recommendations, but the fundamental changes remained.

Perhaps the most important changes were the bypassing of the states and their agencies and the combining of the university sector with that of the colleges for advanced education, wiping out policy differences in the treatment of the individual institutions—and the decision of all of the states except Victoria and Western Australia to abolish their coordinating agencies and put any remnant functions and staff into their ministries of education. The Commonwealth insisted on dealing with each institution individually, as had been the practice of the old Universities Commission of 1957, and it assumed that a single governmental department could plan, coordinate, and develop the unified national system. To create a unified system of no more than forty institutions, it has cajoled and pressured the states to reduce the number of their universities, colleges, and technical institutions through massive consolidations and amalgamations. By 1991, it had achieved most major consolidations except in Victoria, where its goal was five universities for the whole state.

Opposition to the plan from vice-chancellors and academics has been voluble and has resulted in a few setbacks to it, but by early 1991 the Australian Vice-Chancellors Committee was publicly pleading with the Commonwealth to tighten its relation with their institutions, and they contended that the remaining state coordinating bodies in Victoria and Western Australia were anachronistic. The *Australian* of 13 March 1991 reported that "the federal government is being pressured to free universities from remaining state government controls, including the payment of funding through the states and the influence of state coordinating bodies" and "not to return funding and policy powers to the states." The vice-chancellors feared that federal attempts to get the states to pay part of the expansion costs of higher education would succeed, and the states would reassert some control.

It seems probable that within a few years Australia's colleges and universities, created by its individual states in response to their interests and goals, will be required to meet national ones first. The step-by-step process by which this occurred cannot be attributed to malice or power grabbing by the commonwealth government but rather to a concern for the economy and welfare of the society, to necessary budget decisions resulting from economic downturn, to the self-interests of institutions—especially the traditional universities—and to the failure of states to protect the public interest through effective coordination and the orderly development of their postsecondary institutions.

In sum, the Green Paper of 1987 probably would not have been necessary if the states had created cross-sectoral coordinating agencies and effectively managed expansion developments. Failure to coordinate at lower levels invariably led to coordination at the highest one.

Comparative Observations on State Coordination

The major difference in the development and results of coordination between Australia and the United States was that the United States succeeded in creating effective coordinating agencies, whereas the Australian states (with the partial exception of Victoria) did not. In Australia, the state authorizing statutes were unclear, ambiguous, and incomplete. The functions of the agency over the institutions were not delineated sufficiently for it to know which segments or which institutions were fully included under its aegis. The nature of the coordination and the degree and amount of it across sectors remained unclear even after initial statutes were amended.

In contrast, from the first-formed coordinating agency to the last in the United States, the statutes clearly stated which sectors of institutions were included, listed the powers and duties of the agency, and often "suggested" means for administration. Intent was fairly clear and ambiguities were clarified in subsequent law that tended to increase the powers of the agency.

University disdain of coordination was common in both countries, but for the most part Australia's universities simply did not respond to efforts at coordination. They did not oppose the creation of agencies that were aimed, in the minds of university leaders, to coordinate the "lesser" segments of postsecondary education; instead, they ignored the new agencies and continued exercising their traditional prerogatives and practices.

In contrast, U.S. universities often fought bitter battles against the creation of coordinating agencies. Their political power was strong enough in most states to give them the lion's share of postsecondary funds and programs, but the legislatures' need for aid in settling turf and funding disputes among all postsecondary institutions eventually led to the founding of agencies coordinating higher education in general, including the universities.

The political power structure in Australia was not conducive to involving the universities in coordination. Most state political leaders were graduates of their own state's leading university or a foreign one, not of a college of advanced education or a technical and further education institution. As a result, these leaders respected the autonomy of traditional universities.

In the United States, many legislators and governors were alumni of their state's universities, but the academic origins of U.S. lawmakers were far more diverse than in Australia, and institutional partisanship waned as the need for more orderly development of higher education became increasingly apparent.

Initially in Australia, the limited number of institutions and their fairly clear differentiation into three segments limited the amount of felt need for a coordinated statewide system that would encompass all institutions and segments, despite the fact that much overlap and duplication existed between the colleges of advanced education and the universities on the one hand and, on the other, the technical and further education schools. With few exceptions, the states made no provision for effective means to coordinate cross-sectoral developments; their new coordinating agencies limited themselves to making a system out of the mix of institutions making up the single segment of colleges of advanced education, and their coordination consisted mainly of accepting new schools into college status and getting funds to improve their quality. They were unable to persuade the political leadership that coordination of all three segments was necessary to promote state and student interests.

In contrast, the roles of U.S. institutions became blurred after only a few years of post–World War II expansion. Community colleges became state colleges, state colleges offered advanced degrees and sought university status, universities fought with each other for expensive professional programs and new campuses, and transfer among institutions was seen as socially desirable. Legislators recognized the tremendous financial burdens of chaotic development and their own inability to discern legitimate budgetary differences among the segments and turned the task of cross-sectoral coordination over to comprehensive coordinating agencies.

In Australia, the concept of planning failed to gain much of a foothold and until recently has been avoided in higher education. State governments, the segments, and individual institutions undertook little systematic continuing planning for the rational development of institutions or segments. Instead, to bring about change, the states relied heavily on recommendations and suggestions of national commissions and occasionally on state inquiries into special issues, but no state agency existed outside parliament to monitor institutional compliance with inquiry recommendations.

The United States also rejected planning until World War II, which demonstrated what could be accomplished by it. Then industries quickly implemented planning concepts, and, in time, higher education also did so. The first state coordinating agencies for higher education in the United States received no planning powers, but after 1954 every authorizing statute for coordination gave prominence to planning. State master plans for developing postsecondary education became commonplace in the 1960s and 1970s; these plans, periodically updated, continue to guide sector and institutional developments in almost every state.

Finally, the Australian states had no great incentive to limit the number of institutions nor to coordinate the three segments because from 1974 onward the Commonwealth furnished all of the operating and capital funds for their universities and colleges of advanced education as well as an increasing share of the funds for technical and further education.

The federal government of the United States has provided funds to higher education since the Morrill (or "land-grant college") Act of 1862, which gave emphasis to agriculture, engineering, and other training not part of the traditional university curriculum. By the 1970s, the federal government was paying as much as 20 percent of all higher education costs, although since the mid-1980s that percentage has dropped. At no time has the federal government sought to coordinate or to control higher education. It continues the practice of funding research centers and projects through various federal agencies, and it achieves its goals by attaching conditions, sometimes numerous, for the use of these funds, leaving to the states and their institutions the decision to accept these conditions along with the funds. As a result, the fifty United States remain powerful in coordinating their systems of higher education, while most Australian states have abandoned the effort.

Acknowledgments

Much of this chapter is based on my study of state coordination in Australia from September through December 1987, during which I conducted hour-long interviews in all of the state capitals and in Canberra with sixty-three ministers, heads of coordinating agencies, vice-chancellors, scholars, former officers of the Commonwealth Tertiary Education Commission, and staff in the Commonwealth Department of Education. In November and December 1989, I returned to reinterview certain state and federal officials. I am indebted to these interviewees for their insights; to the scholarly work of Don Anderson, John Anwyl, David Beswick, Grant Harman, Ron Parry, and Don Smart; and to the Centre for the Study of Higher Education at the University of Melbourne, which provided me with office space and research services during my visits.

References

Anderson, Don. 1982. "Planning in a Strait-Jacket: Federal Limits to State Initiatives in Higher Education." In Grant S. Harman and Don Smart, eds., *Federal Intervention in Australian Education*. Melbourne: Georgia House.

Dawkins, J. S., Minister for Employment, Education and Training. 1987. *Higher Education: A Policy Discussion Paper (The "Green Paper")*. Canberra: Australian Government Publishing Service, December.

———. 1988. *Higher Education: A Policy Statement (The "White Paper")*. Canberra: Australian Government Publishing Service, July.

Gallagher, A. P. 1982. *Coordinating Australian University Development*. St. Lucia: University of Queensland Press.

Georgia Code, Title 32, Paragraphs 101–124, 1931.

Glenny, Lyman A. 1959. *The Autonomy of Public Colleges: The Challenge of Coordination*. New York: McGraw-Hill.

Harman, Grant S. 1976. "National and State Co-ordination of Australian Colleges of Advanced Education." Canberra: Australian National University.

Williams, Bruce. 1982. "Governments and Universities since 1959." *Vestes (Federation of Australian University Staff Associations)* 25(1):3–11.

9 The Return to Europe: Issues in Post-Communist Higher Education

LADISLAV CERYCH

The development of European higher education in the 1990s will be shaped by a multiplicity of factors. Two are already seen as of particular importance and as forces with a far-reaching effect. First is the movement toward closer European integration and, more precisely, the impending advent of the large single European market by 1 January 1993, accompanied and supported by the growth of several major higher education programs in the European Community. Second is the opening up of Central and Eastern Europe and its transition to democracy, including the quest for a more or less radical transformation of its higher education systems.

These two developments have different origins and have thus far been largely independent of each other, but a link between them is emerging and will undoubtedly become stronger in the future. On the one hand, this link is due to the very nature of the European Community efforts concerning higher education. According to Clark Kerr, "The EEC endeavor is the greatest of all intentionally planned experiments with the internationalization (or at least regionalization) of learning ever undertaken" (1990, 16). Obviously, this time internationalization will not stop at an iron curtain, which until the late 1980s greatly limited its spread from West to East.

On the other hand, developments in Central/Eastern Europe, including most of its efforts for renewal of higher education, are guided by an objective now commonly labeled the "return to Europe." For a majority of former Warsaw Pact countries, this means a close association with the European

Community and, in the long run (hopefully not too long), full membership.

Thus, interaction and mutual influence between developments on the European Community level and the opening of Central/Eastern Europe can be expected. We shall return to this point in the conclusion of this chapter, which is otherwise exclusively devoted to issues related to the renewal of higher education in Central/Eastern Europe.[1]

The Renewal of Higher Education in Central/Eastern Europe

The Central/Eastern European systems of higher education are in an exceptional situation. An earthquake took place and, officially at least, everybody agrees that major transformations and reforms are necessary: reforms of structures, of curriculum, of staffing, and of numerous other key aspects that shape a system. This by itself is a rather unique opportunity for change or even a great mutation comparable to those that took place on a few occasions in history—for example, in Napoleonic France, at the time of Humboldt in Germany, and after the 1917 revolution in Russia. The big question, of course, is whether this opportunity will be seized. More precisely, will the traditional resistance to change of higher education (anywhere in the world), combined with the weight of the heritage of the past forty and more years, be overcome by the forces of renewal accompanying the opening of Central/Eastern Europe in the late 1980s?

The Heritage

Very few actors in and investigators of the Central European scene would disagree with the statement that probably the most difficult task and challenge they have to face is the heritage of the past forty to fifty years. The challenge is pedagogical, sociological, economic, and political and is of rare scope and complexity. Rigid centralization of and almost total political control of access to the curriculum (except in pure sciences, though to some extent even there), academic staff appointments, institutional management (insofar as it existed), resource allocation—these are just a few characteristics of the old system that require change. Added to them are several structural features that are hardly compatible with modern higher education: the imposition of the Soviet model of institutional separation between teaching and research, the catastrophic effects of manpower planning (or of highly distorted manpower planning), salary levels that imply small and even negative rewards for higher education graduates compared with other groups in the population, and a declining role and weight given to higher education over the last ten or twenty years by the government (in fact, the Party) leading to dramatic shortages of all kinds—of equipment, of supplies, of books, etc.

Many of these inherited shortcomings can and are being changed by decree and/or new legislation. Many cannot be dealt with in this way and will require measures and actions that have yet to be designed, adopted, and implemented; in any case, it will be some time before they have their full effect—and some time before they have any effect at all. The compulsory teaching of Marxism-Leninism to all has been abolished, but what should be done with the thousands of teachers of Marxism-Leninism is another matter entirely. New laws have given full or substantial autonomy to universities, but they could not teach people how to cope with autonomy. This, incidentally, raises what is probably the most difficult problem due to the heritage of the past: the inertia of acquired attitudes—the inertia of being told what to do and what not to do, of not showing any initiative, of not taking any risks.

As mentioned, resistance to change in higher education is a well-known phenomenon that applies to all countries. The problem is probably even more deeply rooted in Central Europe because of at least two circumstances. First, although the principal actors—the ministers, rectors, deans, and student leaders—have been changed, the bulk of those who finally shape the functioning of higher education remain those who were installed by and benefited from the old system or at least were passive "fellow travelers." The commonly expressed opinion in Central Europe is that many of these people deliberately block any attempt at change. We cannot judge how far this is correct, but clearly for many (perhaps the majority) entering unknown territory implies dangers that they would rather avoid.

Second, the majority of people in higher education in Central Europe do not know how to do things differently. They are naturally aware of and even adhere to general concepts such as university autonomy or freedom of teaching, but too often these are merely postulates without practical consequences. Worse, they may be postulates leading to problematic simplifications: autonomy implying simply a return to the prewar situation; a new curriculum meaning just getting rid of the ideological constraints, without moving toward new structures of knowledge (e.g., interdisciplinarity). Thus, the recent statement of a Czechoslovak specialist: "One of the greatest problems is that the majority of teachers are not interested in curriculum change."

All of this applies not only to higher education, but also to many (if not all) problem areas and social subsystems of Central Europe: privatization, transition to a market economy, public and local administration, etc. In a sense, the situation of higher education is only an illustration of a more general problem, though perhaps a particularly serious case.

Partly, at least, this is also due to the highly ambiguous if not paradoxical relation between higher education and the state (the Party) until now. On the one hand, the regime considered universities as one of its key tools of indoctrination, as a privileged means of shaping the young generation according to the norms of the prevailing ideology; on the other hand, it mistrusted universities as seats of potential (and actual) resistance to the monopoly of Party dogmas and control.

The Main Shortcoming: Relations between the State and Higher Education

The list of shortcomings of Central/Eastern European higher education is very long, and only some of them can be mentioned here. We must keep in mind another critical problem: old structures and norms have often been wholly or partly abandoned, but no new ones have yet emerged in their place.

This is true in particular of the new relation between the state and higher education. The old centralization and total Party control have been rejected, and full university autonomy has been formally introduced. However, besides the already-mentioned issue of how to overcome the inertia of acquired attitudes (of "waiting for orders"), a certain vacuum has been created with regard to appropriate mechanisms to set overall policies and priorities. In practice, two dangers exist: on the one hand, that the state will continue—thanks again to the inertia of the old behavior patterns of some of its officials—to regulate in detail the functioning of higher education institutions and maintain financing mechanisms that leave little scope for university autonomy; on the other hand, that the state will abandon its responsibility for the formulation of long-term higher education policy and will restrict itself merely to managing day-to-day problems. The latter might be the result not so much of a deliberate decision, but simply of the quantity of these day-to-day problems to be dealt with by the overburdened officials.

Thus, striking a proper balance between institutional autonomy and state intervention will be a major challenge of higher education in Central/Eastern Europe. Market forces alone, we would argue, will not suffice, and—almost paradoxically when one considers the overall and desirable trend toward deregulation—the state's role in defining and shaping the new balance will be essential.

These considerations are of particular relevance when looking at what, at first sight at least, appears as the most tangible and burning issue of Central/Eastern European higher education: its critical financial situation combined with its obsolescence in terms of modern equipment, access to Western literature, and the like—all this in the context of the most difficult economic situation of the countries concerned.

The lack of resources appears dramatic, especially in some of the countries concerned. In Czechoslovakia, for example, budgets of universities in 1991 have nominally declined by about 5 percent compared to the already low figures of the previous year. Considering the expected inflation rate of 20 to 30 percent, this in real terms will imply cuts of at least 25 percent. No improvement seems possible in the notoriously low salaries of teachers— low not only compared to those prevailing in the West but also in relation to salaries outside higher education, especially in fields and sectors of the emerging market economy, which means that the already low attractiveness of the teaching profession will continue to decline. Funds for the renewal of and for indispensable new equipment, for the expansion and modernization of libraries, and for the badly needed massive increase in international exchange will be even more scarce than in the past.

Most Western universities also had to face more or less difficult financial problems in the 1970s and 1980s. None of them—except possibly in isolated cases—can compare with the financial constraints of Central/Eastern European higher education. The latter, moreover, has only a very small possibility of mobilizing sources of support beyond the central budget. Such sources (e.g., industry or local authorities) are in a similarly difficult financial situation and are highly uncertain about their immediate future. Foreign aid is in this respect an exception—but only to a small extent, because, whatever its size, it can never cover more than a fraction of the need.

A better allocation of available resources, a judicious choice of priorities, and a radical improvement in the efficiency of higher education are obviously the only means to cope with the present financial constraints. But this will take time and will require new mechanisms and rules of resource allocation in the development of which the state, in a new type of partnership with universities, must assume an important responsibility.[2]

The Separation of Teaching from Research

Another critical issue for Central/Eastern European higher education is the already-mentioned separation between teaching and research. These functions are entirely or partly compartmentalized into two different sets of institutions—universities on the one hand and academies of science on the other. Most of the university teachers do little if any research, and most of the researchers are not involved in any teaching. The root of this separation—more pronounced or complete in some countries (such as Czechoslovakia) than in others (such as Poland or Yugoslavia)—is political or even ideological. The Communist regime, especially during the more recent period, recognized the importance of research and accepted—willy-nilly and to a limited extent—one of its prerequisites, namely, a certain freedom for researchers. This was not the case for teachers, those in direct contact with the young generation. Hence, political control of the latter was much stricter than of the former. As a result (not always realized in the West), the quality of teaching deteriorated much more than did the quality of research.

One of the very serious consequences of this separation is undoubtedly the weakness and the occasional absence of postgraduate education in most of Central/Eastern Europe. A more general consequence is teaching that does not take sufficient account of the latest advances of science.

Solutions will not be easy, and hard-fought battles around this issue can be expected—and are already taking place. These battles will have a considerable influence on the future development of higher education. Abolishing the academies is advocated by some, and the minimum goal seems to be the development of new linking mechanisms between them and the universities (joint appointments, common laboratories, etc.). Universities and academies (higher education and science) should be put under the umbrella of the same ministry where this is not the case already.

Needed Growth and Diversification

Growth and diversification of higher education in most Central/Eastern European countries is an issue that, we believe, should attract more attention than it does. In some countries such as Czechoslovakia, Hungary, and Poland, it is widely recognized that the existing higher education enrollment ratios are very low—approximately one-half (15 percent or less) of the Western figures. At the same time, given the already-mentioned financial constraints as well as growing unemployment and/or underemployment of graduates, growth of the system can hardly be envisioned within the short run and the existing structures. The countries concerned need more highly qualified manpower, not only at the very advanced level but across the whole range of qualifications that a modern system of postsecondary education is expected to provide.

Practically all Central European countries, with the notable exception of Czechoslovakia, have both a university and a nonuniversity sector of higher education, as understood by existing international definitions of these terms. In general, however, it seems that the relative prestige of the nonuniversity-level institutions is very low, and frequently they are hardly considered to be part of higher education. Western experience shows that such institutions (e.g., the German *Fachhochschulen*, the French Instituts Universitaires Technologiques (IUTs), the British "Further Education" colleges, the American community colleges) have a strategic role to play from the point of view both of the needs of the economy and of social demand for higher education. Universities or university-level specialized institutions alone cannot cope with either of these two pressures; thus, the existence of a recognized alternative to traditional universities is indispensable.[3]

In the past, a certain degree of diversification developed through a rather strong sector of part-time higher education for employed people. However, over the past decade, this sector has rapidly declined, in part because of the low quality and prestige of its degrees—a trend that seems to continue. This by itself is a powerful reason for the countries concerned to pay great attention to a new type of more vocationally oriented higher education both within and outside existing universities.

Yet another reason is the development of small regional universities. Existing resources are not sufficient to build most of them into full university-level institutions. In these circumstances, it seems much wiser to provide such regional establishments with clearly defined and specific roles and missions (i.e., as an important component of a new nonuniversity sector rather than as third-rate universities). Strengthening or developing this sector, including the building up of distance education, of advanced continuing education, and of "nontraditional" higher education in general, will not be an easy task because the concept of a global diversified post-secondary system is not yet well understood in Central/Eastern Europe.

Obsolete Curricula

Finally, a brief mention should be made of what to many seems to be the most fundamental shortcoming of Central/Eastern European higher education, namely, the obsolescence and rigidity of its curricula. This issue has many aspects: students have to take an excessive number of courses (up to thirty hours or more per week), many of them outdated and offered by a teaching staff without real qualification; there is little room for optional courses and student choice; there are no or very few interdisciplinary courses because of overspecialization of institutions and the absence or extreme weakness of contacts between different disciplines. The list could be extended much further because, of course, certain fields are more affected than others. Humanities and social sciences (including especially economics and law) are in the worst situation. At least some of the exact sciences and engineering—particularly when it comes to their theoretical and basic research components—are generally in a better state and, in some cases, are at a very high level. Even here, however, important gaps exist, particularly with regard to teaching and research relying heavily on empirical and experimental techniques and oriented toward applied work.

Shortfalls in the curriculum area will probably be the most difficult to overcome because two critical conditions must be met: (1) the development of new structures and mechanisms facilitating flexibility and innovation and (2) the spread of new behaviors and attitudes toward change among the higher education staff.

The Prospects for Renewal

Many other problems face Central/Eastern European systems: the acquiring of skills in the management of autonomous, responsible, and responsive institutions and of performance evaluation techniques; the development of a coherent admissions policy and of access criteria adapted to both the cultural and the economic missions of universities in a period of transition of Central/Eastern European societies toward democracy; the extension of the universities' role in continuing education and of their relations with industry—the tasks and challenges seem almost insurmountable. Yet chances for renewal also exist.

First, it might very well be that the very seriousness of the situation is by itself a powerful factor for change. Because so many things do not work, the climate is possibly more favorable than ever before to a radical mutation otherwise so rare in higher education.

Second, in spite of the low standards in many parts of the systems, there are centers of excellence with internationally recognized people and departments at the leading edge of their fields. They might be rare or almost nonexistent in some areas, or they might be small islands with little influence on the rest of the system, but they have the potential to become models for and leaders of the future renewal. Moreover, it should not be forgotten that many academics and students played a key role in the breakdown of the old regimes. They were surely only a minority, but isn't renewal and innovation almost always the work of tiny minorities?

Third, there are some seemingly paradoxical situations that, if properly handled, might be turned into advantages or at least show that there may be light at the end of the tunnel. Staff/student ratios are extremely favorable almost everywhere: as of 1987, 1:8 in Bulgaria, 1:6.4 in Czechoslovakia, 1:6.5 in Hungary (and 1:5.4 in Hungarian universities), and 1:6.2 in Poland. The best in Western Europe is 1:10, and the ratio reaches 1:20 or more in several countries (e.g., France and Italy) (UNESCO 1989).

The case of the Budapest Technical University is a good illustration of this paradox. It enrolls about six thousand students but has an academic staff and a plant roughly equivalent to those of the Technical University of Aachen in Germany, which enrolls close to thirty thousand students. This can, of course, be interpreted as an indication of great inefficiency and "low productivity" of Central/Eastern European academic personnel (similar to the well-known low productivity of agriculture and industry where, in many instances, two to five times as many people are needed to do the same job as in the West). But this also shows that human resources—the most important of all—are available.

Developing a European Dimension of Higher Education

Finally, there is the convergence of the two developments mentioned at the beginning of this chapter: the growing internationalization of higher education in general and the policies and programs of the European Community in particular, with the overwhelming desire of Central/Eastern European countries to join the latter as rapidly or at least as closely as possible. Cooperative schemes with Western institutions imply in most cases innovative ventures that carry not just external aid money but special prestige, helping to overcome local resistance to change and the inertia of inherited attitudes.

Among these, the European Community programs COMETT, ERASMUS, LINGUA, and TEMPUS deserve at least brief mention here. The principal emphasis of COMETT is on the development of university-industry cooperation. It facilitates the placement of students of one country in a company of another country; the appointment of specialists from industry and business as part-time and/or temporary university teachers, and vise versa; and, more generally, the creation of university-enterprise partnerships, always on a transnational basis.

The ERASMUS program aims at strengthening European interuniversity cooperation in general. Its three main tools are support for the development of joint courses—and frequently also of joint degrees—among higher education institutions (in both the university and the nonuniversity sectors) of two or more different European Community countries; support for intra-European exchanges and mobility of students and academic staff (already involving over thirty thousand persons); and European transfer of credit.

The LINGUA program is designed essentially to develop teaching and learning of foreign languages in higher education and in other education sectors (especially in vocational training institutions and through training foreign language teachers employed by companies).

The TEMPUS scheme combines most of the elements of the three above-mentioned programs but focuses on Central/Eastern Europe. Its principal objective is to contribute to the renewal and modernization of higher education in that region. This is to be achieved through so-called "Joint European Projects" that must involve at least one higher education institution in Central/Eastern Europe (the countries of the former Soviet Union are for the moment not included in the scheme) and at least two institutions in two European Community countries. Such projects can cover a wide range of activities: studies of Central/Eastern students in the West, the appointment of Western teachers and specialists in Central/Eastern European universities, curriculum development, intensive seminars or summer schools in areas neglected in the former Communist countries, the creation of new departments or even of new institutions, the supply of modern equipment and the improvement of libraries, advice and courses on the management of universities, and the like.

The total budget of TEMPUS for the 1991–92 academic year represented an equivalent of over $70 million in U.S. funds. The budgets of the three other programs range from some $40 million to over $70 million annually.

Financially this support, as well as the aid of many bilateral agencies and private foundations, is far from negligible, but—as already stressed—it can cover only a small fraction of the need. More important is its potential catalyzing power. In this respect, the European Community programs and, in fact, the approach of post-1992 Europe represent a dynamic and, one hopes, a strong factor of renewal of Central/Eastern European higher education. The responsibility of transforming the potential of this factor and the hopes related to it into an actual trend and reality lies with both Central/Eastern European actors and their Western partners.

Notes

1. For an analysis of the effect of European Community programs and policies primarily on Western European higher education, see "Higher Education and Europe after 1992" (1989).

2. It can, of course, also be argued that the state (the Ministry of Finance) should give greater priority to higher education in the distribution of its overall resources. However, many sectors—environmental protection, health, industrial restructuring, communication, and the like—can and do make the same claims, and higher education is in this respect seldom in a favorable competitive position in spite of many official statements concerning its importance for the nation's future.

3. Among the many publications on this subject, see in particular the recent report of the Organization for Economic Cooperation and Development entitled *Alternatives to Universities* (1991).

References

"Higher Education and Europe after 1992": Special Issue. 1989. *European Journal of Education,* 24(4).

Kerr, Clark. 1990. "The Internationalization of Learning and the Nationalization of the Purposes of Higher Education: Two Laws of Motion in Conflict?" *European Journal of Education,* 25(1):5–22.

Organization for Economic Cooperation and Development. 1991. *Alternatives to Universities.* Paris: Organization for Economic Cooperation and Development.

UNESCO. 1989. *Statistical Yearbook, 1989.* Paris: UNESCO.

III Changing Constituencies

10 Faculty: Differentiation and Dispersion

BURTON R. CLARK

[handwritten margin note:] Bc of inc. tech., will there soon be a weeding out of great professors. Will these jobs ever be completely eliminated?

The academic profession is a multitude of academic tribes and territories. As in the days of old, it is law, medicine, and theology. It is now also high-energy physics, molecular biology, Renaissance literature, childhood learning, and computer science. Built upon a widening array of disciplines and specialties, it hosts subcultures that speak in the strange tongues of econometrics, biochemistry, ethnomethodology, and deconstructionism. Driven by a research imperative that rewards specialization, its fragmentation is only slowed, not fully arrested, by limited resources to fund all of the new and old lines of effort in which academics would like to engage. Subject differentiation, already very great, will increase in the future.

No less important in the differentiation of the academic profession in America is the dispersion of faculty among institutions in a system that is inordinately large, radically decentralized, extremely diversified, uniquely competitive, and uncommonly entrepreneurial. A high degree of institutional dispersion positions American faculty in many varied sectors: some one hundred "research universities" of varying research intensity; another one hundred "doctoral-granting" universities that offer a limited number of doctorates and possess limited research dollars; six hundred "comprehensive universities and colleges"—a catch-all category of private and public institutions that have graduate as well as undergraduate programs, offering master's degrees but not doctorates; still another six hundred "liberal arts colleges," nearly all private but varying greatly in quality and in degree of

[handwritten margin note:] Will there still exist in the future such a wide variety of Univ. or is colleges steering us in a different path?

163

concentration on the liberal arts; a huge array of some fourteen hundred two-year colleges, mainly public, whose comprehensiveness stretches from college transfer programs to community-center offerings; and finally a left-over miscellany of some six hundred specialized institutions that cannot be fitted into the above basic categories.

All of these major categories in turn contain much institutional diversity. For example, buried within them are historically black colleges, Catholic universities, women's colleges, fundamentalist religious universities and colleges, and such highly distinctive institutions as the Juilliard School (of Music), the Bank Street College of Education, and Rockefeller University. In short, the American faculty is distributed institutionally all over the map, located in the educational equivalents of the farm and the big city, the ghetto and the suburbs, the darkened ravine next to the coal mine and the high hill overlooking the lovely valley.

Disciplinary locations and institutional locations together compose the primary matrix of induced and enforced similarities and differences among American academics. These two internal features of the system itself are more important than such background characteristics as class, race, religion, and gender in determining the thought and behavior of academics. In themselves these primary dimensions of diverse setting turn simple statements about "the professor" in "the college" or "the university" into stereotypes. We deceive ourselves every time we speak of "the college professor"—a common habit among popular critics of the professorate who fail to talk to academics in their varied locations and to listen to what they say. Understanding begins with a willingness to pursue diversity.

Different Worlds, Small Worlds

The disciplinary creation of different academic worlds becomes more striking with each passing year. In the leading universities, for example, the clinical professor of medicine is as much a part of the basic work force as is the professor of English. The medical academic can be found in a cancer ward, interacting intensively with other doctors, nurses, orderlies, laboratory assistants, a few students perhaps, and many patients in a round of tightly scheduled activities that may begin at six in the morning and extend into evenings and weekends. Such academics are often under considerable pressure to generate income from patient-care revenues: they frequently negotiate with third party medical plans and need a sizable administrative staff to handle patient billing. Salary may well depend on group income that fluctuates from year to year and that is directly affected by changes in the health-care industry and by the competitive position of a particular medical school-hospital complex. Hence, salary may not be guaranteed, even in a tenured post. Sizable research grants must also be actively and repetitively pursued, and those who do not raise funds from research grants will find themselves loaded up with more clinical duties.

The humanities professor in the leading universities operates in a totally different environment: teaching "loads" are in the range of four to six hours a week. Office hours are at one's discretion; administrative assignments vary considerably with one's willingness to cooperate. The humanities academic typically interacts with large numbers of beginning students in lecture halls, in an occasional turn in introductory classes; with small numbers of juniors and seniors, in specialized upper-division courses; and then with a few graduate students in seminars and dissertation consultation around such highly specialized topics as Elizabethan lyric and Icelandic legend. Much valuable work time can be spent at home, away from the "distractions" of the university office.

About what is one thinking and writing? Attention may center on a biography of Eugene O'Neill, an interpretation of what Jane Austen really meant, an effort to trace Lillian Hellman's political passions, or a critique of Derrida and deconstructionism. Professors seek to master a highly specialized segment of literature and to maximize individual interpretation. The interests of humanities professors are reflected not only in the many sections and byways of such omnibus associations as the Modern Language Association, but also in the specificities of the Shakespeare Association of America, the Dickens Society, the D. H. Lawrence Society of North America, the Speech Association of America, the Thomas Hardy Society of America, and the Vladimir Nabokov Society. Tocqueville's famous comment on the propensity of Americans to form voluntary associations is nowhere more true than in the academic world.

Disciplinary differences are of course not limited to the sharp contrast between life in a medical school and in a department of English. The work of Tony Becher (1989) and others on the cultures of individual disciplines has shown that bodies of knowledge variously determine the behavior of individuals and departments. Disciplines exhibit discernible differences in individual behavior and group action, notably between "hard" and "soft" subjects and "pure" and "applied" fields; a simple fourfold classification distinguishes between hard-pure (physics), hard-applied (engineering), soft-pure (history), and soft-applied (social work). Across the many fields of the physical sciences, the biological sciences, the social sciences, the humanities, and the arts, fieldwork reveals varied work assignments, symbols of identity, modes of authority, career lines, and associational linkages. More broadly, great differences in the academic life often appear between the letters and science departments and the many professional school domains in which a concern for the ways and needs of an outside profession must necessarily be combined with the pursuit of science and truth for its own sake. Far from the popular images of Mr. Chips chatting up undergraduates and of Einsteinian, white-haired, remote scholars dreaming up esoteric mathematical equations are the realities of academic work that helps prepare school teachers, librarians, social workers, engineers, computer experts, architects, nurses, pharmacists, business managers, lawyers, and doctors—and, in some academic locales, also morticians, military personnel, auto mechanics, airport technicians, secretaries, lathe operators, and cosmetologists. For over a century, American higher education has been generous to a fault in admitting former outside fields and new occupations into the academy—a point made by historians of both higher education (Metzger 1987) and the professions (Wiebe 1967).

Because research is the first priority of the leading universities, the disciplinary differentiation of every modern system of higher education is self-amplifying. The American system is currently the extreme case of this self-amplification; its great size, decentralization, diversity, and competitiveness prompted Eliot at Harvard and others in the old colleges of the day to speed up the nascent evolution from the age of the college to the age of the university. This evolution turned professors loose to pursue specialized research and to teach specialized subjects at the newly created graduate level, even as students were turned loose to pick and choose in an array of undergraduate courses that was to become ever more bewildering. The reward system of promoting academics on the grounds of research and published scholarship has become more deeply rooted in the universities, would-be universities, and leading four-year colleges with every passing decade. The many proliferating specialties of the disciplines are like tributaries flowing into this mammoth river of the research imperative.

The most serious operational obstacles to this research-driven amplification are the limitations of funding and the institutional need to teach undergraduates and beginning graduate students with packages of introductory materials that they can understand. Then, too, there remains in the American system the longstanding belief in the importance of undergraduate liberal or general education. The saving remnant of academics who uphold the banners of liberal and general education are able to sally forth in full cry periodically—the 1920s, the late 1940s, the 1980s—to group some specialties into more general course offerings; narrow the options in distribution requirements from, say, four hundred to one hundred courses; insist that teaching take priority over research; and in general raise a ruckus about the dangers of the specialized mind. Meanwhile, however, campus promotion committees continue their steady scrutiny of the record of research and scholarship. Central administrators work to build an institutional culture of academic first-rateness as that is defined competitively across the nation and even internationally on the basis of the reputation of noted scholars. Sophisticated general educators and liberal arts proponents in the universities recognize the primacy of the substantive impulse and learn how to work incrementally within its limits.

Institutional Differentiation

As powerful as are the self-amplifying disciplinary differences in dividing the professoriate, institutional diversity now plays an even more important role. This axis of differentiation places approximately two-thirds of American academics in settings other than that of doctorate-granting universities; over a fourth of all faculty are in the comprehensive colleges and universities that offer degree work as far as the master's degree; a small number, about 5 percent, teach in the private liberal arts colleges; and a major bloc of a fourth to a third teach in the nearly fourteen hundred community colleges.

These major locales exhibit vast differences in the very basis of the academic life, namely, the balance of effort between teaching and research. Teaching loads in the leading universities come in at around four to six hours a week, tailing down to two to three hours—a class a week, a seminar a week—rather than rising above six. The reciprocal is that faculty commonly expect to spend at least half of their time in research, alone or in the company of a few advanced graduate students. We need not stray very far, however, before we encounter teaching loads that are 50 percent, 100 percent, even 200 percent higher. The "doctorate-granting universities" often exact teaching loads of nine to twelve hours. So too for liberal arts colleges, especially outside the top fifty. In comprehensive colleges, loads of twelve hours a week in the classroom are common. In the community colleges, the standard climbs to fifteen hours, and loads of eighteen and twenty-one hours are not unknown. And, as we move from the top of the institutional hierarchy to the bottom, faculty involvement shifts from advanced students to beginning students, from highly selective students to open-door clientele, from young students in the traditional college age group to a mix of students of all ages in short-term vocational programs as well as in course work leading toward a bachelor's degree. In the community colleges, students in the college-transfer track are now numerically overshadowed by students in terminal vocational programs, and both are frequently outnumbered by nonmatriculated adults who turn "college" into "community center."

The burdens of remedial education are also much heavier as we descend the hierarchy. The open-door approach, standard in two-year colleges and also operational in four-year colleges that take virtually all comers, confronts college teachers with numerous underprepared students. Then, to add insult to injury, as we descend the hierarchy, we encounter more part-time academic work. During the last two decades, the ranks of the part-timers have swollen to 200,000 or so—a fourth to a third of the total academic work force—with heavy concentrations in the less prestigious colleges and especially in community colleges, where a half or more of the faculty commonly operate on a part-time schedule. At the extreme opposite end of the institutional hierarchy from those who serve primarily in graduate schools and in graduate-level professional schools in the major universities are the full-time and part-time teachers in English or mathematics in downtown community colleges who teach introductory and subintroductory courses over and over again—the rudiments of English composition, the first course in mathematics—to high school graduates who need remediation and to adults struggling with basic literacy.

With the very nature of academic work varying enormously across the many types of institutions that make up American postsecondary education, other dimensions of the academic life run on a parallel course. If we examine the cultures of the institutions by discussing with faculty members their basic academic beliefs, we find different worlds. Among the leading research universities, the discipline is front and center, the institution is prized for its reputation of scholarship and research, and peers are the primary reference group. A professor of physics will say: "What I value the most is the presence of the large number and diverse collection of scientists who are constantly doing things that I find stimulating." A professor of biology tells us that his university "has a lot of extremely good departments. . . . There are a lot of fascinating, interesting people here." A political scientist adds that what he values most "is the intellectual level of the faculty and the graduate students. . . . Good graduate students are very important to me personally and always have been, and having colleagues that are smart is important." And a professor of English states that his institution "is a first-rate university. . . . We have a fine library, and we have excellent teachers here, and we have first-rate scholars." Academics in this favored site have much with which to identify. They are proud of the quality they believe surrounds them, experiencing it directly in their own and neighboring departments and inferring it indirectly from institutional reputation. The strong symbolic thrust of the institution incorporates the combined strengths of the departments that in turn represent the disciplines. Thus, for faculty, disciplinary and institutional cultures converge, a happy state indeed.

The leading private liberal arts colleges provide a second favored site. Here, professors often wax lyrical in interviews about the small college environment tailored to undergraduate teaching: "It is a very enjoyable setting. The students are—the students we get in physics—a delight to work with"; "I can't put it in a word, but I think that it is one of the least constraining environments I know of"; "It is a better form of life"; or "My colleagues are fantastic. The people in this department are sane, which in an English department is not always the case." These institutions retain the capacity to appear as academic communities, not bureaucracies, in their overall integration and symbolic unity.

But soon we encounter sites where faculty members are troubled by inchoate institutional character and worry about the quality of their environment. In the lesser universities and especially in the comprehensive colleges that have evolved out of teachers colleges, at the second, third, and fourth levels of the institutional hierarchy, the setting is often summed as follows:

> I think the most difficult thing about being at an institution like [this one] is that it has a difficult time coming to terms with itself. I think the more established institutions with strong academic backgrounds don't have the problem that an institution that pretty much is in the middle range of higher educational institutions around the country does. I'm not saying that [this place] is a bad institution, but it certainly doesn't have the quality students, the quality faculty, the quality programs of the University of Chicago, Harvard, Yale. . . . When it talks about standards, what sort of standards? When it talks about practicality, how practical does it have to be? . . . It doesn't have a strong sense of tradition.

Compared to the research universities, the overall institutional culture is weaker and less satisfying for many faculty members, at the same time that disciplinary identifications are weakened as heavy teaching loads suppress research and its rewards.

In these middle-level institutions, professors often speak of their relationship with students as the thing they value most. Students begin to replace peers as the audience of first resort. That shift is completed in the

[Handwritten margin note, right side upper:] Should all univ.s have an equal code of unified standards that stud. cuts must obtain?

[Handwritten margin note, right side lower:] But, maybe some professors are happier and gain greater fulfillment from teaching in the classroom.

community colleges, with the identifications of faculty reaching a high point of student-centeredness. In a setting that is distinctly opposed to disciplinary definitions of quality and excellence, pleasures and rewards have to lie in the task of working with poorly prepared students who pour in through the open door. For example: "We are a practical teaching college. We serve our community and we serve . . . the students in our community, and give them a good, basic, strong education. . . . We are not sitting here on our high horses looking to publish"; and "I really do like to teach, and this place allows me to teach. It doesn't bog me down with having to turn out papers." In the community colleges, the equity values of open door and open access have some payoff as anchoring points in the faculty culture. But in the overall institutional hierarchy, where the dominant values emphasize quality, selection, and advanced work, the community college ideology can play only a subsidiary role. The limitations cannot be missed: "It would be nice to be able to teach upper-division classes."

As for work and culture, so go authority, careers, and associational life. To sum the story on authority: at the top of the institutional hierarchy, faculty influence is well and strong. Many individuals have strong personal bargaining power; departments and professional schools are strong, semi-autonomous units; and all-campus faculty bodies have dominant influence in personnel and curricular decisions. University presidents speak lovingly of the faculty as the core of the institution and walk gently around entrenched faculty prerogatives. As we descend the hierarchy, however, faculty authority weakens and managerialism increases. Top-down command is noticeably stronger in the public comprehensive colleges, especially when their genetic imprint is that of a teachers college. The two-year colleges, having evolved mainly out of secondary systems and operating, like schools, under local trustees, are quite managerial. Faculty then feel powerless, even severely put upon. Their answer has been unionization. The further down the hierarchy of prestige we go, the more widespread do unions become, especially among public sector institutions.

To sum the associational life of faculty: in the leading universities, faculty interact with one another across institutional boundaries in a bewildering network of disciplinary linkages: formal and informal; large and small; visible and invisible; local, regional, national, and international. When university specialists find "monster meetings" not to their liking, they go to participate in a smaller division or section that best represents their specific interests, or, as of late, they find kindred souls in small, autonomous meetings of several dozen people. The jet set is everywhere, from physicists pursuing high-energy physics to professors of English off to a conference in

Paris on structuralism. As we move down the hierarchy, however, there is less reason to be involved, less to learn that is relevant to one's everyday life, and the travel money is gone from the institutional budget. Then, academics do not go to national meetings, or they go only if the national association comes to their part of the country and develops special sessions on teaching—or they break away to form associations appropriate to their sector. Community college teachers have been developing associations in such broad areas as the social sciences and the humanities and in such special areas of teaching as mathematics and biology and doing so on a home-city or home-region as well as national basis.

All in all, institutional differentiation interacts with disciplinary differentiation in a self-amplifying fashion that steadily widens and deepens the matrix of differences among the faculty that leads to their different, small worlds.

Systemic Problems

When we pursue the different worlds of American professors by emphasizing disciplinary and institutional conditions, deep-rooted problems come to the fore that are otherwise relegated to the background or only dimly perceived. Already evident in the foregoing account, five systemic concerns may be briefly stated as problems of secondarization, excessive teaching, attenuated professional control, fragmented academic culture, and diminished intrinsic reward and motivation.

Secondarization and Remediation

The long evolution from elite to mass to universal access in American postsecondary education has not been without its costs. One major undesirable effect is a change in the conditions of the academic life that occurs when academics confront poorly educated students who come out of a defective secondary school system and flow into higher education by means of open access. Academic work then revolves considerably around remedial education. Faced with students in the college classroom whose academic achievement is, for example, at the level of ninth or tenth grade English, faculty first have to help the student progress to the twelfth grade or traditional college-entry level, thereby engaging in the work of the high school. Mathematics instructors may even find themselves facing students whose achievement bogged down about the fifth or sixth grade and hence need to complete some elementary schoolwork as well as their secondary education. Well known by those who teach in nonselective four-year colleges and especially in community colleges, this situation may seem surprising, even shocking, to others. But, like the night the day, it follows from the structure and orientation of American secondary and postsecondary education. If secondary schools graduate students whose achievement is below the twelfth grade level and if some colleges admit all who approach their doors, then college faculties will engage in K–12 work. Remedial education is spread throughout American higher education, from leading universities to community colleges, but it is relatively light when selectivity is high and quite heavy when selection is low or even nonexistent.

The problem of teaching poorly prepared students is compounded in the two-year college by its concentration on the first two years of the four-year undergraduate curriculum and on short-term vocational and semiprofessional programs. This curricular context calls for repetitive teaching of introductory courses. Since community colleges experience much student attrition during and after the first year of study, due to a variety of personal, occupational, and academic reasons, teaching is concentrated in first-year courses. In each department it is preeminently the general beginning course or two that must be taught over and over again, with little or no surcease. Upper-division courses, let alone graduate courses, are rarely available. Some course diversity can be found at the second-year level, but the departmental task is to cover the most introductory materials semester by semester, year in and year out. The teaching task is then more like that of the secondary school than that of the selective university. The task of remedial education adds to the downward thrust, requiring subcollege instruction on a plane below first-year introductory instruction.

Inherent in current American education, this teaching context is so infrequently mentioned in public discussion and print as to constitute a virtual institutional secret, that the life of the higher education scholar is reduced in considerable measure to a life of secondary school teaching. With due respect to the difficulties of the work and to the often deep devotion of involved staff to the welfare of underprepared students and immigrant populations, this widely found situation amounts, in blunt terms, to a dumbing-down of the intellectual life of professors. Educational euphemisms allow us to blink at this undesired effect of American-style comprehensive secondary education and universal higher education, but they do not allow us to escape it. The situation marginalizes faculty. Eroding "the essential intellectual core of faculty work," it deprofessionalizes them (Seidman 1985, 275).

Excessive Teaching

The complaint that professors do too much research and too little teaching has been abroad in the land for almost a hundred years. When William James wrote about "the Ph.D. octopus" shortly after the turn of the century, he pointed to the increasing preoccupation of professors in the emerging universities with specialized research, graduate students, and doctoral programs. Since then the cry of too much research has been a perennial battle cry of the American reformer seeking more emphasis on undergraduate programs and especially on their general or liberal education components. The 1980s saw a strong resurgence of this point of view inside and outside the academy. Careful critics beamed their messages at research universities, would-be universities, and even four-year private and public colleges that have opened their faculty reward systems to the research imperative and its expression in publication and participation in research networks. Even in the more carefully stated cases, however, critical comment tends to turn into a generalized charge that "professors" should do less research and more teaching. In the academic press and in the popular press more generally, careful targeting is entirely foregone. In the extreme, a minimization of teaching by professors is portrayed as part of a "scam."

But across the dispersed American professorate, the reality is the reverse: more academics teach too much than teach too little. Fifteen hours of classroom teaching each week is far too much for the maintenance of a scholarly life; even twelve hours is quite excessive. But, as noted earlier, most institutional sectors present such loads, specifying assignments that are two to three times greater than that of professors in research-based institutions. Twelve and fifteen hours a week in the classroom at the college level tends to push professors out of their disciplines. A sense of being a scholar is reduced as the "physicist" becomes entirely "a teacher of physics," the "political scientist" becomes a "teacher of political science," and then they both become mainly teachers of the introductory courses in these fields. Academics stop going to meetings of their disciplinary associations; interest flags and travel funds are not available. There is good reason to think that excessive teaching loads are now a source of academic burnout, importing into higher education the teacher burnout long noted as a problem in the K–12 system. A 1989 Carnegie Foundation faculty survey found that the share of the full-time faculty "intending to retire early" was 25 percent in research universities, 26 percent in liberal arts colleges, and a huge 49 percent in two-year colleges (Carnegie Foundation for the Advancement of Teaching 1990). Hence, settings characterized by heavy introductory teaching propel academics toward early retirement twice as much—one-half of total staff!—as settings where professors have light teaching loads, involvement in research, and more of the scholarly life as traditionally defined.

Weakened Professional Control

As indicated earlier, command structures are not unheard of in American colleges and universities. Professors in research universities and leading private four-year colleges certainly encounter trustee and administrator influence. But they generally have strong countervailing power of a professional kind that is rooted in personal and collective expertise. Department by department, professional school by professional school, they exercise primary influence in personnel and curricular decisions. They expect to be consulted in many matters rather than to receive orders from those in nominally superior positions. As we move to public and private comprehensive colleges and then especially to the community colleges, however, the foundations of authority change. Subject expertise becomes more diffuse, in the extreme amounting only to sufficient knowledge in the discipline to teach the introductory course to poorly prepared students, while at the same time the role of trustees and administrators is strengthened, in the extreme approaching the local top-down supervision found in school districts. Such managerialism is particularly evident in public sector institutions, especially when they are exposed to state assertions of accountability.

Adding greatly to the vulnerability of academic professionals to political and administrative dictate is the marginal position of part-time faculty. In all institutional sectors, part-timers have always been with us. But their use grew greatly during the last two decades as a form of inexpensive and dispensable labor, particularly in public two- and four-year colleges. In 1990, it was common in the community college sector for a majority of the faculty in a college to be serving part-time. The part-timers are marginal in influence; their large numbers weaken the influence of full-time faculty vis-à-vis trustees and administrative staff. A proletariat exists in American academic life, centered in poorly paid part-time employment in staffs devoted to introductory teaching.

Fragmented Academic Culture

All-encompassing academic values are increasingly abstract and hard to find. The claims frequently made by reformers that academics must somehow find their way back to agreement on core values and assume an overarching common framework become more unrealistic with each passing year. But in lieu of values powerfully held throughout the system, perhaps we can still find structural and symbolic connections that indirectly and in a complex fashion serve to provide some integration of academic culture.

For one, considerable center-to-periphery influence exists among different types of institutions. Institutionally, the hard core of academic values in the American professorate is found in the leading research universities and top liberal arts colleges. The first exemplifies modern science and advanced scholarship. Since it also trains most of the faculty for all of the other sectors, its socialization of graduate students diffuses its models of orientation and behavior. The second leading sector upholds the much-respected tradition of liberal education for undergraduates. It becomes the model in public circles for what undergraduate education would be if properly carried out. These two dominant sectors emit value rays that radiate first to adjacent types of institutions and then in weaker force to sectors more divorced in character. In short, the many different types of institutions do not operate as watertight compartments. At the level of ideas and orienting values, they overlap.

The many disciplines and specialties also connect one to another, both as modes of reasoning and in coverage of empirical domains. As portrayed in several acute analyses, they may be seen as connecting in "chains of overlapping neighborhoods," thereby producing "a continuous texture of narrow specialties," a "collective communication," and "a collective competence and breadth." In short, as elsewhere in ever more differentiated societies, academia may be partially integrated through "interlocking cultural communities." (For a fuller account of these metaphors and perspectives offered respectively by Michael Polanyi, Donald T. Campbell, and Diana Crane, see Clark 1987, 140–142).

Thus, some partial but substantial integration of academic culture in a fragmented academic system may come from bit-by-bit overlap of separate memberships and specific identities. Disciplines and institutions may serve as mediating institutions that tie individuals and small groups into the whole of the system. Such forms of integration are likely to be pursued and valued only when observers give up the search for unifying common values and surrender the expectation that academics should behave as if they were members of a national corps.

Diminished Intrinsic Motivation and Reward

Under all the strengths and weaknesses of American academic life, we can sense the persistent problem of the professional calling. When academic work becomes just a job and a routine career, then such material rewards as salary are placed front and center. Academics stay at their work or leave for other pursuits according to how much they are paid. They come to work "on time" because they must; they leave on time because satisfactions are to be found after work is concluded. But when academic work is a calling, it "constitutes a practical ideal of activity and character that makes a person's work morally inseparable from his or her life. It subsumes the self into a community of disciplined practice and sound judgment whose activity has meaning and value in itself, not just in the output or profit that results from it" (Bellah et al. 1985, 66). A calling transmutes narrow self-interest into other-regarding and ideal-regarding interests: one is linked to fellow workers and to a version of a larger common good. The calling has moral content; it contributes to civic virtue.

Professionalization projects seek to provide vehicles in which multitudes of workers are transported to a calling, there to find intrinsic motivation as well as the glories of high status and the trappings of power. The academic profession is lucky in that it has natural sources of intrinsic motivation in abundance in the fascinations of research and the enchantments of teaching. Many academic contexts offer a workaday existence rich in content and consequence. As a confederate gathering, the academic profession's continuing promise lies considerably in the provision of a variety of contexts that generate "absorbing errands"—a metaphor attributed to Henry James. In that promise lies the best hope in the long term for the recruitment and retention of talent. But when such contexts fade away or become severely weakened, the errands run down and talented persons search for other fascinations and enchantments. The systemic problems I have identified—of secondarization, excessive teaching, weakened professional control, fragmented academic culture—tell us where to look and what to look for in determining the conditions that run down the academic calling.

Bureaucracy is needed in academia, since formal organization is necessary if researchers are to do research, teachers are to teach, and students are to learn. But if the tools of professionalism are to be put to good use in the promotion of academic activity, the supporting organization must be essentially profession-driven, offering conditions that heighten the intrinsic rewards of teaching and research and the intrinsic satisfactions of the academic life. Thus, academic work must be full-time, not marginalized as fleeting service. Devolution of power is essential, from state to institution and from institution to department, leaving much decision making in local hands cognizant of local needs and conditions. Accountability can be defined over

[Handwritten marginal notes: "But, this motivation may not be enough if so many professors are burnt out at com. colleges" and "Idea of tenure or renewed contracts"]

long periods of time, carried out, for example, by an eight-year review of each program—not made a yearly affair or elaborately prefigured in myriad rules requiring close compliance. Trust in professionals hired for their expertise and competence is, of course, the prime condition. Only professional norms and practices are positioned, person by person, in everyday activity constructively to shape motivation and steer behavior. Grasping this point, wise academic leaders seek to create the conditions of professional inspiration and self-regulation. Failing to grasp the logic of the profession (indeed, the very requirements of an effective modern system of higher education), "managers" attempt to substitute the nuts and bolts of bureaucratic regulation. Then the calling is reduced, the errand loses its fascination.

In our cultural world the academy is still the place where the devotion to knowledge and intellectual integrity remains most central, where it not merely survives but has great power. Caught in this devotion, many academic men and women find—as Max Weber once put it—a "demon who holds the fibers of their very lives" (1946, 156). Hence there is reason for optimism about the condition of American faculties in the 1990s and beyond the year 2000. But adverse conditions can do much damage to this core devotion. Supportive organization for faculty commitment is always necessary. It may even be the central component of viability in individual colleges and universities and in the welfare of the higher education system as a whole.

Acknowledgments

This chapter is based largely on a study, carried out between 1983 and 1986, that gave rise to my book, *The Academic Life: Small Worlds, Different Worlds* (1987), and on two articles in which I sought to highlight the primary findings and interpretations of the study: "Listening to the Professorate" (1985) and "The Academic Life: Small Worlds, Different Worlds" (1989).

References

Becher, Tony. 1989. *Academic Tribes and Territories: Intellectual Enquiry and the Cultures of Disciplines.* Milton Keynes, England, and Philadelphia: Society for Research into Higher Education and Open University Press.

Bellah, Robert N., Richard Madsen, William M. Sullivan, Ann Swidler, and Steven M. Tipton. 1985. *Habits of the Heart: Individualism and Commitment in American Life.* Berkeley and Los Angeles: University of California Press.

Carnegie Foundation for the Advancement of Teaching. 1990. "Early Faculty Retirees: Who, Why, and with What Impact?" *Change,* 22(4):31–34.

Clark, Burton R. 1985. "Listening to the Professorate." *Change,* 17(4):36–43.

———. 1987. *The Academic Life: Small Worlds, Different Worlds.* Princeton: Carnegie Foundation for the Advancement of Teaching.

———. 1989. "The Academic Life: Small Worlds, Different Worlds." *Educational Researcher,* 18(5):4–8.

Metzger, Walter. 1987. "The Academic Profession in the United States." In Burton R. Clark, ed., *The Academic Profession: National, Disciplinary, and Institutional Settings,* pp. 123–208. Berkeley and Los Angeles: University of California Press.

Seidman, Earl. 1985. *In the Words of the Faculty: Perspectives on Improving Teaching and Educational Quality in Community Colleges.* San Francisco: Jossey-Bass.

Weber, Max. 1946. "Science as a Vocation." In H.H. Gerth and C. Wright Mills, eds., *From Max Weber: Essays in Sociology,* pp. 129–156. New York: Oxford University Press.

Wiebe, R.H. 1967. *The Search for Order, 1877–1920.* New York: Hill and Wang.

11 The President: A Precarious Perch

JUDITH BLOCK McLAUGHLIN
AND DAVID RIESMAN

Listening to the recent crescendo of attacks on higher education, one would hardly know that the American nonsystem of higher education remains one of the more innovative and reasonably independent areas of American life. American colleges and universities remain a magnet for students and faculty from all over the world, a vote of confidence from overseas not matched by the chorus of complaints at home.[1] As the essays in this book illuminate, among the reasons for this are the enormous diversity of institutions, the unique nature of the lay governing board, and the adaptability of many colleges and universities to changes in society. Additionally, one important hallmark of American higher education is the nature of the college and university president. The leeway given the college and university presidency, disaggregated by locale and degrees of independence, creates a different constellation than one finds in other countries such as the United Kingdom and Germany, which also have advanced systems of higher education. In this chapter, we consider how the position of president has evolved over time, assess the changes in recent years in how presidents are chosen and who has become president, and suggest some of the significant challenges and dilemmas confronting presidents today.

The Growth of Responsibilities and Constituencies

In 1636, when Harvard College was created by an act of the Massachusetts General Court, legal responsibility for the new college was vested in a

board of overseers. One of the first actions of this board was the appointment of a president of the college. Although Harvard had been modeled
after Emmanuel College at Cambridge University, the position of president
in the new colonial college differed from the role of master in Emmanuel
College, for the British governance structure had to be adapted to the very
different circumstances of the new country. Whereas teaching fellows at
Cambridge elected the master and decided most institutional policies, no
similar educated group of faculty members existed in the new colonial
colleges. Classes were taught by young men studying for the clergy. Hence,
in the new American model of governance, the authority for governing the
institution rested with a lay governing board and the president whom this
board selected.

In these first colleges, the president comprised the entire administrative
staff of the college. He was the chief executive officer, the senior—and
typically only—member of the faculty,[2] the college chaplain, the institutional disciplinarian, and the liaison to the local community. As Joseph
Kauffman noted, "The early college president was the college. Its identity
became a reflection of his character, leadership, and personal success"
(1982, 13). But while, as it has sometimes been put, these colleges appeared
to be the "lengthened shadow" of their presidents, these eminences were by
no means immune to revolts from below, illustrated in Harvard's own case
by Bernard Bailyn's account of presidents who were ousted (Bailyn 1986).
Indeed, it was not long before there began the development of a student
culture—Phi Beta Kappa was an early example of student initiative—
which went its own way, relatively independent of disciplinary regulations
and helping to give rise to a phenomenon, an example of "American excep-
tionalism," namely, the alumni.[3]

Until the second half of the nineteenth century, the president remained
the central figure of college life. In the post–Civil War period, however,
American higher education underwent an extraordinary growth, resulting
in more students, more faculty members, more facilities and curricular
offerings, and, concomitantly, a substantial increase in management responsibilities and problems that the president could not handle alone. In
the 1870s, Presidents Andrew Dickson White at Cornell and Charles W.
Eliot at Harvard appointed faculty members to the newly created positions
of dean on their respective campuses. Within a few years, deanships existed
at most colleges, often both a dean of the faculty and a dean of the college
(the latter in charge of student concerns), to be followed shortly thereafter
by other administrative posts, including such positions as registrar and

librarian. The growth of "the administration" is perhaps best appreciated by such figures as these: the number of administrative officers at American colleges leapt from three to four in the 1880s to nearly sixty for large universities by 1930.

Much of our current, often nostalgically colored memories of presidents who were "great men" reflect the leaders who developed the first universities, including Charles W. Eliot at Harvard, Daniel Coit Gilman at Hopkins, and others whose work was made vivid to us in the accounts by Laurence Veysey (1965) and Frederick Rudolph (1962). Burton R. Clark's *The Distinctive College: Antioch, Reed and Swarthmore* (1970) described the salvation of the senescent Antioch by Arthur Morgan and his introduction of the off-campus co-op program; Reed's start under President William T. Foster as the serious nonplayboy, nonathletic campus it remains; and how Frank Aydelotte, refracting his experience at Oxford and managing by one vote to escape dismissal, transformed Swarthmore College from a local Friends' and also friendly college through the Swarthmore Honors Program, which, although embattled as "elitist," survives to this day.[4]

These strong presidents were not without their critics, however, the most vocal of them being members of their own faculties. The establishment of the American Association of University Professors as a monitoring group in 1915 was one indication of the growing power of faculty members. Faculty members held their greatest influence in the research universities, a genre of institution which has greatly expanded in the decades following the Second World War to include not only most of the land-grant institutions but also many private and public aspirants to doctorate-granting status. When the post–World War II G.I. Bill and the baby boom resulted in substantially increased enrollments at America's colleges and universities, faculty members found that they possessed still greater leverage. One result of this "academic revolution" (Jencks and Riesman 1968) was that decisions about academic matters, once made with varying degrees of consultation by presidents, their top administrators, and with decreasing involvement by boards of trustees, became almost entirely a faculty prerogative.

The "academic revolution" was quickly followed by the student revolutions of the 1960s, with their new demands for inclusion in institutional governance. Many presidents were forced out of office when they refused to bow to "nonnegotiable demands" made by activist students (almost invariably supported by faculty or other adult sponsors) or, on the contrary, when they were considered too complacent or compliant by the general public. One lasting result of this period of upheaval was the appointment of students to faculty and administrative committees. Another was that the radicalized and countercultural campuses also became the targets of a growing Right Wing backlash. During the past decade, as the numbers of prospective traditional age college students have dwindled, students (and their parents) have become an even more important constituency to which presidents must attend.

Presidents' lives also have grown increasingly complicated in the latter half of the twentieth century because of the larger role of the federal government in higher education. The G.I. Bill and subsequent federal arrangements for grants and loans to students along with growing support for university research right after World War II which has multiplied greatly since then have in recent years been accompanied by an increased monitoring of higher education, even in areas where the government has not been providing support. For example, the federal government has enforced affirmative action imperatives through the Equal Employment Opportunities Commission, bringing a new kind of external pressure and authority into the lives of presidents.[5] In 1990 the Department of Justice unsuccessfully brought suit against Virginia Military Institute, charging that its all-male status violated the equal protection clause of the Constitution. The Department of Justice also brought a suit under the antitrust laws against consortia, which include some of the most eminent Ivy League universities and private liberal arts colleges, charging that their tuitions were agreed upon in a monopolistic way (a charge without foundation and not actively pursued) and that their financial aid packages were handled in a cooperative fashion rather than through market competition—a charge the institutions accepted but defended as a legitimate arrangement that spread financial aid to those who really needed it, rather than bestowing it in a bidding war for capable and wealthy students. State and federal governments alike now demand of campuses much more in the way of reporting than was the case earlier. For example, crimes, including sexual assaults, must be reported annually and disclosed to prospective students and the press.

Such developments have meant that presidents, especially those who head research universities that depend heavily upon federal grants, must spend much larger chunks of their time focused on actions in Washington than ever before. Presidents have had to build larger administrative teams, routinely denounced as bureaucratic waste by faculty members and outside observers. The general disappearance of *in loco parentis* has been accompanied by an expansion in student services. Affirmative action officers have been necessary to see to compliance not only with what is juridically expected, but also with what is locally demanded and sought. In-house legal counsel advise the president and other administrators on issues of liability, reporting, response to campus protests, conflicts over so-called "hate speech," and disciplinary rulings. It takes a large staff to compile and report the data required by the federal, state, and sometimes also local government monitoring groups.

This increase in administrative positions has occurred even while parents, students, and much of society rage against the rises in tuition, public as well as private. Often criticized as being more than the rate of inflation, these tuitions reflect the fact that the costs of labor-intensive human services necessarily increase faster than the rate of inflation. What seems to us extraordinary has been the ability of presidents and their development offices to find new sources of philanthropic support, not only parents as important financial contributors, but even grandparents, to whom some colleges have begun to send fund-raising letters.[6]

Presidents have always been expected to be "all purpose people," able to perform a multitude of functions, available and responsive to all constituencies. But in other respects, the president of the contemporary college or university has little in common with his or her predecessor in the early American college. As a result of the increase in the extent and scale of responsibilities, the growth in number and power of constituencies, and the heightened expectations placed upon higher education, presidents today find themselves at the fulcrum of conflicting constituencies, internal and external, and differing values, interests, priorities, and perspectives.

Presidential Succession and Roles

Clark Kerr reported that when he was president at Berkeley he traveled to Bloomington, Indiana, to understand why it was that Indiana University had been able, like Harvard and only one or two other locales, to recruit a valued faculty member from Berkeley; he discovered Herman B. Wells, the courageous, inventive president whom in a recent essay he compared with John Hannah at Michigan State University (1991). These men were near-contemporary illustrations of the longevity of many college and university presidents in an earlier era. Today, by contrast, a five-year term is average and a fifteen- or twenty-year term exceptional.[7]

During the time of transition in leadership, the remembered past and the often tense present and feared or hoped-for futures all become engaged with the process of choosing a successor. Faculty members often insist that the next president must be a distinguished scholar with classroom and research credentials, while administrators and some trustees may emphasize the need for actual experience in higher educational administration. Local business leaders or state politicians may or may not insist that the next president have political connections, but they are among the constituents who insist that he or she have political savvy and skill.[8] Students may argue that the president should be someone who is visible on campus and regularly attends student functions, including major athletic events; alumni look to the president to personalize the institution and to maintain the traditions—academic, athletic, social, sometimes pastoral—they have come to value. But the priorities are not invariably as stereotypical as this suggests. On some campuses, for instance, it is the trustees who speak in favor of strong academic leadership while members of the faculty prefer a president who devotes time largely to raising money and leaves all educational decisions to them, and alumni may be divided among themselves as to whether their institution should stay the same as that idyllic place, frozen in memory, or be at the forefront of changes in society.

The first structured conversations about the role of the president typically occur early in the selection process when the search committee drafts a statement of qualifications for the position. This "wanted poster," called a job description, should more aptly be named a "person description" since it is an attempt to delineate the characteristics that the new president should possess. One sees these lists in the *Chronicle of Higher Education* each week: "President for such-and-such college," they begin and soon state, "Requirements for the position include . . ." Many times, the lists contain every conceivable virtue: the president should be a strong leader, a consensus builder; a fund-raiser with a track record of success and a distinguished scholar; should possess a commitment to affirmative action, evidence of collegial decision making, experience with collective bargaining, demonstrated competence in fiscal management, and the ability to articulate a vision for the institution.

Many lists represent attempts to be egalitarian, occasionally even listing the criteria for the presidency in alphabetical order, so as not to give more weight to one than another by its placement on the list. But lists of criteria are also so lengthy because they reflect popular expectations that the president somehow will manage all these roles effectively, will succeed at being all things to all people, and will do all things, if not equally well, then certainly all competently and some superbly.

It is easy to be cynical about these arguments concerning criteria and to forget the anguish of responsible members of the board of trustees, especially but not only in the independent sector, as they struggle with their responsibilities. For this very reason, trustees might find a certain relief in the cynical view of the presidency itself expressed by Stanford Professor James A. March over the years and more recently by Professor Robert Birnbaum, namely, that the office is more important as symbol than as substance, for in their view the president has little influence upon what Cohen and March in *Leadership and Ambiguity* referred to as an "organized anarchy" (1986). March counseled presidents to feel less apprehensive in their often anxiety-provoking settings, since in his view they can neither do very much harm nor very much that is useful (1980). Birnbaum discovered in interviewing presidents that they almost uniformly believed they had made a greater difference in their institutions than their predecessors had done (1986). Cynicism aside, surely there is merit in these observations as a counterweight to exaggeration of the role of the leader in a singularly "flat" semi-organization. Most of us believe that we have more free will than evolutionary biology and current theories of artificial intelligence suggest. Yet we ourselves have studied enough institutions where presidents have made a difference to believe that they can and often do. This is in no way inconsistent with their role as a symbolic statement about the kind of institution they nominally and in some measure actually direct. They are an institutional logo. In a universe of institutions, many but by no means all of which are aspiring to become better and certainly not to fall in esteem, the fact that the president is a nationally recognized scholar or has degrees from prestigious institutions may be important not because of the academic know-how or connections these may suggest, but because these insignia can reflect glory on the entire institution.[9]

Yet when we refer to a "nationally recognized scholar," we are pulled up short by the realization that we live in an age of mass elites, that the people who are nationally recognized are celebrities of entertainment, famous for longer or shorter spells—and *spells* is the right term for the charisma of these stars of a consumer society; virtually all of them—like that star of stars, Ronald Reagan—have risen from humble beginnings and seem therefore in a sense like everybody else and not anything so formidable as a "nationally recognized scholar" with "degrees from prestigious institutions." This celebrity world is not new. Walter Lippmann recognized its hazards in the 1920s, and so have students of charismatic movements. But it is only in the "postindustrial" television age that these celebrities seem to have eclipsed memory even among students in some of the most selective colleges and universities. When asked to recommend commencement speakers, these students often suggest actors or celebrities. Presidents can occasionally, by virtue of locale and their own talents, court in that league, but they cannot compete in it.[10]

Making the Choice

Presidential searches are generally the work of two groups: the governing board and the search committee. In a number of public institutions and less frequently in private colleges or universities, there will be a two-tier arrangement: the search committee whose membership is drawn from the governing board has ultimate power, and a subordinate but still presumably influential committee comprising representatives of campus constituencies will be assigned the initial screening and interviewing of candidates. More commonly today, however, there will be a single search committee that includes members of the governing board and representatives from the campus. If this committee includes major influential board members, it will be able to make a presumptively final decision, subject to pro forma ratification or, only in the rarest cases, rejection by the full board. Questions about the constitution of the search committee or committees and about which constituent groups will have how many representatives can embroil a campus in controversy at the very outset of the process. In many states, the search committee is, like the list of criteria, a potpourri with as many as two or three dozen members, including administrators, faculty members, representatives of the staff, students, alumni, and perhaps representatives of local business concerns.

Often the most desirable candidates are not especially eager to move to a new job, and they are almost never people desperate to leave their present posts. Yet only in the rarest circumstances can the person chairing a large committee create an ambience of candor and comity among its members which would make colloquy with candidates invitational and illuminating. Indeed, the assumption is commonly made that the main task of the search committee is to issue criteria, to advertise, to look at those who turn up, and then to make a choice, rather than recognizing that the most desirable prospects need to be persuaded to become candidates and then assiduously courted. Some states complicate the courtship further in their public sectors where, as in the State University of New York and the Massachusetts system, it is the local trustees who must choose the presidents, yet their choice needs to be confirmed by the system chancellor and the Board of Regents—a statewide governing group that will influence the resources and opportunities the new incumbent might mobilize. Most people chosen as system heads have been campus heads, sometimes within the system, more commonly from elsewhere; there is a widespread failure to recognize that the qualities requisite in a system head are not identical to those desirable to lead a campus. To the system head, the "constituents" are the campuses, not their individual faculty members or student bodies. Yet because they are so often chosen from former campus administrators, they frequently compete for visibility with the presidents of the flagship campuses, particularly when they have their own headquarters in Madison, Wisconsin; Tuscaloosa, Alabama; Boulder, Colorado; or Durham, New Hampshire.

The growing recognition of the traps for the unwary that a search presents—to candidates as well as to search committees—has led in recent years to an increasing use of professional assistance from consulting firms. Although board members with corporate backgrounds have long been familiar with the use of executive search firms, only recently have they begun to employ such firms in higher education; it is only within the past decade that there has been a proliferation of firms, both for-profit and not-for-profit, bidding to assist in presidential searches. What consultants do and are asked to do varies enormously. Some help the board and the search committee to understand their own institution, sometimes discovering problems and dilemmas not previously recognized; often such consultants write a description of the institution to help inform candidates as well as the board. Capable consultants can help the search committee appreciate how their institution is perceived from the outside and realize that, although they may believe they are offering a splendid opportunity, the most desirable candidates may not see it that way. Consultants use their own contacts to expand the roster of recruits, expend varying amounts of energy on checking references, facilitate the interview process with the most viable candidates, and occasionally—too seldom, in our own view—help with final arrangements. In a few cases, the decision as to which of the many aspirant search consultant firms to hire can become a kind of trial run for the final selection of candidates, while in other cases the selection by trustees of what faculty members regard as corporate-style "headhunters" can create friction at the outset. Altogether, approximately 60 percent of presidential searches currently hire a search consultant.

Perhaps no other issue in the selection process is as complex and as controversial as the question of the degree of confidentiality vis-à-vis candidates and vis-à-vis discussions and votes by the committee and the board. Under Florida's "sunshine law," nothing is supposed to be confidential, not letters of recommendation, not meetings with candidates, not discussions on the search committee or on the Board of Regents. Other states' "open meeting" and "open record" laws sometimes grant exemptions for personnel, and these are interpreted to permit searches to be conducted with confidentiality; Arizona's legislation has been interpreted by the Arizona Supreme Court to allow confidentiality for applicants and nominees until the point at which they are contacted by the search committee or its representative. For a number of years, efforts to obtain an exemption have failed in Florida in the face of pressure from the media, but in Texas the combined power of the University of Texas system and the Texas A&M system achieved exemption by a recent statutory amendment. Even in private institutions or in public institutions where confidentiality is not prohibited by law, however, it is not always attained. Leaks occur by maneuver, malice, mishap, or the combination of journalistic ingenuity with good luck, as, for example, when a private plane is spotted at a small airport, leading to a hunch about the search at a nearby college. Confidentiality for members of the search committee and the board is essential if they are to be candid with each other rather than performing for their constituents. Confidentiality is also salient when one seeks to recruit sitting presidents or others whose effectiveness depends on the belief that they are loyal to their institutions and not shopping around in search of something better. Yet instances arise where those conducting the search must choose between complete confidentiality and assuring the legitimacy of the search. Both private and public institutions sometimes bring from two to five "finalists" to campus to help reassure constituents that their participation is wanted, while also providing the visiting candidates with a varyingly representative, although generally exhausting, set of glimpses into the institutional subcultures. In addition to the danger that such a procedure will lead some prospects to withdraw, there is a further hazard, namely, that the serious deliberations and inquiries of the search committee will be undercut by the plausible campaign for a candidate favored only by a small minority of the search committee, and even by them not as a first choice.

It is often said by the journalistic and academic defenders of public scrutiny of candidates that it is just such scrutiny that they will have to endure as presidents, so that it is important to see how they manage, or stage-manage, the process when they come as candidates. We have already made clear that presidents need to be adept at managing many publics. They cannot afford to be diffident and reclusive. But it is obvious that there are other ways to gauge the public persona of potential presidents than to ask them to assume the risks associated with disclosure of their candidacy. For example, John DiBiaggio as president of the University of Connecticut had already exhibited his adeptness in dealing with the legislature and state executives. However, when he agreed to become a candidate in a "sunshine" search for the presidency of the University of Florida, came to the campus as a finalist, and then was not chosen, he was not only deprecated in Connecticut for making evident his lack of institutional loyalty, but also flawed as someone whom the University of Florida had rejected. Only with the help of a consultant and the promise of complete confidentiality did he agree to become a candidate for the presidency of Michigan State University. In fact, confidentiality was so important to him that he did not visit the campus until after he had accepted the offer of the presidency.

Even someone who has been a president needs help in appreciating the differences between the former and the present institution. In our book on presidential searches (1991), we contended that this is an important role consultants can play, although they almost never do. The person who has chaired the search committee has often found it an exhausting and even nerve-wracking opportunity—and we have seen a number of cases where this person has taken off on a vacation trip or in any case regards his or her task as accomplished. Moreover, the departing president is often not particularly helpful to the successor. There may be resentment and the fear of being outshone. Or it sometimes occurs that the predecessor holds back out of what we regard as a false sense of what is appropriate, fearing to prejudice the successor, for this understandable outlook demeans the newcomer by assuming that what the departing president says will be accepted without any further inquiry. The new incumbent is often lonely, facing problems that look simple but may not be. We are reminded of one president who, on his arrival, observed that the cars parked in the roadway outside the administration building disfigured the stunning landscape and suggested that they be removed; he was lucky to be informed by his executive assistant that the dean had for many centuries parked his car in just that spot, whereupon he canceled the order of removal! In large matters and in small symbolic ones, the newcomer can easily go astray, sometimes from assuming that the current scene is similar to the one he or she has just left. Only on rare occasions do consultants help newcomer presidents in working out with the chairman of the board such touchy matters as repair of the assigned presidential house or the privileges and responsibilities of the spouse, for the newcomer does not want to appear greedy or inept—and in any case will have major institutional issues, whether enrollment decline or a projected fund drive or curricular revision, to cope with. Given the scarce resources that presidents are—and the relatively short time on average that they now spend on a particular campus—they need all the coaching they are willing to accept, a role the consultant can sometimes play without being thought to represent a particular vested interest.

Who Becomes President?

Consultants are often chosen in part because they offer an assurance that the choice will not be a parochial one, either in terms of geography or in terms of gender or origin. When Nicholas J. Demerath, Richard W. Stephens, and R. Robb Taylor published *Power, Presidents, and Professors* in 1967, they reported that well over half of presidents did not travel very far geographically, but either got their education or had worked not far from their current locales. There are still such local choices, but it is now rare for such an outcome to be foreordained. In 1991, the definitions of who is eligible for the post of president are much broader for many institutions than they were several decades, and even one decade, ago. To illustrate: the inaugural class of the Harvard Seminar for New Presidents in the summer of 1990 included many presidents who were "firsts" for their institutions. Five of the six women in the seminar were the first women to serve as president of their college or university (four of these are presidents of coeducational colleges; one is the first woman president of a women's college). Other presidents who were "firsts" for their institutions included an African-American president of a state university, an Asian-American president of a state college, and a native American president of a community college. Additionally, there were several "first" Jewish presidents and one president who was the first lay president of his college.

Right through to the first part of this century, all of the presidents of Boston University had been Methodist ministers (this tradition is one of the reasons why Martin Luther King, Jr., was attracted there for his doctoral work), but it is hard to find a trace of the Methodist connection now in any of the once-Methodist string of urban institutions that includes Boston University, American University, Washington University, Syracuse University, Southern Methodist University (which has a Catholic president), the University of Denver, and the University of Southern California. A number of the smaller Protestant colleges have sought to maintain links with their denominations, notably in the South, where Trinity University in San Antonio and Davidson College have kept their ties with the Presbyterians and Birmingham-Southern and Austin College have kept theirs with the Methodists; just as in Utah Brigham Young University remains firmly within the orbit of the Church of Jesus Christ of Latter Day Saints. Wake Forest University has curtailed its ties with the Southern Baptists, and Furman and Baylor universities are straining against those ties as the Southern Baptist conventions have moved in the fundamentalist direction. Among Catholic institutions degrees of change in the orbits of choice vary, even though as of this writing each of the twenty-eight Jesuit institutions has managed to find a Jesuit to lead it,[11] but the trustees of many other Catholic institutions—already a laicized and relatively independent group—have recognized that the insistence on a priest or nun may greatly limit choice. Even so, some institutions have elected to retain their stipulation that the president be a priest, or even a priest of a certain order. When, after many exuberant years, Theodore Hesburgh, C.S.C., announced his intention to retire from the presidency of Notre Dame, several priests of that order were brought in to become, as it were, apprentices; one of these, Father Edward Malloy, C.S.C., was eventually chosen to succeed Hesburgh. The diocesan University of St. Thomas chose Dennis J. Dease as its new president in 1991, out of a pool of twenty-four priests. Other Catholic institutions, seeking a wider orbit, have chosen to look outside religious circles.

Another widening of orbits is in terms of the backgrounds from which presidents come. Those vaulting directly from professorial life to a presidency in the mode of Bart Giamatti at Yale and Nannerl Keohane at Wellesley—the latter had chaired the Stanford University faculty senate but not held an administrative position—are rare. Most presidents are seasoned administrators by the time they reach the presidency. Another change in the background of presidents is that more have the Ed.D. degree than ever before. The chief executives of two leading state systems—David Gardner of the University of California, Bruce Johnstone of the State University of New York—have Ed.D degrees. In part, this new acceptance of a degree other than the Ph.D. has to do with recognition of the legitimacy of leading doctoral programs that give the Ed.D. It also reflects the increased emphasis on having people in the presidency with significant background in educational management, in contrast to those whose primary focus has been research and teaching in an academic department. Law school deans have in recent years become presidents of leading liberal arts colleges, as well as of major universities, including Berkeley, Columbia, Dartmouth, Harvard, Indiana, Santa Cruz, and Yale. Thomas Kean, notable for his interest in education when he was governor of New Jersey, is now the president of his alma mater, Drew University—an example of local choice of someone with a national reputation.

There are also more "repeaters" in the presidency today, presidents who are serving as the chief executive officer of their second or third institution. Examples abound: Princeton's Howard Shapiro came there from the presidency of Michigan and Dartmouth's James Freedman from the presidency of Iowa. James Robinson moved in the reverse direction—from a small private liberal arts college to the public sector—when he departed the presidency of Macalester College for the presidency of the University of West Florida. Gordon Gee at Ohio State was previously president of the University of Colorado system and before that of West Virginia University. Marguerite Ross Barnett is president of the University of Houston after having been chancellor of the St. Louis campus of the University of Missouri. Janet Greenwood was president of Longwood College in the Virginia state system and is currently president of the University of Bridgeport in Connecticut, which is private. Robert H. Edwards, one of many lawyer-presidents, served nine years as president of Carleton College, then on the staff of the Aga Khan's charitable and educational enterprises in Paris, and in 1990 became president of Bowdoin College. Daniel H. Perlman went from the urban commuter campus of Suffolk University in Boston, which had started out primarily as a night law school, to the presidency of Webster University, once a Catholic women's college.

Appreciation of the complexity of the task of the president has increasingly led to the choice of someone who has been a president heretofore, recognizing that the institution cannot afford to wait while a new recruit learns for the first time on the job how to be a president. For presidents themselves, the interest in assuming another presidency may be not only the desire to assume new challenges in a new setting but also the fact that there are only limited postpresidential options. Today it is more difficult even for full-time scholars to keep current in their academic discipline, and the intense demands on the presidency make it extremely unlikely that one can retain a substantial tie to one's research (unless that is in the field of higher education itself); it is somewhat less difficult, though still hard, to schedule what many presidents most enjoy, an opportunity to teach or co-teach a seminar for freshmen or another undergraduate course.

Almost wherever we look on the academic landscape, we see the exercise of entrepreneurial talents—presidents who take risks to rescue failing or moribund institutions. When our fellow contributor, David Breneman, was president of Kalamazoo College, he helped persuade the board and the rest of the institution to remain a liberal arts college rather than cultivating the enormous market for undergraduate business courses chosen by as many as half of the students in many private colleges. Kalamazoo, with 1,270 students largely from within the state and right next door to Western Michigan University, tempts its students away from immediate undergraduate professionalism by requiring them to have off-campus experience in internships in the United States and in many overseas settings, exposing them in this way to the "real world" and to many career opportunities. Robert Knott took over at Tusculum College in Greeneville, Tennessee, nearly failing and threatened with closing. President Knott persuaded the faculty to adopt the Colorado College plan of focusing on a single subject at a time; the college discovered that this radical rather than marginal differentiation from its rivals proved attractive in high degree. By not stereotyping "the students," Tusculum discovered an audience extending well beyond its Tennessee orbit. To help sustain Chatham College, a faltering women's college in Pittsburgh, first Alberta Arthurs and then Rebecca Stafford as presidents recruited older women who could live in the dormitories along with their children, not only helping keep the college afloat, but also introducing a new diversity, namely, students in an expensive private liberal arts college who are not between the ages of seventeen and twenty-three.

There have also been transformational presidents at institutions where mere viability was not an issue. Three success stories come to mind. The University of California at San Diego was inaugurated in 1964 as one of the three new campuses initiated under Clark Kerr's presidency of the system; in a very short time it attained enormous scholarly eminence. George Mason University began as a campus separate from the University of Virginia in 1972 and benefited from the growth of population in its northern Virginia location. Emory University is another success story, also located in an area of in-migration and economic growth. Each has attempted to do more than "follow the leader," whether defined as Berkeley, Duke, or the University of Virginia. Each has been shaped by its leadership toward distinctiveness as well as distinction.

Not all entrepreneurial activity goes unpunished. On 22 March 1991, the former president of the University of South Carolina, James B. Holderman, was indicted in Columbia, South Carolina, on charges of illegally using the presidency for personal gain (Smothers 1991, 6). When he became president in 1974 Holderman was determined to rival Chapel Hill in terms of national visibility. He also sought to deprovincialize the institution, bringing such people as Henry Kissinger and Jihan Sadat, the widow of the assassinated Egyptian president, Anwar Sadat, to lecture and offer symposia on the Columbia, South Carolina, campus. Large fees were paid to these individuals and to other celebrities. And Holderman himself apparently believed that it took money and the look of money to bring in money: he lived lavishly and courted donors with expensive gifts, escorted them in rented limousines, and took princely suites in hotels when he traveled, using funds—also a supplement to his salary—of the Carolina Research and Development Foundation, which, not dependent on "taxpayers' money," did not need to open its accounts to journalistic exploration. The media were in hot pursuit. When Holderman resigned under pressure, leaving to enter business in Florida, scrutiny continued, and the indictment suggests that he did exploit his position for personal gain, introducing the president of the Dominican Republic, whom he had brought to the campus, to members of a local law firm, which reimbursed Holderman for making the connection.

Such instances of personal gain are rare. It was not personal gain that caused Brunetta Wolfman to be forced out of Roxbury Community College in Boston when she drew on foundation funds to pay her way at fundraising events for local politicians who might help the college. Even more clearly it is not personal gain when presidents are forced out because of what are seen as overluxurious repairs to the president's house. When Kenneth Keller was president of the University of Minnesota, he was charged with elitism for wanting the university to focus on things it might do superbly well and abandon others; when revelations appeared in the press, day after day, about the costly renovations in the president's not especially stately campus house and in his newly redecorated offices, he was forced to resign.[12]

What Presidents Face

In his book on the *ancien regime,* Tocqueville observed that revolutions occur not when things are getting worse, but when they are getting better— but not better fast enough to meet rising expectations. Much of higher education unevenly across the country seems to be in this position today. It survived and even grew astonishingly during a period of demographic decline in the number of young people of college age, in part by ingeniously turning to adult education and making good on the promise of America, namely, that we are not only a second but even a third chance country, where people can have multiple careers, each boosted by a further round of adult education. However, as more and more academic "firms" entered the competition for students, higher education became more costly as tuition was discounted by financial aid and as state and federal support for financial aid declined in relative and in some states even in absolute terms. Some private colleges are now in the position where the cost of each additional recruited student almost equals what that student can be expected to contribute in the way of tuition, no matter how that tuition is financed, and where the high attrition of marginal students often means that the student will hardly have paid off the costs of recruiting him or her before departing.

Another market many institutions entered was that for private funds from corporations, foundations, and individuals. It was once the case that a certain tacit treaty existed between the public and the independent sectors, in which the former would maintain low tuitions and keep out of the market for philanthropy. Now, however, although public tuition—while rising—is still inconsequential in comparison with most private tuition, public institutions are going after the same private philanthropy that is being courted by the independent sector.[13] To counter the increasing odds against them, college and university development offices have come up with sophisticated techniques for discovering where the money is. For major gifts the president is an essential player—and meeting the budget is a never-ending preoccupation. It is important to add that many presidents discover to their astonishment that they enjoy raising money. If they have come from academic life, it is a route to meeting new kinds of people and, escaping the loneliness on campus, even making new friends.

No matter what the pressures to raise money, there are judgments as to what is good money and what is bad money, with many people refusing to accept the premise that has long supported American philanthropy, namely, that "bad money" is well laundered by doing "good"! The issue of investments in companies that do business in South Africa has been an ongoing debate on many campuses. In 1990, at Derek Bok's next to last commencement as Harvard University's president, he announced that the university would divest all stocks in tobacco companies. Pharmaceutical companies may be deemed inappropriate donors if they support research making use of animals over the opposition of animal rights activists.[14]

Viewed from a perspective other than philanthropy, animal rights incursions on a campus illustrate the crises—what might be termed the *industrial accidents*—that can unseat a president. A publicized fraternity hazing, a gang rape, a professor's sexual misconduct, a complaint by a black student of a professor's racism, a suicide, or any concatenation of these events can plunge a president into a situation in which capitulation to demands or a perceived failure to respond to demands may each lead to forced resignation.

The president is generally the central figure around whom such issues revolve. It is in presidents' offices that sit-ins frequently occur, often on issues of race, although occasionally on other matters such as opposition to ROTC or military recruitment on campus because of the military's refusal to accept homosexuals. During the McCarthy era, on those few generally more visible campuses that were touched by the issues, there was a considerable degree of unity among the more eminent faculty, united in the defense of academic freedom. Presidents who shared in that defense might be toppled by trustees or state officials. Those who, like Robert M. Hutchins at the

University of Chicago or Harold Taylor at Sarah Lawrence College, defended academic freedom had most of the faculty on their side.[15] Today, in contrast, it is the campus itself that is divided, and the president, despite or indeed because of efforts toward comity, is often caught in the crossfire. There is a fierceness to the debates about diversity, as well as a strong backlash, seen recently in the outcry over allegations of "political correctness." The questions are often morally ambiguous; "right" and "wrong" are not easily determined.[16]

Athletic overemphasis is not a new menace to presidential equilibrium. It has been there for many academic generations.[17] New are the enormous amounts of money that can be obtained through television coverage, as well as the ancillary moneys from coaches and stars endorsing athletic shoes or other consumer goods. Furthermore, when institutions need support from alumni and, in the public sector, from the legislature, it helps to have winning teams and badly hurts to have losing ones—again, especially in football, but among some circles, particularly the smaller Catholic colleges, in basketball as well. The University of Connecticut surprised itself and the state by having a fabulous basketball season in 1989–90, thus winning needed support statewide at a time of drastic curtailment of budgets for all public institutions in depression-prone New England, with Maine as the lone exception.

The revenue shortfalls of recent years have caught by surprise even some of the more reflective presidential planners. In an independent college, some searing publicized episode on campus can lead to a dramatic falloff in applications for enrollment, resulting in empty dormitories and bewilderment as to whether to cut staff who might be needed should conditions improve next year. State cuts can be draconian and sudden as higher education competes with ever more costly health care, prison and police services, and the not infrequent success of public employees, including schoolteachers, who use or threaten strikes to improve wages and what are often the more costly but less visible constraints of the union contract. The tightening fiscal situation is accompanied by demands for increased audit and accountability throughout the public sector, at the federal and at the state and local levels as well. Tuitions seem to be reaching a ceiling, up against not only the fiscal pressures on students' parents, but also ideological resistance. Part of this resistance reflects the widespread belief that most professors, rather than a highly visible but numerically small cohort, spend their time in societally unproductive research, rather than attending to the young people, especially to the undergraduates. The assumption in these attacks, such as Charles Sykes's widely circulated *ProfScam* (1988), is that the students are eager for contact with the professors and, but for the latter's shoddy neglect, would emerge from college thoroughly well prepared and highly motivated. Here again presidents are in the midst of cross-pressures, much as school superintendents have been for quite a while, faced with expectations from adults, including parents, which the adults themselves are unprepared to enforce upon their own and other people's adolescent, superficially sophisticated young people.

Beleaguered presidents are often under pressure to provide a more culturally diverse and more international curriculum and, at the same time, to reduce teaching "loads"—that interesting term. In the better liberal arts colleges, many presidents find it difficult to recruit faculty members, especially since so many are partners in two-career families, who have the time and energy to devote at once to intense undergraduate teaching in small classes, the demanding committee service required by participatory/democratic governance, and their scholarly aspirations, which they hold in part as protection toward an uncertain future. Back at the ranch, so to speak, where these faculty members are prepared, at Stanford and at Harvard, presidents have worked hard to reconcile the demands of teaching and of research, responsive, for example, to critiques such as that of Ernest Boyer in *College* (1988) and *Scholarship Reconsidered* (1990).

Presidents in this last decade of the twentieth century are considerably more vulnerable from the inside—because of vastly increased faculty power coupled at times with mobilized student power—and perhaps less vulnerable, if only marginally so, extramurally. The cuts that presidents have to make, the disappointments they have to bestow, create a situation in which they are constantly disappointing constituents who, in the American fashion, hold rising expectations. As the one person with perspective on the entire institution, the president is also the one person most likely to be blamed. We suspect that we may be seeing some presidents with foreshortened terms of office because, once they have executed the budgetary decisions, they cannot survive the anger directed at them. Yet we continue to meet presidents who are sanguine even in such settings, for whom the challenges mean that there are many exasperating but hardly any dull moments. Moreover, despite the maze of constraints, the president retains veto power and influence on appointing power at every level and, when financial circumstances improve, a measure of initiating power, though subject in some degree to faculty veto. We have known many presidents who are sufficiently secure with their own boards of trustees and able to exercise leadership well beyond the orbit of their own institutions, whether in seeking to reform intercollegiate athletics or in mobilizing institutions toward the teaching of ethics. Many presidents persist—and succeed—despite the manifold problems facing them, and their institutions are the fortunate beneficiaries of their commitment, talent, and prodigious energy.

Notes

1. See Kerr (1991) for a description of this stability.

2. Harvard existed for more than eighty-five years and Yale for fifty years before either had a full-time faculty member other than the college's president. See Martin Trow, "The University Presidency: Comparative Reflections on Leadership" (1984, 19).

3. When, in the recent years of Margaret Thatcher's stringency vis-à-vis higher education, Oxford conceived the notion of soliciting support from alumni, they turned in the first instance to the Rhodes scholars from the United States, whose undergraduate educations had already socialized them toward the expectation of responsiveness vis-à-vis the philanthropy sought by "their" college. On the general development of independent student subcultures, see Helen Horowitz (1987).

4. For the importance placed by undergraduates on their fellow students being friendly and how odd this requirement appears to non-Americans, see the account of contemporary student culture by the anthropologist Michael Moffatt, who lived as a fieldworker in Rutgers College dormitories, *Coming of Age in New Jersey* (1989), and also his pictorial account and commentary on Rutgers history (1985).

5. In University of Pennsylvania v. EEOC, the United States Supreme Court, in a unanimous decision, declared that, when gender or ethnic discrimination is charged, confidential tenure files must be made public; the tone of the opinion suggested that there was nothing special about universities; nothing to distinguish them from a law firm or an accounting partnership, and no reason why their procedures should have more privacy than those of a business. The unexpected unanimity of the decision, as well as the tone of the opinion, along with the antitrust suit mentioned in the text, seem to be signals that higher education is suspect and deprecated, so to speak, Left, Right, and Center.

6. On the massive entry of state universities into the fund-raising competition, even while their still very low tuitions subsidize many well-to-do students, especially in the "Public Ivies," see the interview by Russell Edgerton with Riesman (1989). The private sector has now been reduced to less than one-fifth of the total number of enrolled students.

7. Marian Gade, who co-authored two studies with Clark Kerr, *The Many Lives of Academic Presidents* (1986) and *The Guardians* (1989), suggested that the shorter tenure of presidents today may be an illusion, since so many presidents continue on to assume other presidencies. If their total years of presidency were considered, they would be as long-serving in the presidency as many presidents of yesteryear. In an age of second marriages and more frequent moving from corporation to corporation than ever before, she commented, a similar transfer rate in the presidency should hardly be surprising.

8. In his 1918 volume, *The Higher Learning in America: A Memorandum on the Conduct of Universities by Businessmen,* Thorstein Veblen saw university presidents as engaged in "a faithful travesty" of business, "peculiarly open to the appeal of parade and ephemeral celebrity, and peculiarly heedless of the substance of their performance"—the nature of the office made ambiguity the "dominant note of his [the president's] official life," and he becomes "an itinerant dispensary of salutary verbiage." (Veblen 1918; for discussion, see Sowell 1986).

9. In his chapter, "The Academic Procession," in *Constraint and Variety in American Education* (1956), Riesman portrayed colleges and universities as moving in a "snake-like procession," in which those in the rear sought to imitate where they mistakenly believed the head of the procession—Harvard, Michigan, Chapel Hill, Cal Tech, Berkeley—to be, failing to perceive the changes in those taken to be the leaders. He believes that this was an exaggeration. There are many institutions that are not in this sense aspirant, preferring to hold the market niche they already have rather than to clamber after others. While there may be a number of institutions which have their eyes on what is now a national "marketplace" of eminences, others remain much more local and less distracted by what they believe to be voguish.

10. When he was president of American University in Washington, D.C., Richard Berendzen, by academic profession an astronomer, courted big names as part of his drive to raise the visibility at once of his university and himself and to raise the funds needed to build a sports-and-conference center. He described a segment of this ceaseless quest in his autobiography, *Is My Armor Straight? A Year in the Life of a College President* (1986). The well-to-do with whom he associated did not always welcome one another; for example, Adnan Kashoggi, frequently attacked as an Arab "arms merchant," was hard to bring into colloquy with many gift-prone Jews. Four years after the publication of his memoir, Berendzen was disclosed as having made obscene telephone calls to a woman in northern Virginia. Berendzen was required not only, of course, to resign from the presidency, but also to surrender the settlement the trustees had offered him in exchange for his tenure as professor of astronomical physics. As a result of these events, Berendzen appeared in *People* magazine and became far more visible, to his and the University's embarrassment, than he had ever been hitherto.

In the winter of 1990–91, two distinguished presidents of eminent institutions— Donald Kennedy at Stanford and David Baltimore at Rockefeller University—became nationally visible for what seemed to be quite different sorts of scandals. After faculty members at Stanford had complained about Stanford's 80 percent overhead charge on government grants for its research, auditors from the Office of Naval Research discovered that the pool dubbed "overhead" included such impolitic expenses as $2,000 a month for the upkeep of Donald Kennedy's garden and $2,000 a month for the laundry for the president's home, as well as expenses for the university's yacht. The complicated story of how the overhead at Stanford was actually calculated and the arguments as to why presidential entertaining might be considered a legitimate cost of "doing business" got lost in the swell of outrage. In the summer of 1991, though convinced he had done nothing wrong, Donald Kennedy, in an effort to limit the continuing damage, resigned his decade-long presidency.

When David Baltimore, a Nobel Prize winner, was at M.I.T., he co-authored a scientific paper with Thereza Imanishi-Kari; later another M.I.T. scholar, Margot O'Toole, a postdoctoral researcher, came to Baltimore and said that she doubted the accuracy of Imanishi-Kari's data. Here also the issue is a complicated one and includes inquiries by M.I.T. itself and by the National Institute of Mental Health. Congressman John Dingell, who is a fierce pursuer of real or alleged dubious practices by universities and is also involved in examining the legitimacy of overhead charged the federal government on research contracts, put the Secret Service onto the case; they concluded that Imanishi-Kari was not simply careless, as Baltimore and she herself had declared, but had apparently fabricated data. At this writing, David Baltimore is still president of Rockefeller University, but many faculty members, originally not happy with his appointment, are calling for his resignation.

11. However, in 1990, the Jesuit University of Detroit merged with Mercy College, conducted by the religious Sisters of Mercy, to become the University of Detroit/Mercy College, just as earlier Loyola University in Los Angeles had merged with a Catholic women's college to become Loyola Marymount University.

12. During the years now apparently ending of increasing real estate values, to live in a house one does not own has been costly to presidents if, as in virtually all cases, they left before death. The irony of the president's mansion is that it appears luxurious to many on the faculty and in the locality even while the family that inhabits it often finds its privacy invaded as curious guests, during the many occasions when the house is used for public hospitality, wander upstairs to inspect the "private" quarters and, as many report, sometimes walk off with items easily concealed, including the silver! We have noticed a tendency, not yet strong enough to be called a trend, for new presidents to insist on having their own homes off campus rather than living in the institutionally provided one. For the view of one ironic spouse, see Jean Kemeny's memoir, *It's Different at Dartmouth* (1979).

13. In litigation by the *Albuquerque Tribune* to open the records of a presidential search at the University of New Mexico, there was constant reference to the "public's right to know" because "taxpayers' money" was involved. We were surprised to discover that, although the University of New Mexico is not a major research university, only 30 percent of its support comes from "New Mexico taxpayers' money"; the rest comes from tuition and fees, federal and other research grants, and the kinds of philanthropy we have just been discussing. The University of Vermont receives only 17 percent of its money from the state.

14. This cohort of groups ranging from the mild to the terrorist has become an increasing burden for the leaders of institutions with medical schools or where other research is carried on—and in fact much research has actually come to a virtual halt because it has involved the use of chimpanzees. Supporters include many who attack "speciesism," the notion that humans have superior rights to other forms of life and particularly their close evolutionary kin, the chimpanzee.

15. This short text has to substitute for a more nuanced account, for example, Paul F. Lazarsfeld and Wagner Thielens, *The Academic Mind: Social Scientists in a Time of Crisis* (1958) and Riesman's "Field Report" therein, based on visits to some fifty campuses and interviews on the effect—absent in the majority of less scholarly colleges—of the national-al and local McCarthyite attacks.

16. A number of presidents have supported campus codes that mandate freedom from harassment, sometimes including freedom from "hate speech." These codes get entangled with legal issues and First Amendment rights—one of the many arenas in which presidents today, much more than was the case even a few years ago, find themselves in the presence of a cohort of college or university counsel whose guidance the president needs to cope with affirmative action issues as well as to be prepared for injuries incurred on the university's premises, whether in a dormitory, in a laboratory, or on a playing field. Many colleges and universities that in the past used an outside firm for only episodic legal advice have had to develop their own permanent counsel. Harvard's Office of Legal Counsel, headed for the past twenty years by Vice President and Counsel Daniel Steiner, now has a dozen lawyers.

17. Football goes back a century (Riesman and Denney 1951). Basketball is more recent. It has been interesting in just these last months to observe colleges and universities that have stayed out of competitive football, emphasizing soccer instead in the case of some liberal arts colleges, almost as an antidote to the frequent brutality of football,

decide that if they are going to appeal for funds not only to their alumni but locally, they must, while recognizing the hazards, enter the competition.

References

Bailyn, Bernard, Donald Fleming, Oscar Handlin, and Stephan Thernstrom. 1986. *Glimpses of the Harvard Past.* Cambridge: Harvard University Press.

Berendzen, Richard. 1986. *Is My Armor Straight? A Year in the Life of a College President.* Bethesda, Md.: Adler and Adler.

Birnbaum, Robert. 1986. "Leadership as Learning: The College President as Intuitive Scientist." *Review of Higher Education,* 9:381–395.

Boyer, Ernest. 1988. *College: The Undergraduate Experience in America.* New York: Harper and Row.

————. 1990. *Scholarship Reconsidered: Priorities of the Professoriate.* Princeton: Carnegie Foundation for the Advancement of Teaching.

Clark, Burton R. 1970. *The Distinctive College: Antioch, Reed and Swarthmore.* Chicago: Aldine.

Cohen, Michael D., and James A. March. 1986. *Leadership and Ambiguity.* New York: Harper and Row.

Demerath, Nicholas J., Richard W. Stephens, and R. Robb Taylor. 1967. *Power, Presidents, and Professors.* New York: Basic Books.

Edgerton, Russell. 1989. "The Next Academic Revolution: David Riesman on the Next Generation of the Professoriate." *AAHE Bulletin,* 42(1):4–8.

Horowitz, Helen. 1987. *Campus Life: Undergraduate Culture from the End of the Eighteenth Century to the Present.* Chicago: University of Chicago Press.

Jencks, Christopher, and David Riesman. 1968. *The Academic Revolution.* New York: Doubleday.

Kauffman, Joseph. 1982. "The College Presidency—Yesterday and Today." *Change,* 14(3):12–19.

Kemeny, Jean. 1979. *It's Different at Dartmouth: A Memoir.* Brattleboro, Vt.: Stephen Greene Press.

Kerr, Clark. 1991. "The New Race to Be Harvard or Berkeley or Stanford." *Change,* 23(3):8–15.

Kerr, Clark, and Marian Gade. 1986. *The Many Lives of Academic Presidents.* Washington, D.C.: Association of Governing Boards of Universities and Colleges.

————. 1989. *The Guardians: Boards of Trustees of American Colleges and Universities: What They Do and How Well They Do It.* Washington, D.C.: Association of Governing Boards of Universities and Colleges.

Lazarsfeld, Paul F., and Wagner Thielens. 1958. *The Academic Mind: Social Scientists in a Time of Crisis.* Glencoe, Ill.: Free Press.

McLaughlin, Judith Block, and David Riesman. 1991. *Choosing a College President: Opportunities and Constraints.* Princeton: Carnegie Foundation for the Advancement of Teaching.

March, James A. 1980. "How We Talk and How We Act: Administrative Theory and Administrative Life." David D. Henry Lecture, University of Illinois, Urbana, September.

Moffatt, Michael. 1985. *The Rutgers Picture Book: An Illustrated History of Student Life in the Changing College and University.* New Brunswick, N.J.: Rutgers University Press.

———. 1989. *Coming of Age in New Jersey: College and American Culture.* New Brunswick, N.J.: Rutgers University Press.

Riesman, David. 1956. "The Academic Procession." In *Constraint and Variety in American Education.* New York: Doubleday.

———. 1958. "Field Report." In Paul F. Lazarsfeld and Wagner Thielens, eds., *The Academic Mind: Social Scientists in a Time of Crisis.* Glencoe, Ill.: Free Press.

Riesman, David, and Reuel Denney. 1951. "Football in America: A Study in Culture Diffusion." *American Quarterly,* 3:309–325.

Rudolph, Frederick. 1962. *The American College and University: A History.* New York: Random House.

Smothers, Ronald. 1991. "Ex-Leader of University Is Charged with Malfeasance in South Carolina" *New York Times,* 23 March, p. 6.

Sowell, Thomas. 1986. "Veblen's Higher Learning after Fifty Years." In *Education: Assumptions versus History,* pp. 175–187. Stanford, Calif.: Hoover Institution Press.

Sykes, Charles J. 1988. *ProfScam: Professors and the Demise of Higher Education.* Washington, D.C.: Regnery Gateway.

Trow, Martin. 1984. "The University Presidency: Comparative Reflections on Leadership." Ninth David D. Henry Lecture, University of Illinois, Urbana, October.

Veblen, Thorstein. [1918] 1965. *The Higher Learning in America: A Memorandum on the Conduct of Universities by Businessmen.* Stanford, Calif.: Academic Reprints.

Veysey, Laurence R. 1965. *The Emergence of the American University.* Chicago: University of Chicago Press.

12 Students: Interests, Culture, and Activism

PHILIP G. ALTBACH

Students are central to the academic enterprise. Along with professors, they are at the core of the educational equation. They play a profoundly important role in shaping the ethos, culture, and orientation of colleges and universities everywhere. For centuries, universities existed only to teach students, and even after research became a function of academic institutions in the nineteenth century, students have constituted an essential element in higher education. Indeed, they are the defining characteristic of higher education: Without them, colleges and universities would be only research institutes or faculty clubs.

Despite the importance of students, the literature on higher education is far more extensive about the influence of higher education on students than about the influence of students on higher education. Research concerning the effect of college on students is well established (Feldman and Newcomb 1973; Astin 1977; Pascarella and Terinzini 1991). Student culture has received some modest attention (Levine 1980; Horowitz 1987; Boyer 1990; Moffatt 1989), and a good deal of research emerged concerning student political activism in the aftermath of the student revolts of the 1960s (Lipset 1967; Altbach 1974a, 1989a). But the overall influence of students on the academy has received considerably less attention. This chapter stresses how student interests, attitudes, culture, and politics influence both their institutions and society. It takes a worldwide perspective, but it pays particular attention to the United States, which, with twelve million students enrolled in postsecondary education, has the largest and perhaps the most diversified student community in the world.

Expansion and Diversification

A hallmark of higher education worldwide since World War II has been expansion. Growth in student numbers has inevitably meant increased diversity in the student population, and the growth of diverse institutions has significantly affected student enrollment and choice. As Martin Trow pointed out (1972), higher education is no longer the preserve of the elite. In many countries universities have become mass institutions, and a few nations—notably the United States—now provide virtually universal access to academically interested and financially secure young adults. The United States now enrolls half of its age cohort in institutions of higher education, and Japan enrolls 30 percent, while most Western European countries have reached around 20 percent. The developing countries of the Third World have also expanded their academic institutions rapidly—more dramatically than the West, in terms of proportional growth—but in general enroll under 10 percent.

Privileged groups in all societies continue to be significantly overrepresented in higher education everywhere, but student populations in virtually every country have diversified in the process of expanding. In Europe, students from the working class are for the first time attending universities in large numbers. In the Third World, more and more students from rural areas are enrolling. In India, social policy has provided special quotas for students from disadvantaged castes and tribes—thereby increasing diversity but also heightening intergroup tensions and problems (Agarwal and Agarwal 1991).

In the United States, prior to World War II the student population was relatively homogeneous: largely male, overwhelmingly white, and mostly Protestant. Opportunities existed for children of immigrants and blue-collar workers to gain access to higher education in the expanding public institutions, but higher education was largely an enterprise of the American middle class. Since the Second World War, however, America's colleges and universities, like all others, have been subjected to a multitude of changes in their students. Never before had the student population increased so rapidly—and never again in the foreseeable future will it expand as much. Between 1960 and 1970, with the maturation of the post–World War baby boom, the number of American college students more than doubled—from 3.8 million to 8.5 million. During the decades from 1970 to 1980, enrollment grew by less than half, and it remained virtually unchanged at 12 million between 1980 and 1990.

Despite this numerical "steady state" of the past decade, the American student population has become more diverse in all respects. The proportion of women has increased so that now half of all American students are women—although significant variations in male/female ratios still exist across fields of study. Most all socioeconomic strata are now represented. And ethnic minority representation has not only increased dramatically but also promises to grow still more. The minority mosaic is extraordinarily complex. Hispanics, blacks, and native Americans are still underrepresented in the student population, but Asian Americans are underrepresented only in graduate study. In fact, Asian Americans are the fastest-growing ethnic group in the student population, having doubled their numbers between 1976 and 1986 (Hsia 1988). Hispanic enrollments have also increased dramatically, almost doubling during the decade. In contrast, black enrollments stagnated during those years at one million, despite programs to increase the number of underrepresented minorities (Trent 1991), and the number of black graduate students actually declined during the 1980s.

The American student population has also become more diverse in terms of age. Increasing numbers of "nontraditional" students have entered higher education. In fact, during the 1980s, older students enrolled in sufficiently large numbers to prevent an earlier predicted downturn in overall student numbers. Older adults have considerably different needs, orientations, and interests than students of traditional college age. They are often not full-time students, do not participate as actively in campus activities, and tend to be more career oriented than their younger compeers.

A growing number of students hold full-time jobs while enrolled, and the proportion of part-time students grew from 17 percent of undergraduates in 1970 to 25 percent in 1988 (National Center for Education Statistics 1990, 165). The number of students who "stop out" (interrupt their studies for varying periods) and in other ways do not fit the "traditional" mode of full-time students who complete their baccalaureate degrees in the "standard" four years has increased. This changing profile of American students has profound implications for the curriculum and for how academic institutions deal with their students.

Hand in hand with this worldwide diversification of students has come an increasing diversity of educational institutions. Postsecondary education now takes place not only in traditional colleges and universities but also in community colleges, polytechnics, specialized institutes, and a wide variety of other institutions. The rise of "open universities" in a number of countries—pioneered in Britain and now operating in such countries as Thailand, India, Israel, and others—has been a major innovation in distance education over the past twenty years but almost completely removes the student from the campus and makes an autonomous student culture impossible, since students are not clustered together. In the United States, one-third of the student population is educated in community colleges, which have traditionally not had an active extracurricular life.

This great diversity of students and institutions has meant that the student community is less of a community. There are fewer common bonds among students and less of a common culture. The recent report of the Carnegie Foundation for the Advancement of Teaching, *Campus Life* (Boyer 1990), noted increased ethnic divisions on campus, declining participation in extracurricular activities, and a need to build a greater sense of community on campus. The growth in importance of racial and ethnic organizations on campus is one reflection of this development, as is the rise in racial tension in many universities (Altbach 1991). There is also increased debate concerning the content of the undergraduate curriculum, reflecting in part a decline in commonly shared values among students—and perhaps among faculty as well ("Race on Campus," 1991, 18–47).

It was perhaps predictable that there would be some reaction against increased diversity in higher education. This reaction is occurring in many countries, including the United States. As higher education, especially in the public sector, has become more expensive, there has been a reaction in government against increased postsecondary expenditures. An increased share of the cost of higher education is being shifted to individuals, and in many countries private institutions are educating an increasing proportion of the student population. As the cost of higher education to individuals increases, access will be limited, reversing a trend of a half-century. The expansion that has characterized the postwar period may also come to an end.

There have also been reactions by students themselves against some of the programs that have resulted in a more diverse student population. A continuing crisis in India concerning the reservation of places in colleges and universities for students from underrepresented castes, tribes, and classes has resulted in violent protests, including the suicide of a number of students from upper-caste groups who have felt excluded by current government policy (Srivastava 1989, 3). In the United States, increases in minority enrollment have created some tensions and engendered considerable controversy over affirmative action policies and special admission programs that have been aimed at increasing the enrollment of minority students. White students have claimed that these efforts are unfair, cost too much, and take away opportunities in competitive institutions from students admitted solely on the basis of "merit" (Altbach 1991). These reactions, seldom reflected in direct political actions, have contributed to the deteriorating sense of civility on campus.

Segments of the academic profession have also reacted against the increased diversity of higher education. In the United States, this resistance has taken several forms. Some professors have been notably unenthusiastic about affirmative action guidelines, special programs for minority students, and other programs aimed at increasing diversity, feeling that these programs dilute the quality of higher education and bring into the appointment and admission process values that violate meritocratic norms. There has also been protest against including in the undergraduate curriculum a wider range of readings or the establishment of mandatory new courses that deal with racial and gender concerns, with critics claiming that such courses are politically motivated and should not be required. These reactions from some faculty as well as students are not surprising from a historical perspective, since the changes on campus have been significant and have affected not only student culture but the traditional ways in which academic decisions are made.

Student Interests

Students affect higher education through their choice of institution and field of study. In the United States, with its large number of competing colleges and universities, students have many choices available to them and, since academic institutions are to a significant extent market driven, these choices have an immediate effect. Arthur Levine pointed out a decade ago that American college students were becoming more oriented toward vocationalism and individual concerns (1980). According to the annual surveys of the University of California, Los Angeles, and the American Council on Education, 41 percent of American college freshmen in 1968 valued being very well off financially as a life goal, compared to 58 percent in 1977 and 73 percent in 1988—an increase of 45 percent over two decades. Career choices also changed over time. Interest in engineering as a profession almost doubled, and that in law and other professional fields rose similarly, while interest in teaching declined drastically—from 17 percent in 1969 to only 7 percent in 1978 and then increasing slightly to 9 percent by 1988. Only 7 percent of students wanted to be business executives in 1969, compared to 8 percent in 1979 and 12 percent in 1988 (Braungart and Braungart 1988).

As a result, the 1970s and 1980s saw a large shift away from majors in the social sciences and humanities and toward such fields as management and engineering, which were perceived to have more relevance in the job market. In 1970 approximately 20 percent of undergraduates earned degrees in the social sciences, but by 1978 only 7.7 percent of freshmen were expressing interest in majoring in those fields—a percentage that increased to 9.5 by 1989. Similar changes can be seen in business studies, where 13 percent of the bachelor's degrees were awarded in 1965, whereas fully one-quarter of freshmen wanted to major in business and related fields by 1989.

At the end of the 1980s, students continued to be quite apprehensive about their economic prospects in a difficult job market, with three-quarters of freshmen mentioning getting a better job and making more money as important reasons in their decisions to attend college (Levine and Hirsch 1991). However, their career interests shifted slightly away from business and toward teaching and other service-oriented careers (Astin 1991). And today's students show a modest increase in support for participation in activist movements. Levine and Hirsch recently indicated that a growing number of students are participating in social service activities (1991), and they reported sensing a noticeable trend toward social concern on American campuses, indicating a slight but significant break from the careerist and privatist trends of the past two decades.

Over those decades, many small private American colleges have been unable to attract a sufficient number of students in an increasingly competitive market and have had serious financial difficulties as a result—and a few have closed. European countries, with very few private institutions and with a strong tradition of university autonomy, have been, in general, somewhat less market sensitive. They have been less willing to make significant changes in the curriculum, and their funding is less directly affected by immediate enrollment trends. Yet, in the long run, universities everywhere are affected by student opinion and enrollment trends.

Another example of the effect of student opinion has been the demise of *in loco parentis*. Until the 1960s, this legal expectation—literally translated "in lieu of the parents"—was deeply ingrained in American colleges and universities, especially those that provided residential facilities for students. It meant that colleges were expected to provide a satisfactory intellectual, moral, and social experience for their students. This institutional commitment to guide the social development of students as well as their academic development resulted in a myriad of rules and regulations concerning student life, from "lights out" times in dormitories to restrictions on campus social activities. In the 1960s, however, student opposition to institutional paternalism along with a more relaxed attitude among American adults were instrumental in convincing academic institutions to reduce if not abandon the concept.

Student Attitudes and Culture

It has been said that student culture is by its nature oppositional—"antinomian," as Edward Shils put it (1969, 1–34). Student culture tends to question authority and look for alternative perspectives on a range of issues—from politics and social issues to interpersonal relationships and preferences regarding music. This sense of questioning is common among many students, although the nature of the questions and the framework for asking them varies significantly.

It is difficult to generalize about students' attitudes internationally or, for that matter, within large and diverse national academic systems, since only a few publications have focused on the topic—among them, Klineberg et al. (1979) and Liebman, Walker, and Glazer (1972). Yet several observations can be made.

First, students are part of an international youth culture that affects their values, attitudes, and lifestyles. There are observable similarities in campus cultures throughout the world—from Stockholm to Stanford. This culture has to do with what students think, what they value, and what they buy. It is centered in the Western industrialized nations and especially in the United States, but it has spread around the world. Student cultures in many Third World nations are only peripherally influenced by it, but its effect is there nonetheless. Just as universities exist in an international academic culture, students are clearly affected by international trends, and international influences play a role in shaping student culture.

Second, student attitudes are important not only for their campus but also for society, since students are a bellwether group in the population and may be a harbinger of future societal trends. Further, they represent a group that will eventually assume positions of significant power and wealth in society. In this respect, their opinions count.

Third, with some notable exceptions, student attitudes generally stand somewhat to the left of the opinions of society. This has been the case for virtually all industrialized societies over the past half-century. On American campuses, student culture is modestly more liberal than the nation as a whole, although it generally reflects the values and norms of the American middle class. Over the past thirty years, student attitudes have become more conservative on some social issues. In 1969, for instance, 54 percent of American freshmen favored the abolition of the death penalty, but a decade later only 34 percent supported its abolition, and by 1988 only 23 percent did so. Similarly, support for the legalization of marijuana declined from 52 percent in 1977 to 19 percent in 1988. Yet, overall, American students remained staunchly liberal during the past three decades in their views on such "lifestyle" issues as abortion, premarital sex, homosexuality, and health care. Support for legal abortion increased nearly ten percentage points from 55 percent in 1977 to almost 65 percent by 1989, when almost 80 percent of freshmen supported a national health care plan (Astin 1991, fig. 6). Perhaps the most significant change related to attitudes concerning the role of women in society, with much greater support for gender equality at home and in the workplace (Braungart and Braungart 1988, 54). It may be significant that the most recent surveys note a modest swing in an even more liberal and activist direction among American students, although the trend is not yet well defined or clear. Despite this apparent shift in attitudes, a majority of students continue to focus on their career and on personal issues rather than social or political issues.

Fourth, student attitudes about politics are generally fairly stable over time, with shifts of only modest proportions concerning basic ideology. In the United States, the political attitudes of college students have remained remarkably stable over almost a century. The major changes seem to have occurred in the 1930s and between the 1960s and the 1990s. In terms of political persuasion, during the volatile 1960s American students moved noticeably toward liberal and left ideological viewpoints, with 30 percent identifying with a liberal philosophy and 3 percent with the Far Left. In the more conservative 1970s, however, those identifying with liberals declined to 23 percent while the Far Left declined to 2 percent. In 1988, at the height of the Reagan era, the liberals declined one percentage point to 22 percent, but the Far Left increased slightly to 2.3 percent. At the same time, fewer than 20 percent chose conservative or far-right ideologies. Thus, over three decades, the only significant increase came in the "middle of the road" ideological position (Braungart and Braungart 1988, 55).

Fifth, European students are, not surprisingly, generally to the left of their American compeers—probably reflecting a more general societal trend to the left in these societies and the existence of large Socialist political parties and movements and, in recent years, of powerful environmental movements such as the Greens in Germany. European student attitudes also seem to swing somewhat more sharply than is the case in the United States, although stability is the main trend as well. France, for example, has seen strong student support for the "intellectual right" since the 1970s. While some students have been involved in the environmental movement, the several incidents of recent mass activism in France have focused on opposition to educational reforms proposed by the Socialist government. The students were, in this case, able to stop the reforms from being implemented. Generally, however, throughout the industrialized world, there has been a general move toward centrist politics in the 1970s and 1980s and a notable lack of interest in activist participation.

Sixth, while there is a significant degree of continuity in student attitudes over time, there is also the potential for dramatic and often unforeseen shifts in direction. External—and occasionally campus—events may quickly stimulate activism. International trends affect students and institutions most directly during periods of crisis. During the 1960s, for example, there was a worldwide consciousness of the "student movement," with political issues and tactics ranging from nonviolent resistance to violent confrontation being communicated internationally (Caute 1988). The war in Vietnam was a rallying cry for students not only in the United States but in Europe and Japan as well. Student demonstrations led by the Zengakuren in Japan as well as by Students for a Democratic Society in the United States were communicated worldwide, and the dramatic French student revolt of 1968 had an immediate international effect.

Seventh, student attitudes differ significantly across institutions. Indeed, some students choose the university that they attend in part on the basis of perceived campus attitudes. In England, Oxford and Cambridge have distinct student cultures but exhibit many similarities when compared to other British universities, largely because of their historic social class traditions. Japanese students are well aware of the variations in student culture between different universities—for example, between private Waseda University and public Tokyo University, both prestigious institutions but with very different traditions. In India, some universities, such as Banaras Hindu University and, more recently, Jawaharlal Nehru University in New Delhi, have especially strong campus-based traditions of political activism. At Banaras, local conditions and grievances tend to dominate student attitudes; at Jawaharlal Nehru, however, ideological politics play a key role (Kumar 1989). In the United States, students at the University of California, Berkeley, and the University of Wisconsin-Madison inherit a longstanding tradition of student political activism, whereas other institutions, such as

Reed College and the University of Chicago, reflect a recognizable intellectual tradition, and still others—particularly fundamentalist institutions—have a recognizably conservative campus culture.

Student Activities and Organizations

Students carry on their own culture primarily through organizations. In many countries, students have control over significant funds for extracurricular activities and organizations. Student organizational networks are often large and complex—and yet are seldom considered by those who analyze trends and directions in higher education. Apart from Trow (1975), Horowitz (1987), and Moffatt (1989), few historians or social scientists have analyzed the nature of student organizations and the changes that take place in them over time. In American higher education, campus organizational culture is a particularly powerful force. Many American universities are homes to more than a hundred largely independent student organizations, including religious groups, sports clubs, newspapers and other publications, political organizations, nationality and ethnic societies, cultural associations of all kinds, and fraternities and sororities that usually provide residential accommodations as well as social activities for their members. Officially recognized student organizations are often funded by institutions through student fees or other means. In a large and often impersonal institutional environment, such extracurricular groups provide an anchor for student allegiance. They often have a more significant influence on student values and attitudes than the faculty or the curriculum, and they sometimes operate in opposition to academic expectations.

A large number of American students—some estimates indicate 40 percent—work at least part time, and many enroll as part-time students because they work full time. This has a major influence on campus organizational culture, since students whose full-time commitment is not to their academic institution will naturally participate less in campus activities than other students and consider the institution less central to their lives. Among America's colleges and universities, wide diversity exists in the extent of student activities and organizations, with highly selective residential institutions tending to exhibit an active campus life and much emphasis on extracurricular activities, often with considerable staff and financial support, while nonresidential "open-door" institutions generally have fewer such activities and less interest in them among their students. Indeed, it may no longer be appropriate (if it ever was) to consider American higher education as having a common "student culture," since such vast differences now exist among institutional cultures. Diversity in all realms has clearly weakened the unity and even the existence of an identifiable American student culture.

Campus organizations change on the basis of broad social and political trends as well as specific academic ones. For instance, most of America's student political organizations that flourished during the 1960s virtually disappeared during the following two decades, while fraternities and sororities, which had been in eclipse, revived (Moffatt 1989). Student religious organizations seem to have increased, although the proportions of students participating in them is unknown. More recently, ethnic and racially based groups have become more numerous, visible, and active.

In most other countries, the organized campus culture is less "dense" than it is in the United States. There are fewer organizations, a less well-developed infrastructure, and, generally, less money for campus groups and activities. Continental Europe never had a tradition of in loco parentis. From the medieval period, its universities provided few facilities and little encouragement for extracurricular activities—one reason being that European students started their university training later than has been the norm in the United States, and they have traditionally been treated as adults. Continental universities historically had one mission—to teach—and their students came to study. Indeed, the concept of a "campus" in the American sense of a separate and identifiable location for the student-faculty community is foreign to the older European universities. As newer European universities have been built outside the city centers and their student populations have become larger and more diverse, they have paid more attention to the provision of facilities and services for students along Anglo-American lines.

In many Third World countries, universities do not have the facilities or the staff to support anything but classroom instruction. Expansion has absorbed all available resources, and funds are insufficient to devote to student services. In the Third World as well as in Europe, the direct costs paid by students for their university education are very low—in some countries tuition is virtually free—and the entire cost of higher education is borne by the state. In such circumstances, there is limited willingness to allocate funds to student services of any kind.

Student Political Activism

Student political activism is characterized by significant national variation, yet some common themes are evident (Altbach 1989b). First, student activism is almost always a minority phenomenon, even during periods of great intensity. Student predilections toward an oppositional perspective and broad liberal or radical views can be a fertile ground for activist politics, and, if conditions are right, they may result in significant social unrest. But only rarely do a majority of students on campuses participate in activist demonstrations, and politically committed students constitute only a small minority of the student population.

Second, student activism is almost always sporadic. It does not seem possible to keep campus activist movements going for long periods. Student generations change, and the pressures of examinations and academic programs are so great that most institutions have no significant tradition of continuously ongoing student political activism. Even the two key periods of major activism in the United States—the 1930s and the 1960s—can be seen in a broad context as aberrations (Altbach 1974a). Although American students had a significant influence on public opinion concerning civil rights and the Vietnam war during the 1960s, student political activity has not continued to be an important social force in the United States. This lack of a viable historical tradition on campus—and of an accompanying sense of legitimacy of student politics in society—is a significant but not overwhelming obstacle to the emergence of the kind of massive student political movements that can have an influence on national policy.

Third, student activism has the potential for creating significant social dislocation quickly. Students are relatively easy to mobilize, and, even where there is not a great deal of overt political consciousness on campus, there is often an undercurrent of political concern. Moreover, students are able to gain access to mass media relatively easily. In all countries, students come disproportionately from the upper socioeconomic classes and are able, in part for this reason, to have easy access to the elites.

Fourth, student activists, in virtually every society, seem to come from identifiable groups in the student population (Lipset 1967). Social science students are much more likely to be involved in student activism than are students in professional programs. Students in the most prestigious universities—and usually in institutions located in the metropolitan centers—are more politically active than those in more locally oriented and rural institutions.

Fifth, with some notable exceptions, student political activism tends to be aimed at societal issues and broad political concerns rather than campus questions, although activism can be stimulated by many different issues. In India, for example, campus conditions are the most common stimulant for activism, and in the United States, as well as in Western Europe, the rapid expansion of higher education and a sense of alienation on campus helped spark the student movements of the 1960s. In France during 1967–68, general leftist politics combined with a perceived crisis in both higher education and the society to stimulate the unprecedented activism of the period (Schnapp and Vidal-Naquet 1971; Touraine 1971). In the United States, the moral imperatives of the civil rights movement and doubts about the morality of the Vietnam war were required to push a generally liberal campus population toward activism.

Sixth, while student movements are most often independent of established political parties, they sometimes align themselves with parties. In such cases, student leaders may achieve a measure of societal power.

Seventh, while student movements are generally on the left, this is by no means an unalterable rule. Currently, the overwhelming trend among Muslim students in the Islamic world is toward Islamic fundamentalism—a conservative tendency that has political as well as theological implications. Elsewhere, religious fundamentalism, very often with political implications, stands in sharp contrast to the general liberalism and scientific orientation of the academic world. No general surveys of student attitudes in the Islamic countries are available, so it is impossible to know what proportion of Muslim students holds fundamentalist views and the nature of the diversity of perspectives among them, but secular and nationalist viewpoints undoubtedly also exist, since these views earlier dominated Islamic student activism. (For one of the few detailed studies of Arab student political attitudes and activism, see Barakat 1977.) The influence of anti-Western movements in the Islamic world—perhaps especially the Iranian revolution—combined with significant frustration over the failure of traditional politics to achieve either modernization or a settlement of the nagging Arab-Israeli conflict probably have played a role in fostering fundamentalism among Islamic students.

Eighth, Third World students tend to be more politically active than those in the industrialized nations, with more powerful traditions of student activism. Third World students are always a force to be reckoned with; their activism is often endemic to the political life of their society, and it has the potential for major political upheaval (Barkan 1975). Several reasons explain why student activism in the Third World is so powerful. Third World students see themselves as members of an "incipient elite," with a legitimate role in national politics. They view themselves as a politically effective class with the ability to play a societal role. Perhaps because they tend to stem from the elites, they have little fear of massive repression. Politics and ideology are more salient issues for them, in part because of political traditions and in part because of everyday social realities. With some notable exceptions, their attitudes tend to be further to the left as well, with significant proportions of students expressing revolutionary opinions. Moreover, they are often an accepted element in the political equation—their involvement may date back to their nation's struggle for independence. The student community is often relatively small and fairly homogeneous in terms of aspirations and backgrounds. It is concentrated in a few universities located near the center of power. Universities are often located in the capital city, and students are easy to mobilize for political action. In addition, many Third World nations do not have a full range of political institutions—the press and media may be limited, literacy rates low, trade unions rare, and the educated middle class small. In this vacuum of competing interest groups, students naturally assume considerable influence. Finally, the governmental structures themselves may have only limited legitimacy. In such a context, it is not surprising that student movements are powerful political factors.

In industrialized countries, the situation is far different and, as a result, students are seldom able to wield much political influence. Students do not consider themselves as "incipient elites" and therefore have lower expectations of political involvement. Student populations are large, diverse, and more difficult to mobilize. Most students are vocationally oriented and have the expectation that their academic degrees will result in remunerative careers. They do not expect to wield political influence, and they worry about being unemployed. They have few traditions of successful activism and are not considered legitimate political actors. Industrial societies are dense with competing interest groups—the media, a vast array of political and social organizations, and the like. Established mechanisms exist for orderly political change. Political institutions are accepted by the bulk of the population, and politics are fairly stable within established political parties. Moreover, students in industrialized countries do not have the potential to overthrow the government, and sporadic activism seldom threatens its stability.

Ninth, the results of student activism vary widely. In the Third World, students can frequently precipitate a crisis and often force the downfall of a regime. Indeed, the list of Third World countries where governments have been toppled by students is long. In 1990 alone, the government of Bangladesh was overthrown by student demonstrations, and the king of Nepal was forced to establish a parliamentary system. Sometimes, student movements are successful and the traditions of student political involvement are strengthened, as in Bangladesh, where elections have been held and the country has moved toward democracy. Similarly, during the late

1980s, South Korean students forced a dictatorial government to call elections that have resulted in a slow move toward democracy, and continuing student agitation during 1991 put pressure on the government to democratize further. But students are never able to pick up the pieces, in that political power flows elsewhere. Repressive forces can take the initiative, and democratic gains can be lost. In 1990, Burma was rocked by student demonstrations that forced an election, but Burma's military rulers refused to abide by the election results and have engaged in severe repression of the student population, torturing many students and closing the universities for an extended period. The demonstrations in Beijing's Tiananmen Square in 1989 resulted in massive repression by China's leaders. Governments in Kenya and Zimbabwe closed down the universities to limit unrest and arrested hundreds of student demonstrators. In several Latin-American countries, military dictatorships took power in the wake of student unrest in the 1960s, and severe repression by military governments in Argentina and Uruguay virtually destroyed their student movements (Levy 1991).

Tenth and finally, student activism can have a direct effect in terms of social change, if not political change. It can also have a more subtle influence through attitudinal change and training for organizational politics. During the 1960s, students forced Western societies to pay attention to some social issues and educational problems. In both West Germany and France, students achieved their goal of university reform, which included student involvement in academic governance (Altbach 1974b; Nitsch et al. 1965). In terms of politics, however, the student movements of the 1960s were less successful. The American student movement was instrumental in building up public opposition to the Vietnam war, but it was unable to end the war, and this resulted in considerable frustration and in the end serious demoralization among the activists (Gitlin 1987). These students were most successful in projecting a set of ideas about lifestyles and social mores. Thus, the women's movement emerged from the ferment of the 1960s, as did the popularization of rock music and a certain liberalization of attitudes concerning drugs and interpersonal relations. Most commonly, student activism has influenced the nature of academic governance and the curriculum. In Latin America, since the great reform movement of 1918, students have had a key role in institutional governance in the public "autonomous" universities—although that role has been weakened in the aftermath of the 1960s and especially with the rise of Latin-American private higher education, where students play only a minor direct role in university governance. In most other developing countries, students are basically excluded from any direct participation in governance. In European countries such as

France, Germany, and Sweden, students have gained a significant number of seats on various governance bodies. In the United States, the activism of the 1960s resulted in the recognition that students have a contribution to make in academic governance and a trend to involve students in institutional decision making, but activism won students no more than a token voice, typically with one or two seats on institutional committees and councils.

The Future

Based on this analysis, it is possible to speculate on the future of the student community. While it is difficult to generalize internationally, some trends are evident at least with regard to the United States. The student population is becoming more variegated, complex, and diverse. Racial, gender, and age variations have increased. These variations have created tension in some instances and have made a sense of community more and more difficult.

Further, the academic system itself has become more diversified and less oriented to a sense of community. Fewer students study full time. The expansion of community colleges and urban universities that serve a commuter population has also reduced what little sense of campus cohesiveness they may have once had. For these reasons, it seems increasingly difficult to maintain the sense of campus community life that once was so prized in American higher education. Only in residential institutions are students much involved in campus life, and there the possibility for maintaining much campus community still exists.

For most students, the experience of higher education is likely to be more anomic, career oriented, and part time. The traditional idea that the college years were for total involvement in the student experience—both educational and social—will hold for a smaller and smaller proportion of the student population. Those in the traditional age groups attending top-tier institutions will remain fully involved in campus culture. The ever-increasing proportion of students who attend community colleges and nonselective urban institutions, who come from nontraditional age groups, and who are minorities will have less commitment to this culture.

While the majority of institutions have not seen significant outbreaks of ethnic racial prejudice, a sense of tension has been growing on many campuses. The decline of community and increased competition for admissions and for grades in a highly competitive job market may increase these tensions. Indeed, these tensions and the incidents that they generate may be among the major crisis points for higher education during the coming decade. Otherwise, a basic configuration of student liberalism on social and lifestyle issues combined with middle-of-the-road to liberal politics is likely to predominate.

In the mid-1980s, a brief activist movement developed on a number of campuses in opposition to the apartheid racial policies in South Africa, and students urged their institutions and American corporations to divest their investments in South Africa. Only a limited amount of campus political concern emerged at the time of the Persian Gulf crisis in late 1990 and early 1991, with opinions mixed but with considerable opposition to American intervention. Had the war continued for an extended period, it is likely that activism would have become more widespread, but it is an open question as to whether it would have reached significant levels. Overall, it seems unlikely that American universities will become hotbeds of politics unless a major foreign policy crisis erupts.

As this chapter is being written, there is a kind of struggle going on for the soul of the university in the United States. Although there is no flash point of political crisis, as was the case in the 1960s, the American university is profoundly divided. Undergraduate students are bifurcated into increasingly separate ethnic and racial enclaves. A not insignificant proportion of white students resent perceived "special opportunities" for underrepresented minority students and fear undue competition from high-achieving Asian-American students. With many students working while studying and most more concerned with private concerns than with community issues, there is no center to campus life. Many students are worried about future job prospects, and many suffer from a seeming lack of direction, reflected in their taking more and more time to complete their degrees. Meanwhile, the faculty, beset by cutbacks and the usual pressures to do research and publish, plays little role in the development of a cohesive campus culture.

It is unclear whether American campuses are a tinderbox beset by tensions waiting to explode or whether the apathy and general privatism that is evident on their surface is an accurate reflection of long-term trends. One reason is that, although students are a force that shapes their campus and sometimes society, relatively little is understood about the nature and orientation of student culture. Increased research on student attitudes and values is essential to understand both the educational orientation of students and the ways their institutions can meet their educational needs.

References

Agarwal, S.P., and J.C. Agarwal, eds. 1991. *Education and Social Uplift of Backward Classes.* New Delhi: Concept Publishing.

Altbach, Philip G. 1974a. *Student Politics in America.* New York: McGraw-Hill.

———. 1974b. *University Reform: Comparative Perspectives for the Seventies.* Cambridge, Mass.: Schenkman.

———, ed. 1989a. *Student Political Activism: An International Reference Handbook.* Westport, Conn.: Greenwood Press.

———. 1989b. "Perspectives on Student Political Activism." *Comparative Education,* 25(1):97–110.

———. 1991. "The Racial Dilemma in American Higher Education." In Philip G. Altbach and Kofi Lomotey, eds., *The Racial Crisis in American Higher Education,* pp. 3–18. Albany: State University of New York Press.

Astin, A.W. 1977. *Four Critical Years: Effects of College on Beliefs, Attitudes, and Knowledge.* San Francisco: Jossey-Bass.

———. 1991. "The Changing American College Student: Implications for Educational Policy and Practice." *Higher Education,* 22(2):129–144.

Barakat, Halim. 1977. *Lebanon in Strife: Student Preludes to the Civil War.* Austin: University of Texas Press.

Barkan, Joel D. 1975. *An African Dilemma: University Students, Development, and Politics in Ghana, Tanzania, and Uganda.* Nairobi: Oxford University Press.

Boyer, Ernest L. 1990. *Campus Life: In Search of Community.* Princeton: Princeton University Press.

Braungart, Richard G., and Margaret M. Braungart. 1988. "From Yippies to Yuppies: Twenty Years of Freshmen Attitudes." *Public Opinion,* September/October, 53–56.

Caute, David. 1988. *The Year of the Barricades: A Journal through 1968.* New York: Harper and Row.

Feldman, Kenneth A., and Theodore M. Newcomb. 1973. *The Impact of College on Students.* Vol. 1: *An Analysis of Four Decades of Research.* Vol. 2: *Summary Tables.* San Francisco: Jossey-Bass.

Gitlin, Todd. 1987. *The Sixties: Years of Hope, Days of Rage.* New York: Bantam.

Horowitz, Helen Lefkowitz. 1987. *Campus Life: Undergraduate Cultures from the End of the Eighteenth Century to the Present.* Chicago: University of Chicago Press.

Hsia, Jayjia. 1988. *Asian Americans in Higher Education and at Work.* Hillsdale, N.J.: Lawrence Erlbaum.

Klineberg, Otto, Marisa Zavallon, Christiane Louis-Guerin, and Jeanne BenBrika. 1979. *Students, Values, and Politics: A Cross-cultural Comparison.* New York: Free Press.

Kumar, Anand. 1989. "The Student Movement since Independence." In Amrik Singh and G.D. Sharma, eds., *Higher Education in India,* pp. 177–187. New Delhi: Konark.

Levine, Arthur. 1980. *When Dreams and Heros Died: A Portrait of Today's College Student.* San Francisco: Jossey-Bass.

Levine, Arthur, and Deborah Hirsch. 1991. "Undergraduates in Transition: A New Wave of Activism on College Campuses." *Higher Education,* 22(2):119–128.

Levy, Daniel C. 1991. "The Decline of Latin American Student Activism." *Higher Education,* 22(2):144–155.

Liebman, Arthur, Kenneth N. Walker, and Myron Glazer. 1972. *Latin American University Students: A Six-Nation Study.* Cambridge: Harvard University Press.

Lipset, Seymour Martin. 1967. "University Students and Politics in Underdeveloped Countries." In Seymour Martin Lipset, ed., *Student Politics,* pp. 3–53. New York: Basic Books.

Moffatt, Michael. 1989. *Coming of Age in New Jersey: College and American Culture.* New Brunswick, N.J.: Rutgers University Press.

National Center for Education Statistics. 1990. *The Condition of American Education.* Washington, D.C.: U.S. Department of Education.

Nitsch, Wolfgang, et al. 1965. *Hochschule in der Demokratie.* Berlin: Luchterhand.

Pascarella, Ernest T., and Patrick Terin Terinzini. 1991. *How College Affects Students.* San Francisco: Jossey-Bass.

"Race on Campus: A Special Issue." 1991. *New Republic,* 8 February, pp. 18–47.

Schnapp, Alain, and Pierre Vidal-Naquet. 1971. *The French Student Uprising, November 1967–June 1968.* Boston: Beacon Press.

Shils, Edward. 1969. "Dreams of Plentitude, Nightmare of Scarcity." In Seymour Martin Lipset and Philip G. Altbach, eds., *Students in Revolt,* pp. 1–34. Boston: Beacon Press.

Srivastava, S. 1989. "Season of Campus Agitations." *Indian Express,* 4 July, p. 3.

Touraine, Alain. 1971. *The May Movement: Revolt and Reform.* New York: Random House.

Trent, William T. 1991. "Student Affirmative Action in Higher Education: Addressing Underrepresentation." In Philip P. Altbach and Kofi Lomotey, eds., *The Racial Crisis in American Higher Education,* pp. 107–135. Albany: State University of New York Press.

Trow, Martin. 1972. "The Expansion and Transformation of Higher Education." *International Review of Education,* 18(1):61–83.

———, ed. 1975. *Teachers and Students: Aspects of American Higher Education.* New York: McGraw-Hill.

13

Governing Boards

JOSEPH F. KAUFFMAN

Among the several distinguishing features of higher education in the United States are its evolution from mostly private, religious colleges; its relative autonomy from the federal government; its diversity, comprehensiveness, size, and accessibility; and the relative independence of the constituent parts of its individual institutions, such as departments, professional schools, and research institutes (Ben-David 1972).

Certainly one would have to include in any listing of distinguishing features of American colleges and universities their structure of governance. A governing board of laypersons representing the public interest constitutes the highest authority of the institution. Whether called *trustees* as in most independent institutions, *regents* as in many public institutions; or even *curators, visitors,* or *overseers,* the citizen governing board is a major feature of American higher education decision making. Over forty-one thousand citizens serve as unpaid, part-time volunteers in this capacity, with many obligations and responsibilities. Their service and contributions have been controversial, however—more often than not because of confusion over their special obligations and responsibilities.

The Development of American Governing Boards

America's colonial colleges were created primarily by Protestant denominations that utilized the concept of a lay board, at first mostly clergy, to control them. This approach was consistent with the pattern of lay boards for Protestant churches in northern Europe, in contrast to cleric-controlled Catholicism, and it was also a pattern developed in Protestant Holland and Scotland for their universities, compared to the English university tradition of internal collegial control and occasional "visitation" by an appointed nonacademic outsider. The absence of bodies of mature scholars in the new colonies made this adaptation of English practice necessary and practical as well as theologically acceptable.

It has been said that, in the eighteenth and for much of the nineteenth centuries, trustees were the dominant force in American higher education, with the latter decades of the nineteenth and the early decades of the twentieth centuries being an era of presidential dominance, which was superseded by the growing triumph of the faculty by midcentury. Certainly, governing boards were in control at first. Only later did they delegate some authority to presidents to act as their agent. Understandably, many early presidents spoke harshly of experiences with trustees. Among them, Francis Wayland, president of Brown University from 1827 to 1855, once wrote to a friend, "How can colleges prosper directed by men, very good men to be sure, but who know about every other thing except about education. The man who first devised the present mode of governing colleges in this country has done us more injury than Benedict Arnold" (Rudolph 1962, 172).

Despite their often conflict-laden experiences with boards, throughout the nineteenth century presidents were the interpreters and justifiers of lay governing boards to their faculties. Increasingly in the twentieth century, however, presidents had to become the interpreters and justifiers of faculty members to their governing boards. The pivotal years for this shift in the relationship of boards, presidents, and faculty seem to have been from 1915 to 1920—beginning with the creation of the American Association of University Professors (AAUP) on the first day of January in the earlier of those years and ending with a major case of faculty academic freedom in the latter year: Harvard's Board of Overseers learning from Harvard President A. Lawrence Lowell that, if the board demanded the resignation of Harold Laski as a visiting lecturer because of Laski's support of the 1919 Boston police strike, Lowell would submit his own resignation in response.

The next year—1921—saw the creation of the Association of Governing Boards of Universities and Colleges (AGB). Faculty members had their AAUP, presidents shared experiences in institutional membership organizations such as regional accrediting associations, and now trustees had an association to provide support for their work. Yet the AGB restricted its membership to boards of public institutions, and it did not have a salaried staff or a permanent national office until 1963, when it voted to appoint its first full-time executive, J. L. Zwingle; establish its headquarters in Washington, D.C.; and open its membership to the governing boards of independent institutions. (In this regard, it is ironic that a complaint about the AGB today is that it is dominated by the boards of independent institutions.)

Under the leadership of Zwingle's successor, Robert L. Gale—who assumed AGB's presidency in 1973—the association has vigorously pursued a greater leadership role on the national scene. Its conferences, workshops, publications, and services to governing boards have contributed to trustees' orientation, knowledge, and acquaintance with model practices. Its *Handbook of College and University Trusteeship* (Ingram et al. 1980) is the standard work in the field, as are its specialized reports by such authors as John Nason (1982) and Clark Kerr and Marian Gade (1989). Although some presidents worry about the AGB's exhortation that trustees should play a more active role in their institutions, most of them cannot deny that the association has contributed greatly to the strength of their boards and, thereby, of their institutions.

Today, in contrast to earlier eras of antitrustee sentiment among many faculty and students and some presidents, the concept of the lay governing board is widely accepted within higher education. As the Carnegie Foundation for the Advancement of Teaching concluded in its 1982 essay, *The Control of the Campus: A Report on the Governance of Higher Education,* despite ambiguities over the specific responsibilities of trustees, "the governing board constitutes the keystone in the governance structure of higher education" (p. 72).

The Responsibilities of Governing Boards

The functions of boards of trustees or regents have changed over the years, but some basic principles about their role in academic governance are accepted by most analysts, if not by all state governors and legislators. Most observers would agree that the activities of virtually all human organizations can be differentiated into three kinds: (1) the work to be done, (2) the administration of that work, and (3) the establishment of policies to guide it. Governing boards of organizations take responsibility for the third kind of activity to assure the success of the other two. For example, Cyril Houle (1989, 3) labeled organizations as "tripartite" systems in his recent book about governing boards in nonprofit and public organizations, including colleges and universities, wherein the faculty and staff carry out the primary work to be done, the president is chief executive or administrative officer, and the board monitors performance and either makes policy or sees that policy gets made. Wise boards know that they can neither administer their institution themselves nor carry out its work, but instead must provide support and guidance for those other activities.

In 1966, the American Association of University Professors took the lead in working with the American Council on Education and the Association of Governing Boards to develop a Joint Statement on Government of Colleges and Universities that outlined the respective roles of the governing board, president, faculty, and students in institutional governance. The statement was then recognized by all three associations as worthy of attention by faculty, presidents, and trustees. Drafted at the height of faculty dominance of institutional governance but with growing signs of student unrest and governmental intrusion, the statement put forth the principles of joint effort, extensive communication, and shared but differentiated participation in governance among all constituents of the institution to achieve three goals—developing a generally unified view of the institution, maintaining the welfare of the institution, and solving its educational problems. According to the associations, "The variety and complexity of the tasks performed by institutions of higher education produce an inescapable interdependence among governing board, administration, faculty, students, and others. The relationship calls for adequate communication among these components, and full opportunity for appropriate joint planning and effort."

The statement recognized the board as the "final institutional authority" with "a special obligation to assure that the history of the college or university shall serve as a prelude and inspiration to the future," but it expected the board to delegate its authority widely. Its principles of board activity deserve quotation in full.

> The governing board of an institution of higher education, while maintaining a general overview, entrusts the conduct of the administration to the administrative offices, the president and deans, and the conduct of teaching and research to the faculty. The board should undertake appropriate self-limitation.
>
> One of the governing board's important tasks is to insure the publication of codified statements that define the over-all policies and procedures of the institution under its jurisdiction.
>
> The board plays a central role in relating the likely needs of the future to predictable resources; it has the responsibility for husbanding the endowment; it is responsible for obtaining needed capital and operating funds; and in the broadest sense of the term it should pay attention to personnel policy. In order to fulfill these duties, the board should be aided by, and may insist upon, the development of long-range planning by the administration and faculty.

It feels as if Boards do not recognize the importance of faculty, students & staff think they can run a university on their own.

It doesn't seem that either faculty or board members acknowledge other's importance.

When ignorance or ill-will threatens the institution or any part of it, the governing board must be available for support. In grave crises it will be expected to serve as a champion. Although the action to be taken by it will usually be on behalf of the president, the faculty, or the student body, the board should make clear that the protection it offers to an individual or a group is, in fact, a fundamental defense of the vested interests of society in the educational institution (AAUP 1966).

Other than the AAUP's addition of two footnotes to the statement in 1978—one on multicampus boards and the other on collective bargaining—the three sponsoring associations have not modified it since 1966. Thus it remains the common standard for shared participation in policy making within higher education. What with all that has happened in institutional governance since 1966, the statement sounds antiquated to an increasing number of trustees and administrators. Nonetheless, its principles of joint effort, communication, and participation have made sense not only in higher education but in other organizations, including business and industry. Its creators may not have realized it, but they were developing an alternative to the conventional "labor-management" dichotomy in profit-making corporations. What would have seemed radical to industry in the 1960s has in more recent decades come to be accepted not only for the governance of professionally based organizations such as hospitals or research-and-development companies but also for automobile assembly plants and other factories.

Since 1966, several analysts of academic life have commented on the specific responsibilities of college and university governing boards. In 1973, the Carnegie Commission on Higher Education issued its report, *Governance of Higher Education: Six Priority Problems,* in which it stated that the board of trustees "at its best" serves six functions (p. 32): (1) it holds and interprets the "trust"—the responsibility for the long-run welfare of the total institution; (2) it acts as a "buffer" between society and the campus, resisting improper external interference and introducing a necessary contact with the changing realities of the surrounding society; (3) it is the final arbiter of internal disputes involving the administration, the faculty, and the students; (4) it is an "agent of change" in what is historically a conservative institution, deciding what changes should be encouraged and when; (5) it has the basic responsibility for the financial welfare of the campus; and (6) above all, it provides for the governance of the institution.

Nine years later, in a volume for the Association of Governing Boards that is a source of wisdom for trustees and others, John Nason listed thirteen major responsibilities of boards, as follows (1982, 19–46): (1) to maintain the integrity of the trust; (2) to appoint the president; (3) to make certain that the institution is well managed; (4) to approve the budget; (5) to raise money; (6) to manage the endowment; (7) to assure adequate physical facilities; (8) to oversee the education program; (9) to approve long-range plans; (10) to serve as bridge and buffer between campus and community; (11) to preserve institutional economy; (12) to serve as court of appeal; and (13) to be informed.

Most recently, James L. Fisher, former president of Towson State University and of the Council for Advancement and Support of Education, listed these thirteen responsibilities and the reasons for them in his book, *The Board and the President,* for the American Council on Education (1991, 93–105):

1. *Appointing the president:* "Failing in this, the most important responsibility of the governing board, is among the major problems in American higher education today."

2. *Evaluating the institution:* "Unless the governing board or a newly appointed president insists, institutions are rarely evaluated by external review."

3. *Assessing board policies:* "The policies of a board may change through practice and amendation, or a board may make no alternations in policy in spite of changing institutional needs. Both conditions set the stage for serious problems. A board can prevent these problems by insisting on a periodic review of its bylaws and practices."

4. *Supporting the president:* "The board should give the president both psychological and substantive support. Both are essential and often overlapping, but are too often unappreciated or taken for granted by a board."

5. *Reviewing the performance of the president:* "Although this responsibility is second in importance only to appointing the president, most boards do a poor job of it. Either they do no presidential evaluation or they do it poorly. In spite of the importance of presidential evaluation, it is infinitely better for a board to do nothing than to do a poor one."

6. *Reviewing the mission of the institution:* "At least every five years, the board should ask the president to commission a review of the objectives of the institution that will be presented to the board for discussion. That is, the board should not do it but should ensure that it is done."

7. *Approving long-range plans:* "Long-range planning is the strategy for achieving the mission of the institution. . . . The long-range plan should be written and updated annually, . . . prepared by the president in consultation with administrative associates and faculty, staff, and students."

8. *Overseeing the educational program:* "The curriculum and research

activities are the core of the institution and the basic trust of the board; the test against which all things should be measured."

9. *Ensuring financial solvency*: "Money is the board responsibility to which no one objects. . . . The board must see that the budget is balanced, and that in the last analysis, income equals expenditures. The board must also be concerned about the property of the institution and the investment of institutional monies. . . . Every board member should be concerned with raising financial support for the institution."

10. *Preserving institutional independence*: "By nature a college or university is controversial as well as important, and outside groups often try to use an institution for special purposes (political, bureaucratic, personal, business, etc.). Because it is also vulnerable, an institution needs a strong board to protect its independence."

11. *Representing the institution and the public*: "It is the trustees who interpret the campus to the external community and provide the legitimate link to those who might otherwise object. . . . Conversely, trustees represent the view of the external public to the staff and, in so doing, enhance the breadth and view of the institution."

12. *Serving as a court of appeal*: "On rare occasions a board of trustees must be pressed to sit in judgment over an institutional dispute."

13. *Determining board performance*: "Once a year the board in executive session should ask the president, 'How are we doing?' . . . At least every five years, the board should engage an outside consultant to help answer questions regarding the performance of the board. While board performance is usually addressed in an institutional evaluation and in a presidential review, the board chair should specifically ask the outside evaluator to assess the board itself."

Acting as bridge, buffer, or agent between the institution and its public or the state can put boards in awkward positions. Some public boards can legitimately be criticized for viewing their bridge role as that of a conduit for implementing the wishes of elected political officials. Public institutions and their boards are increasingly under scrutiny, as are other structures of state government. From 1985 through 1990, at least twenty-seven states conducted major studies of their higher education systems by blue-ribbon commissions, consultants, or special legislative task forces, and fourteen of the states made actual changes in their systems (McGuinness 1990). But overwhelmingly the expectation remains that, whether public or independent, board members should be true trustees—holding in trust the purposes and assets of institutions and acting as stewards or guardians of their essential integrity on behalf of future generations.

The Issues Addressed in the 1980s

If one were to select a major theme of educational concern among trustees as well as the public over the past decade, it would certainly be that of quality. In 1983, the National Commission on Excellence in Education, created by the Secretary of Education, issued its report, *A Nation at Risk,* that illuminated the deterioration of quality and standards in American education and called for major reform. Although the report dealt primarily with elementary and secondary schools, it had clear implications for postsecondary education, including improvements in teacher preparation and admission standards for four-year colleges and universities. Moreover, it did not leave the responsibility for action solely in the hands of educators; instead it demanded action by citizens and elected officials.

Within months, a stream of national reports followed concerning undergraduate college and university education. These, too, focused on quality and, for the most part, were highly critical of current standards and practices. Chief among them were *Involvement in Learning* (Study Group on the Conditions of Excellence in American Higher Education 1984), *To Reclaim a Legacy* (Bennett 1984), and *Integrity in the College Curriculum* (Association of American Colleges 1985). More were to follow throughout the 1980s. While faculties, generally, were defensive about these criticisms, there was great pressure on governing boards to reexamine quality in general. This was done primarily through reviews of general education and the curriculum as a whole. By 1987, the annual survey of the American Council on Education, "Campus Trends," revealed that 95 percent of the nation's colleges and universities had "recently made changes in the curriculum or are currently doing so" (1987, 3). Further, there was renewed emphasis on undergraduate education in general and the freshman year in particular (Upcraft et al. 1989). In research universities there was mounting pressure to restore the balance between research and teaching, reexamine their responsibility for undergraduate education, and ensure proper training and utilization of graduate teaching assistants. Board members questioned institutional and system priorities and the allocation of resources.

Implicit in these critiques was the charge that too many institutions simply did not know the outcomes of their efforts to induce learning. As a result, the 1980s saw the flowering of the assessment movement. In some states, assessment became a condition for receiving state funds. Despite early skepticism and some resistance, most institutions have instituted some forms of assessment beyond the traditional recording of course grades. As the decade progressed, assessment began to be seen as more than the use of national tests for accountability purposes. More and more institutions developed their own instruments and techniques to enable improved instruction and learning. Early identification and remediation of basic skills deficiencies, the utilization of value-added concepts, and improved learning environments are now a part of the activities of most institutions. Further, governing boards increasingly expect to receive regular reports on such matters and what is being done to assure continuing improvement in educational outcomes and academic programs. Equally important, boards have come to realize the importance of periodic assessment of institutional operations, presidential performance, and their own stewardship.

Part of a governing board's credibility comes from its awareness of how things are going, but until the 1980s it was quite common for boards to avoid any kind of assessment of their own performance. Now, trustees cannot claim that competency assessment is for everyone else. While the art of performance review of governing boards may not be well advanced and criterion problems remain, it is possible to review the effectiveness of boards. The AGB has developed criteria or bench marks that can be used by boards of various types of institutions—private, public, multicampus, and the like—for self-study and self-evaluation. In addition, a trustee audit instrument can also be used in such efforts. Particularly if guided by an external consultant or mentor, board self-evaluation efforts have been constructive, especially when there is time to discuss and reflect on needed improvements, as in retreat settings.

Some public boards have gone beyond self-evaluation and authorized independent advisers or consultants to conduct external reviews. In such a process, constituent representatives, public officials, community leaders, and other relevant persons are asked for their views on board performance. Most recently, the Board of Regents of the University of Minnesota underwent such an assessment. It engaged four independent persons to conduct the review, with Harold L. Enarson, president emeritus of Ohio State University, as chair. Using a modified set of the AGB criteria, the assessment committee conducted interviews in January 1991 with representatives of faculty, students, alumni, senior administrators, other staff, and several regents emeriti. At the conclusion of its deliberations, the committee prepared a report for the chair of the Board of Regents, which is now a public document ("Assessment of the Board of Regents," 1991). In it, the regents came out looking very well.

Even if governing boards are reluctant to undergo such a public assessment, it must be argued that a periodic review of board performance is a constructive undertaking. Boards can benefit from reflecting on perceptions of their conduct and effectiveness. Respondents can be wrong in their judgments and attitudes, but ignorance of those judgments and attitudes cannot be defended.

The Current Concerns and Criticisms of Governing Boards

As is to be expected, governing boards have been criticized over the years for their unrepresentative membership, aloofness, performance, and more. Regarding unrepresentativeness, studies of the characteristics of board members show them to be overwhelmingly white, Anglo-Saxon, and primarily business and professional men in their fifties (Nason 1982). Encouragingly, the board membership of public institutions is more varied than that of independent institutions—particularly those that are self-perpetuating without significant opportunity for members' election by alumni or other constituents.

Regarding aloofness, many faculty members and administrators rightly express concern about boards crossing the line between policy and administration or engaging in "micromanagement," as uneducated boards perennially want to do—interfering in decisions ranging from the appointment of visiting lecturers and individual faculty members to the recognition of particular student organizations. Today, however, critics more often charge boards with ineffectiveness than with interference. In many cases, the extensive delegation of board authority to presidents and by presidents to faculty bodies has inhibited legitimate board action. Thus, in his extensive list of criticisms of the boards of nonprofit organizations and academic institutions, Houle reported that they are seen as ineffectual rather than too intrusive (1989, 17–20).

In *The Guardians: Boards of Trustees of American Colleges and Universities* (1989), Clark Kerr and Marian Gade identified areas of praise and concern about boards that were mentioned by the respondents to a survey they conducted regarding trustees. Despite concern over politicization in the public sector, the respondents give overall commendation to boards for the provision of academic freedom. Not surprisingly, however, inadequate funding—either from fund raising or state appropriations—is a frequently mentioned area of concern. In addition, faculty leaders tend to believe that there is inadequate communication between boards and faculties, and some student leaders express similar sentiments in regard to board communication with students.

What the 1990s Will Bring

Issues of the 1980s—quality, assessment, general education require-ments, and the like—will continue to confront governing boards during the remainder of this decade. In addition, the proportion of present faculty who will retire in the 1990s will rise sufficiently to challenge institutions in finding new faculty. Faculty salaries, market factors, tenure, and the use of part-time faculty will all be issues for revisitation by trustees. Yet fiscal matters will most likely be top priority. The majority of states are faced with serious revenue problems that will affect state tuition assistance programs for students at private colleges as well as appropriations for state institu-tions. Tuition levels will rise, although the tuition gap between independent and public institutions will remain, if not widen. In some states, problems of access will recur as enrollment caps accompany budget reductions. In all of this, boards will be urged, more and more, to take charge. Fund raising, capital campaigns, and the reallocation of resources to address priority needs will be the central concerns of board members. As people with expe-rience in business and public affairs, most trustees are comfortable applying their experience to such matters. With the aid of competent presidents, most of them will be able to translate effectively their business orientation to the nonprofit world.

Probably the most controversial issue for governing boards that will develop as the decade unfolds is that encompassed by the word *centraliza-tion*. This issue will affect the boards of independent colleges and univer-sities somewhat differently than those of public institutions, where political officials will have their own agenda.

Centralization in Independent Colleges and Universities

The trustees of independent colleges and universities will continue to struggle, as they always have, with institutional budgets, deficits, and other fiscal matters, but as the decade progresses they will be urged by many voices to inject themselves more actively in academic decision. In some interesting ways, this will be a return to the proposal by Beardsley Ruml in his 1959 *Memo to a College Trustee*—a controversial document that attract-ed wide attention in independent liberal arts institutions. Ruml, a distin-guished former educator and prominent management expert, had been asked by the Ford Foundation's Fund for the Advancement of Education to look at the problems and challenges of liberal colleges and suggest changes in both their financial and their organizational management. His analysis of the problems resulted in his call for trustee action concerning the curriculum, long ago delegated to the faculty. "The weakness of the liberal college today and the measures both internal and external that must be taken to give the college the strength it badly needs require a change in the traditional management of the overall program of the liberal college. . . . The Trustees . . . must take back from the faculty as a body its present authority over the design and administration of the curriculum" (p. 13).

His proposal elicited much comment. The *Journal of Higher Education* published a symposium on it in the November 1959 issue, wherein eight prominent educators commented on it. J. Douglas Brown, dean of the faculty at Princeton University, criticized Ruml for attempting to apply "the techniques of mass production of the automobile industry" to the liberal arts college by having the trustees assume jurisdiction over the curriculum and class size (p. 412). "The number of departments or courses to be established in a college or university is not a proper decision for the board, the president, or the faculty to make in splendid isolation," he stated (p. 416)—arguing for "joint determination" of such matters or what had come to be called "shared governance" by the time of the Joint Statement on Government of Colleges and Universities seven years later.

In 1975, John Corson agreed with Ruml that boards should "reclaim from their faculties powers that had been entrusted to the boards and for the exercise of which they are responsible" (pp. 270–271). Corson did not agree with unilateral board decision making in isolation from the faculty and the president, but he called for much greater board questioning of institutional performance in all areas, including the academic.

During the 1990s, proposals with some of the same flavor as that of Ruml will most likely be made, especially the call for trustees to take back authority they have previously delegated to the faculty. Ruml's call for "informed trustees" (p. 77) and Corson's call for boards to question institutional performance obviously make sense, but little will be gained if trustees disregard the concerns of J. Douglas Brown and the principles of the 1966 Joint Statement regarding some participation of all involved institutional constituents in major institutional decisions. Brown was correct in the title of his response to Ruml: "Mr. Ruml's Memo: A Wrong Approach to the Right Problems." While boards retain the inherent right to take jurisdiction over all aspects of institutional operation, exerting this jurisdiction by themselves would be dysfunctional unless all parties clearly accept the circumstances as an emergency.

The Centralization of Public Colleges and Universities

Most observers of academic government discuss governing boards as boards for single institutions. Although that is true for almost all independent colleges and universities, it is increasingly not applicable to most public institutions. In a bit of prophecy in his 1975 book, Corson stated that "the prospect seems clear that the boards of individual public institutions will either be eliminated or their functions delimited and their status lowered in the years ahead. Only the private institutions will likely have boards of trustees by the year 2000" (p. 270). Already, only one-third of America's public campuses remain freestanding institutions with their own governing boards. All the rest are parts of multicampus universities or systems. In speaking of their governing boards, we may be referring to an entity that governs two campuses (the University of Illinois) or twenty-six (the University of Wisconsin System). Some systems have an overall governing board (Board of Governors) along with a board of trustees for each individual institution in the system, with responsibilities delegated by the superior board, as is the case in Massachusetts. There, the boards of trustees of individual state institutions have very little authority other than that delegated to them by the consolidated Board of Regents of Higher Education—in practice, presidential selection, assessment, and campus operation. (At this writing, the new Governor of Massachusetts is thinking of eliminating the superior Board of Regents entirely.) Some states have one governing board for each of their separate segments of higher education. Thus, California has three statewide boards: the Regents of the University of California (9 campuses), the Trustees of the California State University (20 campuses), and the Board of Governors of the California Community Colleges (107 institutions in 71 community college districts, each with its own board of trustees).

For public institutions within such multicampus systems, the consolidated governing boards pose special problems. One difficulty is that they become less an advocate for their institutions and more an impartial body attempting to reconcile conflicts within the system and be responsive to the concerns of legislators and governors. In 1984, John Millett noted that, from the standpoint of state government, one criticism of consolidated governing boards was that they were perceived as identified with institutional interests rather than state interests: "State governments wanted statewide governing boards to order presidents to behave differently and to tell them not to expect ever-increasing state financial support. The statewide governing boards perceived that they were being asked to make unpopular political decisions that state government officials, especially state legislatures, were unwilling to make" (p. 242). Certainly, the concept of trusteeship as applied originally to boards of independent colleges is strained, if not distorted, by the many conflicting expectations for consolidated governing boards. They cannot be expected to be knowledgeable about or sensitive to the concerns of individual campuses, and communication—even with faculty and students—tends to be centralized and filtered through system administrators and political leaders of faculty and student organizations.

To moderate some of these problems, Kerr and Gade urged the appointment of campus-based boards "with appropriate delegated authority" within consolidated systems (1989, 123). They argued that "campus-based boards can give more intense consideration than system boards to buildings and grounds issues; to relations with faculty, students, alumni, and local communities; to fund raising; to the performance of the campus head; and to the appointment of officers below the CEO level." The sixteen-campus University of North Carolina is a good example of this arrangement. The statute creating the university's Board of Governors as a single governing board for all of its senior institutions also provided for institutional boards of trustees with whatever powers the board itself might delegate. In 1972, the board approved an extensive list of delegations of power to the campus-based boards of trustees. As Philip G. Carson, who has served as the chairperson of the board, has stated, the board "kept for itself exclusive control in three areas only: approval of new degree programs, budget requests submitted to the General Assembly, and approval of key personnel appointments" (1987). One has to be impressed with this effort to provide as much campus decentralization as possible in what is classified as a consolidated board system.

Beyond the creation of multicampus systems, twenty-seven states have established coordinating or regulatory agencies or commissions for higher education that are concerned with long-range planning, budget review, program authority and approval, and the like. These coordinating commissions are, in effect, agencies of the state operating as an instrument between the governor and legislature and the governing boards of public institutions. Their executive officers are the members of the association of State Higher Education Executive Officers, which works closely with the Education Commission of the States. While these commissions are not governing boards, there can be considerable ambiguity as to what constitutes coordination and what remains governance. For example, Maryland has a consolidated University of Maryland System that includes all senior institutions but two, and those two have their own individual governing boards. In addition, the Maryland legislature has created the Maryland Higher Education Commission as a coordinating and planning body. A careful examination of the commission's 1988 enabling legislation shows several areas of overlapping authority between it and the three governing boards. Moreover, and perhaps most significantly, the executive officer of the coordinating commission sits as a member of the governor's cabinet. In the best of circumstances, institutional boards, statewide boards, and coordinating commissions, along with their executive staffs, can work together and reach agreement in ways that state statutes may not describe. Otherwise, the effect of coordinating commissions on the role of governing boards will be further diffusion of responsibility for institutional decisions.

In still other ways, the boards of public institutions seem to be losing authority to centralized state agencies and public officials, both elected and appointed. Some states treat their public colleges and universities as routine state agencies, with controls over purchasing, personnel positions, the filling of vacancies, the carryover of unexpended funds from one fiscal year to the next, and various versions of line-item budgeting. To economize, New Hampshire once sought to impose the same state menu on the inmates in its prisons, the patients in its mental hospitals, and the students in its colleges—despite the fact that, unlike the prisoners and patients, the students were paying for their board and room. Even salaries may be set within the same framework and context as that of all other state employees. D. Bruce Johnstone, Chancellor of the State University of New York, has commented in this regard: "The consequence of wages and salaries being set (with or without collective bargaining negotiations) by the state and not by the public university trustees or administration is that the university itself loses control over about 80 percent of its costs" (1991, 23B).

Beyond such controls, governors and legislators seek more direct ways to link state institutions with state economic development goals. They can create a variety of incentives and disincentives in state budget and financing policies that provide leverage for institutions to change in ways that coincide with state policies—accountability, quality, assessment, curricula, graduation requirements, teacher training, and cooperation with public schools and other public agencies. Obviously, if there is one chief state higher education officer and one governing board for state higher education, such mandates and controls will be more easily achieved than with a variety of boards and executive officers. Public colleges and universities are clearly vital to a state's quality of life and economy, but they are more than instruments of a state's political policies, and their governing boards have to guard their essential integrity as academic institutions. No one else is charged with that responsibility.

Two related problems may increase during the 1990s along with this trend toward state centralization. One concerns the responsibility of governing boards to act as the court of last resort for disputes within the institution. Patrick M. Callan observed that this responsibility, too, is eroding in public institutions.

> As state legislatures have moved to more frequent and longer sessions and as their staffs have increased in size, legislators have become more willing to play the role of courts of last appeal for those who are disaffected by institutional decisions in public colleges and universities. Presidents and governing boards have come to recognize that, often, the instigators of legislative intrusion into institutional decision making are the faculty, staff, and students, sometimes supported by professional lobbyists and political action committees (Callan 1991, 20B).

The second problem involves the notion of individual trustees serving as representatives of special group or political interests. Many observers, this writer included, have noted with concern that the trustee or guardian function expected of boards has been eroding as board members perceive of themselves as representatives of specific state, political, or group interests. Kerr and Gade have warned, "We see a particular threat in the public sector of higher education in the gradual but by now significant shift from independent guardian-type boards to politicized representational boards. Direct public control through governors and legislatures may easily come to appear to be more protective of the overall public interest and more subject to an effective system of checks and balances than a system of local boards representational of different special interests varying by time and place" (1989, 108–109).

I do not attribute malevolence to the steady movement toward greater centralization and additional layers of decision making and control in public higher education. In fact, many of the goals sought by such actions seek legitimate public policy outcomes that are inherently supportable. The concern, however, is with the cumulative effect of all such actions, whereby not only are governing boards weakened, but also so many different parties are involved that, ultimately, no one is accountable. No one has expressed this concern more forthrightly than Kerr and Gade in noting how centralization runs counter to the trend toward decentralization in both American economic policy and governmental theory here and abroad (1989, 117).

Conclusion

There may have been a time when serving as a trustee or regent meant letting your name be used on a letterhead or showing up at commencement to hear a report from the president and be wined and dined. William A. Dees, Jr., a distinguished former chairman of North Carolina's Board of Governors implied as much when he addressed the state's assembled institutional boards of trustees in 1987: "Some folks see the position of trustee only as a position of honor—a reward for past service—honorific." But he went on to say, "If you see it that way, you would be rendering a service to yourself, the university, and the state, to resign now. The position of trustee is one of service and responsibility." My own experience as a consultant to many governing boards and a discussion leader at many board retreats has convinced me that most trustees and regents want their service to make a significant contribution to their institution. They do not want to deal with trivia or be rubber stamps.

Despite the reality that presidents are employees of governing boards, presidents must assume more responsibility for what board members understand about their role and what they experience in this role (Kauffman 1980). Board members must understand that effective governance and management of an institution represent means to an end—and that they are not ends in themselves. The central purposes of academic institutions have to do with scholarship and learning. All of the efforts of boards, as well as faculty and administrators, are for the central purpose of having learning take place. Evidence of that achievement is satisfaction enough for most governing boards.

References

American Association of University Professors. 1966. "Statement on Government of Colleges and Universities." *AAUP Bulletin,* 52:375–379.

American Council on Education. 1987. "Campus Trends, 1987." *Higher Education Panel Report Number 75.* Washington, D.C.: American Council on Education, August.

"Assessment of the Board of Regents of the University of Minnesota." 1991. Harold L. Enarson, Chair of Assessment Committee. Report Submitted to the Board of Regents, 7 February.

Association of American Colleges. 1985. *Integrity in the College Curriculum: A Report to the Academic Community: The Findings and Recommendations of the Project on Redefining the Meaning and Purpose of Baccalaureate Degrees.* Washington, D.C.: Association of American Colleges.

Ben-David, Joseph. 1972. *American Higher Education: Directions Old and New.* New York: McGraw-Hill.

Bennett, William J. 1984. *To Reclaim a Legacy: A Report on the Humanities in Higher Education*. Washington, D.C.: National Endowment for the Humanities.

Brown, J. Douglas. 1959. "Mr. Ruml's Memo: A Wrong Approach to the Right Problems." *Journal of Higher Education*, 30:412–416.

Callan, Patrick M. 1991. "Reflections on Cost Control in the Public and Private Sectors." *Policy Perspectives*, 3(2):20B–21B.

Carnegie Commission on Higher Education. 1973. *Governance of Higher Education: Six Priority Problems*. New York: McGraw-Hill.

Carnegie Foundation for the Advancement of Teaching. 1982. *The Control of the Campus: A Report on the Governance of Higher Education*. A Carnegie Foundation Essay. Washington, D.C.: Carnegie Foundation for the Advancement of Teaching.

Carson, Philip G. 1987. Unpublished speech given at the Conference on Trusteeship, University of North Carolina at Wilmington, 8–9 October.

Corson, John J. 1975. *Governance of Colleges and Universities*, rev. ed. New York: McGraw-Hill.

Dees, William A., Jr. 1987. Unpublished speech given at the Conference on Trusteeship, University of North Carolina at Wilmington, 8–9 October.

Fisher, James L. 1991. *The Board and the President*. New York: American Council on Education/Macmillan.

Houle, Cyril O. 1989. *Governing Boards: Their Nature and Nurture*. San Francisco: Jossey-Bass.

Ingram, Richard T., et al. 1980. *Handbook of College and University Trusteeship*. San Francisco: Jossey-Bass.

Johnstone, D. Bruce. 1991. "Productivity and Cost Containment: The Challenge of Public Sector Budgeting." *Policy Perspectives*, 3(2):22B–23B.

Kauffman, Joseph F. 1980. *At the Pleasure of the Board: The Service of the College and University President*. Washington, D.C.: American Council on Education.

Kerr, Clark, and Marian L. Gade. 1989. *The Guardians: Boards of Trustees of American Colleges and Universities*. Washington, D.C.: Association of Governing Boards of Universities and Colleges.

McGuinness, Aims C., Jr. 1990. "State Coordination and Governance of Higher Education—1991." In *State Postsecondary Education Structures Handbook*, pp. 1–26. Denver: Education Commission of the States.

Millett, John D. 1984. *Conflict in Higher Education: State Government Coordination versus Institutional Independence*. San Francisco: Jossey-Bass.

Nason, John W. 1982. *The Nature of Trusteeship: The Role and Responsibilities of College and University Boards*. Washington, D.C.: Association of Governing Boards of Universities and Colleges.

National Commission on Excellence in Education. 1983. *A Nation at Risk*. Washington, D.C.: U.S. Department of Education.

Rudolph, Frederick. 1962. *The American College and University: A History*. New York: Knopf.

Ruml, Beardsley. 1959. *Memo to a College Trustee: A Report on Financial and Structural Problems of the Liberal College*. New York: McGraw-Hill.

Study Group on the Conditions of Excellence in American Higher Education. 1984. *Involvement in Learning: Realizing the Potential of American Higher Education*. Washington, D.C.: National Institute of Education.

Upcraft, M. Lee., John N. Gardner, et al. 1989. *The Freshman Year Experience: Helping Students Survive and Succeed in College*. San Francisco: Jossey-Bass.

IV Evolving Curriculum and Disciplines

14 New Dimensions for General Education

VIRGINIA SMITH

Curricular issues that dominated the 1980s and promise to play a major role in the 1990s relate to that portion of the undergraduate experience outside students' majors or fields of specialization—particularly that portion most commonly referred to as "general education." During the eighties, majors in the undergraduate curriculum increased, separated, formed new unions, and generally responded both to the explosion of knowledge and to market demands. Clearly, some majors declined in importance. Classics disappeared from a number of curricula, as did geography. Fewer students majored in the humanities, and concerns increased about the decline in foreign language enrollment. While these issues and the range, scope, and quality of majors received some attention and discussion, the national debates and campus improvement efforts of the last decade focused, for the most part, on what else besides the major is represented by a baccalaureate degree.

The State and Scope of General Education

In 1978, Arthur Levine opened his chapter on general education in his *Handbook on Undergraduate Curriculum* with the assertion that "general education is a disaster area" (p. 3). Several national reports reinforced this assessment either by roundly criticizing what existed on the nation's campuses or by urging improvements that suggested the widespread lack of excellent programs. Indeed, the 1980s were studded with a whole galaxy of reports, not about the structure of our colleges and universities, not about governance, not about how to finance higher education, but about curriculum. Reports and discussions in the 1950s and 1960s about structure, governance, and finance were somehow clearer and in many ways less heated than those about curriculum. If recommendations about structure, governance, and finance meet with favor, at least some of them can be accomplished by higher education administrators or governmental agencies. But debates on curriculum go to the very heart of the enterprise, and— even more important—implementation of any recommendations on curriculum requires faculty involvement and often faculty initiative.

In his glossary of definitions, Levine equated *liberal education* and *general education*, saying that liberal education was the most frequent synonym for general education (Levine 1978, 525–528). In a book published a decade later, *The Meaning of General Education,* Gary Miller explored the historical roots of these two concepts and urged readers to understand their fundamental differences. He characterized general education as instrumentalist, with a focus on problem solving and acquisition of skills and abilities, and liberal education as rationalist, being more concerned with the life of the mind as the arena for learning. He described general education as psychological, with its interest in individual and social change, whereas liberal education, on the other hand, is basically logical, targeting on the mental processes involved in thinking through abstract ideas. And, perhaps most important, to Miller liberal education is essentialist: it seeks, studies, and tries to understand truths that are universal, that are essential (1988, 183).

Miller's comparison stated the distinctions in the extreme, but these extremes help us identify the differential effect of the two paradigms. Liberal education is less affected by changes in the society in which it exists; educationally, it operates as a conserving force. It relies more on the past than on the present and the future, whereas general education must take the present into account in terms of both the students that come to it and the society in which it operates.

Are these useful distinctions between liberal and general education? For Miller, the distinctions provided a way of characterizing the underlying assumptions in the reports of the last decade. He identified the report of the National Institute of Education's Study Group on the Conditions of Excellence in American Higher Education, *Involvement in Learning* (1984), as close to the general education model. The report of the National Endowment for the Humanities, *To Reclaim a Legacy* (Bennett 1984), was to Miller more clearly a liberal education model, with its *50 Hours* (Cheney 1989) being nearer to the general education model than the early endowment report but still essentially following a liberal education model. The Association of American Colleges published *Integrity in the College Curriculum* (1985), a hybrid, but the association's subsequent report, *A New Vitality in General Education* (1988), drew more heavily on the general education model.

As analytically helpful as these two carefully contrasted models might be, Miller's distinctions have not been widely used in current discussions on campuses about the nonmajor component of undergraduate education, nor have these distinctions been used in achieving the kind of consensus needed for improvements. It can be argued, in fact, that many campuses are not utilizing either model but have developed their curricular design to serve a purpose that is a relatively small element by itself in either perspective— that of simply providing some exposure to subjects outside the student's major.

To achieve a better understanding of how campuses are approaching general education and what steps they are taking to improve their programs beyond the major, the Exxon Educational and the Ford Foundations have funded a study, "Exploring Good Practices in General Education," that is sponsored by the Society for Values in Higher Education and directed by Virginia B Smith, Lee Humphreys, and David C. Smith. The study has two phases: (1) a brief questionnaire about general education addressed to chief academic officers at each of the nation's universities and colleges and (2) team visits to selected campuses whose general education programs received multiple nominations as admirable programs by academic officers at other colleges and universities. Specialized institutions such as Bible institutes and medical schools were not included in the first phase of the study.

Table 14.1 shows the response rate to the phase 1 questionnaire by Carnegie Commission classification.

In order not to limit the responses to any particular a priori view of general education, the survey did not provide its own working definition of that phrase. Instead, several questions asked the chief academic officers for their views about general education. Responses to these questions indicated that little consensus exists about the meaning, purpose, and content of general education, but the responses also provided substantial evidence for why there should be considerable variety in implementing general education programs.

Table 14.1   Rates of Response to the Questionnaire about General Education

Carnegie Class	Total Number of Coded Records in Class	Number in Class Responding	% in Class Responding
Comprehensive universities 1	404	251	62.1
Comprehensive universities 2	167	98	58.7
Doctorate-granting universities 1	46	28	60.9
Doctorate-granting universities 2	59	29	49.2
Liberal arts colleges 1	139	87	62.6
Liberal arts colleges 2	418	219	52.4
Research universities 1	70	35	50.0
Research universities 2	33	15	45.5
Two-year colleges	1,151	477	41.4

The Purposes of General Education

Although much of the national debate on general education has focused primarily on curricular design and the subject-matter content to be included in it, responses to the questionnaire established that many chief academic officers see curricular design as only one aspect of a much broader set of educational techniques and conditions that support and ultimately make up the resulting program of general education. From their open-ended responses to a question about the purpose of general education at their institution, we were able to distinguish six different purposes for general education.

1. *Heritage*: To provide a common core of great ideas or great books; to pass on a common western heritage
2. *Counterpoint*: To expose students to a broader range of subject matter than they would find in their majors; to achieve breadth—at its best, an enriching context for the major; at its worst, simple exposure to a series of fragments

3. *Instrumental*: To develop particular skills, such as writing, speaking, and critical thinking
4. *Development or Empowerment*: To develop the whole learner, in contrast to emphasis upon specific skills, particularly to develop the basis for becoming a lifelong learner
5. *Social Agenda*: To infuse the general education component with some social purpose or purposes such as global awareness, environmental sensitivity, preparation for responsible citizenship in a democratic society
6. *Valuing*: To perceive what values are operating in a situation, how values are determined, and at a few institutions even to inculcate certain values.

Most colleges use some combination of two or more of these purposes, with the particular combination of purposes varying from campus to campus.

At a recent Council of Independent Colleges Institute for Deans, the participants were given this list of six purposes and were asked to rank the importance or priority of each of the six purposes as demonstrated by the educational strategies used to accomplish general education on their campuses. Table 14.2 shows the resulting rankings.

The purpose most closely related to Miller's ideal model of "liberal education" we have labeled Heritage. Only 29 percent of the respondents put this in the top two priorities. Counterpoint, on the other hand, was placed in the top two priorities by 56 percent. A full paradigm for "general education" as developed by Miller would probably address the purposes of Skill Development, Empowerment, Social Agenda, and Values, yet none of these purposes except Skill Development, which was identified in the top two priorities by 69 percent, received high priority ratings by the deans.

There seems little question that the purposes of Counterpoint and Skill Development are the most common objectives of general education on

Table 14.2   Relative Importance of Six Priorities in General Education

Priority	A (Highest)	B	C	D	E	F (Lowest)
Heritage	7%	22%	25%	19%	12%	15%
Counterpoint	39	17	12	12	10	10
Skill development	32	37	9	12	5	5
Empowerment	7	5	19	27	29	14
Social agenda	7	7	14	10	27	37
Values	9	12	22	20	17	20

American campuses today. The usual way of implementing these purposes is through distribution requirements. Given the organizational structure of most campuses, distribution requirements may be the only type of implementation that can be used for general education without making significant organizational changes.

The Organizational Status of General Education

Although most educators probably assume that general education is an important element on their campuses, in organizational status it is accorded far less importance than the lowliest discipline-based department. General education is the only undergraduate program that affects all students, but even the smallest discipline-based department has someone designated as chair (and usually that is that person's only academic administrative responsibility). The same is rarely true for general education; information from our 1987 survey shows that less than 3 percent of America's colleges and universities have a designated academic administrator whose sole responsibility is general education. Similarly, the chairs of discipline-based departments normally have a budget and hire faculty, and the faculty within each department design the curriculum for that department. Yet discussions in the field following up on our question of organizational status suggest that few colleges have separate budgets for general education, faculty are not hired to teach general education courses as such, and faculty members are seldom hired because of their understanding of or ability with reference to general education needs.

The lowly internal organizational status of general education did not seem to trouble the administrators responding to our survey. In response to a question about what they would do to improve general education on their campuses, assuming they had the resources to make such improvements, fewer than 5 percent said they would modify the organizational status of general education.

Whatever general education is on the nation's campuses, in most instances it is inappropriate to think of it as a program. It rarely has any of the structural or resource supports required for program development and maintenance. Instead, on many campuses general education is nothing more than a catalog construct: a construct sometimes made up of designated courses but more frequently made up of directions to take courses in certain designated departments. It is a construct whose shape is determined by putting together pieces of a curriculum usually designed for some other primary purpose (such as the lower-division courses in a major). The selection of the pieces is often the result of intricate faculty politics involving faculty slots and protection of turf rather than being a response to an identified educational purpose.

An analysis of the responses to our survey affirms the idea that general education on many campuses cannot be viewed as a curricular program. Indeed, in the survey, chief academic officers did not think about general education as only, or even as primarily, a curricular program. One survey question asked, "In your judgment what is the most notable aspect of your general education program?" About half of the responses to this question referred to features we would ordinarily think of as curricular design features, but the remaining half highlighted noncurricular design aspects such as a requirement for work experience, an emphasis on outcomes, cultural experiences outside classrooms, assessment, advising programs, the quality of the faculty, and skill development purposes within courses or across courses.

Whether general education is viewed as a curricular program or as a set of institutional responses to educational purpose might be seen simply as a question of semantics. What real difference does it make what name we give to the phenomenon? It makes a great deal of difference. The way we characterize general education determines the questions we ask about it, and the answers we obtain to those questions often pave the way for its evaluation. If a college is using a strategy far broader than a simple curricular design to achieve its undergraduate educational purposes, then rating that college's general education program on the basis of whether or not it has a core curriculum, asking questions about the content of the core, and determining if there is a sequence in the core completely miss the college's own way of responding to the educational needs of its undergraduate students. These questions might tell us whether the Heritage purpose is being served. By themselves, however, without reference to pedagogy, assessment techniques, or institutional support systems, these questions about "core" cannot satisfactorily tell us whether other purposes listed above are being served—purposes identified as important by many college and university academic officers.

Examples of Good Practice

Another question on our survey asked respondents to identify one or two colleges that had admirable general education programs. Over 826 citations were made, naming 344 colleges with general education programs considered admirable by at least one other chief academic officer. Analysis of the citations revealed that 3 colleges received almost 20 percent of the citations; 13 colleges received almost 40 percent of them, and 27 colleges received over 50 percent.

The three colleges receiving 20 percent of the citations were Alverno College in Milwaukee, Wisconsin; Brooklyn College of the City University of New York; and St. John's College in Annapolis, Maryland, and Santa Fe, New Mexico. Alverno and St. John's are private, identify themselves as liberal arts colleges, and are both relatively small in enrollment. Brooklyn College is public and has sixteen thousand students, twelve thousand of whom are undergraduate. The current program at St. John's is the oldest of the three, Alverno's was developed in the early 1970s, and Brooklyn College developed its program in the early 1980s.

The three programs differ markedly from one another, but there are a few strikingly similar features in the programs of Alverno and St. John's, including the importance of assessing student achievement. A major element of Alverno's program is the carefully calibrated student assessments that are embedded in its curriculum. Its assessment system relates to the eight abilities that infuse the Alverno curriculum—communication, analysis, problem solving, valuing, social interaction, responsibility for the global environment, effective citizenship, and aesthetic response—and that shape the pedagogy and collegiate structure as much as do the academic discipline-based courses and departments. The Alverno catalog states (p. 2):

> Alverno's student evaluation method, called assessment, helps a student and her teachers judge her command of the subject matter and mastery of the eight abilities. Unlike tests, assessments evaluate not just what a student knows, but how well she can apply what she knows. . . . A student does not receive grades as a result of assessments. The validation she receives when she has successfully completed an assessment indicates that she has met the detailed, rigorous requirement set by the college.

In conversations with students at Alverno, we gathered that they feel that they learn much more from the assessment than from grades. They gain information about how to improve and what they do well, and they are judged against a standard rather than being ranked or compared with others by being given a score or grade that, in itself, yields little information and often provides neither motivation nor guidance on how to improve.

St. John's also has a unique approach to the assessment of student performance. Its catalog states (p. 34):

Within the College, the most important form of evaluation is the don rag. Once a semester, freshmen, sophomores and juniors meet with their tutors in the don rag. The tutors report to one of the seminar leaders on the student's work during the semester; the students are then invited to respond to their tutor's report and comment on their own work. Advice may be requested and given; difficulties may be aired, but grades are not reported or discussed. In the junior year, students may request a conference rather than a don rag. In that case, students report on their own work and then the tutors comment on that report. By the time students are seniors, it is assumed they can evaluate their own work and there is no don rag unless the tutor believes there is a special need for one. . . . The tutor's comprehensive judgment of the student is reported to the Dean each semester as a conventional letter grade, A, B, C, D or F, where C indicates that the work is at a satisfactory level. . . . Within the College, grading is not of central importance. Students will be told their grades only on request. They are encouraged, however, not to work for grades, but rather to develop their powers of understanding.

In both of these colleges the assessment technique has a profound influence on pedagogy. Although quite different in detail, both of the approaches are similar in the key role that assessment plays in the educational experience and are also similar in the diminished value given to letter grades.

In our study, less than 5 percent of all colleges and universities indicated that they had developed comprehensive individual assessment systems other than the usual letter grades in courses. Almost all of the colleges that have developed such systems turn out to be among the twenty-seven colleges that received 50 percent of the citations for having admirable general education programs.

Alverno and St. John's also place great importance on the fusion of the pedagogical approach with educational philosophy. At neither institution is the teaching approach left to the *sole* determination of the individual faculty member. The unified vision of educational purpose leads to concern for and, finally, some agreement on the most suitable instructional styles and strategies to accomplish the shared educational purpose, as well as some agreement on the most suitable assessment technique to evaluate achievement of this purpose.

The two colleges are contrasted, however, in terms of educational purpose. As the Alverno catalog states, Alverno's purpose was reached by faculty asking themselves in the early 1970s:

What will best enable [our students] to succeed in their careers? What insights will most enrich their lifetimes? What abilities will make a lasting difference in their homes, their families and communities? What will equip them to continue as independent learners who can adapt to and grow with the fast-changing world?

Gradually faculty reached common agreement on what students need most for success after college. Knowledge and the abilities to apply it became the twin goals of their teaching. Working as a group, they restructured the entire curriculum from start to finish to assure that every course helped students advance in both. To unify their teaching, they organized the entire curriculum around eight abilities that require a broad range of knowledge and a great deal of practice. . . . The eight abilities give backbone to Alverno's curriculum, uniting it with a common purpose for teaching and an organizing framework for learning (p. 1).

St. John's states its purposes as follows (p. 6): "Liberal education should seek to develop free and rational men and women committed to the pursuit of knowledge in its fundamental unity, intelligently appreciative of their common cultural heritage, and conscious of the social and moral obligations."

St. John's is close to Miller's paradigm for liberal education, whereas Alverno is close to the paradigm for general education. For St. John's, the most important unifying dimension is in the great books approach, although the development of liberal arts understandings and intellectual skills (discussion, translation, writing, experiment, mathematical demonstration, and musical analysis) are also given deliberate attention.

For Alverno it is the eight abilities and their assessments that provide the principal unifying dimension for the educational experience, but certainly the acquisition and understanding of knowledge is given substantial importance as well. The educational plans of both colleges, along with those of several other colleges in the group of twenty-seven receiving the highest number of citations, are highly integrated, requiring substantial active collaboration among faculty and also requiring that students understand the educational strategies of the institution.

Brooklyn College's program requires continuing collaborative work by the faculty through an annual faculty/curriculum development seminar held each summer. That the core requires this constant attention and thus provides opportunities for studying integrative teaching techniques, for sharing a common purpose, is one of the core's greatest strengths and, according to many faculty on the campus, has led to the revival of collegiality.

The core at Brooklyn defines one-quarter of each student's work at the college. It represents an admirable model at a large university. Although often cited as a core that defines the general education knowledge each student is expected to acquire, the Brooklyn program is also concerned with skill development, particularly methodological and expressive capabilities. Even in its core, the Brooklyn effort is not as integrated as the programs at Alverno and St. John's, but it is far more integrated than the typical general education programs at most public universities and four-year colleges and at many liberal arts colleges. Implementation of its program has required supplemental organizational structures, including a standing committee on the core and core course coordinators appointed by the president.

Organizational structures at Alverno and St. John's also differ from those at most colleges. At Alverno, every faculty member belongs not only to a department but also to an ability group. For instance, a faculty member might introduce herself as a professor of history and a member of the problem-solving group. Group membership may change from year to year, but what does not change is that patterns and networks of faculty collaboration are at least two dimensional. All faculty members have responsibility for teaching both knowledge and abilities and have numerous needs and opportunities to discuss both instructional and assessment strategies with other faculty members.

The other twenty-four colleges that make up the most frequently cited colleges share in varying degrees the educational strategies described above. Examining the educational programs of all of these institutions in detail leads to the inescapable conclusion that colleges that are seen as having excellent programs have been quite idiosyncratic in working out their own purposes and strategies to address them. Furthermore, it would be impossible to obtain any real understanding of the genius of these programs by asking questions related only to curricular design. Many of the programs cited as good examples by the respondents to our survey do not even use the term *general education* with reference to their undergraduate programs, nor do they respond to the same educational purposes. Among the twenty-seven frequently cited are colleges that place substantial emphasis on co-curricular programs outside their curricular design. To judge the quality of those educational programs only by curricular design would be to fail to take into consideration very strong elements. In each case, the college implemented its educational purpose with an appropriate strategy, uses different unifying techniques to create an integrity in the educational experience, and evidences an understanding and acceptance of their purposes and strategies across constituencies on the campus, although not all have the same degree of success in these efforts. And in those cases where programs seem the strongest, there is evidence that either the administration and faculty have a fairly clear understanding of their students and their learning needs or the mission of the college is so explicit that most of the students who come are good fits with the program.

Developments Affecting the Future

Certain emerging developments lead to optimism about the shape of the curriculum in our nation's colleges in the twenty-first century. First, there is growing dissatisfaction, both on the campuses and in the public arena, with distribution requirements as the only or primary design for general education. It is true that distribution is an excellent strategy for responding to the Counterpoint purpose, but, in the light of all the purposes we would like undergraduate education to serve, this particular purpose increasingly appears trivial. Even the language often used to describe it seems weak and ineffective: "the exposure of students to a range of disciplines." In most cases, when people talk about "exposure," they hope that the person exposed doesn't catch anything. In this case, educators hope that students catch *something*, but they seem willing only to specify the exposure and leave the rest up to chance.

Second, taking all of the information from our survey and site visits into account, it seems that many institutions are infusing their educational programs with techniques for improving skills, with more interdisciplinary courses, with specially designed freshman courses and senior capstone courses, with greater integration of off-campus learning into the educational experience, and with a movement away from relegating general education to an isolated block of the curriculum. There also seems to be some movement toward addressing common (non–major based) learning needs across the entire undergraduate education program both inside and outside the major and over all four years of the program.

If our faculties are actually led into real discussion of purposes, we may see in the twenty-first century greater cohesion and integrity in all of our undergraduate programs. Unfortunately, thus far much of the debate on the improvements has been limited to strategies rather than purposes. Watching the curricular debates in the last decade, both on campus and in the public arena, reminds me of the marvelous caricature of a discussion between the old and the new education in Aristophanes' *The Clouds*. You may recall that the debate got under way with the old and the new hurling invectives at one another, somewhat reminiscent of today's hot exchanges about what should be in a core curriculum or whether there should be a core. In *The Clouds*, when the debaters finally got down to their basic arguments, the old tradition of education based its claim on the fact that it had educated the heroes who were needed to fight at Marathon—that it had inculcated in the citizens of Athens the necessary attitudes and qualities of character for them to take heroic action. But the new traditions saw the times and the needs differently, claiming that the need now was not for mental homogeneity or adherence to rules, but for intellectual agility. The societal need was not for heroes in the field but for political leaders and orators. The old and the new were agreed that the curriculum had some responsibility to serve the social agenda, but their disagreement was deeper than the curriculum and deeper than methods of pedagogy; this was indeed a conflict about the social agenda for Athens, about ends. Most of their explicit discussion, however, had been about means. Similarly, the curricular debates today have underlying tensions about inclusivity or exclusivity, about pluralism or amalgamation, even about a civil society or a civilized society and, increasingly, about the role of the United States in a global society.

Virtually every effort at improvement starts as a response to a perceived problem. Thus, the elective system of the late nineteenth century was a response to too much rigidity, while the emphasis on distribution requirements in the early twentieth century was a response to too much specialization. Today, one of our great concerns is too much fragmentation. It is natural, then, that there are demands for greater coherence in the curriculum. Preliminary to determining what strategy for coherence should be employed, we need to agree on answers to essential first questions—coherence for whom, and about what, and for what purpose? Many seem to want to find today's coherence by using yesterday's patterns let out a bit at the seams because we've grown a little, inserting a gore here and there to accommodate non-Western culture, including in the syllabus a female writer, but essentially keeping the same pattern.

If coherence is to be merely coherence of knowledge, then instructors feel that they can make the final determination on what knowledge is important and how it should be organized. The students are the receivers. Coherence organized in this fashion is essentially an authoritarian approach that can be modified at the periphery but hardly at the core. On the other hand, if general education is thought of as a way of organizing a learning experience and if the coherence sought is in the learning experience itself, then the student can be taken into account—indeed, *must* be taken into account—in designing the experience.

If knowledge and its organization are alone at the heart of understanding, then the pedagogy likely to be used will probably be didactic with the learner passive. This does not have to be the situation, but if the teaching style is left to the individual faculty member, as it often is in most institutions, the didactic style will be used in many courses. Furthermore, the structure of many institutions, the evaluation processes used, and the size of classes also make it likely that the didactic approach will be the only logistically possible approach. If knowledge is the means and not the end of learning—a raw material along with the student in the learning experience—then the resulting pedagogy is far more likely to require active participation of the student.

As long as our questions on general education focus primarily on how many courses are required and what content is included in those courses, we will neither be able to develop appropriate remedies for fragmentation nor uncover the ways in which some colleges have developed unusually effective undergraduate programs. To suggest that the major purposes of general education can be achieved in a certain specified array of courses is unrealistic. The sweep of the recommendations made in two recent reports from the Association of American Colleges—*A New Vitality in General Education* (1988) and *The Challenge of Connecting Learning* (1990)—amply demonstrate both the desirability and the need to examine the undergraduate educational experience as a whole.

What should be the questions that we ask of colleges in the twenty-first century? At least four should be asked of every institution, with the first two concerning aims and outcomes.

1. What are the *purposes* of the undergraduate educational program?
2. What are the *educational* results of the program?

The combination of the answers to these two questions should provide the goals for the college with sufficient clarity to permit them to be used as a framework for developing curriculum, selecting instructional approaches, developing co-curricular activities, and identifying assessment needs.

The third question involves the means to ends and outcomes:

3. What are the essential *unifying strategies* that are used to provide coherence and essential meaning to the educational experience?

Unifying strategies need not reside only in the curricular design, although that is certainly a reasonable place to expect at least some of these strategies. The unifying strategies form the glue for the entire undergraduate experience. At Alverno, they are the framework of the eight abilities and their assessments. At St. John's, they are the consistent instructional approach and the great books. At Berea College in Kentucky, where the curriculum is very typical of many liberal arts colleges, some of the unifying strategies are outside the curriculum and are found in its work program, its compulsory convocations, and its strong links with Appalachia. At Colorado College, the block system is probably the pivotal force, and at the Evergreen State College in Olympia, Washington, the interdisciplinary one-course terms that create a working community of learners are a powerful unifying force.

The fourth and final question involves evaluation:

4. What *assessment techniques* are used to ensure that the purpose is well served, that the hoped-for educational results are obtained, and that the unifying strategies are working well?

Effective assessment systems at some stage require collaboration among faculty members. They should serve as aids for student and program improvements, not simply as ranking systems.

Answers to these four questions on each campus will be shaped by the history of the institution, the nature of its student body, and its physical and human resource patterns, but ultimately they will be shaped by the dominant values that underlie major educational decisions on that campus.

In the twenty-first century, it is anticipated that the answers to these questions—at least at independent institutions—will become more differentiated than in past decades. As economic pressures demand more effective use of resources and as competition for students demands more distinctive educational profiles, we may actually gain new dimensions to the diversity of higher education in the United States. If the campus responses to these questions lead to real diversity in the next century, then we might even see the emergence of multiple scales for excellence, scales related to the four questions above and not related primarily to selectivity of students enrolled or to richness of resources. The first few decades of the century could be a period in which all of us work more consciously, more deliberately, and more collaboratively on our campuses to understand the interplay between our values and the expression of them through our educational programs.

References

Alverno College. 1990. *Learning at Alverno: Alverno College Catalog, 1990–92.* Milwaukee: Alverno College.

Association of American Colleges. 1985. *Integrity in the College Curriculum.* Washington, D.C.: Association of American Colleges.

———. 1988. *A New Vitality in General Education.* Washington, D.C.: Association of American Colleges.

———. 1990. *The Challenge of Connecting Learning.* Washington, D.C.: Association of American Colleges.

Bennett, William. 1984. *To Reclaim a Legacy.* Washington, D.C.: National Endowment for the Humanities.

Cheney, Lynne. 1989. *50 Hours: A Core Curriculum for College Students*. Washington, D.C.: National Endowment for the Humanities.

Levine, Arthur. 1978. *Handbook on Undergraduate Curriculum*. San Francisco: Jossey-Bass.

Miller, Gary. 1988. *The Meaning of General Education*. New York: Teachers College Press.

St. John's College. 1988. *St. John's College Catalog, 1988–89*. Annapolis and Santa Fe: St. John's College.

Study Group on the Conditions of Excellence in American Higher Education. 1984. *Involvement in Learning: Realizing the Potential of American Higher Education*. Washington, D.C.: National Institute of Education.

15 The Humanities in the 1990s

ALBERTA ARTHURS

Through the 1970s and 1980s, scholars in the humanities in the United States developed two distinct and challenging methods of study that have changed their fields profoundly and perhaps permanently. One was the development of "specializations of difference" the newly segmented areas of ethnic studies, minority studies, and women's studies. The other was the "blurring of the genres," to use Clifford Geertz's now famous phrase of 1980—the blurring of the traditional boundaries and borders across the disciplines of the humanities: a development that has nudged anthropologists and literary critics, historians and economists, for instance, to converse in new ways.

These two parallel developments make themselves visible in quite different ways. The specializations of difference build up canons of new or neglected works and findings for discrete populations, asserting their separate meanings and paralleling them to existing canons and acknowledged fields. In contrast, the blurring of the genres breaks down the established lines of work in intellectual inquiry, suggesting intersections, overlays, juxtapositions, fresh formulations across disciplines, and ways of working. Between them, these large movements of the last two decades have shifted knowledge dramatically and have made possible new uses and new openings for humanities scholarship in the society at large.

The Specializations of Difference

In an influential 1986 article tracking changes in American historical study, Thomas Bender asserted that "the most innovative work done in the past fifteen years, whether by social historians or by intellectual historians, has explored the culture of groups in American society" (p. 127). Many observers agree and would push the observation further. Peter Stearns, for instance, claimed that one of the basic characteristics of social history as a field today is "a substantial focus on groups out of power" (1985, 322). Similar statements are made about discovery in literary studies and in other areas of the humanities. The implications of such work are extensive. As Lucy Lippard wrote in *Mixed Blessings: New Art in a Multicultural America*—a volume useful in understanding all the humanities today— "The boundaries being tested . . . are not just 'racial' and national. They are . . . those of gender and class, of value and belief systems, of religion and politics" (1990, 6). And John Higham, in his epilogue to *History: Professional Scholarship in America,* which provides a useful gloss on the changes in historiography in the 1970s and 1980s, spoke of a new "pluralist paradigm" in an effort to describe this fundamental change in areas of knowledge (1983, 261).

In the 1990s considerable speculation is emerging that this new work has been too separate, that the work of humanists has become fragmented and hermetic, that each social group is creating its own terms and networks, and that there is need for a new synthesizing principle or set of principles to place these separate scholarships within a frame or collectivity of humanistic understanding. It seems clear that a new challenge of this sort is next. Bender argued the need for it. Nell Painter, in response to Bender, welcomed "the genuine syntheses that have begun to appear that recognize discrimination and encompass the conceptual insights, as well as the subject matter, of the new histories of the last twenty years" (1987, 111–112). Roy Rosenzweig worried that perhaps it is too soon for synthesis; that we cannot expect "synthetic work to emerge before the monographic social and cultural studies of the past two decades are either completed or assimilated" (1987, 120). Debates about the content or the timeliness of synthesizing approaches in the humanities will deepen, but the search for synthesis—for the combining of the new specializations, for a theorizing about difference in the broad context of American society, will surely continue. Reviewing the developments in recent scholarship, veteran historian William McNeill stated that "the scope and range of historiography has widened, and that change looks as irreversible . . . as the widening of physics that occurred when Einstein's equations proved capable of explaining phenomena that Newton's could not" (1986, 9). Making an integral history out of this work—a widening that keeps intact the separate discoveries that have been made and reflects the crucial repositioning of groups that the new scholarships have achieved—is the stuff for scholars now.

What marks the specializations of difference—ethnic, minority, women's studies—is that, at base, they are foundational. They have come into being, one after another, as the diverse populations of this country have matured within it. Black studies began as an insistent, provocative voice allied—like the women's studies movement—directly to the political demands of the populations it studied. The successive stages of learning, of penetration, and of change are shown in its vocabulary, in the movement from "black studies" to the more descriptive "African-American studies" and now to "Africana studies," which incorporates into the field the worldwide diaspora of black peoples and the diverse products of that diaspora. Within the academic institutions of the United States, Chicano, Latino, Asian-American, and native American studies are pressing forward, many still in emergent stages, at the same time that black studies and women's studies are consolidating their gains of the last twenty years, advancing theory, perpetuating their newest ideas from deep within their originating disciplines, and making new work that is international in scope. The synthesis that is being called for will be a radically updated version of the "voluntary pluralism" that Lawrence Fuchs described in his recent book on race and ethnicity in America, *The American Kaleidoscope*. Fuchs called "voluntary pluralism" the "invention of Americans . . . in which individuals were free to express their ancestral affections and sensibilities, to choose to be ethnic, however and whenever they wished, or not at all" (1990, 5). That pluralism, as Fuchs made clear, depended on similarities in origin. Americans who could not achieve such invisibility had no choice, and had—within this definition of pluralism—no flexibility and no mobility. In the United States of today, "voluntary pluralism" must be newly defined. It will be based on the acceptance of difference, rather than on the masking of it; on interaction rather than integration; on celebrating difference rather than tolerating it. Fuchs used the image of a "kaleidoscope" in place of the "melting pot" in describing the scope of participating populations, concepts, and expectations in the United States today. (The first three chapters of his book are especially relevant reading.) Humanists have been instrumental in effecting these race, class, and gender repositionings through their development of the specializations of difference.

The Blurring of Boundaries

At the same time that these studies of difference have been building, another development in scholarship has been relocating the very lines and paths of knowledge. In his important 1980 article, "Blurred Genres: The Refiguration of Social Thought," Clifford Geertz predicted a "culture shift," a "jumbling of varieties of discourse," that amounts—as he analyzed it—to a whole new way of thinking and relating ideas. Rather than facing a set universe of disciplines and clear demarcations of knowledge, Geertz saw the social scientist and the humanist, even the scientist of the late twentieth century, "surrounded by a vast, almost continuous field of variously intended and diversely constructed works that we can order only practically, relationally, and as our purposes prompt us." This fluidity of ideas and models means that thinkers from all schools and specialties can borrow and swap, poach and plunder each others' territories "to distinguish the materials of human experience" (pp. 165–179).

In this "refiguring," the disciplines of the humanities become central to the intellectual efforts deemed most important in our times; they achieve a fresh centrality in the work of social sciences and even in the sciences. Much more of the "imagery, method, theory, and style" of intellectual inquiry is drawn from the humanities than had been true; the intellectual communities change; the humanist is less distanced, less confined, less rarefied. In the irony of uncertainty that underlies this refiguration, humanists are also less essentialist and less convinced of the sanctity of their methods and subjects. In the 1970s and 1980s, as Geertz saw with clarity, the old rules for understanding were broken. The disciplinary lines of work became less clear. The humanities could shift their ground and still not lose it. The challenge to humanists was great, and Geertz made no effort—in 1980—to predict whether this jumble, this "culture shift," would engage them positively.

It seems to be the need for new understandings and new answers in the 1970s and 1980s that carried scholars out of their usual spaces and into new, shared territories. The sciences and social sciences had moved much more closely in their inquiries to the humanistic questions: to unknowables, to value questions, to judgments based more on interpretation than on calculation. Geertz may have been seeing sooner than most observers the sense of unease that visits the sciences now and the increasing movement of the social sciences into comparative cultural studies that question the roles, the personae, of social scientists themselves within their own inquiry. Certainly he and others foresaw the questioning of scientific authority that is coming to characterize the pre-twenty-first century and the questioning of social and political authority that is taking place everywhere today.

The disaggregating of the disciplines brings the humanities into new importance in the late 1980s and the 1990s as they break away, bleed, or blur into other disciplines of study and into other sectors. The good old fields, like the good old boys, do not remain untouched. Gerald Graff affirmed this when he claimed that by the 1990s a great deal of recognized humanities research would not have qualified as "research" or "scholarship" at all at an earlier time, because it is bolder, more relevant to contemporary events, and less tidily derived from the disciplines than it once would have been (1992). Graff confirmed Geertz's idea of a "culture shift." So did James Clifford in *The Predicament of Culture,* when he discussed "modernity's inescapable momentum," people and things and disciplines "out of place" (1988, 5). Ethnography is done by anthropologists now, but also by poets and historians, collectors and curators, and by the travelers, immigrants, refugees, and natives whom they study. In the 1990s, the displacements Geertz described will transcend the disciplines and force startling conjunctions and reconceptions. "There is a Third World in every First World, and vice-versa," wrote the artist-scholar Trinh Minh-ha in one clear voicing of the shift (1986–87, 3).

These changes have not taken place without controversy. As humanists head into the twenty-first century, they will be prominent among the analysts of the radical readjustments going on worldwide. As environmental concerns force the reexamination of modern technology and of the principle of progress that has motivated change in this century, questions about cultures and about values become critical. As human populations move, realign, simultaneously mix and maintain their identities, ideas that the humanities disciplines have conventionally examined become burning issues for our times. Scholars differ on the dangers of such developments. Many humanists lament what they see as the irrevocable damage to their disciplines that such engagement brings. Others claim that the new positioning of the humanities disciplines and the relevancies of the disciplines are overdue, exciting, and full of opportunity.

The Domains of the Humanities

One way of examining this controversy, the debates about these developments, is to examine the very ground, the platform, on which the humanities stand. It has been most common to define the humanities as they have grown and matured in the United States as separate and distinct fields of study. A useful and famous list, dispensed by the National Endowment for the Humanities since its establishment by Congress in 1965, concretizes the disciplines in this way: "history; philosophy; languages; linguistics; literature; archaeology; jurisprudence; the history, theory, and criticism of the arts; ethics; comparative religion; and those aspects of the social sciences that employ historical or philosophical approaches" (National Foundation on the Arts and Humanities Act 1965).

In a profound sense, this taxonomy becomes the paradigm. By setting such a platform, the list defines not only what humanists study, but how they study (within their specialties) and how the results will be received (by other specialists). Of course, such a definitional paradigm, or platform, is useful. Providing categories of these kinds helps discovery and discourse by keeping research on track and forcing precision. But, equally, this kind of definitional paradigm is limiting. It encourages jargon, coterie research, and mild-manneredness concerning large ideas. It is an adequate but not a sufficient paradigm for the times.

Other conventional ways of describing the humanities are not much more illuminating. In addition to listing their parts, humanists sometimes describe themselves in numbers (journals or books published during a period of time or about a period of time; the numbers of subfields, professors, majors, or graduate students) or by their sociology (the job market, the openings in specific fields, the availability of funds, the politics of the academy or of the funding agencies). There is a large degree of comfort in repeating these taxonomies or definitions, and they have been in place, satisfactorily enough, for a long time. But they are challengeable by the new developments in scholarship during the last twenty years. On the very face of it, such static definitions are inadequate to the growth of new specialties and the extensive shifting of disciplinary boundaries that have been described.

It is important to ask, then, whether there are additional ways of thinking about humanities studies? Is there a better way of understanding the findings, the tools of analysis, the perspectives that are developing? Is there an analysis of the specialties that can better show their new connection to other specialties and fields? Can the humanities be described in ways other than their disciplines without becoming merely reductive or overly universalist or losing the fine subtleties, the speculations, that specialization affords?

A taxonomy more appropriate to these questions can be made by examining the functions and the effects of the humanities. Such an analysis takes the disciplines past the usual categories and into a consideration of their consequences. In an essay on higher education that has provided the analytic model for this section of this chapter, Clark Kerr once wrote that "higher education is more often described than evaluated" (1978, 158), and he proceeded to examine the actual consequences of higher education as a way of providing a more worthy measure of it. Similarly, an effort to examine the functions of the humanities provides a fuller measure of them. The examination of their actual consequences over the past quarter century demonstrates that the humanities, like the higher education community within which they sit, have more effects, more functions, and more force than they usually affirm.

Examined this way, the humanities also reveal the reasons for their own rifts, the sources of the controversy and debates in their ranks. If there is more force or power coming from the humanities than is usually acknowledged, it is inevitably accompanied by pain, resistance, and reaffirmation of the familiar. New work is stimulated; scholarship and society shift, but—equally—embedded expectations are frequently shredded or discarded or moved away from the center. The traditional functions of the humanities are crowded by new priorities. A list of the functions or consequences of the humanities reveals these tensions and provides insights into the dynamics of the 1990s. Moving from the most venerable to the most venturesome the functions of the humanities in our time look like this:

1. *Advancement of learning*: Including preservation and interpretation of the past, this is the classic function of humanities research. Adjusting the contexts of knowledge through the discovery of new knowledge and the reformulation of ideas has been the traditional pursuit of humanists.

2. *Enhancing quality of life and providing public service*: Traditionally associated with the humanities, these functions include appreciation of the arts and offerings of them (plays, poetry readings, lectures, libraries, museums), nonscholarly travel, language use, historical study, the making of social and artistic institutions, and civic contributions of many kinds.

3. *Aiding individual growth*: The transmission of information and ideas from a learned to a learning generation aids individual growth.

4. *Articulating ideals for society*: The disciplines of the humanities have traditionally dealt with societal ideals as subjects of study. In so doing, however, they become arbiters of those ideals and provide the battlefield for discussions of democracy, capitalism, human rights, progress, religion, justice, and a battalion of other big ideas. Although it is common for humanists to insist upon their distance from the real-life implications of such debates, they are actually in the thick of it. Functionally speaking, people listen to what the experts say, for instance, about the American experience, its im-

portance, its beliefs, and values. People tend to bound their own understandings by what the experts tell them.

5. *Adjusting the contexts of authority*: In recent years, the nature of the new scholarship has had effects beyond scholarship. Whole fields of study have begun. The creation of women's studies, feminist studies, and, now, gender theory is an example, as is the creation of black studies and its evolution into Afro-American studies and now into Africana studies. More recently, reflecting the emerging specialties in the United States of Hispanic-American, Asian-American, and native American studies, the field of ethnic studies is synthesizing much scholarship, and American studies is being reformulated. Other examples of changing specialties are urban studies, social history, and the addition of film to arts scholarship. All of these fields have drastically changed scholarship, but they have played out with equal force in politics, social structures, cultural and employment patterns, and family and gender relationships by giving the power of decisive new ideas to the society.

6. *Inspiring social change and activist concerns about justice*: The disciplines of the humanities have traditionally studied these subjects. But, especially in the newer scholarship, learning about these subjects has been accompanied by activities to bring them about. Hence, the humanities become instruments for reevaluating the roles of women and minorities, establishing better representation within academic and other communities, fighting discrimination and poverty, providing access to education and rights for newly immigrating or emerging groups, and responding to the needs of diverse cultures.

7. *Mediating across sectors of the society*: This is a relatively new function, one that can no longer be masked merely as "interdisciplinary studies" and that carries well past the "blurring of the genres" described by Geertz. Philosophers contribute to medical ethics; science and its history, technology, and society become professional specialties; a prestigious journal devotes an issue to environmental history; a Spanish language department offers contemporary Hispanic-American and Latin-American literature; anthropologists and ecologists hold a joint conference. At one level, these interactions are extensions of academic inquiry, as Geertz described. At another level, through such activity the humanities are mediating complicated middle grounds across sectors. Examples of such mediating work are to be found increasingly within the academy. It is being pressed particularly by the growth of cultural studies as a field and as an influence on other fields. The consequences are alignments of thinking that may illuminate tough, even intractable, problems that will not yield to insights from any

single sector. These mediating conversations are beginning to take place across radically unlike sectors. As scientists and environmentalists and development practitioners, for instance, ask their questions for the next century, they are seeking humanists to help them.

8. *Mediating across cultures*: The study of Western cultures has a rich academic tradition within language departments and in such fields as history and literature. Less familiar cultures, from the nations of Latin America and the East to indigenous tribal peoples, have conventionally been the subjects of such fields as area studies, international relations, and anthropology. Humanists have usually confined their attention to the early history of such cultures when they have examined them at all. Most recently, such traditional divisions of the world are being challenged by more interactive and searching definitions of cultures and their relations to each other. Interactions between cultures and nations are being reshaped. The humanities are central to such reexaminations of cultural perceptions.

What can be learned from this functional way of looking at the humanities is that humanist scholars have more power both on campus and off than they are comfortable claiming. It comes as less of a surprise—looked at this way—that books about humanities education are best-sellers or that the battle of the books goes on at a score of campuses in the 1990s. Ideas about justice and inclusion are the stuff of the humanities as they are the subjects of these debates. Beliefs, values, and ideals are rightly debated by humanists. The balances between tradition as a good and change as a good are fit argument and fit activity for humanists, and the national character is their historical subject.

It becomes less surprising, too, that humanist scholars are being called to testify in courts of law about rights, about discrimination, about freedom of expression. The courts are another theater for the configuring of ideas in our society and for debates about change; the courts, indeed, are the most basic of those theaters in the making of American society. Humanists belong in the company of those who are debating issues of equity, probity, and First Amendment rights. Looked at this way, it becomes less important who's right or wrong, what the curriculum becomes, or which reading list prevails. It is the immediacy, the centrality of humanistic debate in contemporary circumstances that matters. It is the fact that the debates occur with humanist input, the functions of discovery that they serve, that is important. It is the engagement in such debates that marks the humanities today and sets the agenda for their work.

Humanists must accept this definition of their role. Given the rapidly changing and difficult circumstances in which we live, more calls on humanists can be expected. And given the changes and developments that have taken place in the scholarship itself during the last quarter century, the knowledge is ready for use.

Engagement in the World and the Collapse of Consensus

Unprepared as they may be for the engagement, humanists are equipped and they are needed to comment, for instance, on rain forests and biotechnology research, on governance structures in Eastern Europe and South Africa, on indigeneity, on Islam, on the making of a civil society in China and a score of other places, on the culture of Hispanic Americans, on the African diaspora, on the role of women in technologically based development. Acknowledging the true consequences of their work will help humanists use their knowledge for the world's advantage, expressing their ideas not only on their campuses, but also within the corridors, courts, and contests of power worldwide, where they have functions to perform. This is not the first time that the venues and the vocabularies of humanists have been put to such use, but it is a particularly important time because it is explosive in terms of redefining world structure and ideas.

To the extent that a functional analysis of the humanities is determined by the times and by the particular historical and cultural circumstances within which such an audit is made, it also becomes clear and is unsurprising that the standards of objectivity and unanimity of vision that once were claimed for the humanities seem outmoded today. In this complex, internationally interdependent, culturally textured half century, as has been shown, a multiplying of points of view seems appropriate and necessary. The development of the new scholarships has provided a multiplicity of perspectives, and scholars' reactions to those developments have themselves been diverse. More generally, as historian Peter Novick documented persuasively, the "ideological consensus" that had provided the foundation for historical scholarship has "collapsed." Opposition, even partisanship, opinion as well as interpretation, have come to mark the humanities professions. The claim to objectivity, based on the basic respect for science that has characterized the twentieth century, had become suspect by the 1980s, replaced by the accommodation of "conflicting truths" and the emergence of "transient, interpretive communities" (Novick 1988, 415ff.). This shift in the humanities' stance surely reflects the prevalence of the inchoate, complicated, uncategorizable ideas afloat and needing analysis in the 1990s.

Also, in this half century, as this analysis of the functions of the humanities demonstrates and as the new developments in scholarship make possible, the study of cultures can no longer be Euro-centered. Humanities perspectives are becoming manifold and adaptive—they must include sophisticated considerations of identity and of difference, a broad and nuanced internationalism, the acknowledgement of the reciprocal markings of cultures by each other. The force of the humanities is toward arranging knowledge and transmitting it in the context of past events and of cumulative findings. But the force of the humanities today is also toward the reexamination of longstanding assumptions about cultures, their dominance of each other, and their unique perturbations across time and in the current world situations.

It is also worth stressing that these properties and perspectives relate quite specifically to functions of the humanities in the here and now. It might all be different in the next quarter century. Such a temporal sense of reality is also a shock to the traditional suppositions that humanists used to make about the permanent and continually additive nature of their work. A list of the functions or effects or consequences of the humanities made two decades ago would have been half as long as that of today. In the functions that they fill in the eighties and nineties, the humanities are responding to change, shifts, and dynamic redefinitions. Closure on any question is not expected. Consequences are themselves rapidly changing; effects lead to new effects, and change itself could become the constant.

Humanists and Nonhumanists

Most thinkers who influence the world we live in are not humanists, and they do not touch on the humanities as a topic of concern. It might seem to follow that there is nothing that humanists can learn about the humanities from these thinkers. Perhaps it is enough for humanists to read only other humanists or those few nonhumanist thinkers who do cite history, quote poetry, name a philosopher, or, even, deplore their own failure to use such sources. But, if we are to get things straight, discourse between humanists and other thinkers is essential. What can be learned from experiencing nonhumanists is that the humanities are embodied in analysis even when they are unmentioned, that contemporary situations cannot be addressed without the humanities. What can be learned is that humanists must take their clues and their courage and make their connections from the most challenging ideas advanced, regardless of the intellectual contexts out of which they come.

An example is the need for sophisticated international ideas in the 1990s. This is a need known and now being articulated by forward-looking humanist scholars. As recently as 1989, Akira Iriye entitled his presidential address to the American Historical Association, "The Internationalization of History." In this challenge to professional historians, Iriye commented on "three aspects of internationalization . . . closer ties with foreign historical communities . . . the promotion of comparative history . . . the problem of cultural consciousness on the part of the historian." He made a call for historians' attention to international subjects and suggested that explorations of contemporary situations by historians can address implications "for the stability or instability of the world as a whole" (1989, 1–10). Iriye prodded historians toward international problem solving from the very center of the profession.

More recently, W. R. Connor, the head of the National Humanities Center, wrote of the failure of area specialists in the United States to predict events in China, the Soviet Union, and the Middle East, and he eloquently pointed to the fact that culturally thin, pragmatic, and presentist analysis cannot help anticipate such changes or understand them when they come. What is needed, Connor wrote, is a "greater attunement to emotional and moral factors, to the persistent claims of primary attachments, and of religious, ethnic, and national identities . . . a fresh approach to the understanding of the world situation . . . grounded in a serious study of culture and the nature of long-term historical change." This is again a call for action to humanists from the center of their establishment. In the act of interpreting current events from a humanist perspective, Connor evidenced his point that "scholarship in the humanities and related social sciences . . . has immense public ramifications" because "cultural issues are . . . as central to political life as are . . . economics, foreign relations, military matters" (1991, 175–184). Both Iriye and Connor urged their colleagues in the humanities to take to heart their responsibility for public discourse and policy formation in the 1990s.

Significantly, it was a full decade or two decades earlier that educators and policy makers from outside the humanities were urging the importance of creating better mechanisms for studying global problems and urging scholars—particularly those in languages and related international studies—to form international communities and to make international commitments. Nonhumanists were suggesting the essential need for humanist interpretation of contemporary world problems because they recognized the dangers inherent in the country's insularity and egoism. Had humanists been more alert and bolder, the contributions they are now beginning to make might be well under way. Scientists, engineers, economists, and other professionals have grown used to seeing the implications for their involvement in national and world events; they are skilled at listening to and interacting with nonspecialists, policy makers and practitioners. Humanists must now find their places at those tables as well and trade their truths there because, without better cultural and historical understandings, the broad interrelationships needed in today's world circumstances will not materialize. Nonhumanist commentators can help humanists grasp the realities and seize the day. Nonhumanists can be visionary on behalf of the humanities.

Early in the discussion, thinkers outside the humanities also took the lead in advocating improved education in American public schools. In doing so, such commentators helped to prepare the way for humanistic involvement in school reform. Now well embedded in the work of the Organization of American Historians and the Modern Language Association, in a range of professional activities, and on a large number of campuses, the involvement of scholars in the school improvement efforts of the 1980s and 1990s might not have materialized without pressure from nonhumanists. They were instrumental as well in tying the need for renewing the schools to the increasing cultural diversity and the multiple nations of origin of the American citizenry itself in the 1980s and 1990s. Such examples as these—and there are many—evidence the importance for the humanities of heeding intelligent, forward-looking, broad, and inclusive ideas from many sectors. As provocateurs, as allies and partners, as visionaries from within their own specialties, smart people outside the humanities must be allowed to help humanists and must be helped by them. What can and should be shared across the sectors, in and out of the humanities, and in and out of the academy is a passion for making things better.

One additional lesson can be learned from outside the disciplines. Without ever having become historians or theologians by training, or scholars of literature or art, or philosophers—by philosophers' standards—or cultural anthropologists, or other "soft" social scientists, many of the most true and telling commentators of our times are humanists. In reexamining the role and the goals of the humanities, it is not only their definition that must swell. Their ranks must also swell to include a range of thinkers and theorists who contribute ideas broadly. As we reexamine world problems from cultural and historical (humanistic) perspectives, we should be prepared to find humanists among the scientists, religious leaders, journalists, artists, government officials, lawyers, and schoolteachers who are working on these problems, as well as in the institutes, the museums, the libraries, and the conferences that contain the professional humanists—those of the disciplines. The practical humanist is characterized by a rationality that is inclusive, temperate, patient, idealistic; by a vision of the sense of what's needed next; by a human-centered definition of progress; by a determination to be an informed citizen of the world. Finally, what humanists can learn from nonhumanists is that we are not alone.

References

Bender, Thomas. 1986. "Wholes and Parts: The Need for Synthesis in American History." *Journal of American History,* 73(1):120–136.

Clifford, James. 1988. *The Predicament of Culture: Twentieth Century Ethnography, Literature, and Art.* Cambridge: Harvard University Press.

Connor, W.R. 1991. "Why Were We Surprised?" *American Scholar,* 60(2):175–184.

Fuchs, Lawrence H. 1990. *The American Kaleidoscope: Race, Ethnicity, and the Civic Culture.* Hanover, N.H.: University Press of New England.

Geertz, Clifford. 1980. "Blurred Genres: The Refiguration of Social Thought." *American Scholar,* 49(2):165–179.

Graff, Gerald. 1992. "The Scholar in Society" In Joseph Gibaldi, ed., *Introduction to Scholarship in Modern Languages and Literatures,* 2d ed. New York: Modern Language Association.

Higham, John. 1983. *History: Professional Scholarship in America.* Baltimore: Johns Hopkins University Press.

Iriye, Akira. 1989. "The Internationalization of History." *American Historical Review,* 94(1):1–10.

Kerr, Clark. 1978. "Comparative Effectiveness of Systems: Unknown and Mostly Unknowable." In John Millett, Burton Clark, Brian MacArthur, Howard Bowen, and Clark Kerr, eds., *Twelve Systems of Higher Education: Six Distinctive Issues,* pp. 157–177. New York: International Council for Educational Development.

Lippard, Lucy. 1990. *Mixed Blessings: New Art in a Multicultural America* New York: Pantheon Books.

McNeill, William H. 1986. "Mythhistory, or Truth, Myth, History, and Historians." *American Historical Review,* 91(1):1–10.

Minh-ha, Trinh T., ed. 1986–87. *Discourse,* no. 8, (Fall/Winter).

Novick, Peter. 1988. *That Noble Dream: The "Objectivity Question" and the American Historical Profession.* Cambridge: Cambridge University Press.

Painter, Nell. 1987. "Bias and Synthesis in History." *Journal of American History,* 74(1):109–112.

Rosenzweig, Roy. 1987. "What Is the Matter with History?" *Journal of American History,* 74(1):117–122.

Stearns, Peter N. 1985. "Social History and History: A Progress Report." *Journal of Social History,* 19(2):319–334.

16 Hearts, Brains, and Education: A New Alliance for Science Curriculum

MARIAN CLEEVES DIAMOND

Every normal human infant is a potential scientist, if curiosity and discovery are considered to be the fundamental tools for the beginnings of a scientist. A baby gets to know about its own body by watching a wiggling arm that can be controlled as it extends from the body . . . a stimulus and a response . . . a first experimental observation! Such an action is one step in directing the development of a precious mind with limitless possibilities to receive and assimilate information freely toward creative efforts for a lifetime, if given an open chance. The ability to question and the excitement of discovery are there from the beginning.

Then, as an example, why is it that in later years only one-third of the students who enter freshman chemistry at the University of California at Berkeley graduate in this discipline? Their curiosity and motivation to explore scientific principles have helped them reach the university. What happens as experts in chemistry attempt to continue to excite them with knowledge about the molecular building blocks of their world? The students soon turn their attention toward such fields as biology, anthropology, political science, and economics, but not to the physical sciences. The desire to learn is not the problem. These students continue to have this craving. The switch cannot be only for money because these other disciplines do not necessarily guarantee a higher income. The problem must be the manner in which the information is presented. Are there one or more ingredients missing from the content and delivery of the material? Is the problem in the fact that too much material is being offered so that appropriate analysis is impossible? Is the fun of science no longer present? Are the sciences so difficult to understand that the majority of the students cannot grasp the concepts? This cannot be true because most children can readily work with various types of complex problems if they are presented appropriately. After all, the students have reached the college level, having satisfied all of the science prerequisites. Is the material being offered out of human context so the answers do not mean anything? In other words, are the science lectures being delivered in such a way that they neglect parts of the human equation?

After spending an afternoon watching nine-year-olds working out new programs at their computers, there is no doubt in my mind that the youngsters enjoyed the abstract concepts they shared actively with their peers. In the first place, no one had previously informed them that computer science was difficult. No negative stage was originally set. The joys of the acquisition of knowledge, skills, and human companionship were all positively intertwined. Given the equipment and some basic directions by the well-informed and caring instructor, their nimble minds were discovering satisfaction by working together creatively for hours. Here in one small room were a group of children who had the potential to become not only scientifically literate but possibly professional scientists some day. They were demonstrating their interest and abilities quite readily. What happens somewhere in the educational system that causes students either to switch to fields other than science or to leave school altogether? The realization that they eventually have to make use of their skills to survive enters into the equation. Many students learn in spite of the system because they realize that once they obtain the essential degree they can proceed on their own in many directions.

New Approaches to Science and Knowledge

The above discussion illustrates why new approaches to science and knowledge in the academic setting from kindergarten through college are being actively examined in the United States today. American educators are seriously comparing our teaching methods, course content, and "end products" with those in other nations because of the lack of acceptability of what our educational system in general offers and in turn produces.

I chose the title, "Hearts, Brains, and Education," for this chapter because I think it is essential to develop the cooperative, compassionate, and caring side of learning as we promote the intellectual side of science education. I use *hearts* here in the metaphorical sense. In my language as a brain investigator, a positive integration between the limbic system that deals with emotions and the cerebral cortex that deals with higher cognitive processing is essential for human beings to work well together in any society and especially in a highly technical one.

Efforts to this end in science education are occurring in many classrooms. Here let me offer three examples of where I see active, caring, cooperative, experimental progress taking place in science education from a firsthand point of view. One is in the Lawrence Hall of Science—the curriculum research and development center for elementary and secondary school science at the University of California at Berkeley; the second is at the Lawrence Livermore National Laboratory in Livermore, California; and the third is in my own recently formed department at Berkeley—Integrative Biology—and my anatomy classrooms there for over thirty years.

The Lawrence Hall of Science

Unfortunately, most elementary school teachers have had little science training. In the past, science was frequently introduced as a difficult subject, so fear as an inhibitory learning factor rather than discovery as an excitatory factor was the rule. Primary teachers and consequently their students were not exposed to the joys of science surrounding every moment of their existence. Over twenty years ago the idea of the Lawrence Hall of Science was conceived to introduce the young of every age to the pleasure of hands-on exhibits of scientific principles, primarily physics and chemistry in those days. Today all areas of science are introduced.

In certain situations people first learn best by interacting with their subject, thus the reason for beginning with hands-on exhibits. A great deal of satisfaction is derived from knowing that you can put the puzzle together or work the computer to get the answer, but in doing so new questions or problems arise. (I often wonder about the neural connections between hand-eye coordination and the pleasure centers in the brain.)

"What science knows is less interesting than what it does not yet know" is a statement from the *Economist* of 16 February 1991 (p. 4). Following this line of reasoning, the exhibits in the Lawrence Hall awaken the mind to scientific inquiry so that people want to gain further knowledge. Science classes can be developed to enlighten both teachers (twelve thousand per year come to the Hall) and students (eighty thousand each year receive hands-on science) with further information on the subject. The classes in themselves are experimental, being revised until the material presented is clear and easily accessible at the appropriate level for the pupil. Everyone is encouraged to interact with the activities. Once the classroom materials, including the hands-on experiments, reach an acceptable standard, they are written up for publication and dissemination throughout the nation and overseas. They become available for K–12 teachers everywhere who want to introduce the fun of science in a basic fashion into their own curriculum. Some of the publications are suitably called GEMS guides ("Great Explorations in Math and Science"). GEMS activities have been trial tested by hundreds of teachers nationwide to ensure their classroom applicability. They are designed to be presented by teachers without extensive science or math background and use easy-to-obtain materials.

At present, GEMS guides reach one-quarter of the nation's elementary schools. Subjects covered include "Hide a Butterfly" to learn about protective coloration for preschool to third grade, "Crime Lab Chemistry" for fourth to eighth grades, and "Convection: A Current Event" for grades 6–9. The most recent GEMS guides deal with acid rain and global warming to alert youngsters to present environmental challenges. Not only basic scientific principles but, in addition, modern scientific problems and teaching methods can be introduced through GEMS for teachers.

Satellite teaching for primary and secondary schools is a field that is actively developing and will have tremendous influence in the future. GEMS guides, as well as FOSS ("Full Option Science System," another hands-on science program for fourth through sixth grades), will be used for two initial programs for students and their teachers, one in several states in the Pacific Northwest, including Alaska, and one in the state of California. With activity kits to accompany the television displays, the importance of hands-on participation can reach an untold number of individuals. Direct phone interaction will be introduced with satellite teaching. The potential for this kind of teaching throughout the world is extremely exciting, reaching individuals who otherwise might never touch the modern world.

"Family Math" and "Family Science" provide new directions for families to learn these subjects together. I once surveyed women scientists, who reported that the single most important subject for them was math. Family Math has sold over ninety thousand copies during the past few years. Family Science is still in the production stage, but who knows what its influence will be? Perhaps the slogan will arise that "the family that studies together stays together"! Families acquiring knowledge together may answer many social problems. In Alvin Toffler's 1990 book, *Power Shift,* he stated that, "today, in the fast-changing, affluent nations, despite all inequities of income and wealth, the coming struggle for power will increasingly turn into a struggle over the distribution of and access to knowledge" (p. 20). Francis

Bacon wrote at the end of the sixteenth century that knowledge is power. Will our children appreciate this unprecedented tool called *knowledge* as they face the challenges that lie before them?

The IISME program ("Industry Initiatives in Science and Math Education") at the Hall allows teachers to enter the community industries during the summer with paid salaries. The experience gained during their interactions with ongoing industrial productions allows them to bring "real-world" information back to the classroom. Most dedicated teachers want to be perpetual learners so they will have unique opportunities to share with growing minds. Their students in turn can reach their intellectual potential whether they are healthy or have some kind of disability.

At the Hall, specialized equipment and new procedures were developed to ensure full access to science learning for visually impaired children. It was discovered that these project materials worked with students with other disabilities as well. At present these interdisciplinary, multisensory science enrichment programs have been used effectively with blind and visually impaired, orthopedically disabled, learning disabled, developmentally disabled, emotionally disabled, hearing impaired, and, yes, non-disabled students, too!

The staff's inquiring, productive minds are continually moving in new directions in science and math education at the Hall. Science museums play an important role in awakening young minds of every age throughout the world. New science museums are being established in China, Korea, Thailand, Spain, and Venezuela, to mention just a few. Integrating the school programs with those of the science museums offers dimensions of unmeasured value.

The Lawrence Livermore National Laboratory

In 1990 the secretary of the Department of Energy, Admiral James Watkins, made a strong plea for the national laboratories operated for the federal government to play a more active role in science education. Decades before his request, since the 1960s, one of these national laboratories—Lawrence Livermore National Laboratory—has been engaged in science education for the school districts in its area and across the nation. This laboratory now has more than fifty-five different kinds of active programs in the schools.

Each year about thirty-five thousand precollege, college, and graduate students and three hundred faculty members and postdoctorates benefit from the educational programs sponsored by Lawrence Livermore. People usually associate the function of this impressive institution with secret weapons research for national defense, but in 1991 less than one-fourth of the laboratory's activities dealt with classified information.

A program called LESSON (Lawrence Livermore Elementary School Science Study of Nature) was started by Lawrence Livermore employees in 1969 for the kindergarten-through-eighth grade schools in Oakland, California, long before educational efforts became popular for the national laboratories in general. Laboratory scientists entered classrooms with "traveling science" shows. Now this program trains teachers in such subjects as biology, physics, chemistry, and electromagnetism, emphasizing aspects of safety and encouraging the participation of women and minorities. For years LESSON focused only on schools with large minority enrollments. Now LESSON is expanding to include more schools.

In recent years an average of seventy-five teachers per year have participated in this program. LESSON provides them with instruction in science concepts taught by laboratory scientists. The teachers gain confidence in their ability to teach science from doing their own experiments because all lesson plans have accompanying kits. Originally the students were taught how to make their own equipment, such as microscopes, but now they can buy inexpensive plastic ones. Technology is becoming more accessible for all of the schools.

In 1987 Lawrence Livermore began a Summer Science Institute in which scientists talk with local schoolteachers in grades 5 and 6, who in turn develop their own science curricula. What a marvelous opportunity for these teachers to learn directly from scientists! At present, Lawrence Livermore programs reach school districts within a forty-five-mile radius around the laboratory.

The laboratory's latest educational experiment, which began in 1988, is called "Global Climate Change." This program is an attempt to develop an interdisciplinary curriculum that integrates the physical and biological sciences with the social and political sciences and economics for children in grades K–12, grouping K–5, 6–8, and 9–12. The program involves using themes such as energy, evolution, and environment and will attempt to tear down the walls that separate science-based disciplines and those of the liberal arts. Global Climate Change parallels the California State Science Framework for grades K–12 in using themes, but, with the Lawrence Livermore project, the scientists will be working directly with teachers! Teachers in this program are now offering workshops to train other teachers on the use of the curriculum and kit materials.

I am anxious to learn the success of the program because it has such promise, provided that the young brains are mature enough to integrate the material adequately. Having adults with long-term training in these disciplines attempt to produce a summation of specific topics at different grade levels in an interdisciplinary curriculum of this nature is a task of monumental proportions. If it is successful, a revolutionary step in enhancing modern education will have been taken. All of us at every level of academic activities will benefit, as will society in general.

The University of California at Berkeley

Having illustrated several of the ongoing science educational programs for kindergarten through grade 12, we will now examine some of the evolutionary directions at the college level. Again, I rely on programs close at hand—namely, those on the University of California campus at Berkeley.

In the 1980s, both internal and external review committees met to make recommendations for the reorganization of the biology departments on the Berkeley campus. Since the biological sciences were undergoing a remarkable revolution, it was essential to reexamine the present and future directions for this branch of science. Which disciplines were advancing in an explosive manner? Molecular genetics and cell biology emerged as separate disciplines. Biochemistry had demonstrated the underlying similarities in the chemistry of all living things. Utilizing model computer techniques, population biologists were able to integrate concepts that infused new life into the fields of systematics, evolution, and ecology. At the same time that these individual fields were emerging, it was essential to keep in mind that quantitative biological science has a substructure of overlapping disciplines with broad general applications. A study of all organisms includes their biochemistry, genetics, cell biology, ecology, and population dynamics. With the many advances in medicine that have benefited from new knowledge in modern biology, biotechnology companies have been formed to take advantage of the recent discoveries. Pharmaceutical, chemical, agricultural, and energy industrial firms are investing actively in the various applications of biological technology.

Universities now have the obligation to adjust their teaching and research programs to meet the demands of preparing their students for entrance into the work force in these diverse yet interrelated biological fields. Not only do the teaching and training programs have to be revised, but the building facilities need remodeling as well. The report of the external review committee in April 1981 summarized the direction of the biological sciences quite clearly. "The biological sciences constitute a gathering force that will affect every aspect of our society, a force which may have even greater impact than those of chemistry and physics in the past. Those institutions that play a leading role in the development of this force and its application to the great problems of society will benefit greatly, both within themselves and the society they serve" (p. 7).

The Berkeley undergraduate biology curriculum was considered to have unnecessary duplication, fragmentation, and specialization because of the disconnected departmental structure. Such problems could no doubt be rectified with considerable reorganization. Utilizing the information from all of the review committee reports, three new departments were established after dismantling the existing ones. The new departments include Integrative Biology, Plant Biology, and Molecular and Cell Biology. The subdepartments within these new departments are the following:

- *Integrative Biology*: Track 1: Morphology, Physiology, and Development. Track 2: Behavioral Biology. Track 3: Systematic Biology, Paleontology, Genetics, and Evolution. Track 4: Ecology. Track 5: Integrative Human Biology
- *Plant Biology*: none
- *Molecular and Cell Biology*: Biochemistry and Molecular Biology; Cell and Departmental Biology; Cell Physiology and Biophysics; Genetics, Immunology and Tumor Biology; and Neurobiology

It was amazing to see how well the faculty in general adopted their new departments and carried on business in their new environment. Several reasons were undoubtedly responsible for the ease of this transition. During the reorganization, faculty had the opportunity to form affinity groups as well as choose space in close proximity to former colleagues either from their home department or from others within the campus. In most cases the course content was not modified significantly, with the exception of a few new courses that took advantage of the reorganization. Because the professors continued to teach essentially the same course but in a new department, the stress of becoming established in a new department was not unusually severe. Perhaps the need for reorganized course material will come in the future.

What do I find of value in my new department after having worked in my original one—Physiology-Anatomy—for over thirty years? First, it might help to note which departments were recombined to form the new Integrative Biology Department. These included Physiology-Anatomy, Botany, Genetics, Zoology, and Paleontology. From this new mix, the faculty works surprisingly well together on both general university business and departmental matters. Faculty meetings are obviously more heterogeneous in nature, and faculty seminars cover a much broader spectrum of topics than when the original departments existed.

This subject bears some expansion to illustrate specifically what I have found of value with my new department. At one seminar, I sat next to a botanist who was attempting to understand the role of the protein calmodulin in plants. I asked if he was familiar with the role of calmodulin in the animal nervous system. After learning from me that calmodulin interacts with calcium to assist the movement of vesicles in the nerve fibers toward their terminals, he wondered if the same function was true in plants. Now one reads that a proposed mechanism for a plant's growth pattern may be due to increased calcium in the cytoplasm. One of the genes that has recently been isolated in plant codes for calmodulin has been shown to combine with calcium ions. The calcium-calmodulin complex redirects the axis of the cell dimension by rearranging the ingredients of the internal skeleton of the cell. Is it possible that this is happening in the nerve fiber as well, resulting in a rearrangement of the cytoskeleton to direct the vesicles toward the terminal nerve membrane?

Why was it important to present this conversation is such detail? To illustrate that it is refreshing to integrate knowledge from a completely new source in a departmental seminar setting. To me it is a very exciting event to learn that common mechanisms are occurring in both plants and the mammalian nervous system. If my department had not reorganized at this time, such integration of biological systems might have remained unknown to me. Such material can be of greater use because eventually it becomes integrated into lectures in the classroom.

With such beneficial outcomes after reorganization, one wonders if other tightly disciplined departments might consider dismantling and regrouping. If parts of physics, chemistry, and biology risked integrating, what new combination of efforts might emerge? Traditional science departments might find that not only would their particular research disciplines benefit, but also the teaching curriculum would gain new directions. This kind of integrative action might be more beneficial for the older members of the faculty who have their basics well established and could more easily combine the subject matter.

To risk reorganization takes a good deal of courage. The feeling of instability is not only painful but frustrating at first. It is as if one's whole academic carpet had been pulled out from under. But now that the process has been successfully attempted at one large, major university, others might follow in even more bold directions. The time commitment to develop new integrated scientific lectures would be great, but the results have exciting potential. If the scientists at the Lawrence Livermore National Laboratory are willing to attempt curriculum integration for grades 6–12, to continue at the university level with integrated scientific disciplines would offer a fresh approach to science education. The potential is provocative!

The Human Dimension in Science Education

Now to return to the human dimension in science education. Early in this chapter, I examined the multitude of reasons why naturally curious human beings do not flock to science courses. One question was, "Is the material being offered out of human context so the answers do not mean anything?" Certainly a subject like human anatomy is as close to human context as any could possibly be, but to my knowledge most anatomy professors do not relate the curriculum to the students who are learning it. In other words, they do not suggest introspection to learn about oneself by studying the structure and function of the parts of one's own body. By teaching in this manner, by adding the personal side to the equation, teachers will help students gain an appreciation for the magnificent persons that they are and also gain knowledge that will last them a lifetime. The answers are built into them and consequently are always there either to help themselves or, as concerned citizens or professionals, to help others. The curriculum can be designed to introduce the material in such a way that the personal human factor is included.

All of the students who come into my office for letters of recommendation for medical school say that they want to become doctors because of the human interaction. Here is a scientific profession that has no problem attracting students because it deals closely with people. Is there a way to introduce science curriculum to schoolchildren to include the human factor in the very early stages? One very simple way is to have the children learn to teach each other. Our motto is "Each One Teach One." Even kindergartners can learn to obtain information well enough to teach each other. Such a habit learned early can last a lifetime. The children learn the joy of cooperation, shared creativity, and collective benefits from individual experiences, all combined with caring human interaction. Since no two human brains are identical, the collective efforts of children working together can be most satisfying. The electromagnetic energies between people are not yet clearly understood, but, when positive, they can add to the enjoyment of learning together. We have found that freshman students at the university can learn their material well enough to teach sixth graders. Each freshman had to learn three major concepts about the brain, since this was a "Build a Brain" class, to teach the elementary children on a one-to-one basis when they came to the university. The result was spectacular. The freshmen were frightened and, at the same time, prepared. The sixth graders were anxious to learn from the college students. In other words, the traditional method of sitting in class listening to a lecture was modified so, once the material was learned, it was shared with someone else. More variety in teaching methods at the university are needed to keep the students interested in the science curriculum.

By combining "heart" and "brain" functions with science in classrooms and science museums and by sharing with peers at every level in the educational process, we have learned that these methods do provide satisfaction for those involved. Unconventional, exciting ways to deal with science education do exist and should be introduced whenever possible. Everybody gains.

References

"Report of the External Review Committee." 1981. Berkeley: Biological Sciences, University of California, April, p. 7.

"A Survey of Science—The Edge of Ignorance." 1991. *Economist,* 318(7694).

Toffler, Alvin. 1990. *Power Shift.* New York: Bantam.

V   Critical Issues

17 Improving the Quality of Instruction

K. PATRICIA CROSS

The biggest event in education during the decade of the 1980s was the publication of *A Nation at Risk* in 1983. Its sometimes bombastic rhetoric made its way almost immediately to the front pages of newspapers across the nation. Phrases such as "a rising tide of mediocrity" and "unthinking unilateral educational disarmament" entered the national vocabulary, and states scrambled to appoint blue-ribbon commissions to study the quality of education in their own schools.

The "evidence" of poor student learning that they found consisted largely of conclusions similar to those in *A Nation at Risk* (National Commission on Excellence in Education 1983, 8, selected items):

- International comparisons of student achievement, completed a decade ago, reveal that on nineteen academic tests American students were never first or second and, in comparison with other industrialized nations, were last seven times.
- Some twenty-three million American adults are functionally illiterate by the simplest tests of everyday reading, writing, and comprehension.
- About 13 percent of all seventeen-year-olds in the United States can be considered functionally illiterate. Functional illiteracy among minority youth may run as high as 40 percent.
- Average achievement of high school students on most standardized tests is now lower than twenty-six years ago when Sputnik was launched.

- The College Board's Scholastic Aptitude Tests (SATs) demonstrate a virtually unbroken decline from 1963 to 1980. Average verbal scores fell over fifty points, and average mathematics scores dropped nearly forty points.

Within three years after the appearance of *A Nation at Risk,* there were more than thirty national reports calling for educational reform, and the fifty states had appointed a total of some three hundred task forces to make recommendations for achieving educational "excellence"—arguably the most popular term of the decade. In 1986, the National Governor's Association issued *Time for Results.* And the decade ended with an "Education Summit" called by an "education" president to give "education" governors an opportunity to set an agenda for "excellence" in education.

Although the political guns of the 1980s were aimed largely at the public schools, higher education entered the fray with a quick succession of "reform reports" of its own. In 1984, the Study Group on the Conditions of Excellence in American Higher Education, appointed by the National Institute of Education, offered its research-based recommendations for students' *Involvement in Learning* (1984). The Association of American Colleges called for *Integrity in the College Curriculum* (1985). The National Commission on the Role and Future of State Colleges and Universities declared "ignorance . . . the enemy of democracy" and called for improved education *To Secure the Blessings of Liberty* (1986). And the Education Commission of the States called for *Transforming the State Role in Undergraduate Education* (1986).

By the late 1980s, the common refrain, echoed again and again in reports from every quarter—professional associations, legislatures, and special task forces—was a concern about what was perceived as the declining quality of undergraduate education (Cross 1986a). The purpose of this chapter is to look at the reform decade of the 1980s from the precarious perch of the early years of the 1990s. The 1980s were devoted largely to the identification of the problem and the marshaling of forces to deal with it. The decade of the nineties opened with proposals to assess students' learning, to give more attention to teaching, and in general to redirect the resources and commitments of higher education to the improvement of undergraduate education. The major reform activity of the late 1980s was the assessment of students' learning. By 1990, 82 percent of the colleges and universities in the country had some form of assessment activities under way, and two-thirds of them had obtained some results from their assessments (El-Khawas 1990). The second largest plank in the educational reform platform has been the improvement of college teaching. Recommendations for improving undergraduate instruction have tended to cluster in three categories that can be discussed separately: (1) rewarding good teaching, (2) evaluating teaching, and (3) improving programs to help faculty become more effective teachers.

Rewards for Good Teaching

There is widespread agreement, at least in the literature of higher education, that the priorities of colleges are now skewed toward research and graduate education and away from teaching and undergraduate education. Documentation of the trend toward relegating undergraduate teaching to the back seat in the reward system of higher education was presented in an influential article entitled "The Faculty at Risk," which was published in *Change* in 1985. In it, Jack Schuster and Howard Bowen reported the results of a three-year study during which they interviewed 532 administrators and rank-and-file faculty members at thirty-eight colleges and universities about their careers and, in particular, their satisfactions and dissatisfactions with academic life. They found "alarming" changes in the working conditions of faculty: "Around 1970, the American faculty's condition probably reached its most robust state. . . . However, in the fifteen years since then, various developments have eroded those hard-won accomplishments and jeopardized the well-being of the academic profession—and with it the quality of American higher education" (p. 13).

Among the most serious problems identified by Schuster and Bowen was the shift in values that triggered a change in campus reward systems. The reward of research over teaching was brought about, in part, by the strong buyers' market of the 1970s that had permitted even the most modest campuses to hire research-oriented Ph.D.s from prestige research universities, causing a large number of institutions to move toward new reward structures for faculty. "The result," concluded Schuster and Bowen, "is a veritable surge toward research," but, they warned, "we doubt that the stampede toward publishable research and scholarship, or what sometimes passes for scholarship, serves the nation's needs, or the longer-term interests of those campuses historically committed to effective teaching" (p. 16).

By 1990, Peter Seldin could write, with little fear of contradiction, that, "despite rhetoric to the contrary, it is clearly a trend that colleges and universities give more consideration to research and scholarly performance than to teaching in their recruitment, promotion, and tenure decisions. . . . Undervalued today, . . . the faculty member more interested in teaching than in scholarly research is soon forced by the institution's reward system to 'go with the program'" (pp. 3, 4).

And Ernest Boyer foresaw a crisis of purpose in higher education (1990, xii, 55).

> The reality is that, on far too many campuses, teaching is not well rewarded, and faculty who spend too much time counseling and advising students may diminish their prospects for tenure and promotion. . . . Far too many colleges and universities are being driven not by self-defined objectives but by the external imperatives of prestige. Even institutions that enroll primarily undergraduates—and have few if any resources for research—seek to imitate ranking research centers. In the process, their mission becomes blurred, standards of research are compromised, and the quality of teaching and learning is disturbingly diminished.

The paradox is that faculty themselves claim a high interest in teaching, yet they fail to reward it. An oft-quoted survey by the Carnegie Foundation for the Advancement of Teaching found that 70 percent of all professors say that their primary interest is in teaching rather than research. But 55 percent claim that it is difficult to receive tenure in their departments without publishing scholarly work (Carnegie Foundation Survey 1985).

In sum, as the 1990s opened, research was clearly the prestige activity for institutions and faculty members. For institutions, it resulted in money and prestige; for faculty members it resulted in promotion and mobility, discretionary funds for equipment and extra secretarial help, travel funds, and visibility with their own disciplinary peers. It is going to take substantial effort to revise the reward system of higher education to give undergraduate education its due. Two approaches are visible in the 1990s. One is to try to reestablish parity between research and teaching. The other is to try to redefine the missions of higher education, giving institutions that once emphasized teaching undergraduates pride in the importance of that mission.

Reestablishing Parity between Research and Teaching

The first approach, calling for boosting the recognition of teaching in the reward system, is most visible in research universities—or perhaps their high visibility simply leads to more publicity about their efforts to restore undergraduate teaching to a place of honor in the research university. In any case, the presidents of Harvard and Stanford launched programs that were given wide coverage in both the popular and the professional press. In 1987, Derek Bok announced to the faculties of Harvard University that Harvard undergraduates and their parents needed to know what kind of education they were getting for their money, and he launched a university-wide assessment effort focused on collecting data about the learning experiences of students at Harvard (Light 1990). In 1990, Stanford University President Donald Kennedy said in a speech to its academic council, "It is time for us to reaffirm that education—that is, teaching in all its forms—is the primary task" of higher education (1990). Within a year, Kennedy had raised $7 million to redirect the Stanford reward system toward recognizing the value of outstanding teachers.

Despite David Riesman's qualification earlier in this volume to his 1956 assertion that institutions of higher education form a "snakelike procession," in which institutions low in the prestige hierarchy tend to imitate those higher up, his 1956 observation remains largely true, and the actions of Stanford and Harvard should boost the prestige of teaching in most of academe.

Redefining the Missions of Higher Education

The second approach—that of trying to redefine the missions of higher education—is currently led by the Carnegie Foundation for the Advancement of Teaching. In a report entitled *Scholarship Reconsidered*, its president, Ernest Boyer, put it this way (1990, 13):

> What we are faced with, today, is the need to clarify campus missions and relate the work of the academy more directly to the realities of contemporary life. We need especially to ask how institutional diversity can be strengthened and how the rich array of faculty talent in our colleges and universities might be more effectively used and continuously renewed. We proceed with the conviction that, if the nation's higher learning institutions are to meet today's urgent academic and social mandates, their missions must be carefully redefined and the meaning of scholarship creatively reconsidered.

Boyer's Carnegie Foundation report has been widely read and is mildly controversial. It endorsed faculty scholarship and sought to redefine it in ways that are more congruent with the mission of undergraduate teaching institutions. In it, Boyer proposed defining faculty scholarship to include four functions—the scholarship of discovery, the scholarship of integration, the scholarship of application, and the scholarship of teaching.

1. The "scholarship of discovery" is what we think of as traditional research—that is, the advancement of knowledge in the academic disciplines. Boyer does not wish to diminish the emphasis given to the role of traditional research, contending that it is the "very heart of academic life

and the pursuit of knowledge must be assiduously cultivated and defended" (p. 18). He does, however, argue for broadening the definition of faculty scholarship beyond research to value other forms of intellectual activity—in particular, the following three activities.

2. The "scholarship of integration" involves faculty in making connections across the disciplines, illuminating and interpreting data, and bringing new insight to bear on original research. While the scholarship of discovery asks the questions, "What is to be known; what is yet to be found?" the questions for those engaged in integration are "What do the findings mean?" and "Is it possible to interpret what's been discovered in ways that provide a larger, more comprehensive understanding?" (p. 19).

3. In the "scholarship of application," the questions are "How can knowledge be applied to consequential problems?" and "Can social problems themselves define an agenda for scholarly investigation?" The meaning of this form of scholarship comes closer to what is currently scantily rewarded as "service"—but Boyer called for a scholarly sort of service that is "serious, demanding work, requiring the rigor—and the accountability—traditionally associated with research activities" (p. 22).

4. Finally, the "scholarship of teaching" recognizes the intellectual, dynamic work involved in building bridges between teachers' understandings of their disciplines and students' learning. It requires pedagogical knowledge as well as disciplinary knowledge, and it goes beyond transmitting knowledge to transforming and extending it through helping students learn how to make use of it.

It is hard to predict what influence this redefinition of scholarship will have on a system of higher education that is seriously searching for a restructured faculty reward system. Questions have already been raised about whether the "scholarship of application" will change the currently poorly rewarded function of "service" or how defining teaching as "scholarship" will enhance its prestige in the academy. Some critics will contend, I think, that Boyer has defined the three other forms of scholarship as supporting the research function—integrating research, applying the findings of research to practical problems, and teaching the knowledge gained through research. That appears to leave research as the kingpin of academic work.

Although Boyer called ultimately for rethinking the missions of higher education, especially for "teaching institutions," accomplishing that task will depend heavily on restructuring of the reward system. Faculty will continue to give time and attention to activities that provide status, mobility, and prestige. If teaching and other forms of faculty scholarship are to be rewarded, credible measures of evaluating them must be devised. Boyer himself insisted that each form of scholarship must be documented as serious scholarly work for it to take its proper place in the reward structures. Only if credible, practical criteria for evaluation can be developed and sold in the academy will his new definitions of scholarship have the desired effect.

The Evaluation of Teaching

The battle shaping up over the reward of teaching, whether as a scholarly activity or as a neglected mission of higher education, will ultimately be fought over the credibility of the evaluation system. There are those who contend that "teaching can be assessed as rigorously as research and publication" (Seldin 1990, 6). Others contend that "the criteria for judging other factors (scholarship, publication, service, etc.) are more clear cut, easier to use, and to many, more objective" (Centra et al. 1987, 1).

Enormous energy and effort have gone into the search for valid measures of teaching effectiveness and into educating faculty members and administrators to use what is known about the evaluation of teaching. There are literally thousands of research studies on the validity, reliability, and usefulness of various measures of teaching effectiveness—thirteen hundred articles on student ratings alone (Cashin 1990, 93).

In fact, the research literature on the evaluation of teaching is now so extensive that it is tempting to use Boyer's four forms of scholarship to illustrate the breadth of "scholarship" on the evaluation of teaching. In the 1970s, most of the literature consisted of "scholarship of discovery" to answer questions such as these: What are the characteristics of effective teachers? (Abrami 1985; Centra 1979; Feldman 1976; Wotruba and Wright 1975). Are student ratings reliable, valid, and unbiased (Centra 1976; Centra and Creech 1976; Costin, Greenough, and Menges 1971; Feldman 1976; Frey 1976; Kohlan 1973; Marsh 1984)? Is there agreement among students, administrators, and colleagues on the quality of teaching? (Blackburn and Clark 1975; Centra 1973b, 1975; Marsh, Overall, and Kesler 1979). Are student ratings related to student learning? (Centra 1977; Cohen 1981). How do faculty view their own teaching? (Centra 1973b; Cross 1977).

So much research was done in the 1970s and 1980s on teaching effectiveness that many publications consisting of meta-analyses and syntheses of this research—the "scholarship of integration"—have now appeared (Cohen 1980, 1981; Cross 1988; Cashin 1990; Dowell and Neal 1982;

Feldman 1977; Gleason 1986; Levinson-Rose and Menges 1981; Marsh 1980; McKeachie et al. 1986; Menges and Brinko 1986; Murray 1985).

The "scholarship of application" has also not been neglected in the effort to inform college faculties of the relevance of research to practice. (See, for example, Cashin 1990; Centra 1973a; Gleason 1986; Gleason-Weimer 1987; Grasha 1977; McKeachie et al. 1980; Skeff 1983.)

Finally, all of this knowledge derived through various forms of scholarship is making its way into the "scholarship of teaching." Special handbooks are being written for faculty members (Braskamp, Brandenburg, and Ory 1984; Centra et al. 1987; Davis 1988). Courses in higher education administration are teaching this body of knowledge, and offices for instructional improvement or faculty development probably have at least a five-foot shelf on teaching evaluation.

Indeed, the problem now is that any faculty member or faculty committee conscientiously concerned about devising a credible and appropriate teaching evaluation scheme is easily drowned in information and advice. The advice almost always includes recommendations to use more than one measure. Although most faculty members now accept student ratings of instruction as one measure of teaching effectiveness and most colleges have adopted systematic student ratings in the evaluation of faculty performance (Seldin 1984), handbooks typically lay out the options and recommend multiple evaluation measures (see, for example, Cashin 1990; Davis 1988; Centra et al. 1987).

One of the more interesting schemes is that devised by the Center for Instructional Development at Syracuse University, under the direction of Robert Diamond. The purpose of its manual is "to help improve the process of evaluating teaching for use in tenure and promotion decisions" (Centra et al. 1987, 1). The manual starts with one of the many research-derived lists of the qualities of effective teaching. (There are now a large number of studies of student perceptions of effective teaching, all of which come out with lists remarkably similar to others regarding the characteristics of effective teachers.) Syracuse uses the six characteristics of effective teaching derived by Wotruba and Wright (1975) from a synthesis of twenty-one research studies and adds one more criterion of its own—"appropriate student learning outcomes"—to arrive at these seven qualities of effective teaching:

1. Good organization of subject matter and course
2. Effective communication
3. Knowledge of and enthusiasm for the subject matter and teaching

4. Positive attitudes toward students
5. Fairness in examinations and grading
6. Flexibility in approaches to teaching
7. Appropriate student learning outcomes

Using these seven qualities as criteria, Syracuse then goes on to suggest what data can be gathered, from which sources, to provide credible information about the extent to which individual teachers exhibit the characteristics of effective teachers. Data collection methods include self-assessments, classroom observations, structured interviews, student ratings of instruction, tests or appraisals of student achievement, content analysis of instructional materials, and review of classroom records. Sources of evaluation include self, students, faculty, dean or department chair, alumni, and other appropriate administrators.

My conclusion, after reviewing exhaustive (and exhausting) amounts of research on teaching effectiveness and how to apply it in the evaluation of teachers, is that there is little excuse for any knowledgeable person to maintain that we cannot reward good teaching because we cannot evaluate it. Although the will to reward good teaching may not yet exist in higher education, the way to do so is clearly present in the literature of higher education.

Programs to Improve Teaching

Programs to improve teaching are highly variable in both scope and intention. At the institutional level, they range from rather modest approaches for making library or media services available to instructors who request help through the creation of an office for the improvement of instruction to massive institution-wide reform (McCabe and Jenrette 1990; Loacker, Cromwell, and O'Brien 1986).

Many national organizations reach across institutions to work directly with faculty on the improvement of teaching. Publications abound on the teaching of English, psychology, engineering, and other disciplines, as do conferences on everything from remedial education for community college teachers to the training of teaching assistants for graduate school departments and deans. Since 1986, the American Association for Higher Education has been especially active in providing a range of programs and publications to encourage the improvement of undergraduate education. National conferences on assessment, the improvement of teaching, and the training of teaching assistants have been enriched by foundation-funded projects and a series of reports and publications addressed to faculty members and administrators.

Given the amount of activity and the high visibility of projects to improve the quality of instruction, it seems likely that, if the 1980s was the decade for appointing study commissions and writing reform reports on the quality of undergraduate education, the 1990s will be a decade of implementation of programs to improve the performance of both teachers and students.

The optimist will look at the energy and commitment behind the very substantial number of programs to improve instruction; the pessimist will look at the relatively small influence such innovations have had on the reward systems of the great majority of American colleges and universities. But the evidence exists that major educational reform is possible and successful in all kinds of institutions—from small liberal arts colleges with clear missions and a faculty dedicated to teaching, to huge universities and multipurpose community colleges. Since space prohibits more than a sampling of current efforts to implement the teaching/learning reforms called for in the 1980s, I will describe briefly two programs, one institution based and the other directed toward classroom teachers across the disciplines.

The Teaching/Learning Project at Miami-Dade Community College

Perhaps the most impressive effort to improve the quality of teaching and learning in higher education is taking place in an institution where reform would seem most difficult and frustrating—at a huge multipurpose, multicultural community college in one of America's most rapidly changing urban environments. The Teaching and Learning Project at Miami-Dade Community College is entering its fifth year of operation with an impressive list of goals and accomplishments. (A brief and excellent chapter on the project is available in McCabe and Jenrette 1990, and an annual summary report has been issued each year since 1986–87.)

The vision and the leadership for the Teaching and Learning Project came from Robert H. McCabe, president of the college since 1981 and executive vice-president before that. McCabe's assumption of academic leadership was consistent with Clark Kerr's observation that faculty and boards of trustees alike are looking for stronger presidential leadership. Over eight hundred interviews conducted by Kerr and his associates for his extensive study of the American college presidency indicated that many college presidents were losing influence over academic affairs by default (1984, 8). "The president should be the chief academic officer in fact, and the president has a special obligation to innovate and initiate academic policy from the special point of view of the long-term and overall welfare of the campus, which the president is in the best position to understand and to foster."

McCabe's vision for the institution was ambitious. He encouraged a program in which "the college would attempt systematically to change the way that it does business in order to raise the status of teaching; improve teaching and learning at the college; relate all of the reward systems to classroom performance; and change the decision-making process such that the first priority is teaching, learning, and the classroom environment" (McCabe and Jenrette 1990, 183).

Basically that says it all. Especially important in the context of this chapter is the strong commitment to revision of the reward system for both faculty and administrators. Decisions and performance are rewarded to the extent that they support and enhance teaching and learning at the college. The point I wish to make here is that this is no modest affair; it involves dozens of committees, the commitment of resources—and promises to raise additional funds, an evaluation plan for faculty promotion and tenure submitted to an all-faculty referendum, and ultimately a reward structure that is serious and credible about making teaching and learning the first priority of the institution.

The project itself is almost a textbook-perfect implementation of reform. Miami-Dade did everything the textbooks say must be done:

- Vision and leadership came from the top.
- Everyone was involved, from custodians to trustees.
- Resources were committed—released time for faculty serving on committees, a full-time project director, off-campus retreats, endowed teaching chairs, etc.
- Ownership was established—two-way communications implemented, referendums conducted.
- Structures were put in place for continuing operation of the program—recruitment, selection, and orientation of new faculty members, annual reviews of teaching performance, required graduate level courses on teaching and learning.

The Miami-Dade case refutes the thesis that large, complex organizations are too unwieldy to be innovative. It offers evidence that presidents can assert the power of leadership in academic affairs. It shows that faculty will accept and promote an evaluation of teaching that is perceived as fair and that leads to clearly defined rewards in promotion and tenure.

While some will complain that the Miami-Dade program can move for-

Table 17.1 Primary Teaching Role as Perceived by Two- and Four-Year College Teachers, by Discipline

Primary Teaching Role	All	Humanities	English	Basic Skills	Social Science	Business	Medicine	Science	Math	Arts
					Percentage of 2700 Respondents					
Higher-order thinking skills	**28**	**32**	**47**	13	**44**	26	17	28	35	20
Facts and principles	**28**	31	17	8	35	28	18	**55**	**44**	24
Jobs/careers	17	2	3	7	4	**32**	**44**	10	2	11
Student development	17	24	19	20	14	12	12	3	7	**37**
Basic learning skills	7	6	15	**51**	2	1	1	3	9	3
Role model	3	5	2	2	3	1	8	2	3	5

ward because teaching is the clear-cut mission of a community college, they should remember that there are thousands of "teaching institutions" in this country that have not clarified their mission and that do not operate with clear incentives and rewards for good teaching. It will take commitment and leadership if teaching and undergraduate education are to be restored to a position of priority in American higher education.

Classroom Research

A quite different approach to the improvement of instruction— "Classroom Research"—works across institutions, attempting to influence faculty as individual classroom teachers and as specialists in the teaching of particular academic disciplines. Classroom Research was introduced in 1986 at the national convention of the American Association for Higher Education as an assessment tool that can be used by discipline-oriented teachers in their classrooms to obtain feedback on what their students are learning (Cross 1986b). The premise of Classroom Research is that teachers can improve their teaching by obtaining a continuous flow of information from students in their classes about how well they are learning what the teacher is trying to teach. It requires that teachers know what they want students to learn from them and that they be able to use some fairly simple assessment techniques to find out if they are accomplishing their teaching goals.

Thus, one of the first aims of the Classroom Research project was to develop a Teaching Goals Inventory that would help teachers articulate their teaching goals. Teachers, it turns out, have very different priorities in their teaching—among them, teaching students facts and principles of the subject matter, providing a role model for students, helping students develop higher-order thinking skills, preparing students for jobs or careers, fostering student development and personal growth, and helping students develop basic learning skills. When we asked more than twenty-seven hundred teachers from thirty-three two- and four-year colleges which of these six teaching roles they considered primary, we got the results shown in the first column of percentages in table 17.1. As can be seen, "helping students develop higher-order thinking skills" and "teaching students facts and principles" are the two leading role preferences—each attracting just 28 percent of the teachers—but there is wide variety in the goals that teachers consider primary.

Table 17.1 also shows that teachers' perceptions of their role are closely related to the subjects they teach, with the highest percentages in each column printed in bold. Indeed, the most highly significant differences

Table 17.2 Three Top-Priority Teaching Goals, by Discipline

						Percentage of 2726 Respondents				
Item	Teaching Goal	Arts	Humanities	English	Basic Skills	Social Science	Business	Medicine	Science	Math
1	Apply principles				59	57	69	73	61	
2	Math skills									84
4	Terms & facts						61	70	60	
5	Wise decisions									
6	Analytic skills			66						73
11	Self-esteem				63					
12	Think for self	66	59	75	65	50				
16	Responsible for self							68		
20	Value of subject		56			52				
22	Concepts & theories								71	
24	Creativity	69								
25	Writing skills			84						
29	Aesthetic appreciation	78	56							
43	Openness to ideas						57			
45	Problem solving									84

among teachers occurred across fields of study. For example, whereas 55 percent of the science teachers said they were primarily concerned about teaching students the facts and principles of their subject matter, only 17 percent of the English teachers saw mastery of facts and principles as their primary goal. Instead, these teachers were far more likely to choose "helping students develop higher-order thinking skills."

Interestingly, teachers of English, the humanities, and the social sciences are most likely to form a cluster around the goal of "helping students develop higher-order thinking skills," whereas those in mathematics and the sciences are most likely to try to "teach students facts and principles of the subject matter." Not surprisingly, teachers of business and the health professions (in this case, mostly nursing and allied health) see themselves as "preparing students for jobs and careers." Those in the fine and performing arts see their primary role as "fostering student development and personal growth," which seems appropriate given the personal expression that lies at the heart of the arts. Teachers of basic skills are, of course, largely concerned about the "development of basic learning skills."

Perhaps today's college teachers are just modest, but, despite all of the talk about mentors and role models, few teachers see themselves as role models for their students. And women and minorities are no more likely to see themselves as role models than are white men.

In addition to asking this question about their role as teachers, the Teaching Goals Inventory asks college teachers to select one course that they are currently teaching and to rate the importance of each of fifty-two goals to their teaching of that course. What teachers want students to learn from them also varies greatly with the discipline taught but only occasionally with gender, age, or full-time versus part-time teaching status.

Table 17.2 shows the three most highly rated goals for each disciplinary group. You can see the pattern of clusters that is formed. Goal 1 in the inventory, which is stated as "develop ability to apply principles and generalizations to new problems and situations," is strongly endorsed by teachers in science-based subjects. Teachers in English, the humanities, and the arts, in contrast, emphasize the goal of developing a "capacity to think for oneself." Interestingly, social scientists and basic skills teachers share common goals with both the sciences and the humanities, giving high value to the application of principles and to developing the capacity of students to think for themselves.

Business teachers have a profile similar to that of the scientists. Both groups value highly item 1—applying principles and generalizations to new situations—and item 4—teaching terms and facts. Scientists, however, are high on teaching students concepts and theories (item 22), whereas business teachers are interested in the pragmatic development of problem-solving skills (item 45).

Teachers in the fine and performing arts show one of the more distinctive profiles, valuing, as we might expect, the development of aesthetic appreciation (item 29). In fact, 78 percent of them select aesthetic appreciation as essential to their teaching, while 69 percent also give creativity high priority. The health professions also have a distinctive profile, emphasizing personal responsibility more than any other discipline. They are the only disciplinary group to give top priority to these two goals: "develop capacity to make wise decisions" and "cultivate a sense of responsibility for one's own behavior."

The profile shown here for English teachers is particularly instructive. Despite all of the talk about writing across the curriculum, improving students' writing skills is seen by English teachers and, I might add, by almost everyone else as the primary responsibility of the English department. Eighty-four percent of the English teachers in our sample considered the improvement of student writing skills an essential goal of their teaching. Although not shown in table 17.2, only 27 percent of the humanities teachers and 14 percent of the business teachers considered the improvement of student writing an essential goal of their teaching. Math teachers similarly accept most of the responsibility for teaching math. Even science teachers do not rate the improvement of math skills very high; only 17 percent consider it essential to their teaching.

The differences in instructional goals among teachers is one reason for encouraging college teachers to engage in classroom assessments of their own design. If a teacher receives regular feedback on whether students are learning what that teacher thinks it is important to teach, then the results of the assessment should be helpful in self-analysis of teaching effectiveness.

Most teachers do get feedback from students, of course, in the form of results from tests and quizzes, facial expressions, participation in class discussion, and the like. But such feedback is not systematic and is not designed to provide the kind of information that informs teachers about whether they are accomplishing their own teaching goals. To get teachers started on classroom assessment, Tom Angelo and I prepared a handbook for faculty consisting of thirty easy-to-use assessment techniques that can be employed in the classroom by teachers of any subject (Cross and Angelo 1988). One very simple classroom assessment technique is called the "One-Sentence Summary (WDWWHWWW)." This assessment device requires

Table 17.3 Sample of the "One-Sentence Summary (WDWWHWWW)" Assessment Technique

---

Topic: Classroom Research

The summary in matrix form:

QUESTION	RESPONSE
Who?	Teachers
Do What?	Assess
To What or Whom?	Their students' learning
How?	Using classroom assessment techniques
When?	Regularly during the semester
Where?	In their own classrooms
Why?	To understand and improve learning by improving their own teaching

The summary in sentence form:

Teachers assess their students' learning by using classroom assessment techniques regularly during the semester in their own classrooms to understand and improve learning by improving their own teaching.

---

students to synthesize information about a given topic into an informative sentence—albeit frequently a long one. The task, familiar to journalists, is to answer the questions represented by "WDWWHWWW" (Who Does What to Whom, How, When, Where, and Why?). After a class session on Classroom Research, for example, the assessment might consist of asking students to construct a one-sentence summary in which the teacher would be looking for understandings such as those in table 17.3 (1988, 62).

My personal favorite among the thirty assessment techniques is one of the easiest to administer, yet it provides very rich and useful data. It was originally proposed by Charles Schwartz, a professor of physics at the University of California, Berkeley, and is called "Minute Papers." Here is how it works: A few minutes before the end of class, Professor Schwartz asks students to write the answers to two questions: (1) What was the most important thing you learned today? (2) What questions are uppermost in your mind as we conclude this class session?

I have used Minute Papers in my own graduate classes at Harvard and Berkeley. Inevitably, the first time I use them in class, some students are hard put to articulate anything of importance that they learned in the class sessions and, much to my dismay and disappointment, they seize desperately on the last thing said. Some students pick up something that I thought was fairly incidental but that had a particular meaning for them since it made some connections with what they already knew. A few students synthesize beautifully, picking up the major themes, articulating them clearly, and then raising some rather interesting questions. And some, to my delight, choose as significant something that they learned, not about content, but about themselves as learners.

I find that Minute Papers are a good teaching technique as well as a useful feedback device. Even among graduate students, Minute Papers done early in the semester tend to bring forth fairly low-level cognitive learning. Some students, for example, cite specific facts or content that they deem significant. As the semester progresses and I feed back to students the responses of their classmates, students who formerly thought largely in terms of facts begin to model the higher stages of cognitive learning shown by other classmates. They begin to look for broader principles and concepts and to articulate them as among their most significant learnings.

In addition to providing information about what students are learning while there is still time to make midcourse corrections, the simple device of Minute Papers carries some strong pedagogical messages. It puts students on notice that they are expected to be able to synthesize and articulate their learning—and that they should be active learners, raising questions and thinking about the implications of the lesson.

I have also found that opening a class session with a review of what students, as a group, found most significant from the previous class session builds a nice bridge of continuity from one class to the next, and it also gives me an opportunity to prepare handouts or otherwise clarify issues that students found puzzling or provocative.

The point of our handbook on classroom assessment techniques (Cross and Angelo 1988) is not to provide set recipes for self-evaluation, but rather to suggest to teachers how they can be creative in devising assessment techniques that meet their own criteria for relevance and that will provide useful information about their effectiveness as teachers.

From our experience in working with teachers over five years of the Classroom Research Project, we learned the following:

- College teachers are remarkably creative in devising appropriate classroom assessment techniques.
- They find devising assessments and analyzing the data collected intellectually stimulating, and many report that it increases their interest in teaching.

- Their interest in assessing students' learning creates a bond with their students and makes students more aware of and more knowledgeable about themselves as learners.
- Classroom assessment provides an excuse for engaging in intellectual discourse about teaching with colleagues within and across departments.
- Some teachers have gained professional status and recognition for their work in classroom assessment through conducting workshops for colleagues, writing articles for professional journals, and devising ever more sophisticated techniques for engaging in research on teaching and learning.

Changes from the 1980s

While educational reform is never as neat as it looks in hindsight, the 1980s and 1990s are two quite distinctive decades. The 1980s collected criticism from every quarter; the 1990s are embarked upon widespread reform directed at improving the quality of undergraduate education. The criteria for whether reform is being accomplished lie in the vigorous assessment movement: Are students learning what we think they should be learning? The handle for improving students' learning—or at least one vitally important handle—is the quality of undergraduate instruction. That is not an easy handle to get hold of, involving as it does thousands of individual faculty members, all presumably doing the best they know how, given their relative isolation in classrooms across the country, their lack of training for teaching, their values, their perceptions of rewards (intrinsic as well as extrinsic), and the state of the art and science of pedagogy.

Nevertheless, it appears from the perspective of the early 1990s that there is lively discussion, lots of energetic leadership, encouraging support for teaching within and across disciplines, new knowledge being generated in cognitive psychology, and some stories of success. The 1990s will bring a new generation of teachers into a higher education system facing extreme financial stress, and these new faculty members will come from graduate schools and departments variously interested in preparing a new professoriate for teaching. Thus, I am hopeful that the 1990s, with its multifaceted attack on the improvement of instruction, will leave a legacy of pride in the profession of teaching.

References

Abrami, Philip C. 1985. "Dimensions of Effective College Instruction." *Review of Higher Education*, 8:211–228.

Association of American Colleges, Project on Redefining the Meaning and Purpose of Baccalaureate Degrees. 1985. *Integrity in the College Curriculum*. Washington, D.C.: Association of American Colleges.

Blackburn, Robert T., and Mary Jane Clark. 1975. "An Assessment of Faculty Performance: Some Correlates between Administrator, Colleague, Student, and Self-ratings." *Sociology of Education*, 48 (Spring): 242–256.

Boyer, Ernest L. 1990. *Scholarship Reconsidered*. Princeton: Carnegie Foundation for the Advancement of Teaching.

Braskamp, Larry A., Dale C. Brandenburg, and John C. Ory. 1984. *Evaluating Teaching Effectiveness: A Practical Guide*. Beverly Hills, Calif.: Sage Publications.

Carnegie Foundation Survey. 1985. "Who Faculty Members Are and What They Think." *Chronicle of Higher Education*, 18 December, 25–28.

Cashin, William E. 1990. "Assessing Teaching Effectiveness." In Peter Seldin et al., eds., *How Administrators Can Improve Teaching: Moving from Talk to Action in Higher Education*. San Francisco: Jossey-Bass.

Centra, John A. 1973a. "Effectiveness of Student Feedback in Modifying College Instruction." *Journal of Educational Psychology*, 65:395–401.

———. 1973b. "Self-Ratings of College Teachers: A Comparison with Student Ratings." *Journal of Educational Measurement*, 19(4):287–295.

———. 1975. "Colleagues as Raters of Classroom Instruction." *Journal of Higher Education*, 44(1):327–335.

———. 1976. "The Influence of Different Directions on Student Ratings of Instruction." *Journal of Educational Measurement*, 13(4):277–282.

———. 1977. "Student Ratings of Instruction and Their Relationship to Student Learning." *American Educational Research Journal*, 14(1):17–24.

———. 1979. *Determining Faculty Effectiveness: Assessing Teaching, Research, and Service for Personnel Decisions and Improvement*. San Francisco: Jossey-Bass.

Centra, John A., and F.R. Creech. 1976. *The Relationship between Student, Teacher, and Course Characteristics and Student Ratings of Teacher Effectiveness*. Report PR-76-1. Princeton: Educational Testing Service.

Centra, John, Robert C. Froh, Peter J. Gray, and Leo M. Lambert. 1987. *A Guide to Evaluating Teaching for Promotion and Tenure*. Syracuse: Center for Instructional Development, Syracuse University.

Cohen, P.A. 1980. "Effectiveness of Student-Rating Feedback for Improving College Instruction: A Meta-Analysis of Findings." *Research in Higher Education*, 13:321–342.

———. 1981. "Student Ratings of Instruction and Student Achievement: A Meta-Analysis of Multisection Validity Studies." *Review of Educational Research*, 51:281–309.

Costin, F., W.T. Greenough, and Robert J. Menges. 1971. "Student Ratings of College Teaching: Reliability, Validity, Usefulness." *Review of Educational Research*, 45:511–535.

Cross, K. Patricia. 1977. "Not *Can*, but *Will* College Teaching Be Improved?" *New Directions for Higher Education*, 17 (Spring): 1–15.

———. 1986a. "The Rising Tide of School Reform Reports." *Phi Delta Kappan*, 66(3):167–172.

————. 1986b. "A Proposal to Improve Teaching." *AAHE Bulletin,* 39(1):9–15.

————. 1988. "Feedback in the Classroom: Making Assessment Matter." Washington, D.C.: AAHE Assessment Forum.

Cross, K. Patricia, and Thomas A. Angelo. 1988. *Classroom Assessment Techniques: A Handbook for Faculty.* Ann Arbor: National Center for Research on the Improvement of Postsecondary Teaching and Learning, University of Michigan.

Davis, Barbara Gross. 1988. *Sourcebook for Evaluating Teaching.* Berkeley: Office of Educational Development, University of California.

Dowell, D.A., and J.A. Neal. 1982. "A Selective Review of the Validity of Student Ratings of Teaching." *Journal of Higher Education,* 53:51–62.

Education Commission of the States. 1986. *Transforming the State Role in Undergraduate Education: Time for a Different View.* Denver: Education Commission of the States.

El-Khawas, Elaine. 1990. "Campus Trends, 1990." *Panel Report No. 80.* Washington, D.C.: American Council on Education.

Feldman, Kenneth A. 1976. "The Superior College Teacher from the Students' View." *Research in Higher Education,* 5:43–88.

————. 1977. "Consistency and Variability among College Students in Rating Their Teachers and Courses: A Review and Analysis." *Research in Higher Education,* 6:223–274.

Frey, Peter W. 1976. "Validity of Student Instructional Ratings: Does Timing Matter?" *Journal of Higher Education,* 47:327–336.

Gleason, Maryellen. 1986. "Getting a Perspective on Student Evaluation." *AAHE Bulletin,* 38(6):10–13.

Gleason-Weimer, Maryellen. 1987. "Translating Evaluation Reports into Teaching Improvement." *AAHE Bulletin,* 39(8):8–11.

Grasha, A.F. 1977. *Assessing and Developing Faculty Performance.* Cincinnati: Communication and Education Associates.

Kennedy, Donald. 1990. "Stanford in Its Second Century." Address to the Stanford Community, Stanford University, Meeting of the Academic Council, 5 April.

Kerr, Clark. 1984. *Presidents Made a Difference.* Washington, D.C.: Association of Governing Boards of Universities and Colleges.

Kohlan, R.G. 1973. "A Comparison of Faculty Evaluations Early and Late in the Course." *Journal of Higher Education,* 44:587–595.

Levinson-Rose, J., and Robert J. Menges. 1981. "Improving College Teaching: A Critical Review of Research." *Review of Educational Research,* 51:403–434.

Light, Richard J. 1990. *The Harvard Assessment Seminars: Explorations with Students and Faculty about Teaching, Learning, and Student Life. First Report.* Cambridge: Harvard Graduate School of Education.

Loacker, G., L. Cromwell, and K. O'Brien. 1986. "Assessment in Higher Education: To Serve the Learner." In C. Adelman, ed., *Assessment in American Higher Education: Issues and Contexts,* pp. 47–62. Washington, D.C.: U.S. Department of Education, Office of Educational Research and Improvement.

Marsh, H.W. 1980. "The Influence of Student, Course, Instructor Characteristics in Evaluations of University Teaching." *American Educational Research Journal,* 17:219–237.

————. 1984. "Students' Evaluations of University Teaching: Dimensionality, Reliability, Validity, Potential Biases, and Utility." *Journal of Psychology,* 76:707–754.

Marsh, H.W., J.U. Overall, and S.P. Kesler. 1979. "Validity of Student Evaluations of Instructional Effectiveness: A Comparison of Faculty Self-evaluations and Evaluations by Their Students." *Journal of Educational Psychology,* 71(2):140–160.

McCabe, Robert H., and Mardee S. Jenrette. 1990. "Leadership in Action: A Campuswide Effort to Strengthen Teaching." In Peter Seldin et al., eds., *How Administrators Can Improve Teaching,* pp. 181–198. San Francisco: Jossey-Bass.

McKeachie, W.J., Y.-G. Lin, Monica Daugherty, et al. 1980. "Using Student Ratings and Consultation to Improve Instruction." *British Journal of Educational Psychology,* 50:168–174.

McKeachie, W.J., Paul R. Pintrich, Yi-Guang Lin, and David A.F. Smith. 1986. *Teaching and Learning in the College Classroom: A Review of the Literature.* Ann Arbor, Mich.: National Center for Research on the Improvement of Postsecondary Teaching.

Menges, Robert S., and K. Brinko. 1986. "Effects of Student Evaluation Feedback: A Meta-Analysis of Higher Education Research." Paper presented at the meeting of the American Educational Research Association, San Francisco, April.

Murray, H.G. 1985. "Classroom Teaching Behaviors Related to College Teaching Effectiveness." *New Directions for Teaching and Learning,* 23:21–34.

National Commission on Excellence in Education. 1983. *A Nation at Risk: The Imperatives for Educational Reform.* Washington, D.C.: U.S. Government Printing Office.

National Commission on the Role and Future of State Colleges and Universities. 1986. *To Secure the Blessings of Liberty.* Washington, D.C.: American Association of State Colleges and Universities.

National Governors' Association. 1986. *Time for Results.* Washington, D.C.: National Governors' Association.

Riesman, David. 1956. *Constraint and Variety in American Higher Education.* New York: Doubleday.

Schuster, Jack H., and H.R. Bowen. 1985. "The Faculty at Risk." *Change,* 17(4):13–21.

Seldin, Peter. 1984. "Faculty Evaluation: Surveying Policy and Practices." *Change,* 16(3):28–33.

———. 1990. "Academic Environments and Teaching Effectiveness." In Peter Seldin et al., eds., *How Administrators Can Improve Teaching: Moving from Talk to Action in Higher Education,* ch. 1. San Francisco: Jossey-Bass.

Skeff, Kelley M. 1983. "Evaluation of a Method for Improving the Teaching Performance of Attending Physicians." *American Journal of Medicine,* 75:465–470.

Study Group on the Conditions of Excellence in American Higher Education. 1984. *Involvement in Learning.* Washington, D.C.: National Institute of Education.

Wotruba, T.R., and P.L. Wright. 1975. "How to Develop a Teacher Rating Instrument." *Journal of Higher Education,* 46:653–663.

18 Behind the Open Door: Disadvantaged Students

FLORA MANCUSO EDWARDS

The first chapter of the final report of the Carnegie Council, *Three Thousand Futures* (1980), is entitled "The Fears of Some and the Hopes of Others." In the twelve years following the publication of that report, both our fears and our hopes have been realized.

Today, we live in a world with unlimited potential and unprecedented opportunity. What was a generation ago inconceivable is now achievable. Yet we live in a world in which our economy and our educational system are built on shifting sands—in particular, on our shifting demography. The suburbanization of our economic base has left the inner core of our cities with a service economy comprising fewer and fewer low-skilled jobs juxtaposed against a shortage of skilled workers. While thousands of displaced workers and disenfranchised youth languish on our street corners unemployed and unemployable, jobs for those with the prerequisite skills and knowledge go unfilled for lack of an adequate work force.

By the year 2000, one-third of all schoolchildren younger than seventeen will come from minority groups, and almost 42 percent of all public school students will be minority children or children born into poverty. By the turn of the century, 21.8 million of the nation's 140.4 million-person work force will be nonwhite. We anticipated these developments, and some of us tried to prepare for them. We redecorated our campuses by removing the ivy from our hallowed walls and opening our campus gates to those who a generation ago never would have dreamed of pursuing a college education.

Others of us helped create community colleges that now dot the educational landscape from Maine to California. These "people's colleges," unfettered by the constraints of tradition, took unto themselves the awesome responsibility of opening the window of opportunity to those imprisoned in poverty. They heralded a new mission for higher education—that of enfranchising those who were cut off from the mainstream of American life. It would be through our two-year colleges, aided by four-year colleges and universities, that the American dream would come true.

At the same time, far from the recesses of our collective consciousness, a quiet revolution was occurring on the midwestern and western plains. Our forgotten native Americans caught a glimpse of the dream. Higher education would become a vehicle for enfranchising a people described only by the language of despair. Today, twenty-four tribally controlled colleges serve over ten thousand native Americans in eleven plains states. The challenges they face, spelled out in the report of the Carnegie Foundation, *Tribal Colleges: Shaping the Future of Native America* (1989), reflect in microcosm the challenges of all colleges and universities that open their doors to those who have been left behind.

This dream of enfranchisement was very different from the one on which much of American higher education operated. The tried and true philosophy that well-to-do, well-prepared undergraduates are less likely than poorly prepared students to be at risk and hence more likely to succeed academically needs no discussion. That is the traditional model of higher education on which institutional prestige and credibility is based. Colleges and universities are judged primarily by their degree of selectivity: that is, by the profile of their freshman class. The relative homogeneity of such environments is built on a model of exclusion. The challenge our new students brought to our campuses was the recognition that access and excellence had to be mutually interdependent, not mutually exclusive goals.

The report of the Commission on Minorities in Higher Education, *Educating One-Third of a Nation*, reminds us from whence we have come and how far we have yet to travel (1988, 7):

> The 1960s marked the beginning of an experiment in social change unparalleled in American education. The Kennedy-Johnson era sought to use educational opportunity as a mechanism to lift the disadvantaged out of the depths of poverty and deprivation. In less than one decade, people of color, excluded for two centuries from the mainstream of American life, were integrated into schools and many of the nation's campuses. Civil rights laws were promulgated and enforcement procedures put into place; a system of financial aid was established; educational interventions such as Head Start and Trio were launched with measurable

success; and the rise of inexpensive and accessible community colleges made higher education available to more people than ever before. As a result, the combined proportion of American Indians, Asians, Blacks, and Hispanics inside academe grew steadily, reaching a plateau in 1975, when at least one-third of the Black, White, and Hispanic 18 to 24 year old high school graduates enrolled in college.

Not surprisingly, the people responded to our outstretched hands. They brought us their dreams from the tenements of the south Bronx; they came down from the hills of Appalachia; they stood on the plains of the Indian reservations and heeded our call. We told them that through our gates lay the road to fulfill their dreams. All that remained was for us to turn the dream into reality.

That was the challenge we faced. What we have learned since then are the three S's of success for disadvantaged students: Structure, Support, and Service.

Disadvantaged Students Need Structure

We learned that a commitment to open access for academically under-prepared students brings with it a commitment to the development of alternative strategies to ensure success. As public concern grew that the "open door" had become a revolving door, we learned that commitment and motivation cannot make up for fundamental academic deficiencies. Testing, historically viewed solely as a gate, became a tool for retention. Moved from the preadmission phase to preregistration, diagnostic testing of basic skills in reading, writing, and mathematics became the important first step in planning a program for success. During the past decade nine states moved to mandatory basic skills testing to ensure proper diagnosis and placement of students with academic deficiencies.

Across the country, new offerings in educational foundations were created to provide the basic reading, writing, and computational skills for those who had been ill-served by the K–12 system. Four states introduced mandatory basic skills programs for students with academic deficiencies. Programs in English as a second language were expanded to take into account the linguistic needs of our new immigrants, whose academic profile differed greatly from that of our traditional foreign students.

The perceived dichotomy between access and excellence forced us to rethink our criteria and to consider our outcomes. "Accountability" became the watchword of the day, especially for those institutions that had opened their doors to those most in need. The impetus toward accountability was fueled by the new clientele. Once success was no longer ensured by selectivity, the results had to be tied to something other than the freshman class. We learned that the premise that students from disadvantaged backgrounds should be judged by alternative criteria serves only to dilute the quality of our programs and to impugn the credentials they receive. The need to document output increased in direct proportion to the discrepancy between the profile of the new freshman class and that of their more "traditional" counterparts. During the past decade, four states instituted rising junior examinations designed to certify the basic academic competencies of lower-division students. In many ways, the trend toward accountability crystallized the challenge before us. We had to do more than "open the door." Our colleges and universities had to repair the deficiencies of the past and bring our new students to a level of competitiveness with those who had come with success as a birthright.

Disadvantaged Students Need Support

The advent of open admissions implied that higher education would become a right for all, not a privilege for the chosen few. The expansion of federal student aid during the 1960s and 1970s helped implement the new idea. Rates of degree-credit college entry rose by a third or more for high school graduates of medium and lower socioeconomic background and academic skills (Eureka Project 1988, 8). In the 1980s, however, tuition and fees at public and private colleges rose by 70 and 90 percent, respectively, compared to a 3 percent increase in federal student aid (adjusted for inflation). The Pell grant program, our nation's principal need-based program of student financial assistance, now provides 29 percent of the average tuition as opposed to 40 percent a decade ago. More important is that federal financial aid shifted dramatically from grants to guaranteed student loans, thereby subverting the original purpose of the loan program. Rather than low-interest, deferred-payment tuition plans, guaranteed student loans have become an integral part of financing higher education for the needy. The "default rate scandal" of the eighties was the predictable result of a national strategy that forced increasing numbers of poor students into mortgaging their already uncertain futures. That these students, with no credit or employment history, unprepared for the present and unsure of the future, tend to be high-risk prospects for loans should have come as no surprise. The enrollment trends accompanying this shift are more than coincidental. During the mid-1970s, the disparities in college participation rates among whites, African Americans, and Hispanics had all but disappeared. Since then, however, even though minority high school graduation rates have increased, college participation for African-American high school graduates fell from 50 percent in 1976 to 47 percent in 1988; it fell from 49 percent to 47 for Hispanics; and it never rose beyond 17 percent for native Americans. By 1989, only 16 percent of all Hispanic eighteen- to twenty-four-year-olds were enrolled in college, compared with 23 percent of African Americans and 32 percent of whites. The proposed ability-to-benefit regulations of the U.S. Department of Education and its attacks on campus-based minority scholarships tell us a great deal about our national commitment to inclusion. These are in many ways indicative of a national mood that has retreated from the promise of two decades ago.

Our new students felt that mood reflected on our campuses and in our classrooms, and they "voted with their feet." They exited exactly the way they entered—through the revolving door. The message is clear: Too many of our students who come to our campuses lacking the skills and the confidence to succeed leave us exactly the way they came.

Disadvantaged Students Need Special Services

We have learned just how fragile our new students are and how important it is that a learning environment be sensitive and responsive to their needs. We have learned that without support services they will fall through the cracks and disappear without a trace. In the past decade, we have learned that the needs of our new students are very different from those of our traditional students. The challenge that lay before us was keeping them on campus long enough so that they could reap the benefits of our collective efforts. Richard C. Richardson, in a recent study for the Education Commission of the States (1990), identified a number of successful strategies to reduce the barriers to participation, some of which I list here.

- Alternative admissions programs that include strategies for helping nontraditional students overcome differences in preparation
- Expanded recruitment efforts to consider nontraditional sources of underrepresented students
- Emphasis on merit as well as need in awarding financial assistance to underrepresented student groups
- Help for first-generation college students and their families in coping with the procedures and forms for requesting financial assistance
- Development of special orientation programs and other transition experiences, including class scheduling to encourage networking and mutual assistance
- Organization of mentoring programs coupled with intrusive academic advising

- Development of programs to improve the campus climate for student diversity through publications, organizations, and activities that portray cultural differences as a strength
- Development of programs to teach students how to learn through instruction in study skills, note taking, and preparation for tests

Across the country, we responded. Prefreshman summer programs were developed to provide a gradual transition to college life. The one-day freshman orientation program, characterized by speeches and teas, was replaced on many campuses with semester-long programs. These ranged from informal sessions in which students and faculty discussed concerns and difficulties to highly structured programs of study designed to build the necessary skills to negotiate the college environment.

Collaborative learning and group study projects were augmented with peer and faculty mentors to encourage interaction and provide academic and emotional support. Early warning systems were developed to identify students in academic trouble as early as the second month of class. Programs ranging from individual counseling to crisis intervention were developed to assist disadvantaged students in coping with personal and family crises that their middle-class counterparts only read about in the newspapers.

For our new students, career counseling and programs of cooperative education provided more than aptitude testing and work experience. They opened a window on a professional and corporate world that our traditional students took for granted as their birthright and our new students had never seen before. Building on that base, we tapped the goodwill of our partners in business and industry and recruited corporate mentors to work with disadvantaged students to promote the expectation of success.

During the past decade, child care centers on many campuses became as common and as necessary as the campus bookstore as more students came as single parents with no other means of child care. For many of our low-income students, the child care center became the dividing line between college and public assistance.

Despite all of our efforts, our results have been mixed. African Americans and Hispanics still persist in college at much lower rates than whites and Asians. The Minority Status Report, published in 1991 by the American Council on Education, told us that 42.3 percent of Hispanics, 43.5 percent of African Americans, 55 percent of whites, and 60.9 percent of Asian Americans stay in college at least four years.

Our experience of the past ten years should have taught us that, if we are serious about redressing the inequities of the past, we need to look beyond our campus gates for the solution.

An Ounce of Prevention Is Worth a Pound of Cure

If we have learned anything in the past ten years, we have learned that simply "opening the college door" is too little too late. Our failure to rescue those who come to us in greatest academic need is born of years of educational neglect. If we are truly going to make a difference, we need to build the "missing pipeline" that leads from the schoolhouse to the college campus.

- In Texas, Youth Opportunities Unlimited (YOU) is a university-based summer education and work experience program, combined with a range of support services, to provide an eight-week, total-immersion experience for disadvantaged fourteen- and fifteen-year-olds who are entering the ninth and tenth grades.
- In New York, the City University of New York, in cooperation with the New York City Board of Education, sponsors campus high schools for disadvantaged youth. These "middle colleges" combine high expectations for student performance with support and encouragement.
- In Massachusetts, the University of Massachusetts Minority Engineering Program, one of the oldest of the eighty-nine such programs in the country, recruits fifty junior and senior high school students from throughout the country and gives them a glimpse of what it would be like to be a college engineering student.
- In Minnesota, high school juniors and seniors can receive both high school and college credit for classes they complete in postsecondary institutions.

The common thread in all of these programs is that they make a difference. However, as we look upon the face of our nation today, we are forced to admit the harsh reality that despite all of our efforts, all we have managed to do is place a Band-Aid on a hemorrhage.

A Disadvantaged College Student Is an Oxymoron

On each of our campuses from Maine to California, we came to appreciate the strength and courage of our new students—these men and women who came to us with only their dreams. We saw the miracle of change. We saw despair turn to hope, and we saw unborn generations reclaimed from poverty. We came to see our mission in a new light, and many of our colleges burned with messianic fervor. We were to be the vehicle of empowerment. It would be through our colleges and universities that neighborhoods would be reclaimed. We, the educational establishment, would be the architects of the future.

The truth is that, a generation later, the gulf between black and white, rich and poor, continues to widen. Frank G. Pogue, Vice-Chancellor for Student Affairs and Special Programs of the State University of New York, summed it up (1990). "Our prisons and the conditions that give rise to imprisonment are doing a better job of recruiting and graduating men and women who are African American, Latino American and Native American than are most of our institutions of higher education. For a host of well known reasons, it is projected that by the year 2000, some 70 percent of African American males will be in prison, dead, on drugs, or alcoholics."

Our prison system, which houses more than 1.1 million people, now stands out as our country's principal government program for the poor. Black Americans, who represent approximately 12 percent of the entire population, make up over 65 percent of the prison population and 8.2 percent of the college population. Nearly half of state prison inmates, no matter what their race, were jobless or holding only part-time jobs at the time of their arrest. Almost two-thirds of state and federal inmates have failed to finish high school. As of 1986, 60 percent of all those in state prisons had earned less than $10,000 a year before incarceration.

And we have another generation of inmates on the way. Today 14 million children live below the poverty level. Fifty percent of all black children and 40 percent of all Hispanic children are poor; 82 percent of all children eligible for Head Start programs receive no service; 12 percent of all children will be born out of wedlock, and half of these will be born to teenage mothers. Every day, forty teenage girls give birth to their third child. By the year 2000, 20 percent of the girls among today's four-year-olds will become pregnant as teenagers. If demography is destiny, then we are on the road to disaster.

We live in a world brutally divided between those bloated by food and those bloated by hunger. We have replicated this division within our own borders. In New York City's Borough of the Bronx, with a total population of approximately 1.2 million, approximately 15 percent of its adults, or 210,000 men and women, cannot read; intravenous drug users number as many as 53,000; and the borough has 21 percent of New York City's adult AIDS cases and 37 percent of its pediatric AIDS cases, but only 12 percent of the city's population. South Bronx Regional High School, waging a desperate war for the souls of its youth, converted a crack house into a dormitory for homeless students. The school principal said it all: "How can you educate a kid who's got so many problems finding a place to live that education becomes the fourth or fifth priority in his life? . . . If we don't speak to these other needs of the kids, we're not going to have any kids left to educate." That is the true dilemma in providing access to disadvantaged youth.

On 5 June 1990, the New Jersey Supreme Court declared the state's system of financing elementary and secondary education unconstitutional as applied to the poorer urban school districts. The court drew a clear picture of truly disadvantaged students: "Their needs go beyond education. They include food, clothing and shelter, and extend to lack of close family and community ties and support, and a lack of helpful role models. They include the needs that arise from a life led in an environment of violence, poverty, and despair" (Abbott v. Burke, 119 N.J. 287 [1990] [Abbott II] at 369).

What we have learned since the 1980 report of the Carnegie Council is that the term *disadvantaged college student* is an oxymoron. Those we see are only the few survivors. The truly disadvantaged never even approach the campus gate. They fall by the wayside long before we ever see them. They are lost on streets that have no mercy, and it will take far more than a revised curriculum to reclaim them.

The unspoken truth is that we cannot ask our schools to be the sole oasis of hope in a desert of despair. Much less can we ask the educational enterprise to accomplish this in an environment in which the concept of public responsibility as a universal imperative is vastly diminished. During the eight-year period since the release of the landmark report, *A Nation at Risk*, no fewer than three hundred separate commissions have been formed and have issued reports regarding the state of American education. We lack neither the knowledge nor the resources. What we lack is commitment and courage to rise to the challenge.

Six Recommendations to Reclaim the Future

Develop a Marshall Plan for Cities in Distress

The complexity of the problems facing the urban environment calls for new levels of cooperation and leadership from public and private institutions. An urban extension service, modeled after the vastly successful rural extension service, could serve as a catalyst to reclaim our cities. Specialists from colleges and universities could work hand in hand with city governments in action-oriented, problem-solving approaches to a variety of pressing urban needs. A new partnership of federal and city agencies could target priority areas such as housing, infrastructure planning and renewal, community health, drug abuse prevention, literacy and adult basic education, and worker training and retraining. The consolidation of the bureaucratic maze of federal and local programs into a single coherent initiative is the first step to providing an environment in which our young people have a fighting chance to learn.

Create an Improved "Pipeline" from Kindergarten to College

The development of coherent policies to promote articulation and collaboration between the K–12 sector and colleges and universities to promote student achievement and barrier-free movement among them is the first step to building a true educational continuum. Articulation grants should be made to high schools, community colleges, and four-year schools to form partnerships that enable their faculties to build and maintain continuity in learning. The federal Department of Education and the National Science Foundation should work with the Labor Department to help such partnerships respond to the critical skill needs of employers. Similarly, the Fund for the Improvement of Postsecondary Education should be reauthorized with a new focus, giving priority to initiatives and innovations that promote "pipeline" articulation and human resource development.

Build Environments of Inclusion Rather than Exclusion

We have learned that the sensitivity of the campus environment is often the decisive element in promoting the success or failure of at-risk students and that—all of the support services to the contrary—we have changed very little where it truly matters the most. For all students, faculty are intellectual role models, the figures of authority, the yardstick by which they come to judge their potential. Black, Hispanic, or native American students who never see themselves represented on the faculty or in the administration draw sad conclusions about their potential and their future. Similarly, white faculty members who regard an occasional minority colleague as a cultural oddity draw equally sad conclusions about the potential of the minority students in their classes. Yet it will take more than affirmative action programs to increase the numbers of minority faculty across the disciplines. It will take a pool of candidates ready and willing to assume their places at the head of the class. In great measure, the absence of minority faculty on our campuses and the underrepresentation of minority students in our classes are but different sides of the same coin. The absence of the former is merely an indication of the lack of success of the latter in negotiating the academic environment.

The presence of minority faculty is important not only to the survival of our minority students but also to the life of the campus as a whole. The makeup of the faculty in many ways defines the makeup of the academic community, including the focus of the curriculum. The faculty perform a vitally important role in shaping the expectations, values, understandings, and implicit agreements that define the character of the institution. This is the academic infrastructure that lies at the heart of our collective culture as a learning community. That one-third of our nation should be invisible in our classrooms and in our curricula robs all students of the richness of the fabric of American society.

For our minority students, belonging breeds success. Students who feel that they are guests at someone else's banquet soon leave the table. The Eurocentric perspective and the relegation of courses, research, and faculty possessing a non-Western view into "ethnic studies" departments (conveniently so-labeled as something isolated and apart) send a powerful message that only the strongest ego can withstand. Unfortunately, the message is received by those least able to withstand its influence.

The construction of the "pipeline" will, over time, contribute to the diversity of our faculties. However, there is much that can be done in the interim. The Task Force on School Drop-outs of the National Governors' Association offered two recommendations that bear repeating here (1987, 45). The first is a program to forgive all or part of college loans for minority students who enter the teaching profession. The second is the establishment of teacher cadet programs to attract minority high school students to the teaching profession, including summer college tours, follow-up information, career guidance, and orientation to the teaching profession.

Whatever the specifics of the plan, if minority participation and achievement are important goals, then they must be stated clearly and publicly. Without public accountability, the commitment to diversity will never move beyond the stage of rhetoric.

Develop a National Network for Human Resource Development

We need a national partnership between industry and education involving, if necessary, tax incentives for business to invest in our collective future. At the K–12 level, businessmen and women should be mentors and role models to those children who need them most—those who see no future but the street. At the college level, titles I and XI of the Higher

Education Act should be replaced by a national network of employer-college partnerships for human resource development. From cooperative education and youth apprenticeship to tech-prep and advanced placement, flexibility should be the hallmark of partnerships between industry and education. A true partnership with industry can result in a smooth transition from school to work instead of from school to the street.

Eliminate Financial Barriers to Postsecondary Education

Inspired in part by the success of the original G.I. Bill, the Pell grant program has provided access to college for more Americans than any single program of financial assistance. Yet the shift in federal policy from Pell grants to guaranteed student loans has had a chilling effect on participation rates for needy students. Congressman William D. Ford correctly observed that "loans do not buy equity for needy students; they buy more inequity." If we are serious about higher education as a vehicle of enfranchisement, then we need to begin with the basic economic barriers. Pell grants should become an entitlement, designed to ensure that the neediest students can complete at least one year of college without resorting to loans. Moreover, Pell grant eligibility should be maintained for less-than-half-time students, and state financial aid programs should extend to part-time students—permitting more young people to pace their educational programs and to design schedules that give them a fighting chance at success. Apart from grant and loan reform, simplification of financial aid delivery is key to removing the barriers that block access. Countless students are turned away in distress by the complicated forms and the daunting process that each year increasingly defeat the intent and success of the programs.

Commit Our National Leadership

Today, we reap the scant harvest of our collective neglect—a learning deficit that is felt on our campuses, in our corporate parks, and on our streets. However, we have the wherewithal to change things. During a period of less than six months, we recently marshalled our resources, mobilized our troops, brought a foreign power to its knees, and liberated a country the location of which eludes the average high school graduate. We did not question the investment of resources. Nor did we speak of an evolutionary process. Our national interest was threatened, and we could not afford to wait. Skillful political leadership united the country and committed its human and material resources to achieve our objectives. That is the wonder of American ingenuity. That is the embodiment of the American spirit. We need that same skillful leadership to deal with the enemy within our own borders. We cannot afford to write off one-third of our nation without paying the consequences of tearing apart the fabric of our society.

We can change things if we are truly committed and have the will. If we fail in this critical task, it will be a failure of leadership. But it will not be just the failure of our elected leadership. It will be the failure of those of us who are supposed to stand for the hopefulness of our society. If we in higher education are indeed the architects of the future, then our collective voice must carry from the statehouse to the White House. As we approach the dawn of a new century, our greatest contribution will be to forge a national agenda so that every child can claim the future as a birthright.

References

Carnegie Council on Policy Studies in Higher Education. 1980. *Three Thousand Futures: The Next Twenty Years for Higher Education*. San Francisco: Jossey-Bass.

Carnegie Foundation for the Advancement of Teaching. 1989. *Tribal Colleges: Shaping the Future of Native America*. Princeton: Carnegie Foundation for the Advancement of Teaching.

Commission on Minorities in Higher Education, American Council on Education. 1988. *Educating One-Third of a Nation: The Conference Report of the American Council on Education*. Washington, D.C.: American Council on Education.

Eureka Project. 1988. "A Review of Student Financial Aid in California." In *The Critical Difference: Student Financial Aid and Educational Opportunities in California*. Sacramento: Eureka Project, March.

Pogue, Frank G. 1990. "Diversity, Multi-Culturalism, Pluralism: Elements in a Balanced Educational Experience for All Students." Comments presented at the Equity and Diversity Policy Forum Commission on Higher Education, Baltimore, Md., 28 June.

Richardson, Richard C., Jr. 1990. *Promoting Fair College Outcomes: Learning from the Experiences of the Past Decade*. Denver: Education Commission of the States, January.

Task Force on School Drop-outs, National Governors' Association. 1987. *Making America Work: Bringing Down the Barriers*. Washington, D.C.: National Governor's Association.

19 Campus Climate in the 1980s and 1990s: Decades of Apathy and Renewal

ERNEST L. BOYER

While reflecting recently on the history of higher education since World War II, it occurred to me that each decade has had its own distinctive flavor. First came the 1950s, a time when college doors swung open and when academics were dazzled by the prospect of unprecedented expansion. Then came the 1960s, a time when, almost overnight it seems, we went from expansion to a struggle for survival. After a decade of crisis and confrontation, the world of higher learning turned inward, preoccupied with fiscal cutbacks and "retrenchment."

Turning to the decade of the 1980s by scanning back issues of the *Chronicle of Higher Education*—our newspaper of record—it is possible to recapture the mood of that era, a decade that also had its own flavor. Over most of the decade, the *Chronicle* reported student apathy. One story suggested that, in contrast to the 1960s, the focus of undergraduates in the eighties had much more to do with playfulness and self-indulgence than with public policy crusades. "Students are into fun-and-games-type programs," said Bob Davis of the American Program Bureau. "You talk to them about gun control or abortion—they show about as much interest in that as in changing the oil in their car" ("Good-bye 80's," A11).

From the *Chronicle*, the 1980s also appear as the decade when concerns about the quality of campus life dramatically increased. *In loco parentis* had long since been abolished, but what emerged was a climate described by one president as "low-grade decadence" (Carnegie Foundation and American Council on Education 1989). His characterization was a bit harsh, perhaps, but during this period college officials became increasingly concerned about alcohol abuse, which replaced somewhat the so-called drug problems of the sixties. There was a growing worry about crime, as well. And, although robberies and assaults did not reach the epidemic proportions suggested by the headlines, many institutions became deeply troubled about the safety of their students.

Questions of Institutional Responsibility

College officials knew they were no longer "parents," but they also knew that their responsibilities, both legal and moral, extended far beyond the classroom, and many began asking how to balance the claims of freedom and responsibility on the campus.

During the eighties, undergraduates enjoyed almost unlimited freedom in personal and social matters, and responsibility for residence hall living was delegated far down the administrative ladder, with resident assistants on the front lines of supervision. Top administrators were often out of touch with day-to-day conditions on the campus. The problem was that, while colleges were no longer parents, no new theory of campus governance had emerged to replace the old assumptions. Regulations could not be arbitrarily imposed—on that everyone agreed—but what was left in doubt was whether codes of conduct should be established and, if so, who should take the lead. Unclear about what standards to maintain, many administrators sought to sidestep rather than confront the issue.

To complicate matters further, while college and university officials understood that their authority had forever changed, this shift toward a freer climate was not understood or accepted by either parents or the public. The assumption persisted that, when an undergraduate went off to college, he or she would, in some general manner, be cared for by the institution. It is understandable that parents continued to feel that the institution betrayed them if a son or daughter was physically or emotionally harmed while attending college.

Even state legislators and the courts were not willing to take colleges off the hook. When a crime hit the campus, as in the widely publicized Len Bias drug overdose case several years ago, the university was held responsible, at least in the court of public opinion. Indeed, the 1980s brought an unprecedented intervention in response to lawlessness on campus. Congress passed a bill requiring every college and university to provide an annual report on the incidence of crime on campus and to make such information available to prospective students.

Perhaps the most challenging issue of the eighties and the one that seems certain to shape the higher education debate for years to come is related to diversity—the topic of the next chapter in this book. The decade of the eighties brought a rich array of minority students to the campus, along with more women and a veritable army of older and part-time students. And it was widely assumed—innocently, perhaps—that, as students from different backgrounds came and lived together, they surely would learn to know and even perhaps respect each other. But, as Arthur Levine notes in the following chapter, it didn't work out that way. The increased diversity stirred tensions and resulted in a growing separation among students along racial and ethnic lines at a time when there was growing evidence that the push for social justice that had so shaped the priorities of higher education twenty years before had dramatically diminished.

This tension over diversity on America's campuses was, more broadly, a reflection of society at large. At one level, the struggle was part of the nation's effort to resolve the never-ending tension between the individual and the group. At another level, it reflected a growing lack of consensus over the very nature of our community. For generations, there was a shared understanding in this country of what it meant to be an American. While the diversity of our origins was acknowledged and even celebrated as a source of strength, it was unquestioned that all members of society were to enter the American "melting pot." What distinguished the 1980s was the vocal questioning of a shared identity. We were confronted with what Professor Shelby Steele called "the politics of difference" (1989), and the result was not shared understanding but further division as common bonds were weakened. Such a climate, at its worst, triggered harsh misunderstanding, abusive language, and even violence. During a study of campus climate a few years ago, the president of a large public university confessed, "I've been around a long time and frankly I'm more worried today than in the 1960s. Back then, you could meet with critics and confront problems head on. Today, there seems to be a lot of unspoken frustration which could explode anytime" (Carnegie Foundation and American Council on Education 1989).

The Loss of Community

At the heart of this concern was what another president called "the loss of community" (Carnegie Foundation and American Council on Education

1989), a feeling that colleges are administratively and socially so divided that common purposes are blurred or lost altogether. Although every institution had clearly defined academic rules, there remained at most campuses great confusion about the social and civic dimensions of collegiate life. In these areas many questioned where college responsibility began and ended (Carnegie Foundation 1990).

The problem related not just to social life but most especially to the academic program—to what became known as the "multiculturalism debate." Leaders of minority groups charged that the curriculum was biased, and they called for special courses that were more culturally inclusive—Black Studies, Asian Studies, Women's Studies, and so on. Professor Molefi Kete Asante, writing in the *American Scholar,* stated the case for a more inclusive curriculum. "No longer can the structure of knowledge which supported white hegemony be defended: whites must take their place, not above or below, but alongside the rest of humanity" (1991). Traditionalists, on the other hand, argued that these new priorities should be fitted into the regular academic framework. They also insisted that American universities have a special obligation to focus on Western intellectual thought, frequently referred to as "the canon."

In response to this debate, many U.S. colleges and universities added new courses to reflect special interests and give recognition to overlooked cultural traditions, arguing that the curriculum is never static. There was agreement among most academics that the richness of the nation's varied cultures was a reality to be cherished, not deplored. It was argued persuasively on many campuses that to recognize this nation not as one culture but as many, to defend the rights of minorities, and to preserve the freedom to dissent were essentials of a democratic people. And, to the extent that colleges and universities during the 1980s expanded enrollments, broadened curricula, and responded to the diversity of students they enrolled, they, and the nation, could be justly proud.

At the same time, there was a growing feeling in the academy that, if the university were to flourish, it would need to be made up of people who believed that they were working toward common—not competing—goals. Increasingly, it was recognized that a balance was needed between individualism and broader community concerns. And the goal of the university, it was argued, should be to help all students understand that they are not only autonomous individuals with a unique heritage, but also members of a human community to which they are accountable.

I do not wish to suggest that during the 1980s colleges and universities were unresponsive to the new realities of campus life. Indeed, quite the opposite was true. Almost all institutions expanded their student services and recruited more professional staff—counselors, financial aid officers, residence hall supervisors, and the like. Further, most campuses began to shape new codes of conduct, often in consultation with students. Many institutions also created workshops on social issues and organized all-college forums throughout the year. Student personnel administrators deserve especially high praise for their sensitive and creative work, often making decisions under difficult conditions.

Still, hardly anyone is fully satisfied with the current situation. Good work was indeed being done to improve the quality of campus life, but student personnel professionals, who carried most of the responsibility for student conduct, were expected to "keep the lid on" with no overall strategy to guide them. No one expected the campus to be problem free, and surely it was unrealistic to view the modern college as an island divorced from the outside world. But neither could colleges and universities live comfortably with a climate of endless ambiguity about how campus life decisions should be made.

A Renewed Attention to Undergraduate Education

One of the most encouraging developments of the late 1980s was the dramatic shift in the priority of higher education to undergraduate education, with increased focus on the student. Some of this interest may have been self-serving. After all, the market for students was getting tougher, and colleges were concerned about survival. But the larger and more pervasive motivation was the renewal of the institution.

There was widespread recognition that a larger, more integrative vision of community in higher education was required. This new vision should focus not on the length of time students spent on campus but on the quality of the encounter, and it would relate not only to social activities, but also to the classroom.

It is of special significance that higher learning institutions—even the big, complex ones—continued in the 1980s to use the familiar rhetoric of "community" to describe campus life and even to use the metaphor of "family." Especially significant is the fact that 97 percent of the college and university presidents surveyed by the Carnegie Foundation for the Advancement of Teaching said they strongly believed in "the importance of community." Almost all of the presidents agreed that "community is appropriate for my campus" and also supported the proposition that "administrators should make a greater effort to strengthen common purposes and shared experiences" (Carnegie Foundation and American Council on Education 1989).

It was in this context, then, that the Carnegie Foundation, in cooperation with the American Council on Education, launched a study to consider social conditions on the campus (Carnegie Foundation 1990). A search for the renewal of community in higher learning may, at first, have seemed quixotic. After all, America during the 1980s became increasingly divided. Cultural coherence faded, and the very notion of commonalities seemed strikingly inapplicable to the vigorous diversity of contemporary life. Within the academy itself, the fragmentation of knowledge, narrow departmentalism, and an intense vocationalism increasingly became the strongest characteristics of collegiate education.

Still, the challenge could not be avoided. If colleges and universities cannot define their purposes with some precision and if students, faculty, and administrators cannot live with some degree of understanding, how do we expect to have understanding on the city streets? After a year-long study, we proposed that six principles, taken together, define the kind of community that every college and university should strive to be. We proposed that academic institutions, to be effective, must be purposeful, open, just, disciplined, caring, and celebrative.

- By a purposeful community, we mean a place where faculty and students share academic goals and work together to strengthen teaching and learning on campus.
- By an open community, we mean a place where freedom of expression is uncompromisingly defended and where civility is powerfully affirmed.
- By a just community, we mean a place where the sacredness of each person is honored and where diversity is aggressively pursued.
- By a disciplined community, we mean a place where individuals accept their obligations to the group and where well-defined governance procedures guide behavior for the common good.
- By a caring community, we mean a place where the well-being of each member is sensitively supported and where service to others is encouraged.
- By a celebrative community, we mean a place where the heritage of the institution is remembered and where rituals affirming both tradition and change are widely shared.

These principles have to some degree informed decision making in higher education throughout the years. The purpose of the Carnegie Foundation's report was to urge that in the 1990s they be adopted more formally as a campus compact and be used more consistently as the basis for day-to-day decision making on the campus. With this in mind, many campuses have, at the beginning of the 1990s, been considering just how a community of learning might be more carefully defined and how to build a new post–*in loco parentis* framework for governance in higher education, a framework that could strengthen the spirit of community on campus and perhaps also provide a model for the nation.

A Search for Curricular Coherence

The decade of the eighties was marked not only by a search for community on campus, but also by a search for more coherence in the curriculum to be studied. General education experienced something of a revival. Of course, students came to college to follow their own special aptitudes and interests. They were eager to get credentials and jobs; become productive, self-reliant human beings; and, with new knowledge, continue to learn after their college days ended. Increasingly it was recognized, however, that these private concerns, while important, were insufficient. The individual interests of students must be matched by community concerns. And perhaps it is here that we can draw an analogy from the cities. Paul Goldberger, architecture critic for the *New York Times,* observed that, while city life has always been characterized by a struggle between the private and the public sectors, there was once general respect for buildings and spaces "of the public realm." In New York City, for example, this meant Central Park, Grand Central Terminal, the New York Public Library, and the street, subway, water, and sewage systems.

In recent years, however, commitment to the public realm has diminished. As Goldberger put it, there is less commitment "to the very idea . . . that the city is a collective, shared place, a place that is in the most literal sense common ground" (1989, 1). As the inspiration of shared spaces lost appeal—with people retreating increasingly into their own private worlds—many seemed to feel that the public domain in cities could not be reclaimed. Still, a city simply cannot function physically without an infrastructure—roadways, pipes and tunnels for water and waste, basic public services—nor can it survive spiritually without the spaces and places that sustain its intellectual, social, and artistic life. So it is with higher education.

A Reemphasis on Teaching

The 1990s are bringing another fundamental issue to the surface. After years of neglect there is, on many campuses, a renewed commitment to teaching. According to a Carnegie Foundation survey conducted in 1989, 60 percent of the responding faculty members said that they'd rather teach than do research, and an equivalent percentage stated their belief that teaching, not research, should be the primary criterion for promotion and tenure (Carnegie Foundation 1989).

On campuses across the nation, there is a recognition that the faculty reward system does not match the full range of academic functions and that professors are often caught between competing obligations. In response, a lively discussion has emerged about how faculty should, in fact, spend their time. Former Stanford University President Donald Kennedy called for more contact between faculty and students, especially in the junior and senior years, a time when career decisions are more likely to be made. "It is time," Kennedy said, "for us to reaffirm that education—that is, teaching in all its forms—is the primary task" of higher education (1990).

In the late 1980s, the University of California completed a study of lower-division undergraduate education, recommending that more weight be placed on teaching in faculty tenure decisions (1986). In the East, the University of Pennsylvania, in its faculty handbook, stated that "the teaching of students at all levels is to be distributed among faculty members without regard to rank or seniority as such" (1989, 40). In the Midwest, Robert Gavin, president of Macalester College, reaffirmed his institution's view of the liberal arts mission as including not only academic quality, but also internationalism, diversity, and service (1990).

It is this issue—what it means to be a scholar—that has become a central theme in the debate about quality in higher education. For the first time in years, many academics are stepping back and reflecting on the variety of functions that faculty are expected to perform. As Patricia Cross noted in chapter 17 on the improvement of teaching, the Carnegie Foundation issued a report, *Scholarship Reconsidered,* arguing that the term *scholarship* should be given a broader, more capacious meaning that brings legitimacy to the full scope of academic work (Boyer 1991). The work of the professoriate can be seen as having four distinct, yet interrelated functions: the scholarship of discovery, the scholarship of integration, the scholarship of application, and the scholarship of teaching.

The first two kinds of scholarship—discovery and integration of knowledge—reflect the investigative and synthesizing traditions of academic life. The third element, the application of knowledge, moves toward engagement as the scholar asks how knowledge can be responsibly applied to consequential problems. Finally, the scholarship of teaching focuses on the work of the professor as a dynamic endeavor involving knowledge of one's field and of pedagogy. Teaching is viewed as a means not only of transmitting knowledge, but also of transforming and extending it.

Scholarship, then, means more than engaging in original work; it also means stepping back from one's investigations, looking for connections, building bridges between theory and practice, and communicating one's knowledge effectively to students.

Such a vision of scholarship—one that recognizes the great diversity of talent within the professoriate—may, in the future, prove especially useful to faculty as they reflect on the meaning and direction of their professional lives.

An Attention to Assessment

Finally, during the 1980s the spotlight shifted to assessment. Over the decade, concern grew that the pieces of a college education did not add up to a coherent whole. Reports about the need for remediation—the poor basic skills of some students in teacher preparation programs, nursing students who failed to pass state licensing exams, graduates who could not read instructions—sparked what some described as a "crisis in confidence" in higher education. In commenting on this crisis, Chester Finn, former Assistant Secretary of Education of the United States, wrote, "We have essentially no means of gauging how well American higher education as a whole is doing with respect to student learning" (1984, 48).

New questions were being asked. Is it enough for college students to be evaluated in each class, receive grades, and then, when enough credits have been earned, be handed a diploma? Or should colleges seek to measure student progress against larger goals that reflect overall institutional purposes? Are there, in short, outcomes greater than the sum of the separate parts? The governors of the fifty states, at their August 1986 meeting in Hilton Head, South Carolina, declared that they "wanted to hold institutions accountable for the performance of their students." A worthy goal, perhaps, but how is this to be most appropriately accomplished?

A 1986 survey of college and university administrators revealed that 91 percent supported the idea of linking new assessment procedures to the improvement of instruction (American Council on Education 1986). Administrators also agreed that measuring student outcomes would be an appropriate way to evaluate the overall effectiveness of the institution. Grady Bogue, then chancellor of Louisiana State University, captured the spirit of the decade when he said: "To know as much about our students on exit as we know about them on entry hardly seems an extraordinary expectation. . . . How can we possibly give any meaningful leadership to program and service improvement without data on what our graduates know and think?" (1984, 10).

It was hard to argue with this commonsense position. While the notion of better assessment and greater accountability made sense in theory, though, most colleges found it difficult to agree upon the objectives by which the progress of all students might be measured. Nor were the tools available adequate to the task. In 1985, C. Robert Pace at the University of California, Los Angeles, warned persuasively that many testing instruments were not appropriate for use in any evaluation of higher education, "partly because what they measure is not clearly related to educational objectives, partly because some personality traits are rather deeply embedded by the time a student reaches college age, and spending a few years in college is unlikely to change them in an highly visible way" (1985, 10–11).

Further, many academics began to worry that politicians, not educators, would shape the assessment process as funding formulas were linked to narrow yardsticks of achievement. Since the integrity of higher education required that public agencies not control the educational process even indirectly, it was universally agreed that state-imposed "outcome measures" should be resisted. Thus, educators, at the conclusion of the 1980s, continued to search for ways to evaluate their work. They looked for constructive and credible means for public accountability related closely to their purposes.

In the 1990s, we urgently need a continuing debate about the meaning of the undergraduate college and a willingness to make this part of the educational enterprise more vital and enriching. At the same time, the diversity of our system should be acknowledged and protected. The responses to the challenge of enriching the baccalaureate experience will surely differ from one institution to another and, in the end, the quality of the effort must be measured not by the certainty of the outcome but by the quality of the quest.

There is firm evidence that the American college is ready for renewal, and there is an urgency to the task. The nation's colleges have been successful in meeting the needs of individual students. They have been much less attentive to the larger, more transcendent issues that give meaning to existence and help students put their own lives in perspective.

This nation and the world need well-informed, inquisitive, open-minded young people who are both productive and reflective, seeking answers to life's most important questions. Above all, we need educated men and women who not only pursue their own personal interests, but also are prepared to fulfill their social and civic obligations. And it is during the undergraduate experience, perhaps more than at any other time, that these essential qualities of mind and character are refined.

References

American Council on Education. 1986. *Higher Education Panel Report 73.* Washington, D.C.: American Council on Education, August.

Asante, Molefi Kete. 1991. "Multiculturalism: An Exchange." *American Scholar,* Spring, 267–272.

Bogue, Grady. 1984. "Outcomes: An Issue of Caring and Daring." *State Education Leader,* Spring, 10.

Boyer, Ernest L. 1990. *Scholarship Reconsidered.* Princeton: Princeton University Press.

Carnegie Foundation for the Advancement of Teaching. 1990. *Campus Life: In Search of Community.* Princeton: Princeton University Press.

Carnegie Foundation for the Advancement of Teaching. 1989. *National Survey of College Faculty, 1989.* Princeton: Carnegie Foundation for the Advancement of Teaching.

Carnegie Foundation for the Advancement of Teaching and American Council on Education. 1989. "National Survey of College and University Presidents, 1989."

Finn, Chester. 1984. "Trying Higher Education: An Eight Count Indictment." *Change,* 16(4):28–33, 47–51.

Gavin, Robert. 1990. Convocation Speech, Macalester College, 13 September.

Goldberger, Paul. 1989. "Why Design Can't Transform Cities." *New York Times,* 25 June, p. 1.

"Good-bye 80's." 1989. *Chronicle of Higher Education,* 13 December.

Kennedy, Donald. 1990. "Stanford in Its Second Century." Address to the Stanford Community at the meeting of the Academic Council, 5 April.

Pace, C. Robert. 1985. "Perspectives and Problems in Student Outcomes Research." *New Directions for Institutional Research,* 47:10–11.

Steele, Shelby. 1989. "The Recoloring of Campus Life: Student Racism, Academic Pluralism, and the End of a Dream." *Harper's Magazine,* February, pp. 47–55.

University of California. 1986. *Lower Division Education in the University of California: A Report from the Task Force on Lower Division Education.* Berkeley: Office of the President, University of California, June.

University of Pennsylvania. 1989. *A Handbook for Faculty and Academic Administrators: A Selection of Policies and Procedures of the University of Pennsylvania.* Philadelphia: University of Pennsylvania.

20 Diversity on Campus

ARTHUR LEVINE

The decade of the 1980s was a time in which the popular press reported a rising level of racism, sexism, antisemitism, and gay bashing in higher education. Commentators said that divisions among diverse groups on campus were growing. A Carnegie Foundation report lamented the decline of campus community.

In this chapter the state of diversity on America's college and university campuses is reported, based on a study of fourteen diverse institutions of higher education. The schools vary geographically—being located in the Northeast, Middle Atlantic, South, Midwest, and West. They differ in control, including public and private institutions as well as sectarian and nonsectarian schools. They vary in size—from about fifteen hundred to over twenty thousand students. And they include four-year colleges and universities.

At each of the schools, interviews were conducted with administrators, faculty, and students. The study examined diversity in academic life—including curriculum, courses, academic organization, the faculty, and scholarships. It also considered diversity in campus life, including orientation, residence, and the co-curriculum. It looked too at the condition of academic freedom and free speech on campus. The history, climate, politics, and recent initiatives carried out in the name of diversity were matters of inquiry as well.

The Meaning of Diversity

Over the past four decades, diversity has taken on a variety of very different meanings. The earliest conception, a product of the 1960s, is representation in or admission to college. The goal originally was to develop a minority presence on campus. With time, the definition has expanded. The notion of minorities has grown from blacks to include a variety of underrepresented populations ranging across race, religion, gender, and ethnicity. Once thought of largely in terms of students, the focus of diversity has broadened to include faculty, staff, administrators, and trustees. And the idea of presence has shifted from merely increasing the numbers of underrepresented groups to achieving numbers at least comparable to minority percentages in the population.

A second definition of diversity developed in the 1970s is support or retention. The aim is to provide the "new" populations on campus with the sustenance they need to remain in college. This has meant compensatory services, financial aid, diversity support groups and activities, special residential units, and diversity studies departments such as Afro-American and Women's Studies.

A third meaning, a product of the late 1970s and the early 1980s, is integration. The focus is on incorporating historically underrepresented groups, which have become segregated on campuses, into the larger campus population. This has involved the creation of orientation programs for new populations and less frequently for majority students about these populations; the adoption of general education diversity requirements, including scholarship and instruction about diversity within the traditional curriculum; and the addition of a variety of new activities and clubs to the co-curriculum.

A fourth and final notion of diversity, emerging today, is pluralism or multiculturalism. Here the aim is to legitimize both the intellectual and the emotional aspects of diverse cultures in academic and campus life in teaching, research, and service. The goal is equity among diverse cultures and a symbiosis among them.

A majority of the schools in the study emphasized the first two definitions of diversity. However, there were schools with programs in all four categories, and recent efforts at several of the institutions focused on the third definition—integration. No institution, with the possible exception of an historically black college, had achieved any of the definitions fully.

Diversity was an issue of concern on at least eleven of the campuses. The level of interest, however, varied dramatically across the schools—from urgency and broad involvement to disinterest and apathy. There were many new initiatives, and three of the schools were in the process of carrying out large-scale projects. In general, however, rhetoric outstripped action.

The most striking feature of the study, however, was the lack of long-range, systematic planning with regard to diversity on the part of at least three-quarters of the schools. Very few were operating with clear definitions of diversity. There was a tendency to think of diversity as a problem, rather than an opportunity to shape an institution's future. The focus was generally on quick fixes.

The Campus Community

What stood out in this study was the small number of campuses, about a third, in which diversity was a priority on the institutional agenda. Three forces seemed to have the power to increase its prominence. The first was a rather rapid and substantial change in a student body, involving large increases in traditionally underrepresented populations. The second was an overt or public act of racism or sexism. Incidents involving physical attacks on minorities, cross burnings, and hate banners were provoking events on three campuses. A third factor was presidential commitment.

Actually, presidential leadership proved to be essential for any effective diversity initiative. The attributes associated with success were a clear vision, resources to support the vision, appropriate and realistic rhetoric to make the vision compelling, the secured commitment of each institutional constituency to embrace the vision, frequent and continuing publicity and communication regarding the initiative to all segments of the college community, and regular monitoring of progress. A few of the efforts on the campuses involved many of these ingredients, but none involved all. Several of the presidents were eloquent, visionary, and even passionately committed. But in no case had a president managed to secure a commitment from his or her faculty. On most campuses, students were unconvinced of presidential commitment as well. In point of fact, on only two of the campuses did the president assume a leadership role in diversity.

The Students

Students were almost universally the driving force behind diversity on the campuses studied. They prodded their colleges to do more and more.

Many of the campuses studied were tense. The minority students interviewed often expressed a feeling of being uncomfortable and feeling illegitimate in traditionally majority institutions. One young black woman said that she felt "like an unwelcome guest on campus" rather than a member of the community.

The topic of diversity evoked a variety of feelings from whites. Students expressed feelings varying from apathy, anger, and fear to calls for action, approbation regarding current conditions, and helplessness. One of the most poignant conversations was with a diverse group of students who could not figure out how to talk to one another; their differences seemed insurmountable, and no one knew how to get past them. There is a lot of anger on many of the campuses studied—some open, much submerged.

In fact, students tended systematically to underestimate the degree of involvement among diverse groups on campus. When black students were asked how many whites had attended a lecture by a renowned black scholar or whites were asked how many blacks had attended a dance, their estimates were always far lower than reality.

Most of the campuses studied were deeply divided perceptually, if not in fact. It is fair to say that their differences appear larger among students, especially members of diversity groups, than do their commonalities. There are centrifugal pressures both within diversity groups and between groups.

Students perceive on campus no culture or commonality broad enough to bring them together. The academic culture that provides a set of shared beliefs and values for faculty is weak and provides little if any cohesion for students. The only institutions at which this pattern did not hold were Catholic schools. The culture of Catholicism was powerful enough to provide at least a vision of shared campus culture.

Students tended to view themselves in smaller and smaller categories. A social mitosis of sorts was occurring on many of the campuses as student groups broke into increasingly smaller subunits. For example, on one campus the gay student society broke by gender into gay and lesbian clubs. And the lesbian group divided by race into white lesbians and lesbians of color. There was talk of dividing further by major. Because of limited resources at several of the schools, each of these subgroups is being pitted against the others in the search for scarce dollars for activities, scarce physical plant for facilities, and scarce time in the curriculum for classes. At these schools, campus life is becoming a Hobbesian world in miniature—a war of each against all.

There is also a growing sense among students of being victims. The language of victimization was heard again and again among majority and minority students, men and women, Christians and non-Christians, every race and ethnic group. The feeling of being "the other"—left out and discriminated against—is powerful.

The Administration

The diversity issue is frightening for the administrators interviewed. It is a tangled and daunting problem with uncertain contours and broad and explosive potential. Administrators fear what would happen if diversity were dealt with directly, what would occur if the genie were allowed out of the bottle. When talked with confidentially and asked candidly what they would like to see happen with the issue, most senior administrators use the same language. They say they would like it to go away. Diversity tends to be treated by administrators as a series of discrete problems, each arising in isolation. The focus is on quick fixes and Band-Aid approaches.

In general, the administration has delegated the issue of diversity to student affairs. The student affairs people deserve a round of applause for their efforts. No group on campus is doing more to turn the rhetoric of diversity into reality. They have hired staffs that include larger numbers of underrepresented populations than the rest of their campuses, developed staff training programs on diversity issues, established new residence options, added counseling services targeted at underrepresented groups, and created an array of cultural activities for the entire campus community. If student affairs had not filled the void, there is no evidence that any other group on campus would have.

But this is also an area facing huge challenges. Student affairs has an impossible assignment. What makes this task all the more difficult is that student affairs is isolated from much of the rest of the campus community. There is a gulf between student affairs and the faculty, who do not understand the work of student affairs and hold it in low esteem. There is also a gap between student affairs and other senior administrators. As a result, student affairs is being asked to address both the intellectual and the developmental aspects of diversity without the resources and legitimacy to do so.

The Faculty

No group on campus is less involved in the diversity agenda than the professorate. Few teach about or engage in scholarship about diversity. Few seem concerned about diversity. Almost none is engaged in co-curricular activities dealing with diversity.

This is not true of all faculty. There are marvelous examples of engaged professors on almost every campus studied, of faculty, even senior faculty, who are offering classes on diversity issues, integrating new scholarship into their courses, serving key roles on committees, acting as advocates, carrying out research, or working on innovative and exciting ideas for diversity. And on one campus a full fifth of the faculty were regularly attending diversity colloquia. However, it would be accurate to say that the few faculty involved are more likely to be minorities and junior staffers than senior faculty and campus leaders.

There are many reasons for this state of affairs. One is indifference and lack of knowledge about diversity. With this in mind, two of the campuses studied offered voluntary workshops for faculty to enhance their understanding of diversity, with very positive results.

Another rationale is an absence of urgency or pressure. At the moment, the push and pull of this issue is largely between students and administrators. Faculties, because of their atomistic nature, are far more difficult to engage. It is easier for them to opt out. One cynical commentator on a campus studied said that it is almost as if there were an unspoken agreement between administrators and faculty for the faculty to ignore the issue.

Still another cause is the lack of minority faculty on campuses. No institution studied, with the exceptions of a black college and an institution historically committed to diversity, had a faculty even remotely matching the minority population of its region or the nation. And, although several of the institutions were making efforts to gain ground quickly in minority hiring, the result is that nearly all colleges now lack the critical mass of underrepresented peoples to make diversity visible to colleagues, to reduce the level of complacency, to encourage discourse, to provide models for students, and to serve as a catalyst for action. The powerful effect of minority faculty on curriculum diversity could be observed just by walking through any of the campus bookstores.

A fourth consideration is fear. One white faculty member, a historian, said he wanted to teach African-American history, which was not being offered, but he was afraid. Would minority students accept him? Did he have the expertise? Would colleagues, who view ethnic studies as second-class fields, lose respect for him? Would it hurt his chances for promotion? In the end, he found more reasons not to teach the class than to offer it.

One more reality is the lack of incentives for embracing diversity. Programs on the campuses studied offer funds for providing scholarships, developing new courses, remodeling existing courses, encouraging faculty to participate in co-curricular activities, and coaxing departments to hire minorities. Two institutions used mild sticks. On one campus, the chief academic officer asked each department to study the barriers to minorities in its field, discussed the results with the departments individually, and is monitoring progress. On another campus, the departments that did not participate in institutional minority activities were asked to explain why, in person, to the provost. Such efforts are not uncommon but, put simply, the fact is that today there are no systematic incentives for faculty and departments to engage in the diversity agenda.

Programming

The Curriculum

The curriculum at the schools studied remains largely unaffected by concern with diversity. At college after college the programs were described as "Eurocentric." The changes that have occurred in the name of diversity have been largely at the periphery of the curriculum. Several of the institutions have introduced majors and minors in ethnic and gender studies. They have created departments and centers of minority studies. Several schools have added one- or two-semester general education diversity requirements. Two colleges recently sought to adopt such requirements and failed. At least four others are seriously contemplating such a change.

At only one institution, however, had diversity penetrated a significant portion of the course offerings, meaning that classes are being offered on diversity topics; existing courses include diversity scholarship, and reading lists are being expanded with diversity works. At other schools such changes were rare and unusual, occurring only sporadically in the curriculum. Here and there, however, departments in the traditional disciplines embraced diversity in one fashion or another. For example, at a major research university, the English department required all majors to take a course in literature by women or African-American writers, and the history department had established a specialization in African-American history. Perhaps most telling is that, when administrators and faculty were asked what changes had been made in the curriculum to respond to diversity, one of the most common answers was remedial programs.

The Co-Curriculum

Life outside the classroom is a cornucopia, varying dramatically in size from campus to campus, of diversity days, weeks, lectures, meetings, exhibits, films, concerts, workshops, teach-ins, services, theme dormitories, resource centers, counselors, clubs, publications, and meals. Historically, student activities have filled in where the curriculum was weak. That tradition continues.

This broad array of offerings is not without shortcomings. It is immediately apparent that faculty do not participate. In fact, one institution described itself as the Lord of the Flies after five o'clock—no adults anywhere. One consequence is a perceived absence of intellectual leadership. On several campuses, students dismissed the co-curriculum saying, "Sure there is a lot to do, but it isn't serious." The implication is that, if it were serious, it would be part of the curriculum.

Another problem cited on many of the campuses is that groups do not attend each other's events. Minority students regularly complained that white students did not come to their activities and that they felt uncomfortable at majority events. Majority students said they felt unwelcome at minority events. This complaint must be taken with a grain of salt given the student tendency to underestimate participation rates. To some extent, however, the co-curriculum on most campuses seemed to be not a vehicle for encouraging education or interaction among diverse peoples, but rather a mechanism for separating people comfortably according to differences.

Fraternities and sororities deserve special criticism in this regard. They were regularly cited by students and student affairs staff for their deliberate policies of segregation on the basis of individual difference. Stories of objectionable Greek behavior with regard to diversity abounded.

Orientation to college was another much discussed aspect of programming. It suffers from the range of shortcomings associated with the co-curriculum. In recent years, a focus on diversity has been added to the orientation programs at several of the schools studied. It tends to be brief, unconnected to the intellectual life of the campus, and lacking in faculty participation. Minorities were critical of their diversity sessions during orientation, saying that their focus was on "getting minorities ready to deal with the institution." The approach was characterized as one-sided for failing to teach majorities about diversity. However, exceptions to this pattern were found, including an institution with an orientation program several days in length that emphasized diversity and offered sessions for minorities, majorities, and parents, together and separately; in this school the theme of diversity was continued throughout the freshman year in residence hall programs.

Free Speech

Incidents of racism and other attacks on diversity groups were facts of life at many of the institutions we visited. The most frequent victims have been gays, people of color, women, and Jews. Stories were told of ugly public incidents that shook institutions and left long-term scars at a few schools, but far more common were graffiti, name calling, and offensive language. Dormitories were the most common place for such behavior, and classrooms were the least common. It is not clear whether this behavior was occurring more or less often. Some institutions collected numbers; others did not. Some reported increases in hate incidents; others said there were fewer.

Regardless of whether the number of incidents is up or down, campuses have grown increasingly sensitive to the issue. And this situation is encouraging a number of colleges studied, but not by any means a majority, to begin rethinking the standards for free speech which operate on campus. Since the 1960s, most of the institutions embraced the first amendment as their guiding principle. Today, however, several of the schools studied are feeling uneasy about the first amendment approach. Already one has chosen a more limited definition barring offensive talk and acts aimed at individual members of minority groups. Campus conversations lead one to believe that in the next few years debate about the relationship between free speech and diversity will escalate, a number of institutions around the country will consider or adopt standards different from the first amendment, and the courts, as they have already begun to do, will be asked to decide the ground rules.

Conclusions

Several conclusions follow from this study.

- Diversity is poorly defined on campus.
- Goals for diversity are unclear.
- Most colleges and universities lack comprehensive and systematic plans.
- In general, presidents are not providing adequate leadership.
- Students are divided, and tension around diversity is high.
- Faculty for the most part have abdicated.
- Student affairs is being asked inappropriately to assume almost full responsibility for the diversity agenda.
- Diverse populations are highly underrepresented in the student bodies of colleges and universities and on their faculties, senior staffs, and boards of trustees.
- The curriculum has largely peripheralized or neglected diversity.
- The co-curriculum, though rich in diversity programs, lacks intellectual depth, is unconnected with the academic side of higher education, and is largely ignored by the faculty.
- Standards of free speech and academic freedom are being questioned on a number of campuses.
- Academic culture has grown weak and fails to provide colleges and

universities with a shared set of beliefs and values that go beyond differences that divide people.

The Future

Conditions on campus with respect to diversity are explosive today. In the 1990s, the pressure will mount.

An exacerbating factor is changing student character. Recent research by Deborah Hirsch and me shows rising optimism, a rebirth of heroes, increasing activism, and growing social involvement among college students (Levine and Hirsch 1990). In the next few years, this constellation of changes is likely to produce a revival among students of political action, more concern with relevance in the curriculum, and a greater emphasis on campus governance. Diversity is likely to be one of the early issues for activism in the 1990s. This has already begun on a number of campuses around the country.

There is no chance that the issue of diversity will go away in the 1990s as was hoped by so many of the senior administrators in the study. Demographics indicate that our campuses will only grow more diverse as the number of eighteen-year-old whites diminishes and the proportions of people of color and older adults increase during the early to mid-1990s (Levine 1989).

The principal difficulty for the academy today is that the meaning of diversity is uncertain. Its implications are unknown. And its consequences are unfathomable.

Diversity is an issue with no intellectual or emotional center in the academy. Higher education is deeply divided about its meaning, its importance, and what should be done. This is why diversity is such a frightening issue and why it is so tempting to try to ignore it or to offer palliatives.

In the 1990s, the twin pressures of student activism and growing diversity will require that the academy directly confront the issue. Thoughtful, creative, and decisive action are possible now. There is time now. However, as pressures mount during the next few years that is not likely to be the case. Colleges will be forced to react rather than act.

The agenda for colleges and universities in the next several years will be

- to open the campus to candid discourse regarding diversity that embraces the entire collegiate community,
- to demand that presidents provide leadership,
- to define clearly the meaning of diversity,

- to engage the faculty and expand the curriculum,
- to develop a comprehensive long-range plan and associated time line for meeting the diversity challenge,
- ultimately to see diversity as an opportunity, not a problem.

References

Levine, A. 1989. *Shaping Higher Education's Future*. San Francisco: Jossey-Bass.

Levine, A., and Deborah Hirsch. 1990. "After the 'Me' Generation: A Portrait of Today's College Students." Paper presented at the annual meeting of the American Educational Research Association, Boston, April.

21 Standardized Testing in a National Context

DONALD M. STEWART

The issue of testing has so many aspects—public policy and political, social, and even technological considerations—that it will remain a subject of considerable public and professional interest, as well as book-length investigation, for years to come. Rather than an exhaustive overview, this chapter presents a point of view about the evolution of testing in a national context based in part on our experience with national precollegiate examinations in which the College Board has over nine decades of involvement. The chapter explores the public policy environment, which currently has a major influence on testing in the United States, as well as psychometric, technological, and economic trends that are guiding test development for the future.

Challenges to Testing in the Public Policy Environment

Like the other much-debated "t" word of the 1980s—taxes—academic testing is a high stakes, highly technical process that is surrounded by and in part creates a charged social and political environment. During the 1980s, academic journals and daily newspapers, school board meetings and academic conferences all echoed the assertions, put forward by a vocal group of critics, that American students were being "tested to death." Standardized testing in particular came under fire. To cite one example, the tracking of the annual SAT averages became a media event and front-page news. Other kinds of standardized tests for grades K through 12 were attacked as being ineffective or worse, distorting teaching and curriculum. An independent watchdog group, Friends of Education, gained wide visibility by pointing out that all fifty states report test results above the national average on nationally normed achievement tests—a phenomenon that was dubbed the "Lake Woebegone" effect after humorist Garrison Keillor's mythical community in which "all the women are strong, all the men are good looking, and all the children are above average." The situation was further clouded by some misunderstanding among the public, policy makers, and even education professionals about the meanings of "standardized" and "multiple choice" and by the fact that such tests are designed and used in many ways, from measuring rote memorization and computational skills to measuring sophisticated learned abilities and higher-order thinking skills.

On the other side of the coin, the importance and/or validity of test scores was revealed in a variety of ways. In 1983, declines in SAT scores were cited in the seminal report, *A Nation at Risk* (written by a group of educational experts under the aegis of Secretary of Education Terrel Bell and chaired by then University of California President David Gardner), as one of the indicators of declining academic accomplishment of American students (National Commission on Excellence in Education 1983).

The intense efforts during the decade notwithstanding, the attempt to curtail or abolish standardized testing failed, and the public, legislatures, and policy makers continued to look to standardized test results as the most reliable index of the effectiveness of the nation's schools.

The Drive for National Testing

Generally speaking, during the 1980s testing found itself drawn into a fluid and fast-changing environment in which at least three different sets of factors played a role in shaping public perception and professional concern.

Socioeconomic Changes

The first set of factors has to do with changes in the socioeconomic environment and their effects on education. The factors in this group include

- High-technology foreign economic competition, especially from Japan, which has heightened the debatable assertion that the quality of schooling determines America's economic competitiveness;

- A confusion and lowering of academic standards on the part of some high schools as a result of curricular relaxation in higher education;
- A dramatic change in the policy as to who should be considered college bound from a majority to, in the view of some experts, essentially every student;
- International test scores that show American students lagging far behind those of many smaller and economically less-advantaged nations, not to mention students among our trading partners; and
- A tremendous change in the racial, ethnic, and socioeconomic mix of American students. (Some analysts believe that this fact alone, which has resulted in a much broader socioeconomic spectrum of test takers, accounts for falling average test scores.)

Changes with Testing

Along with these socioeconomic forces, a second set of factors has to do with testing itself.

- The development of new psychometric theories
- The arrival of the microcomputer as the essential tool of the age
- Better understanding about the way different kinds of students learn
- An interest in new approaches to testing, such as "authentic testing," "portfolios," and the like (to be discussed later)

Federal Pressures

Finally, there are new federal pressures on education and thus on testing. In September 1989, the newly elected "education" president, George Bush, convened an historic Education Summit with the fifty state governors in Charlottesville, Virginia. As a consequence, six national educational goals were articulated to promote adequate educational preparation of all of America's young people, including assessment of their progress after grades 4, 8, and 12. From one point of view, this activity builds upon efforts made as part of the Great Society legislation of the 1960s, specifically the Elementary and Secondary Education Act of 1965, whose title I—now amended as chapter 1—provides the basis for programs that accelerate the progress of at-risk students, thereby granting a legally enforceable right to a quality education for all low-achieving students. Even though the federal government has yet to commit significant new resources to education (apart from a slight increase in support for the TRIO programs—Upward Bound, Talent Search, and Student Support Services), the change in attitude and the visibility resulting from this renewed federal interest have had a significant effect on public and policy-maker concerns.

Both singly and in many different combinations, these factors have had a great influence on professional and public opinion about testing and education in America. Frankly, not even taxes have been subjected to such a spectrum of pulls and tugs as has testing over the past ten years.

As the zeitgeist moves from a spirit of federal education bashing in the 1980s to a spirit of education building in the 1990s, we see that the pendulum of opinion has swung quite a distance from the testing-adverse attitudes with which the decade began. Rather than being the root of educational evil, testing is now being seen by some highly influential groups in business and government as the *only* effective way by which to bring about educational reform. In this, too, it resonates with its "t"-word cousin as a technique for "engineering" desired social behavior.

This gradual turn in fortune for testing has been caused in part by the politics of frustration, a frustration that, without complete justification, has resulted from the apparently limited progress of the educational reform movement in the 1980s. Notwithstanding the efforts made by states and localities since the warnings sounded so effectively by *A Nation at Risk* and perhaps without full understanding of the progress that has actually been achieved, many policy makers feel that, educationally, America is stalled. As a consequence, a "national test" has been seized upon by significant players in government and business not only as essential to understand the degree of accomplishment of students during their schooling but, even more important, as a way to get education and thus American society and our economy back on track.

During the opening months of 1991, American educators found themselves facing an avalanche of proposals on national testing and assessment. "National" is the key word, even though what it means is uncertain. As used by proponents of new tests, it does not necessarily mean federal, and almost all of those offering proposals eschew the notion of nationalizing the curriculum or constraining state and local prerogatives. Certainly, there is far from universal support for a national test. At a March 1991 meeting of high school principals, a vote on the issue resulted in an expression of opposition by a two to one margin. What is significant, however, is that the debate has been framed in these terms at all, representing a watershed in the history of education in the United States.

Although many factors are at work here, probably the most significant is goal 3 as defined by President Bush and the governors (President's Education Policy Advisory Committee 1990): "By the year 2000, American students will leave grades four, eight and twelve having demonstrated competency in challenging subject matter including English, mathematics, science, history and geography."

In the summer of 1990, the National Educational Goals Panel under the chairmanship of Governor Roy Roemer of Colorado was formed to carry out this recommendation. Since then, the Congress, business, and a host of other players have come forward with ideas. In his article entitled "A National Examination System? In the U.S.?" Lawrence E. Gladieux, head of the College Board's Washington Office, wrote that the debate is so jumbled and highly charged, involving so many forces and actors (who are jockeying for political position), it is quite unclear how testing might be reshaped in the 1990s (Gladieux 1991).

The possible outcomes of this development range from, at one extreme, a true avalanche sweeping away all current testing structure to, at the other end, a rhetorical snow shower that temporarily obscures the logic of the gradual evolution in testing that has occurred during the last several decades.

The new debate clearly springs from deep concerns about the state of U.S. education and the country's future. As is stated in the introduction to the *National Goals for Education* (Office of the Press Secretary 1991): "America's educational performance must be second to none in the 21st century. Education is central to our quality of life. It is at the heart of our economic strength and security, our creativity in the arts and letters, our invention in the sciences, and the perpetuation of our cultural values. Education is the key to America's international competitiveness."

As Gladieux noted, during the past two years key political and business leaders have brought a bottom-line orientation and top-down management style to the task of figuring out how the country should measure educational achievement and progress. An implicit assumption of their proposals is that educational institutions have failed. This is the reason that a new mechanism, national assessment, is being so hotly debated.

Even if a psychometrically sound and economically viable new national test could be developed within reasonable fiscal parameters and an accelerated time frame—and even proponents of the test acknowledge this to be a very big "if"—the evidence is far from compelling that such an instrument would be able to accomplish the transformation of student achievement at the secondary level. The situation is further burdened by other social realities. A report from the Committee on Economic Development entitled *The Unfinished Agenda: A New Vision for Child Development and Education*, released early in 1991, noted that "factors such as poverty, chaotic family structure, substance abuse, and racial discrimination now place as many as 40 percent of U.S. children on the road to educational failure before they ever reach the schoolhouse door." Its contention is based on a number of chilling demographic factors, including the following:

- Between 1970 and 1987, the poverty rate for children in the United States increased nearly 33 percent, and in 1989 close to 25 percent of children under the age of six lived in poverty.
- In 1989, over one-fourth of all births were to unmarried women.
- The poverty rate for a family with children headed by a single woman who is under twenty-five years old and a high school dropout is 90 percent.
- Taxpayers currently spend $16.6 billion annually to support the children of teenage parents.
- Of all Americans in prison, 82 percent are high school dropouts.

The Children's Defense Fund has stated, moreover, that in their view schools are not making perceptible progress in achieving the national educational goals established by the president and the governors.

Taking these factors into consideration, it seems that educational reform, and the role of testing within it, cannot proceed in a manner that will effectively reach all students unless concomitant efforts related to family support, substance abuse, family planning, and prenatal care, through formalized programs such as WIC (Women, Infants, and Children) and Head Start, are in place. Only in this way will the nation be able to reach the very first goal defined by the governors and the president: "By the year 2000 all children in America will start school ready to learn."

Current Issues and Actors in National Testing

In his analysis, Gladieux pointed to almost a dozen players in the evolution of the national testing debate, including these five:

- The President's Education Policy Advisory Committee (of which I am a member) has been working with the president and the governors since the Education Summit and in the fall of 1990 issued a draft proposal for voluntary national examinations in reading and mathematics at selected grade levels.
- The National Assessment Governing Board—the governing board for the National Assessment of Educational Progress (NAEP)—is proceed-

ing with a plan to develop sample-based rather than universal proficiency standards at the fourth, eighth, and twelfth grade levels for each of the subject areas evaluated by NAEP.

- The National Educational Goals Panel, created in the summer of 1990 by the National Governors' Association to monitor progress toward the goals established after the Education Summit, issued a proposal for a national "report card" in the fall of 1991.
- The Secretary of Labor's Commission on Achieving Necessary Skills seems to be heading down a similar track but with a particular emphasis on assessing and setting national standards for "workplace competencies."
- The MacArthur/Pew Consortium has awarded twin grants to the National Center on Education and the Economy (headed by Marc Tucker and based in Rochester) and the Learning Research and Development Center of the University of Pittsburgh (headed by Lauren Resnick) to start the development of a "new student performance assessment system."

The situation is so fluid that it is not at all unlikely that other proposals will be put forward even as this volume is published.

Just as there are a great many proposals, however, there are also a great many questions about a national examination system that remain to be resolved.

- How much would it cost to develop and how would it be financed?
- Who would be tested—all students or a sample?
- What form would the examinations take—standardized/multiple choice or some mix of alternative, performance-based testing?
- How would standards be established, and how would schools, school districts, and states be compared based on the results?
- How would the results help teachers improve the educational process?

A major concern about a new national test at this time (expressed by this author and Gregory Anrig, president of the Educational Testing Service, during congressional hearings in March 1991) is that it does not fully recognize the relationship among curriculum, instruction, and assessment. *What* we teach and *how* we support our students, teachers, and schools must be clearly articulated and financed before the measurement of *how well* we are doing can be meaningful. Furthermore, if the purpose of a new national test is, in part, to send a "tough message" to schools, teachers, students, and parents, we have no evidence that sending that message in this way will change anything. Joe Nathan, Senior Fellow at the Humphrey Institute of

Public Affairs at the University of Minnesota, was reported to say that "a national test will end up stifling the most effective, the most creative, and the finest teachers we have. I would find it ironic . . . if this Administration ended up imposing an extremely disruptive and negative set of tests on the country" (DeWitt 1991).

I, too, believe that the problem faced by U.S. education is not how to assess student performance; rather, it is how to redress the significant inequality of educational opportunity throughout this nation. In considering testing programs for the future, we need to be guided by the following three propositions.

First, while there are many purposes that can be served by assessment, they are all secondary to the improvement of student learning. The democratic and humane values of our society must drive the purposes of assessment. The primacy of improving student learning should be to enable and empower more students, especially minority students and those from disadvantaged economic backgrounds, who are becoming an increasing proportion of our society and whose success is essential for our continued national well-being, to get more and better education.

Second, valuing what we test is not synonymous with testing what we value. Regardless of what our tests measure, over time we will end up valuing what we test. This seems to me to be inevitable. The ethical issue here is for us to make sure that we do not lose sight of those qualities and attributes in students that we value but cannot easily test.

Third and finally, tests cannot make decisions for people; people make decisions. The impulse to rely on test scores is understandable because people perceive tests as being "scientific" because they produce a numerical score, "fair" because all students are required to take and pass the identical test, and "objective" because decisions made from the scores are not greatly influenced by faculty, administrators, or personal biases. But whatever system of national assessment we might devise, we cannot lose sight of the fact that it is only a tool to aid human judgment, not an infallible rule to replace it.

If the nation rushes headlong into an attempt to create a new national test, we could take three years and $200 million (which is probably what it will cost), turn the educational and testing systems on their heads, throw out everything we've used in the past, inaugurate a whole new system— maybe even a better one—and, when it was all over, the kids who do badly now would do just as badly because little will have changed in the education process. This assertion is made recognizing that there are those who believe—although by their own admission without any proof—that tests can be "action-stimulating events, not just speedometers that tell us how fast we're going" (National School Public Relations Association 1991).

Lessons Learned from the Scholastic Aptitude Test

In its recent deliberations about the future of its admissions testing program, the College Board has been guided by the Commission on New Possibilities for the Admissions Testing Program, co-chaired by Derek Bok, former president of Harvard University, and David Gardner, former president of the University of California. While their charge was specifically to evaluate proposed changes to the Scholastic Aptitude Test (SAT), this blue-ribbon group of educators from secondary and postsecondary institutions took a broad view of the testing issue. Among their conclusions, published in their report, *Beyond Prediction,* is the assertion that even if certain criticisms of testing are overstated, those responsible for sponsoring tests need to take the criticisms seriously (1990). The commission's recommendations for the evolution of the SAT seem to me to be equally sound for the development of any national testing system, namely

- to encourage as many students as possible to obtain as much education as their abilities warrant;
- to reinforce sound curricular policies and good study habits in high school by devising tests that emphasize substantive knowledge as well as general ability, while calling for skills of problem solving, writing, and the like as they are actually practiced in college;
- to develop tests that lead students to prepare for them in ways that encourage genuine learning; and
- to respond to increased diversity by helping schools and colleges guide a more varied student population to courses and programs appropriate to their talents and levels of preparation.

Therefore, if we can proceed in a logical fashion, as outlined above, remaining sensitive to the cautions and directives just noted, I believe that we will be able to fashion a system of assessment that works well for us in the future.

The Promise of Technology

The emerging development that has the greatest potential to change the entire landscape of testing is computer technology. There is general agreement among testing specialists and professional educators alike that, certainly by the year 2000 and perhaps well before then, testing by computer will virtually replace current methods of paper-and-pencil testing. The question is no longer whether technology will influence the future of testing but rather how and how fast it will occur. The promise of technology lies not only in the possibilities it creates for improving current testing practices, but, more importantly, in the new capabilities it will create for the assessment of critical skills and abilities that are difficult to assess within the constraints of traditional paper-and-pencil testing. Just as other dramatic advances in technology have not only brought about more efficient ways of achieving traditional functions and goals but also opened the doors to new, previously unimagined services, so too will testing in education be transformed.

Although different observers of the testing scene have different visions of how technology will transform the testing field, certain elements are seen by all as the most powerful forces—among them, the six discussed in the following sections.

Increased Efficiency of Measurement

Perhaps the most immediate benefit of technology is that it is allowing us to design tests and other assessments to measure human abilities and achievements much more efficiently than is permitted by traditional testing practices. Through the sophisticated branching techniques of computer adaptive testing, it is now possible to design tests that route students to those sets of questions that are most appropriate for their levels of ability and thus that result in the most useful information about those ability levels. This is not possible in traditional, paper-and-pencil tests because these tests are inherently linear—they require all students to answer all questions, regardless of the abilities of the students and the difficulties of the test questions. This constraint puts a very real ceiling on the efficiency of measurement, primarily because very little is learned by administering very easy questions to people who are proficient in the skill being assessed or very difficult questions to people who are not proficient in the skill. Recent studies show that it is possible to achieve the same accuracy of measurement in a computer adaptive test with as few as one-quarter to one-half the questions that would be needed on a traditional linear test.

Broader Coverage of Content

Because measurement by computer offers great improvements in efficiency and thus decreases the amount of time required to administer any particular test, new opportunities are created to supplement what is currently measured with additional assessments. At the College Board, for example, we are currently developing long-range plans to integrate via computer the measurement of broad verbal and mathematical reasoning abilities (such as those tested in the current SAT) with the assessment of achievement in more specific subject-matter areas. The vision of a computerized testing program that integrates the assessment of broad reasoning skills with that of subject-matter achievements was articulated most recently by the College Board's Commission on New Possibilities for the Admissions Testing Program. That commission urged the board to continue its efforts to develop such an integrated approach to admissions testing by the year 2000. This kind of integration is made possible only by the application of computer technology, for it is the efficiencies of testing by computer that will allow the board to assess a broader range of abilities without increasing the amount of time devoted to the administration of tests.

Better Diagnostic Information

The power of the computer to test more efficiently has implications for the depth of assessment. Because of its ability to route students to the most appropriate subject matter, the computer offers enormous potential for supplementing general test scores with diagnostic information that pinpoints the exact areas where students seem to be having difficulty. Once again, it is the inherently linear nature of traditional paper-and-pencil testing that sets a very serious constraint on the amount of diagnostic information that can be derived from tests because diagnosis, by its very definition, implies a customizing that is not possible in current tests.

Fuller Integration of Assessment with Instruction

Because of its potential for providing useful diagnostic information about the specific strengths and weaknesses of the learning of individual students, computerized testing offers great opportunities for improving the integration of assessment with instruction. In fact, much of the current research on testing technology is focused on just this issue: how tests can be "seamlessly" interwoven with instruction so that the learner is not even aware of when instruction ends and assessment begins.

Decreased Costs of Testing

Testing by computer also promises to be less expensive than testing as it is done today. This is because a large portion of the expenses of any large-scale testing program are the costs of human labor associated with the actual administration of tests (test supervisors and proctors, for example).

Although these kinds of expenses will not disappear completely in the world of computerized testing, they will diminish sharply and, when combined with the established trend for decreased costs of computer hardware, it is safe to conclude that the economics of testing in the future will be quite different from those of today.

Opportunities for New Kinds of Assessment

The most revolutionary facet of testing by computer will be the opportunities created to assess new constructs. One very important way that future computer-based tests will differ from current tests is that they will be able to assess the processes that people go through in solving problems. Largely because of the capability of the computer both to present to the test taker a lifelike situation rich in detail and to track the test taker's approach to the problem posed, testing by computer can yield a variety of assessments that go well beyond whether or not the test taker arrived at the "right answer." The ability of the computer to track the process taken by the problem solver in approaching a situation can lead to answers to questions such as the following:

- How innovative or creative was the student in generating possible solution paths?
- Did the student make good use of the information presented in the problem, or was the approach inefficient?
- And for problems that may have more than one solution, was the student able to estimate the likelihood of the correctness of various possible solutions?

Although testing by computer is generally acknowledged to be the wave of the future, there are a number of issues that must be considered. Following are some of the issues that need to be confronted and resolved.

Equity. As we move toward the world of computerized testing, we need to be absolutely certain that the technology itself does not introduce inequity or bias into the test-taking situation.

Score Comparability. Regardless of how fast or slowly the move to testing by computer advances, there will doubtless be a transition period during which scores derived from computerized tests will need to be made comparable to scores derived from paper-and-pencil tests. Deriving comparable scores from these two modes of testing is a complex process but will be necessary if these scores are to be used interchangeably.

Test Security. The issues of test security shift somewhat in the computerized-testing world. On one hand, if every test taker receives a fully "customized" test, the dangers associated with students sharing information among one another during test administration are diminished. On the other hand, the dangers of exposure of the entire pool of test questions, which in the computerized world may reside on a single disk, are magnified. These and other issues of test security will need to be resolved before scores from computerized tests can be released with confidence.

Broadening the Methods of Assessment

This survey of current trends in testing in education would not be complete without mention of the push today for alternative assessment methods. This movement in testing goes by many names, including "performance-based" and "portfolio" assessment. Some have even named this movement a search for "authentic" assessment! (How could anyone debate the value of tests so named?)

What is at the heart of this movement in testing? One of the most commonly expressed criticisms of large-scale testing programs is that they are dependent on multiple-choice questions. This format of tests is seen by critics as having two especially deleterious effects: first, the trivialization of learning by stressing only those skills that can be conveniently accommodated by this question format and, second, the "game-like" aspect of multiple-choice questions that invites attempts to devise strategies for outwitting tests, thus further detracting from their educational value.

In fact, the multiple-choice question has survived so long because it has enormous measurement and operational advantages of efficiency, economy, reliability, and objectivity of scoring. Multiple-choice questions are not limited to the testing of factual knowledge. The questions that make up reasoning tests such as the SAT go well beyond the recall of facts to the ability to understand arguments, solve complex mathematical problems, and apply knowledge to new situations.

Despite these advantages, the multiple-choice format continues to suffer from its primary limitation; it requires recognition rather than production, and it is the latter that comes closer to most school and college work and most real-life cognitive tasks. Observers of the current debate on alternative assessment may inadvertently conclude that all educational testing done today is based on the multiple-choice format, yet this conclusion is unwarranted. Many important tests in our educational system currently make use of questions and tasks that go well beyond this format. The tests of the National Assessment of Educational Progress (the nation's "report card") and many state assessment programs, for example, integrate tasks in which students must generate their own answers to questions or problems. One of the largest of the College Board's programs—the Advanced Placement Program—has provided, since its inception in 1955, a model for how multiple-choice testing can be combined with other formats to yield a balanced assessment of student achievement. Each of the twenty-nine different tests that are currently part of the Advanced Placement Program is a careful blend of multiple-choice questions and free-response questions—a structure specifically designed to measure the full range and depth of students' achievement in the fields tested.

The desire to broaden assessment has affected the SAT as well. The new SAT—to be first administered during the 1993–94 academic year—will include two major initiatives to allow students the opportunity to produce their own responses to test questions. The board is now developing plans to broaden the assessments carried out by its other tests as well, through the use of extended free-response sections, student-produced responses in ad vanced mathematics and science tests, and video- and audio-based assessments of achievement in modern languages.

The need to broaden assessment stems largely from a recognition of the fact that testing should be an integral part of the process of learning, not something that comes at the end, as a gateway or hurdle. For testing and assessment to maintain their vital roles in the U.S. educational system, we as educators must ensure that both the content and the format of educational tests be congruent with those educational outcomes of our schools that are most valued by our society. Our task as educators must be to marshal the powers of assessment into an intelligent tool to achieve the critical goals of our schools today.

Of course, the underlying question is how to accomplish this. For the past 217 years, the United States has charted a course involving local control and state oversight of education. We have developed a variety of associations based on nongovernmental, voluntary leadership (as described by the great French observer of America, Alexis de Tocqueville) to resolve larger policy issues. The College Board, now an association of more than twenty-eight hundred schools, colleges, educational systems, and agencies, is one such organization. It was brought into being in 1900 by leaders in secondary and higher education to chart a uniform, national path for precollegiate testing, and it has since been used for similar goals with regard to guidance and counseling, financial aid, and the setting of curricular standards. There is no question that voluntary leadership organizations lack some of the efficiency of large governmental or business mechanisms, but they do include the educators who are ultimately responsible for delivering better educational outcomes, better student achievement. As Gregory Anrig, president of the Educational Testing Service, observed, "Private enterprise has learned the hard way that competitive productivity requires involving the workforce rather than dictating to it. Better student achievement must be developed in the classroom, and only the teacher can do it" (Anrig 1991).

A national assessment instrument created from above and enforced by federal and state law will galvanize the attention of teachers and students. We will indeed come to value whatever we test; that is inevitable. The question is, will such a test improve education? Is it the educational panacea that some are claiming? Or is it, in view of the tremendous power of the microcomputer that will soon be used in the testing process, a rigid and awkward solution, a case of generals fighting the last war? Once computerized testing is a reality, the ability to tailor tests to different students and curricula and to integrate testing with instruction, as noted above, will lead to a resolution of many currently vexing problems. This resolution can be achieved, moreover, without turning our backs on the rich tradition of flexible control and the tremendous resources of educators that reside at the local level, both of which are crucial for educational success in a complex, multicultural society.

Where, it seems to me, the federal and state governments have a critical role to play is in the second part of the equation of (1) what we teach; (2) how we support schools, students, and teachers; and (3) how we measure our results. As the analyses of the Committee on Economic Development and the Children's Defense Fund show, the real point of vulnerability comes long before students ever get to the schoolroom. If we can find the national and state-by-state commitment finally to provide the wherewithal so that, according to the first national educational goal, "all children in America will start school ready to learn," and if we can trust in the ability of properly supported schools and teachers to achieve the outcome of students able to perform according to consensually reached standards, then we will have made great strides in accomplishing our goals. And we will be well along the way toward creating an educated society, which America must have to maintain its economic strength and social well-being in the twenty-first century.

Acknowledgments

I am grateful to Mr. James Lichtenberg and Mr. Lawrence Hecht for their collaborative assistance in the preparation of this chapter.

References

Anrig, Gregory. 1991. "National Test: 'Nay,' Nationwide Assessment System: 'Yea,'" p. 1. Princeton, N.J.: Educational Testing Service.

Commission on New Possibilities for the Admissions Testing Program. 1990. *Beyond Prediction.* New York: College Board.

Committee on Economic Development. 1991. *The Unfinished Agenda: A New Vision for Child Development and Education.* A Statement by the Research and Policy Committee of the Committee on Economic Development. New York: Committee on Economic Development.

DeWitt, Karen. 1991. "National Tests Urged for Public Schools." *New York Times,* 17 January, p. A-12.

Gladieux, Lawrence E. 1991. "A National Examination System? In the U.S.?" *College Board Review,* 159 (Spring): S1–S8.

National Commission on Excellence in Education. 1983. *A Nation at Risk: The Imperatives for Educational Reform.* Washington, D.C.: U.S. Government Printing Office.

National School Public Relations Association. 1991. *Education USA,* 33(29):197.

Office of the Press Secretary (President of the United States). 1991. *National Goals for Education* (Memorandum). Washington, D.C., 26 February.

President's Education Policy Advisory Committee. 1990. "Draft Proposal for Voluntary National Examinations in Reading and Mathematics at Selected Grade Levels." Washington, D.C.: President's Education Policy Advisory Committee, 26 February.

Stewart, Donald M. 1991. Congressional Testimony. Washington, D.C., March.

Afterword: A Personal Note on Clark Kerr

JAMES A. PERKINS

Clark Kerr is an American success story. He comes from a small town in rural Pennsylvania and grew up surrounded by a caring family, warm friends, and his favorite apple trees. From these solid beginnings he emerged as arguably the preeminent leader of higher education in the United States. To paraphrase a current witticism, "He has risen to the level of his increasing competence."

I first met Clark Kerr in 1930 at Swarthmore College, where his family, who prized education highly, supported his enrollment. I pass up comment on his prowess as a fellow member of the soccer team, but I will note that he was, even then, an honor student in labor economics with extraordinary clarity of mind.

For an illuminating capsule of his social philosophy and professional career, I refer the reader to his prologue to the recently published collection of his papers and speeches entitled *The Great Transformation in Higher Education*. While Kerr's prologue is a personal account, his papers are a rich commentary on the development of higher education from 1960 to 1980.

Several highlights of his career in higher education should be singled out here. Kerr was a skillful campus and systems manager. Colleagues of those days say it was his grasp of the nature of the university, combined with a clear-headed fairness and a sense of institutional direction—all of these attributes explain the effectiveness of his leadership.

Perhaps the most visible example of his creative management was the design and effective establishment of the famous California Master Plan for Higher Education. When there was imminent danger of institutional pluralism degenerating into institutional anarchy, he masterminded the Master Plan that assigned niches and sizes to the various institutions in the total system. This arrangement has survived into the present with only minor changes.

Although he left the university under duress, he managed, to use his own words, to leave as he entered, "fired with enthusiasm." It is no small measure of his administrative skill that he arranged to be dismissed by a most unpopular governor and harassed by soon-to-be discredited militant students. He emerged as something of a heroic victim of those twin antieducational pincers. As a result, while his antagonists were descending into the shadows of their just deserts, Clark Kerr has been loaded with honors from his university, where he now maintains his office.

If his presidential tour of duty established Kerr as a creative and effective administrator, as chairman of the Carnegie Council and Commission he made his name as the leading comprehensive scholar of higher education. Presiding over a group of educational administrators, leavened by a handful of business and political figures, he chaired the enterprises that turned out to be a veritable academic cornucopia of some 37 reports and 130 sponsored research studies. Lord Eric Ashby, former vice-chancellor of Cambridge University, has said, "This is the most thorough analysis of a nation's system of higher education that has ever been made." The Queen of England reigns but does not rule. Clark Kerr reigned and ruled over these activities with both profound knowledge and unbelievable patience.

Then, too, he could be an effective policy maker and politician, bringing the California Master Plan from idea to politically supported actuality, an accomplishment clearly the work of one who knew his way around the Capitol and California cities, large and small, with a protective interest in their local institutions. But perhaps his largest political accomplishment came when he led the charge, over the concerted opposition of the education establishment, that resulted in the defeat of the dangerous proposal to provide federal financial support directly to colleges and universities, both public and private. Arguing effectively that the federal allocation and oversight that would necessarily follow would wreck the established relations between public universities and their state governments and would surely damage the independence of the private sector, he was able to convince both the executive and the legislative branches of the federal government to fund higher education through portable student scholarships. Perhaps this illustrates his abiding preference for local rather than central management and market forces rather than central administration. The result is the Pell Grant to Students, currently the centerpiece of federal support for higher education.

Finally, it must be mentioned that Clark Kerr was both a student of and a participant in the expansion of the international dimension of higher education. Under his direction, Professor Barbara Burn of the University of Massachusetts produced the basic text on the subject, *The International Dimension of Higher Education*. And he participated in many conferences with international educators. He was a founding trustee of the International Council for Education Development and lent strength to many international meetings sponsored by that organization. Perhaps uniquely, he was able to add this dimension to this interest without losing his connections with state and national policy making.

It is not to be supposed that Clark Kerr is all mind and administrative skill. He is a very warm human being with wide-ranging interests outside but supportive of his professional life. His extremely able wife, Kay Kerr, has been at his elbow all his life. I know from personal experience that he does not like to travel without her. He loves gardening and especially apples and apple trees. On our trip to the Soviet Union, he was vocally disappointed that our hosts would not include a visit to Alma Ata—the center of apple culture in the U.S.S.R. He is a serious Quaker, a strong and supportive family man, a warm and steady friend, a humane man, and a powerful professional—in short—quite a man!

Contributors

Philip G. Altbach, Professor and Director, Comparative Education Center, State University of New York at Buffalo

Alberta Arthurs, Director for Arts and Humanities, The Rockefeller Foundation

Eric Ashby, formerly Master, Clare College, Cambridge, England, and Vice-Chancellor, University of Cambridge

Ernest L. Boyer, President, The Carnegie Foundation for the Advancement of Teaching

David W. Breneman, Visiting Professor, Harvard Graduate School of Education

Patrick M. Callan, Director, California Higher Education Policy Center Study

Ladislav Cerych, Senior Consultant, European Institute of Education and Social Policy and European Community TEMPUS

Burton R. Clark, Allan M. Carter Professor of Higher Education Emeritus, University of California at Los Angeles

K. Patricia Cross, Elizabeth and Edward Conner Professor of Higher Education, University of California at Berkeley

Marian Cleeves Diamond, Professor, Department of Integrative Biology, and Director, Lawrence Hall of Science, University of California at Berkeley

Flora Mancuso Edwards, President, Middlesex Community College, Edison, New Jersey

Roger L. Geiger, Professor of Higher Education, Pennsylvania State University

Lyman A. Glenny, Professor Emeritus, University of California at Berkeley

Margaret Gordon, Research Economist Emeritus, Institute of Industrial Relations, University of California at Berkeley

Joseph F. Kauffman, Professor Emeritus of Education Administration, University of Wisconsin, Madison; Executive Vice President Emeritus, University of Wisconsin System; and President Emeritus, Rhode Island College

Leslie Koltai, Adjunct Professor, Graduate School of Education, University of California at Los Angeles

Arthur Levine, Senior Lecturer on Education, and Chair, Institute for Educational Management, Harvard Graduate School of Education

Judith Block McLaughlin, Lecturer on Education; Director, Field Experience Program; and Chair, Harvard Seminar for New Presidents, Harvard Graduate School of Education

James A. Perkins, Chairman Emeritus, International Council for Educational Development

David Riesman, Henry Ford II Professor of the Social Sciences Emeritus, Department of Sociology, Harvard University

Neil J. Smelser, University Professor of Sociology, University of California at Berkeley

Virginia Smith, President Emeritus, Vassar College

Donald M. Stewart, President, The College Board

Martin Trow, Professor, Graduate School of Public Policy, University of California at Berkeley

Name Index

Abelson, Philip, 63, 64
Abrami, Philip C., 293, 306
Agarwal, J. C., 204, 220
Agarwal, S. P., 204, 220
Alexander, Lamar, 5
Alfred, Richard L., 107–8, 112
Alsalam, Nabeel, 101, 112
Altbach, Philip G., 203–21
Andersen, C. J., 70, 85
Anderson, Don, 140–41, 148
Angelo, Thomas A., 302, 304, 307
Anrig, Gregory, 350, 358, 359
Anwyl, John, 148
Aristophanes, 254–55
Armytage, W.H.G., 49, 64
Arthurs, Alberta, 193, 259–72
Asante, Molefi Kete, 325, 332
Ashby, Eric, xvii–xxii, 362
Ashcroft, John, 5, 13
Astin, Alexander W., 103, 105, 112, 203, 208, 210, 220
Aydelotte, F., 181

Bacon, Francis, 276–77
Bailyn, Bernard, 50, 64, 180, 201
Baltimore, David, 199
Barakat, Halim, 215, 220
Barkan, Joel D., 215, 220

Barnett, Marguerite Ross, 192
Becher, Tony, 165, 177
Behn, R. D., 91, 98
Bell, Terrel, 345
Bellah, Robert N., 176, 177
BenBrika, Jeanne, 220
Ben-David, Joseph, 222, 238
Bender, Thomas, 260, 272
Bennett, William J., 4, 229, 239, 244, 257
Berendzen, Richard, 199, 201
Beswick, David, 148
Bias, Len, 323
Biedenweg, Rick, 84
Birnbaum, Robert, 185, 201
Blackburn, McKinley L., 21, 35
Blackburn, Robert T., 293, 306
Bloch, Erich, 71
Bloom, David E., 21, 35
Bogue, Grady, 331, 332
Bok, Derek, 8, 18, 81, 84, 195, 290–91, 352
Bowen, Howard R., 98, 289, 308
Bowen, William G., 95, 97, 98, 99
Boyer, Ernest L.: and campus climate, 322–32; and presidents, 197, 201; and students, 203, 206, 220; and teaching, 290, 291–92, 293, 306
Bragg, Stephen M., 18, 19

Subject Index

Designed by Martha Farlow

Composed by The Composing Room of Michigan, Inc., in Berkeley Old Style

Printed by The Maple Press Company, Inc., on 50-lb. Glatfelter Eggshell Cream and bound in Holliston Roxite A